The
Streets
Were
Paved
With
Gold

The Streets Were Paved With Gold

Ken Auletta

Random House
New York

*Grateful acknowledgment is made to the following for
permission to reprint previously published material:*

The Brookings Institution: Excerpt from "The City" by
Richard P. Nathan and Paul R. Dommel.

Harper & Row, Publishers, Inc.: Abridged excerpt from
pp. 123–124 of "Here Is New York" in *Essays of E. B.
White* (1977) by E. B. White. Copyright 1949 by E. B.
White. Reprinted by permission of Harper & Row,
Publishers, Inc.

New England Economic Review: Excerpt from Lynn
Browne and Richard Syron, *New England Economic
Review*, July/August 1977, p. 5.

"More for Less" appeared originally in *The New Yorker*.

"Profile of Abe Beame" by Ken Auletta is reprinted
courtesy of *The New York Times.* © 1975 by The New
York Times Company. Reprinted by permission.

"How the Lies of New York's Political Midgets Are
Destroying the City," "After the Storm, the Hurricane,"
and "What It's Like to Be Dead: A Report from City
Hall" are reprinted by permission of *The Village Voice.*
© The Village Voice, Inc., 1975.

Library of Congress Cataloging in Publication Data
Auletta, Ken.
The streets were paved with gold.
Includes index.
1. New York (City)—Economic conditions. 2. Finance,
Public—New York (City) 3. New York (City)—
Politics and government—1951–   I. Title.
HC108.N7A9   336.747′1   78-21838
ISBN 0-394-50019-9

For Nettie
and Pat Auletta

Acknowledgments

I HAPPEN TO HAVE one of the world's great jobs. As a journalist, people pay me to meet people, travel, get an education, get my name in the papers, have fun. Journalism is prolonged adolescence.

Writing a book is not as much fun. But you get to work with nice people, some of whom I'd like to thank. My close friend, Richard Reeves, goaded me to write this book and painstakingly reviewed the manuscript. When his legs go, Reeves will make a luminous editor. Ray Horton, Howard Samuels, George Sternlieb, Steve Clifford, Dick Ravitch and my agent, Esther Newberg, also took time to read the book and offer valuable suggestions. Mimi Gurbst charitably assisted with fact-checking, as did Mary Schoonmaker. Tully Plesser suggested the book's title. Mike O'Neill, editor of the New York *Daily News*, generously extended my leave of absence with greater frequency than Abe Beame amended his budget deficits. Random House is my publisher because I was anxious to work with Jason Epstein, an educated man. I was not disappointed. His assistant, Sarah Binder, was of great help, as was copy editor Lynn Strong.

Obviously, any blame for this book is mine. If there be any credit, I would like to share it with someone who had a profound effect on my thinking about New York—Howard Samuels. I had the good fortune to work for Howard on and off from 1965 through 1974. In between helping him lose three gubernatorial campaigns, I listened and learned a lot. He is one of the few liberals I have known who knew how to read a budget. As early as the mid-sixties, he was warning of the city's gathering fiscal crisis, of the budget gimmicks, the collapse of New York's economy. At a time when many of us measured the size of a candidate's heart, Samuels was presciently measuring the institutional rot of our governments—their mismanagement, musclebound civil service system, the too-pervasive power of special-interest groups. From the voters, Howard never received the recognition he deserved. From me, he receives both recognition and thanks.

And, finally, I wish to thank Amanda, who spent the better part of a year staring at my back as I pounded away at the typewriter. During that time, she provided equal measures of constructive criticism and love.

Contents

Introduction

A TRIP TO PARIS inspired this book about New York. Walking with a friend along the sun-drenched Seine, stopping to watch boats gently paddle by, passing the majestic Louvre, the hooded outdoor cafés brimming with relaxed, beautiful women, the tiny shops stuffed with treats and treasures—somehow my thoughts drifted back to New York. Not to the gloomy New York—the fiscal crisis, which I had covered since early 1975, the lost jobs, the slums—but to New York's treasures: the meadows and gently rolling hills of Central and Prospect parks; the postcard-perfect Manhattan skyline glimpsed from the Promenade in Brooklyn Heights; the calzone and other Italian treats of Arthur Avenue in the Bronx, the cornucopia of treats along Fifth Avenue in Manhattan. It was hot in land-locked Paris; hotter than it normally was in Coney Island, where I grew up, and where the roar of the ocean made the hum of the air conditioner superfluous.

The daydream terminated when my friend abruptly asked, "When are you going to stop covering a local story and start covering some big national stories?" Weren't New York's fiscal woes so advanced as to be hopeless? Wasn't I bored?

No, I wasn't bored.

No, my continuing anger suggested that I really didn't believe New York was hopeless.

Besides, New York was *the* big story. Maybe it would take a book to convey that. Maybe a detailed probe of New York's difficulties could communicate not just what went wrong here, and why, but what was going wrong in other older cities. Maybe it could illuminate some national, even universal questions: the decline of aging cities; the reasons for the rising taxpayer revolt; the inherent conflict between democracy's social goals and its economic system, between organized special-interest groups and the broader public interest. "You can't get anything through the state legislature in an election year that the unions don't want," Mayor Ed Koch told me in June 1978. "I don't want to paint with a broad brush and say the legislators are in the pockets—in every case—of the union leaders." If they were as honest, the mayor of Atlanta might say the same thing about the Chamber of Commerce, the mayor of Houston about the oil companies, the President of the United States about the arbitrary power of Senator Russell Long, Chairman of the potent Finance Committee. New York's crisis, I thought, tells us about the breakdown of democracy, about politics, greed, bureaucracy, cowardice, the failure of good intentions. About how democratic government does not know how to cope with decline. No, long after we have forgotten the name of the Secretary of HEW or Jimmy Carter's shifting poll ratings, these questions about the nature of government and democracy will haunt us.

Even if there were no broader implications, New York City's economic, fiscal and political crisis would still be a big story. For New York, like a great novel, transcends geographic boundaries or time. It is a world city, the ultimate marketplace. For those with talent, this city is the final test. Many Americans hate New York because they fear it: not just its imposing size but its ruthless competitiveness. The very best lawyers, fashion designers, writers, artists, advertising agencies, publishers, financiers and thinkers ultimately find their way here. Succeed here and you can probably succeed anywhere. From this cauldron of competitive friction, New York charges the nation with more energy than the Tennessee Valley Authority. Constantly, it lifts the limits of our imagination. New York's fashions become the nation's—two years later. Its plays tour the nation—only after passing Broadway's muster. Almost one-third of America's hard-covered books are purchased in New York City. America's largest corporations call it home largely because here is where they find the best legal, advertising, banking and financial services. It's easier to stand out—to be a Big Man on Campus —elsewhere. But if you're good at what you do, at some point you'll probably test yourself against New York.

New York is the ultimate bazaar. Think about other cities: Los Angeles has Hollywood; Pittsburgh, steel; Detroit, automobiles; New Orleans, jazz (and food); Houston, a space center; Nashville, country music. Boston has Harvard; Washington is government; Moscow is the Kremlin; Zurich is banking; Miami Beach is, well, Miami Beach. Think about New York. It cannot be characterized the way other cities can. A single street or avenue or neighborhood can symbolize an entire industry or life style. Wall Street is finance; Broadway is theater; Seventh Avenue is fashion; Madison Avenue is advertising; Fifth Avenue is shopping; Greenwich Village is bohemia; Coney Island is amusement. Everyone has heard of Radio City Music Hall, the Statue of Liberty, the UN, Central Park, the Empire State Building. Once Harlem, and now the South Bronx, defined a slum.

As a bazaar, no other city can compete with New York. Ideas, services, merchandise are placed on sale here, then sold or rejected. But more: the city is a bazaar of cultures, life styles, people. Jews, blacks, Hispanics, Irish- and Italo-Americans, West Indians, Haitians, Malaysians, poor Vietnamese or Continental European refugees, romantic poets, gays, Moonies, feminists, iconoclastic geniuses, nuts, Scientologists, Kreminologists, every shade of political opinion, not to mention addicts, pimps, prostitutes, shopping bag ladies—all flower here. Unlike small towns or homogenized suburbs, New York does not quickly dismiss unusual behavior or ideas as weird. It is almost normal to be abnormal. "On any person who desires such queer prizes," E. B. White has written, "New York will bestow the gift of loneliness and the gift of privacy. . . . New York is peculiarly constructed to absorb almost anything that comes along (whether a thousand-foot liner out of the East or a twenty-thousand-man convention out of the West) without inflicting the event on its inhabitants, so that every event is, in a sense, optional, and the inhabitant is in the happy position of being able to choose his spectacle and so conserve his soul."

New York is also an incubator of the nation's ideals. We are the Statue of Liberty City, gateway to the new world for millions of immigrants. For these pioneers and their offspring, the streets really were paved with gold. Freedom, opportunity, optimism, compassionate government, the melting of class, ethnic and racial divisions—for the multitudes, New York worked. It worked for the Aulettas. My brother, Richard, was the first Auletta to go to college. In Coney Island, we grew up shoulder to shoulder with Jews, Italians, Irish, blacks, Hispanics. My father, Pat, is Italian; my mother, the former Nettie Tenenbaum, is Jewish. Her sister Rose married Pete Dellaquila; sister Sally married William Pagliuga. My father's brother Mike wed Sally Altman. It was terrific. We got the cultural advantage and got to take off from school on both Catholic and Jewish holidays.

Sure, there were racial and ethnic tensions in Coney Island: a black might get his ankles bent if he strayed into Braggo's coffee shop on Mermaid Avenue and West 15th Street, where some pretty tough Italians hung out; a passing Jew might be called a "fairy." But even those who did not want to be were exposed to others in a way that could not help but educate them. Out of this exposure there slowly grew greater tolerance. First for ethnic and racial minorities. Then for ideas, different life styles, for people who in other places might have been branded as "queers." I shall always be grateful to Oswego State Teachers College, it being the only university generous enough to ignore an unpromising high school record for the sake of my then-promising fastball. But one cannot forget the 1963 civil rights protest march into downtown Oswego, when the local *Palladium Times* actually wrote that we were "a bunch of communists"; or Syracuse University, where I completed graduate studies, when the chancellor whacked a peaceful Vietnam war protester with his cane, only to be cheered, not jeered, by student and community leaders. In small towns, protesters were Enemies of the People. They threatened the existing order of things. By comparison, New York had no clearly defined existing order of things to threaten. Strangers, change, growth, waves of migration in and out, rigorous competition—all were normal here.

Yet New York is changing. As kids, we equated New York City with Manhattan. The signs along Shore Parkway in Brooklyn or Grand Central Parkway in Queens pointed to Manhattan yet read, TO NEW YORK CITY, as if the four other boroughs weren't part of the city. Sometimes, on weekends, we would take the BMT to "the City" for a day or night out to see the Rockettes at Radio City Music Hall, to catch a movie six months before it came to our neighborhood theater, to watch the Knicks play basketball on a portable court in the Armory. If I was paying, dinner would be at the Automat—45¢ for a delicious chopped sirloin, 5¢ extra for mashed potatoes. If my parents were paying, we went to the House of Chan, which offered chow mein that wasn't smothered in onions, unlike Taeng Fong's on Bay Parkway. We had annual feasts at our local Lady of Solace church, which was nothing like the Casbah that was Greenwich Village. All of Manhattan seemed to be a feast. Aside from a handful of rich Protestants who we knew lived in Fifth and Park Avenue penthouses, we never assumed people actually lived in Manhattan from the Battery to 96th Street. We didn't think of it as a place with neighborhoods, kids playing stickball or johnny-on-the-pony, knuckles, kick-the-can, ring-a-leaveo; we never imagined there were pool halls or luncheonettes where other kids hung out. What did we know? We were tourists.

As we grew older, many of us gravitated to suburban homes or to apartments in Manhattan. As Brooklyn, the Bronx and Queens stopped growing, as people and jobs fled the outer boroughs, as blight spread there, it came more and more to be true that Manhattan was *the* city. Those living in Manhattan or outside the other four boroughs came to view the other boroughs as we once viewed Manhattan—it was assumed there were no neighborhoods, no stickball, no culture out there. Staten Island was not only close to New Jersey, but its one- and two-family homes made it look the same. Queens was a poor suburb of neighboring Nassau County. The Bronx was no longer renowned for its Grand Concourse boulevard or vast zoo and Botanical Gardens, but for the cancer sweeping north. Brooklyn seemed to die about the same time the Dodgers left. The Hamptons replaced Coney Island as a weekend retreat.

Of course, neither tourist vision represents reality. Manhattan always had street life and neighborhoods, just as the other four boroughs do today. Walk under the El in Corona, Queens, and you'll see a procession of ma-and-pa stores, most owned by Haitians and Dominicans and other immigrants, many of whom probably entered this country illegally. They found that the American Dream still works. Bedford-Stuyvesant is not just abandoned housing or youth gangs. It also contains some of the finest row houses in New York, and one of the most spirited organizations—the Bedford-Stuyvesant Redevelopment Corporation—struggling to transform a neighborhood. Brooklyn is not just the fires of Bushwick, the abandonment of Brownsville; it is also the brownstone revival of Park Slope and Carroll Gardens, the pluck and determination of Northside residents to save their firehouse, the Russian Jews who now find refuge in Brighton Beach, the tree-lined streets of Bay Ridge, the bucolic pleasure of standing in Prospect Park, in the middle of a city, and seeing no tall buildings, nothing but grass and trees and lakes. Little Italy is alive and well in the Belmont section of the Bronx; Irish-Americans compete in old-country sports over in Gaelic Park in the Kingsbridge section of the Bronx; the affluent still consider themselves lucky to land a vacant estate overlooking the Hudson in Riverdale, a stone's throw from the South Bronx. Even Coney Island, which Pat and Nettie Auletta still call home, has not surrendered. There are people there, as in the South Bronx, who we will one day read about and admire. There are poor people, middle-income people, whites, blacks, Hispanics, trying to salvage their communities, leading quiet, noble, unpublicized lives.

For them, as for me and my family, Brooklyn is like a small town in a big city. I remember how we shared the same stoops, the same food and Coke bottles, how we asked permission to spend the night at a neighbor's house. If I didn't hear my mother, a friend would run over and tell me that she had her head out the window and yelling, "Kenny, supper is ready." I think about that a lot now, living as I do in a twenty-story mausoleum on Manhattan's Central Park West. It's pretty, but there are no stoops and, maybe, I know the names of five neighbors.

Sadly, the hub if not the heart of New York has become Manhattan. The boroughs are no longer as unique as they once were. Other cities—like Brooklyn, Queens, the Bronx and Staten Island—enjoy diverse cultures, neighborhoods, working class and poor living side by side, brownstone revivals, Horatio Alger success stories. Increasingly, what is unique about New York is associated with Manhattan. Only Manhattan is gaining jobs. Only Manhattan is the center of commerce, communications, ideas. Only Manhattan is what tourists usually think of when they think of New York. Only Manhattan is what E. B. White thought of when he penned his famous essay "Here Is New York." These are some of the reasons I find myself depressed about the city I live in and love. Blight and decay have not suspended their onslaught. The "renaissance of New York" which Mayor Koch ludicrously talks about—"I feel it as I walk around," he told me—is confined to a relatively few blocks in mid-Manhattan. If you share such cheer, this may be an uncomfortable book. Perhaps my pessimism is excessive.

I understand that a great city lives on hope, as well as facts. Our leaders, unlike our journalists, cannot just shout, "Fire! Fire!" Perhaps the isolation of writing a book, of laboring through lifeless data and budgets, of staring at a typewriter, of challenging conventional wisdom, induces undue hostility on the part of the writer. Perhaps I am reading the evidence too literally—a few years ago, no study or trend line predicted today's resurgence of Manhattan real-estate values.

Beware, dear reader, the writer's biases. In addition to an underlying pessimism, I plead guilty to believing:

■ The most dangerous people in New York are not the Cassandras but the Candides. To solve problems you have to know you have them. That means facing the truth.

■ No one devil theory can explain what has happened to New York. Neither John Lindsay nor Abe Beame, alone, brought us to our collective knees. Nor, by themselves, did the banks, the federal government or historical inevitability.

■ Local decisions, made by New Yorkers, are more to blame for the city's crisis than most of us like to admit.

■ Individuals should be held responsible for their acts.

■ If there are solutions, they will have to emanate primarily from within New York.

Several other disclosures are called for. In writing this book I confronted an intellectual conundrum. Briefly, I oppose bankruptcy. Yet to avoid it, I recognize, requires steps which may be counterproductive and even wrong. Financial institutions need make loans which a prudent investor probably would not make, risking a violation of their fiduciary responsibility. The state of New York need divert funds from desirable tax cuts to even more essential increases in state aid. And the federal government, which has to curb its deficit and say no to special pleaders, somehow has to say yes to New York City's pleas. Inconsistent? Yes. But better, in my judgment, to be inconsistent than to allow America's premier city to go bust.

Some of the material in this book—some pages here, a paragraph or sentence there—is borrowed from earlier work. Chapter 2 expands on a *New York* magazine cover story I wrote in October 1975 ("Who's to Blame for the Fix We're In"). Chapter 3 uses several pages from a December 1975 *New York* cover story ("Should These People Go to Jail?"). Chapter 5 relies on an August 1977 piece in *The New Yorker* ("More for Less"). With the exception of stray paragraphs borrowed from my work in the *Village Voice* (1975–76), the Sunday *New York*

Times, an essay in *The New York Review of Books* or weekly columns in the New York *Daily News* (1977–78), roughly 85 or 90 percent of this book is new. In another sense, it is all new. Forced to wrestle with an entire book, to step back and read and think more deeply, I made connections I had not before made. I could not, in one sentence, tell Stanley Siegel what this book is about.

I also learned—and this is the third caution—that I should not attempt to present an agenda of "solutions." Like most journalists, my business is stating problems, not solving them. Besides, in the process of delineating a problem one sees that the solution is often self-evident. It takes little imagination to proclaim that the antidote to weak leaders is strong leaders. Clearly, it costs too much to do business in New York, and if the city hopes to compete, it will have to somehow reduce taxes and energy costs. A local economic development agenda, including Washington and Albany's role, is a subject I grappled with once in *New York* ("An Agenda to Save Our City: 44 Proposals That Could Turn This Town Around," March 1976). Radical reform of the manner in which the city delivers services, including management, civil service and collective bargaining reforms, I tried to address in *The New Yorker* ("More for Less," August 1977). In truth, while preparing this book I originally intended to include a solutions chapter. I came to fear, however, that it would be misleading. After talking to and reading "the experts," I discovered none had a magic potion, a still-secret plan to restore New York. Increasingly, I became convinced that the sum of the "solutions" would not equal the sum of the problems.

Perhaps Lewis Mumford captured the ambivalence I feel about New York when he said, "I am an optimist about possibilities and a pessimist about probabilities." I am too angry to be cynical, yet too skeptical to be evangelical. So I've just tried to tell the truth as I see it about a very big story.

The
Streets
Were
Paved
With
Gold

Chapter One

The
Rotting Apple

PRINCE PROSPERO was an indefatigable, some might say an impervious man. The plague of the "Red Death" had entered the homes of half his minions, causing rapid bleeding and sudden death. But Prince Prospero remained undaunted. As told by Edgar Allan Poe in *The Masque of the Red Death,* the Prince blithely summoned a thousand of his heartiest knights and dames and retreated to a magnificent castle, where they would defy the contagion.

A lofty wall stood between them and the populace, its gates made of iron and, as an extra precaution, sealed with sturdy bolts. There was no need to step outside the palace:

it was folly to grieve, or to think. The prince had provided all the appliances of pleasure. There were buffoons, there were improvisatori, there were ballet-dancers, there were musicians, there was Beauty, there was wine. All these and security were within. Without was the "Red Death."

Gaiety prevailed. For six months, they partied and danced to the music of a full orchestra, waltzed freely through the seven brightly colored chambers, paused to listen to the chimes from the giant ebony clock, ignored the bright sun which was tamed by thick, beautiful stained-glass Gothic windows. Prince Prospero was content. Yet he wished to do something new, something different, something special. At last he seized on the idea of a masquerade ball. On the appointed evening:

There were arabesque figures with unsuited limbs and appointments. There were delirious fancies such as the madman fashions. There were much of the beautiful, much of the wanton, much of the *bizarre*, something of the terrible, and not a little of that which might have excited disgust. To and fro in the seven chambers there stalked, in fact, a multitude of dreams.

The music ceased when the giant clock struck midnight, the waltzers froze, all dutifully waiting for the twelve chimes to ring. Suddenly, there was a stranger among them:

tall and gaunt, and shrouded from head to foot in the habiliments of the grave. The mask which concealed the visage was made so nearly to resemble the countenance of a stiffened corpse that the closest scrutiny must have had difficulty in detecting the cheat. . . . His vesture was dabbled in *blood*—and his broad brow, with all the features of the face, was besprinkled with the scarlet horror.

The courtiers were confused, torn between rage and horror. Not Prince Prospero, he was simply enraged. "Who dares insult us with this blasphemous mockery?" he commanded, ordering the intruder to be seized and hanged. Still awed, no one moved; all watching as the stranger turned and stalked from the blue to the purple chamber, to the green, the orange, the white, finally halting in the violet chamber. Meekly, the courtiers followed, cringing along the walls, before making a hesitant motion to arrest the intruder. Prince Prospero did not hesitate. Dagger in hand, he bolted through the six chambers, and as he was about to plunge the knife into his victim, the intruder turned. A loud shriek reverberated through the chambers as Prince Prospero fell dead.

Timid no more, the revellers lurched to seize the tall, motionless figure, gasping "in unutterable horror at finding the grave cerements and corpse-like mask, which they handled with so violent a rudeness, untenanted by any tangible form."

And now was acknowledged the presence of the Red Death. He had come like a thief in the night. And one by one dropped the revellers in the blood-bedewed halls of their revel, and died each in the despairing posture of his fall. And the life and the ebony clock went out with that of the last of the gay. And the flames of the tripods expired. And Darkness and Decay and the Red Death held illimitable dominion over all.

A "MULTITUDE OF DREAMS" was loose on New Year's Eve in Manhattan as 1977 drew to a close. Selected guests were invited to pay $300 per couple to attend a masquerade ball at Régine's, the very chic, very *in* Park Avenue discotheque. From behind a peephole, cold eyes screened the guests before the door opened to a room of varnished lights and mirrored ceilings. On regular nights, the menu advertised two scrambled eggs with caviar: "Les Deux Oeufs Poule au Caviar" ($19), "Caviar d'Iran" ($60). A bottle of Chivas Regal could be purchased for $90; a bottle of Coca-Cola, for $6. The disco, owner Régine Zylberberg once told writer Julie Baumgold, "has a whole psychology. You must make people into actors and exhibitionists. . . . People with no names come to see people with names. People with names come to see others they know."

Two thousand elite guests received scroll invitations to attend an unusual New Year's party at Studio 54, the even more *in* disco on the West Side of Manhattan. "Nothing new has been done on New Year's Eve for a long time," explained thirty-three-year-old co-owner Steve Rubell, "and we thought this year was the year to do it." Starting at 3 A.M., and for only $40 per person, Grace Jones would be performing—*The Grace Jones*, who had driven motorcycles onstage, danced half naked in gay discos, her head shaved into a fuzzy cap, her pretty face masked with green and red paint. People were just *dying* to know what she would do next. "I know what I'm doing," Grace said, "and I know there is money to be made at what I am doing."

The plague spreading throughout the rest of New York City remains largely invisible to those sealed off in the castle of mid-Manhattan. All "the appliances of pleasure" are here. Walk along Fifth Avenue, one of the most heavily trafficked pedestrian streets in the world. Window-shop at Gubelin of Switzerland, where a gold Patek Philippe watch retails for $4,900 and gold cuff links for $660; at Godiva's, where a box of Belgian chocolates goes for $35; at Gucci's, with their modest $315 calf billfolds trimmed with 18-karat gold. Stroll past the Olympic Towers' $750,000 cooperative apartments.

One avenue east, on Madison, a rash of new boutiques are opening, many at rents of $50 per square foot. Complice sells special jeans for $65; Ungaro's, silk blouses for $250; Pumpkins and Monkeys, a child's dress for $235. The waitresses in Confetti wear Bill Blass vests.

Manhattan is thriving. Six of the nation's largest banks, employing 120,000 people, are headquartered here, as are nine of the ten biggest ad agencies, all but two of the Big Eight accounting firms, 42 of the 50 leading investment banking establishments, 90 of the Fortune 500 companies, one-third of the nation's 48 largest law firms. According to the real-estate brokers Cross & Brown, Manhattan's real-estate market in 1977 was the highest it had been in five years; nearly 3 million square feet of vacant office space was rented in one year, and prices of $25 per square foot were common. The first new office tower in five years is planned at 487 Park, an avenue that is already a crowded steel-and-glass warehouse for the nation's foremost corporations. Four new office towers will rise on Madison Avenue between 50th and 57th streets. The Chrysler Building is being refurbished, as are other once-abandoned relics. The one-square-block $147 million Citicorp Center was christened in the fall of 1977; rising 59 stories between East 53rd and 54th streets, and stretching from Third Avenue to Lexington, the complex is bursting with ten restaurants and assorted shops, including one that sells imported bonbons.

Housing is also at a premium. In 1977, Manhattan real-estate values soared 30 percent. According to *W*, a publication devoured by people who frequent Régine's, the monthly rent for a two-bedroom apartment in Paris is $729; in London, $720; in Zurich, $500. In chic areas of Manhattan, the same apartment rents for $1,170. The co-op market is at its zenith. On Park Avenue north of Régine's, where white-gloved doormen patrol under shaded canopies, limousines stand at attention and nannies push baby strollers across a wide boulevard lush with tulips and begonias, the average three-bedroom apartment sells for $200,000. Saudi Arabia's Foreign Minister, Prince Saud al-Faisal, tried—and failed—to purchase an eighteen-room apartment at 640 Park for $600,000, with yearly maintenance charges of $25,000.

Manhattan's real-estate boom is matched by its tourism, now New York's second leading industry. More visitors (16.5 million) and conventions (834) were drawn to the city in 1976 than at any time since the 1964-65 World's Fair. They came to spend $1.5 billion and buy 10 million tickets to Broadway's 36 theaters and 500 sister theaters off Broadway, to visit the 400 art galleries, 90 night clubs, 50 institutions for the performing arts, 28,000 restaurants, 30 department stores and 61 museums. Most of these attractions are in Manhattan, where the 100,000 first-class tourist hotel rooms are located. To cope with this surge of tourists, new hotels are in the works. Harry Helmsley plans a fifty-seven-story, 600-room luxury palace—to be called the Palace—on Madison Avenue and is considering another on East 42nd Street. William Zeckendorf, Jr., recently redecorated the Delmonico and McAlpin hotels. The old Commodore Hotel is scheduling a comeback as a Hyatt Hotel, and the New York Hilton is contemplating the addition of 1,200 rooms. Manhattan restauranteurs, whose volume in 1977 was one-third greater than it was in 1976 (a very good year), worry not about customers but about President Carter's proposal to eliminate tax deductions for the "two-martini lunch."

For those fleeing the real or imagined plague abroad, the island of Manhattan is the new Mecca. In 1964, the United States was home for only 11 foreign banks. By July 1977, Manhattan alone had 128 foreign branches, with assets of $44 billion. Thirty-two of these had opened in the last year. Today, almost 70 percent of the total U.S. assets of all foreign banks are sequestered in Manhattan branches. Seventy-eight countries maintain consulates in Manhattan, more than in Washington. There are 131 international law firms and 543 restaurants offering foreign specialties. The twin 110-story towers of the World Trade Center, in lower Manhattan, house 120 foreign companies representing 60 nations. One-third of the new 1977 leases acquired by Rudin Management Corporation, one of Manhattan's premier landlords, were signed by overseas firms. During the first two years of the city's fiscal crisis, 1975–77, foreign companies leased 466,000 square feet of new office space.

An infectious spirit permeates mid-Manhattan. Broadway stars from *Annie, A Chorus Line, The Wiz, The King and I* and *Dracula* volunteer their time to belt out a joyously brilliant "I love New York" television commercial. Sylvester Stallone, Frank Sinatra, Faye Dunaway, Diana Ross and other big names are again making movies here. It seems like everyone, including me, is a Liz Smith addict, reading her New York *Daily News* column to learn if Woody still wears baggy pants, if Halston still adores Liz, Bianca and Liza, if Warren and Diane are nibbling on each other's ears at Elaine's. As I write, Central Park is closed on weekends, a victory over the automobile for the strollers and joggers. Monet is featured at the Metropolitan Museum; Calder and Matisse, at the Guggenheim;

Saul Steinberg, at the Whitney; eighteenth-century Nigerian wood carvings, at the Museum of Natural History just blocks from my home. The Beethoven Society is at Hunter College; Baryshnikov, at the Metropolitan Opera House; film retrospectives, at the Regency; jazz at Hopper's and Jimmy Ryan's. Just about every newspaper and magazine in the world can be found on 42nd Street, as can just about every species of human. Even if you revel in none of these glories, New York can never be boring. It is the eighth wonder of the world. After you've seen the Pyramids, that's it for Egypt. In Manhattan, there's a pyramid on nearly every block.

Occasionally, Manhattan residents or visitors will confront intruders from another world—the world of Eighth Avenue, with its panhandlers, pimps and prostitutes; a stray youth gang snatching purses and gaining attention, as happened in the summer of 1977, by beating up two *New York Times* editors. Most people who run New York, or write about it, live in Manhattan or its suburbs. Without walls or iron gates, they have reason to feel as secure and sealed off as Prince Prospero.

But this Manhattan offers a distorted view of New York City. Outside, a plague spreads, ravaging much of the rest of the city. Two miles from Régine's, where Park Avenue plunges thirty feet, grim railroad tracks suddenly surface to slice the avenue in half. The panorama of glistening office towers, penthouses and tulips gives way to tenements and abandoned, rubble-strewn lots. This is the world of Frank Rivera. Rivera rarely gets to visit south of 96th Street, except to work as a peddler on the sidewalk across from the Plaza Hotel. Fifty-seven blocks away from where he works, Rivera lives in a five-room walk-up at 1646 Park Avenue. The rent is $70 a month. The plaster is peeling. Rats abound. The wail of the subway is the music he has lived with, here, for the last twenty years.

Frank Rivera's home is East Harlem. In nearby Central Harlem, once known as the black capital of America, 24 percent of the residents were on welfare in 1977; 75 percent of the children were born to mothers without husbands. The infant mortality rate, 42.8 for each 1,000 births, is more than twice the citywide average. Each year, 3,000 apartments fall to arson, abandonment, decay.

North of the Harlem River, in the Bronx, a butcher sweeps the sidewalk in front of his store on the Boston Post Road. I ask him directions to Charlotte Street. "That's easy," he says. "You can't miss it. You just drive until you see nothing. Then you know you're there." In much of Manhattan, it's hard to find a vacant apartment. In the South Bronx, it's sometimes hard to find a building. More than 2,000 square blocks are devastated. Fifty-one apartment buildings, housing 3,000 people, once stood on Charlotte Street and its adjoining blocks—just seven miles from Régine's. Today, only nine remain standing, eight of them sealed shut by brick or ruined by fire. Amid the hills of rubble and discarded garbage, 100 people still reside at 1500 Boston Post Road and Wilkins Avenue. Their rents range from $140 to $160 a month for the 39 one- or two-bedroom apartments.

Once, not long ago, this neighborhood was different. There were tennis courts; the local synagogue sported Moorish columns; people darted in and out of Solly Sherman's vegetable and deli market. There was a Rumanian restaurant where a meal of chopped calves' liver, kosher broiled steak, white radishes, pickles and free seltzer came to $1.35. Today, there are no tennis courts, and the synagogue, its columns painted gray, houses the Tremont Crotona Day Care Center. Solly Sherman's and the Rumanian restaurant are gone, destroyed years ago by fire.

There are other Charlotte Streets in the South Bronx. Between 1970 and 1975, the South Bronx lost 16 percent of its housing, or 43,000 apartments, and over the last twelve years 80,000 apartments have been abandoned. Forty percent of all its manufacturing jobs have disappeared. Each day, there are ten fires. Each week, an estimated four blocks succumb to physical decay. The per capita income is 40 percent of the national average; one of three residents is on welfare; only one of four students entering an academic high school actually graduates; the area has lost 10,000 jobs in the last four years.

According to the City Department of Health, the two health districts on the Upper East Side of Manhattan, between Park and Fifth avenues, contain 2,063 doctors. In two comparable South Bronx health districts, Tremont and Morrisania, there are no doctors.

Nothing prepares the eye or ear for such statistics, for the first sight of the "nothing" that is Charlotte Street, for the youth gangs who use moving police vans for target practice. And only a military war prepares the mind for the massive evacuation from the area. Were the Bronx a city, its population of 1.5 million would make it the nation's fifth largest. Yet in fifteen years half its white residents

—mostly middle-income taxpayers—have fled, with the contagion spreading even to the once-glorious Grand Concourse that marches north through the borough.

Brooklyn would qualify as the fourth largest city. Six miles south of Régine's, not far from the water separating the borough from Manhattan, one enters Bushwick. The name derives from the Dutch word *Boswijk*, meaning "town of woods." In the 1800's, Bushwick was primarily an agricultural community. As late as the 1930's, its then-famed Claridge Hotel advertised a "country-like setting"; guests could walk to the Bushwick Theatre, which rivaled the Palace for vaudeville. Immigrants from Northern Europe, and later from Italy, settled here; by 1950, neat one- and two-family wooden houses with small gardens were home for Brooklyn's second largest Italo-American community. In 1960, 77 percent of the residents were white working-class.

Today, 75 percent of Bushwick's residents are black or Hispanic, and nearly half the population is on welfare. The Claridge Hotel is gone, as is the Bushwick Theatre. The South Bronx used to rank number one in fires. No more. Bushwick now claims that distinction because it still has buildings to burn; it averages 6,000 fires a year. In the arson and looting following New York's blackout in the summer of 1977, ninety-two stores on Broadway and Bushwick avenues were razed. The owners of sixty-six of them did not plan to reopen.

It was the fires that finally got to Rose and Jesse Napoli. For forty-five years, Jesse's father, Silvestro, owned their six-family house at 152 Harman Street. Before that, his aunt had owned the eighty-year-old building. Then, on September 22, 1977, an arsonist torched the abandoned building two doors away, igniting the adjoining houses and their own top floor. Across the street, six buildings were already burned; behind them, an entire block. In just three months, Harman Street lost fifty families to safer neighborhoods. And on a sunny October day, Harman Street lost the Napolis.

It used to be that Brooklyn's Bedford-Stuyvesant and Brownsville neighborhoods, alone, looked like sets for a World War II movie. But the plague has spread to Bushwick, as it is spreading to the neighboring community of Williamsburg. In the same month the Napolis departed, the Love Brothers, a not-so-loving youth gang, were terrorizing the 100 tenants of a six-story building on South Fourth Street. They smashed windows, stole furniture and tore out fixtures, peddling stoves for $35, steam radiators for $3. Their reign of terror lasted a week, at the end of which the building was vacant. The youth gangs—some employed by landlords seeking to collect insurance, some just out for kicks—no longer alarm police and are often ignored or overlooked; they have become a normal part of urban life.

South of Williamsburg, on the southern tip of Brooklyn, is Coney Island, where my parents still live. Once the amusement capital of the United States, featuring white sandy beaches, Steeplechase, Luna Park, Ravenhall and Feltman's amusement areas, the 5¢ Nathan's hot dog and a million tourists on hot summer weekends, Coney Island is the next Bushwick. Many of the wooden one- and two-family homes have been ravaged by fire; empty lots abound; youth gangs freely roam the streets, some openly flaunting shotguns. Luna Park burned down, and Feltman's and Steeplechase are gone. A concrete parking lot blankets much of Ravenhall. Most stores along Mermaid Avenue, once the main shopping thoroughfare, are now burned out or abandoned. Nathan's sells fewer hot dogs, and those they do sell cost 75¢. The parachute jump, which can be seen from Manhattan's Empire State Building, has been closed for eight years and is scheduled to be torn down and sold as scrap. At one time, it dominated the skyline; today hundreds of millions of dollars' worth of public housing projects crowd the sky.

The changes in Harlem, the South Bronx, Bushwick, Williamsburg and Coney Island are mirrored in declining neighborhoods throughout the city—East New York, Borough Park, South Jamaica, Long Island City, Corona, Greenpoint, Fort Green, Washington Heights, Crown Heights. Of the city's 340 health districts, almost one-half have less than one physician for every 1,000 residents—one-third the national average and in stark contrast to the average of 42 per 1,000 residents on the Upper East Side of Manhattan. A "successful city neighborhood," Jane Jacobs wrote in *The Death and Life of Great American Cities*, requires "eyes upon the street, eyes belonging to those we might call the natural proprietors of the street." Neighborly eyes ensured safety, a feeling of security, of community. In growing numbers of city neighborhoods, people no longer sit on stoops, no longer venture out at night. Eyes are fixed on television sets and bolted doors. Neighborhoods exist in name only.

Like Prince Prospero's minions, New York has been bleeding—jobs and people. Since 1969, 11 percent of its jobs—more than

600,000—have disappeared. Since 1947, the city has lost one-half its 1 million manufacturing jobs. Since 1952, it has lost 80 percent of its 50,000 longshoreman jobs. Of 161 job categories policed by the federal Bureau of Labor Statistics, 147 registered a loss of jobs between 1969 and 1976. Had the city's economy expanded at the same rate as the nation's between 1965 and 1974, a study by Alan Campbell and Roy Bahl of Syracuse University concluded, it would have gained 25 percent, or 1.03 million jobs.

Since World War II, New York, like many older cities, has been transformed. Almost 2 million middle-income residents have moved out, and almost 2 million mostly poor residents have moved in. The city's tax base has shrunk as its need for services has expanded. In 1960, 78 percent of the city was white; by 1975, 62 percent. And these figures do not include illegal aliens, variously estimated from 500,000 to 1.5 million people. Noting that 60 percent of the city's population under fourteen is black or Hispanic, Bernard Gifford of the Russell Sage Foundation wrote, "It seems likely that the 1980 census will reveal a non-white majority in New York City."

There would be little concern if the melting pot were melting. It is not. Once, New York served as an incubator, nursing the poor and hoisting them into the middle class. But that was when New York was growing, when there were jobs. By the early 1970's, almost 30 percent of the city's population was receiving some form of public assistance. Between 1970 and 1974, former Mayor Abe Beame reported, the income of New York City blacks declined by 3.7 percent.

Like many nations in Europe, New York has developed a permanent underclass, a group of people not easily reachable even if there were adequate jobs and counseling and broad social services. It is, said Senator Ted Kennedy in 1978, "the great unmentioned problem of America today." Michael Harrington wrote eloquently of this new group in his 1962 book, *The Other America*: "If a group has internal vitality, a will—if it has aspiration—it may live in dilapidated housing, it may eat an inadequate diet, and it may suffer poverty, but it is not impoverished. So it was in those ethnic slums of the immigrants that played such a dramatic role in the unfolding of the American dream. The people found themselves in slums, but they were not slum dwellers."

Thirty percent of all New York births in 1976, according to a research study by Nicholas Kisburg of Teamsters Joint Council 16, were illegitimate. That same year, according to the City Health Department, more than 50 percent of all black and 45 percent of all Hispanic births were illegitimate, and in some neighborhoods the figure was higher. In the last ten years, the number of false-alarm fires has zoomed from 37,414 to 249,041. We have a growing number of people, says Deputy Mayor Herman Badillo, "who have no superego, no sense of right or wrong." That is the affliction of seventeen-year-old Francisco Mendez, a Bronx teenager accused of twenty-five counts of murder for setting fire to a Bronx social club, killing twenty-five and injuring twenty-four. When the foreman of the jury announced the verdict in State Supreme Court on February 10, 1978, Mendez smiled, turned to face the spectators, and shrugged.

Confirming the 1968 warning of the National Advisory Commission on Civil Disorders, New York continued to move toward two separate societies—one black, one white. It was not just the rich or some Catholics who sent their kids to private schools. By 1977, only 29 percent of the city's white population attended public schools, and three-quarters went to schools that were at least 50 percent white. According to a Board of Education brief, "The rapidly changing demographics of the city have virtually eradicated the chances for meaningful integration in the Bronx, Manhattan and even Brooklyn." By 1987, says Dr. Richard Vigilante, Director of the Board's Office of Educational Statistics, the white enrollment in all five boroughs will be 14 percent.

There was considerable controversy in 1976 when Housing Administrator Roger Starr proposed a city policy of "planned shrinkage"—reducing services to blighted neighborhoods and encouraging a smaller city population. Instead, New York continues to follow a policy of non-planned shrinkage. Between 1970 and 1975, the city's population shrank by 491,000—one of every 16 residents left. What troubles people like Sam Ehrenhalt, Deputy Regional Commissioner of the Bureau of Labor Statistics, is that those who left were mostly middle-income taxpayers, including many blacks and Hispanics. People moving up the economic ladder are moving out. New York is shrinking, but it's losing the wrong people. There are too many poor people, which means extra services, and too few middle-income taxpayers to pay for them. The city and its ghettos are not perceived as the land of opportunity. A poll conducted in late 1976 for Democratic mayoral candidate Percy Sutton buttresses this gloomy prognosis: 51 percent of black

Democrats who planned to vote in the primary said they're thinking of moving from the city.

The city's fiscal crisis is a result of this dwindling economic base. Mayor Beame tried to hide it, but the city's deficit—like the Red Death—kept spreading. The Mayor's final budget, offered in the spring of 1977, projected a gap of $86 million for fiscal 1978, not counting over $700 million of expenses still financed by the capital budget. Running for reelection, Beame strove to paint the best face on things, claiming that there was "light at the end of the tunnel." Running to get away from political responsibility for the city, the state Emergency Financial Control Board, which since 1975 has been empowered to oversee city finances, claimed that the budget was "technically balanced." Soon after Beame lost the September 1977 primary, the same city officials who tiptoed behind his $86 million claim suddenly discovered that the gap had widened to $468 million. Beame corrected them, giving the new figure of $249 million. In January, the new Koch administration presented to Washington a four-year financial plan that pegged the city's true gap at $1.022 billion, not counting the cost of new labor contracts.

While Beame was painting a rosy picture, the city's official prospectus to potential investors was gloomy. The May 20, 1977, 141-page "Official Statement" received little notice but is worth quoting. By June 1976, it reported, the city's debt totaled an average of $1,476 for each of the city's 7.5 million residents, a sum approached by no other city in the country and representing an increase of 25 percent in one year. And this total $12.6 billion debt did not include the $8.5 billion "unfunded accrued liability" it said was owed future city pensioners. The report also showed that the value of city real estate had declined and that debt as a percentage of the total value of taxable property reached 28.6 percent—up 45 percent in one year.

Manhattan property values soared by over $200 million in 1977, but City Comptroller Harrison Goldin reported in early 1978 that $214.2 million worth of real estate was removed from the tax rolls that year—the third consecutive year in which the value of city real estate declined. Outside mid-Manattan, abandoned housing multiplies like a cancer. There are 25,000 pieces of property—now mostly razed buildings and lots—off the tax rolls. Even more serious, according to Deputy Mayor Herman Badillo, by June 1979 "the city will pick up a minimum of 25,000 buildings this year." These buildings, called IN REM properties, are being abandoned by landlords usually because they lose money. Said Badillo, "That means the city will be forced to take over 150,000 apartments, or over one-half million people this year. That's a disaster. That's a whole city." Shaking his head, Badillo added, "By the end of the year the city could have 50,000 to 60,000 buildings."

Housing Commissioner Nat Leventhal pegs the number at 25,000 and says there are three alternatives: the buildings can be sold to tenants or to landlords, hopefully returning them to the tax rolls, or the city itself must own and manage them. When I asked Leventhal the "optimum" percentage of buildings he thought could be returned to private or tenant ownership with the most vigorous city effort, he answered, "Perhaps 15 percent."

Thus the city program is destined to fail even if it succeeds. For the foreseeable future, the city will be saddled with the fuel and other costs of managing these buildings. Worse, it is deprived of real-estate taxes, its prime tax source. And it has a difficult task in collecting rent. According to one study, only 7 percent of these buildings' tenants paid rent. Mayor Koch, in urging their eviction, said less than half paid rent. Many tenants see little reason to waste rent money on buildings with no improvements. Others know the city cannot easily collect. Many simply can't pay. A 1976 federal study found that between 1970 and 1975 the city's median rent climbed 57 percent—three times faster than the median income of renters. With costs rising, many landlords—particularly those in Brooklyn, the Bronx, north and south Manhattan—can't afford the buildings, while beleaguered tenants can't afford the rent.

Not only are buildings being abandoned, but New York's aging infrastructure is crumbling. The City Planning Commission issued an eighty-nine-page report in early 1978 warning that "renewing the city's capital stock is second in priority only to resolving the fiscal crisis." Alarmed, they found that many of the city's 51 bridges "face collapse," as did some of its 6,000 miles of sewers, 80 sewage pumping stations, 6,200 miles of paved streets, 6,700 subway cars, 4,550 buses 1,695 sanitation trucks, 32 million feet of water tunnel trunk, 20,000 trunk valves, 25,000 acres of parkland. Because of the fiscal crisis, the city could not borrow sufficient funds to finance its capital budget. Even if the federal government were to approve long-term loans to the city, the report noted, Mayor Beame's four-year fiscal plan did not provide adequate funds for capital improvements. Ominously, it concluded, "Yet the city's infrastructure—worth billions and billions of dollars—is an irreplaceable and essential asset. It is the platform on which the economy rests, the basis of all amenities, and the anchor for neighborhoods. Were it to break down, many thriving activities associated with New York City would come to a halt."

Which represents a true picture of New York: booming Manhattan or Charlotte Street? Those neighborhoods coming alive or those that are dying? The burst of tourism or burgeoning abandonment? Is New York's economic decline a snapshot, taken at one point in time and subject to reversal, or a continually moving picture? Like the proverbial glass of water which is either half full or half empty, the answer depends on feelings as well as facts. One can choose to emphasize the rise of Brooklyn's Carroll Gardens or the fall of Coney Island; one can point to the fact that New York has three times as many Fortune 500 companies as its nearest competitor or that its total has fallen from 140 to 90.

No one is immune to subjective judgments, not even Herb Bienstock. The regional head of the federal Bureau of Labor Statistics makes his home in Bayside, Queens, and his living collecting, compiling and interpreting facts. The city has been his home for fifty-odd years, and not even the grim numbers spewing from his computers can blight the beauty he sees in New York. Several years ago, I visited the Bureau's Times Square office to meet with Bienstock and three of his economists. We reviewed the city's depressing facts—the lost jobs, shrinking population, rising taxes and living costs, racial polarization, abandoned housing. After two hours, the three economists and I felt almost suicidal.

Not Herb Bienstock. Slowly, he lifted himself from a deep chair and wandered over to the wide windows overlooking Times Square. Thirty-four stories below stretched a panorama of empty office buildings, abandoned hotels, porn theaters and massage parlors. "Do you really feel New York is deteriorating?" he asked of no one in particular. "It looks pretty good to me."

Today, New York City is looking "pretty good" to a growing number of urban economists and civic boosters. "I'm definitely optimistic about this city's long-term economic recovery," Bienstock told me in early 1978. "The reason I'm optimistic about the mid- and late eighties is that the disasters that have visited us are turning around almost on their own. In the eighties, a lot of politicians are going to be taking credit for improved employment opportunities that had their divine origin in 1962."

In that year, the birth rate began to drop, eventually thinning the ranks of young people looking for work. Projections by the New York State Department of Labor show that another 340,000 jobs will be lost between 1974 and 1985, but Bienstock does not see this as significant. Because of deaths and retirements, he says, there will be a net of 1 million job openings during this period. And fewer youths will be chasing those 1 million jobs. Bienstock also cites the city's more competitive cost of living. "With our high unemployment rate," he explains, "comes a low-level cost-of-living increase. Since 1967, living costs have risen faster in Houston than in New York, though ours are still higher. Between September 1976 and September 1977, New York registered the lowest increase—4.9 percent—of twelve metropolitan areas. The cost of living rose faster in the U.S."

The Bureau's calculations show that though the flight of middle-income residents temporarily ceased in 1976, the city's population was expected to continue to decline; labor and welfare costs, which used to lead the nation, are now more comparable because they are rising faster elsewhere. A 1977 study by the Fantus Corporation, the nation's largest business location consultants, showed that the earnings of industrial workers in New York were below the national average. Manufacturing wages in 1977 climbed only 4.6 percent compared to 7.7 percent nationally. New York city and state taxes have begun to inch down. In an energy-starved nation, New York's density and vast mass transit system become energy savers. No matter what weight is given to somber facts, New York remains the world's premier cultural, port, service and communications center. It is also true that trends suddenly change—two years ago, few predicted the resurgence of Manhattan real estate, Columbus Avenue or Park Slope.

But such optimism can become a narcotic. New York residential housing construction was up 41 percent in 1977; however, that amounted to only 7,600 units—one-seventh the number lost each year to fire, abandonment and demolition. The Bureau of Labor Statistics reports that by 1985 white-collar jobs will increase from 59 to 76 percent of the city's labor force. Yet the blue-collar population, only 60 percent of whom can read at grade level (and this figure does *not* include Hispanics), will be chasing white-collar jobs which many will not be qualified to hold.

Except for the fools among them, the optimists do not argue that New York's economy has been transformed. Implicitly, they're saying that conditions elsewhere are growing worse or that the city's decline has slowed rather than stopped. But decline continues despite the rosy efforts of the Bureau of Labor Statistics. The heading on their 1977 year-end review of New York and the region's economy, for instance, was JOBLESS RATE AT THREE YEAR LOW IN NEW YORK–NORTH-EASTERN NEW JERSEY AND NEW YORK CITY AS AREA PAYROLLS RISE 7,000; INFLATION RATE MODERATES WHILE EARNINGS SHOW RECORD GAINS. Bienstock's summary gushed that New York City's 9.4 percent unemployment rate was "about 2 percentage points below year ago levels, marking the first decline in four years."

Read on, however, and you stumble upon the following:

■ "The job total in New York City was down over the year to a total of 3,164,000." But, they later explain, "The 1976–77 decline was *moderate* [italics added] compared with losses totaling 340,000 in the 1973–76 period."

■ "Factory employment in the City inched down by 3,000 in 1977 following a 7,000 rise in 1976." But this was "a favorable development considering the 1969–75 drop of nearly 300,000."

■ "In New York City, the extent of job loss was down to around 15,000 over the year by September and October, the smallest annual drops for any month since late 1973."

■ "While the City's 1977 jobless rate was below the double digit levels of each of the prior two years, it remained high relative to earlier years, and was about double the 4.8 percent rate at the beginning of the 1970's."

■ While the city lost jobs: "The Nation experienced its second consecutive year of employment expansion in 1977."

What explains the decline in city unemployment despite the loss in 1977 of 41,000 jobs? A smaller population might be one answer, but Bienstock says the population had stabilized. The answer, laments a Bureau official, is that "people are dropping out of the labor force, becoming so discouraged that they give up looking." Or perhaps many subsist more profitably on the streets. We often ignore this because we cannot quantify it and because it is so painful. Unemployment is actually higher than our already bleak statistics suggest.

By early 1978, the Bureau was reporting the good news that city jobs had grown by 16,500 from February 1977 to February 1978. But even this hopeful sign was potentially misleading. Such an increase reflected an expanding national economy, growing at a rate of 4 percent, and obscured the depressing news that New York's job growth of one-half of 1 percent lagged behind that of every major city in America. Deputy Bureau Chief Sam Ehrengalt told me in April 1978 that he expected the city to lose another 250,000 jobs over the next five years. "The bleeding has stopped—for the moment," he said.

That New Yorkers should become dispirited in such circumstances is inevitable, since imperceptibly the outrageous has become normal. Potholes and dirty streets are normal. Poor people are normal. Fear of crime is normal. Corrupt building inspectors, doctors and nursing home operators stealing from Medicaid, city workers not working, pushers and pimps roaming streets as freely as hot dog vendors—all are normal in New York City.

Terrified teachers are normal. While visiting Harren High School one day, I stopped to wait for the elevator on the fourth floor. Classes were in session, and the corridor was empty except for a pretty, middle-aged woman who was also waiting for the elevator. She was a teacher.

"Excuse me," she inquired softly. "Are you going to the first floor?"

"Yes," I said.

"I don't like to walk down the staircase alone," she explained, smiling. "Would you mind escorting me?"

Her nonchalant tone bespoke neither fear nor shame. When I went to high school, we feared bumping into teachers in the stairwells. Today, teachers fear bumping into their dangerous students. To a visitor, that change is a surprise; what's shocking is the teacher's air of resignation. She had come to assume that danger was part of her job.

People may accept danger, but they don't enjoy it. An August 1977 New York Times–CBS survey of city residents revealed that two-thirds rated the city a fair or poor place to live. One month earlier, a similar nationwide poll found that only 6 percent of Americans thought New York City a good or excellent place to live. The attitude becomes a statistic when people pick up and move. "We know the image of New York that many people have is exaggerated," Robert F. Flood, Vice President for Corporate Services of Union Carbide, said just weeks before that giant decided to depart. "We have many employees who live safe and happy lives here. But it is an image we have to contend with. And it isn't just crime and high living costs. It's the city's changing ethnic mix, which makes some people uncomfortable, and the graffiti on the subways, the dirt on the streets and a lot of other things." The company's surveys found that "a substantial majority" of executives and managers, down to those earning $15,000 a year, wanted Union Carbide to move.

It is difficult—no, dangerous—to ignore the economic and social contagion that has swept New York City. The contagion observes few borders. Between 1970 and 1975, New York State lost 2.5 percent of all its nonagricultural jobs. In that same period, the nation's nonagricultural employment leaped 7.4 percent. The state's economic stagnation, a 1977 report by Syracuse University economist Roy Bahl disclosed, meant the loss of $6 billion in potential tax revenues since 1973.

The contagion afflicts most of the Northeast. Since 1934, there has been a massive geographic redistribution of the nation's wealth. Forty-five years ago, New York was in fact the Empire State, its per capita income about 60 percent above the nation's average. Connecticut, Massachusetts, Rhode Island and New Jersey ranged from 37 to 55 percent above the nation. No longer. A 1976 study for the New York State Economic Development Board disclosed that after adjusting for the region's higher living costs, the "real" income of the average citizen of the Northeast was 1 percent below the national average. The region's economic growth rate has lagged behind every other region in the country. Between 1975 and 1977, the Bureau of Labor Statistics reported, employment in the Northeast inched up 2.1 percent—three times slower than the next slowest growth region, the North Central.

Economic stagnation afflicts many older cities. Every time they construct a new building, Detroit and St. Louis, like New York, proclaim the resurgence of their downtown areas; but these downtowns cannot compete with Broadway (ever think of vacationing in Detroit or St. Louis?) nor do they hide the population and job loss mirrored in Cleveland, Philadelphia, Gary, Buffalo, New Orleans, Trenton, and other aging cities. A nationwide Gallup poll, taken in late 1977, found that 36 percent of all urban residents would vacate cities if they could, with overcrowded conditions and crime cited as the chief reasons. The unemployment rate among black Americans, who crowd older cities, is twice that of whites and higher than any time since World War II. The median income of blacks has gone up 105 percent in the last ten years; black poverty has decreased, as has the salary gap between whites and blacks. Still, ten years after the national Commission on Civil Disorders warned that America was moving toward "two societies, one black, one white—separate and unequal," the average median income of a black family ($9,252) is about 60 percent that of the average white family ($15,537). A more recent Rand Corporation study said it was 75 percent. Teenage black unemployment is almost three times greater than for whites—double the gap that existed in the mid-1950's. Nationally, over 50 percent of all black births were illegitimate in 1976; one of every three black youths is supported by welfare. Public schools are more segregated, and the education levels achieved by blacks—central to competing for the growing number of white-collar jobs—is far behind that of white Americans. "A lot of black kids simply feel they don't count, and they don't," says black psychiatrist Alvin Poussaint. "In terms of what makes this society run, they're expendable."

The nation's economy is hardly robust. Inflation is growing faster than income. True, as I write this, the gross national product and consumer spending are expanding, and personal incomes and housing constructions are advancing at a brisk pace; in February 1978, the jobless rate was 6.1 percent, the lowest level in three years. But, here again, we run into the water glass problem. At the end of 1977, 92 million Americans were working; nearly 7 million were not. Looking at those figures, the Commissioner of the federal Bureau of Labor Statistics, Jules Shiskin, told the Joint Economic Committee of Congress, "We ought to be cheering. . . . In terms of unemployment and in terms of gross national product, we are doing better in the current expansion than in any previous expansion in history." The glass was half full, as it was for Gerald Ford when he boasted of growing employment in 1976 (and opponent Jimmy Carter complained of growing unemployment).

To the Chairman of the Committee, Senator William Proxmire, the glass was half empty. "We have lost our sense of outrage, and complacency has set in," he scolded Shiskin. ". . . the continuation of today's high unemployment is a tragedy for nearly 7 million Americans and is costing the federal government some $54 to $60 billion annually."

Some "facts" are hard to dispute. Decomposition, which attacks our older cities, also plagues America's aging industries—often for the same reasons. The lagging productivity of our cities is matched by that of American industry. According to the General Accounting Office, for instance, the average coal miner produced 14 tons a day in 1965 and only 8.5 tons in 1976—yet President Carter's original energy plan called for doubling coal production by 1985. In the first three months of 1978, the productivity of American workers fell 3.6 percent, the steepest decline in four years. Productivity is rising by an average of about 2 percent in the U.S.—three times below the rate in Germany and Japan. As New York or Detroit have trouble competing economically with suburban Connecticut or the Sunbelt, many American industries are getting clobbered by cheaper foreign competition. In 1977, foreign steel imports rocketed 114 percent—up 19.3 million tons. This explains why the steel industry laid off 20,000 employees over a span of just several months in mid-1977. For eighty-five years, steel mills have bordered the Mahoning River in Ohio; today, they are closing—victims of age, Oriental and European competition, and federal neglect. While the federal government decided to subsidize and help mechanize American agriculture, allowing the U.S. to become the world's chief food provider, it made short-term steel decisions. The government occasionally complained about steel prices, but it ignored the industry's pleas for subsidies and protective tariffs. In contrast, Japan planned ahead, subsidizing the modernization of its steel mills and protecting them with tariffs.

The steel-related automobile industry, which used to dominate the world, has seen its share of the American market diminish under the assault of smaller, cheaper foreign cars—often subsidized by their governments. Two million of these cars glut the American market each year. General Motors' profits are up, but the little sister of the big three auto companies, American Motors, is teetering and, like New York and the steel industry, has requested federal loan guarantees.

The hot breath of foreign competition has invaded another American sanctuary, advanced technology. Just as England, which invented radar, lost its technological lead to America after World War II, America is today losing its near-monopoly. Want to purchase a fine camera and lens? The shelves of American camera stores are crammed with Japanese Nikons. A watch? We have trouble competing with the Swiss. A pocket-size tape recorder for journalists? I wouldn't own anything but a Japanese Sony or Panasonic. Japanese radios, phonographs and television sets are more compact and cheaper. The U.S. may have invented the microwave oven and the citizens band radio, but our share of the world market is dwindling. How can American fabricated clothing compete with clothing fabricated in Taiwan for half the price?

It's tough, which explains the clamor from labor and business executives and liberals—who once advocated free trade—for protective tariffs. "Foreign trade is the guerrilla warfare of economics," declares AFL-CIO President George Meany, "and right now the United States economy is being ambushed." Perhaps Mr. Meany had in mind the RCA Corporation, once the world's television giant, now reducing its payroll and shifting much of its operation overseas to tap cheaper labor. Or perhaps he was thinking of Zenith, the country's largest television manufacturer. In September 1977, Zenith announced that it was laying off one-quarter of its domestic work force and transferring "substantial portions" of its TV module board and chassis assembly operations to plants in Taiwan and Mexico, eliminating another 3,500 jobs. Zenith would also buy stereo products overseas because it was cheaper than making them here, thus erasing another 1,500 jobs.

Foreign competition can also be measured by the U.S. balance-of-payments deficit. In 1977, the chasm between our imports and exports reached a record $20.2 billion—double the figure for 1972, the previous record year. Between January and May 1978, 46 percent of all imports were foreign machinery, electronics, transportation equipment and manufacturing goods. These had overtaken oil as the largest drain on America's growing trade deficit. Still, America's dependence on foreign oil remained a profound problem. Before the Arab oil boycott in 1973, the U.S. imported 35 percent of its oil. By 1977, the U.S. imported 48 percent ($44.3 billion), a 25 percent jump over the previous year. And if current trends continue, federal officials caution that this sum will one day multiply to $550 billion. U.S. Energy Secretary James Schlesinger has warned of a "severe economic trauma of the sort we have not witnessed since the Great Depression."

The Secretary's dire words have been sounded by others. Often. Americans consume energy with the same abandon and unconcern for limits once practiced by New York officials toward their budgets. There is alarm—often exaggerated—that Arab oil interests will come to dominate the American economy and alter our traditional foreign alliances; that we will permanently bespoil the environment; that the planet itself is in danger. Despite the chorus of foreboding, despite President Carter's cardigan sweater and proclamation that 1977 was "the Year of Energy," the year ended with his energy proposals mired in Congressional committee.

The same cannot be said for the economy. It seems that no one knows what to do about the twin problems of unemployment and inflation, though President Carter, with a straight face, promised that 1978 would be "the Year of the Economy." The federal government spends money to attack one problem—unemployment—and contributes to another—inflation. The government simply prints more money, and in 1978 the deficit was expected to reach $60 billion. After a brief lull, inflation in early 1978 was raging at a near-record pace. America's trade imbalance also means we are exporting dollars. As the supply of dollars overtakes demand, the value of the dollar shrinks; investors switch to other currencies, driving down the dollar and America's once-dominant economic role even further.

Not that other nations have answers. The new wave of wealthy immigrants flocking from Europe to Manhattan are seeking to escape their own economic plagues. These refugees, unlike earlier immigrants, do not flee famine or religious persecution. But, like their predecessors, they see their old world crumbling. They fear higher taxes, political instability, terrorism and kidnappings. The oceans offer safety. Manhattan offers tax havens, security, the good life. "In 1965 if I saw a friend from Paris, I would cross the street," Jean de Noyer, owner of Manhattan's fashionable La Goulue restaurant, told a reporter. "Now I just wave. . . ."

Wealthy Europeans view their tax laws as confiscatory and the labor unions as too powerful. The British Empire is preserved in history books. France, where the rich can often avoid paying their share of taxes, is beset by political instability. The Left captured 49 percent of the vote in the 1978 elections, and many business leaders fear the deep divisions between classes—not to mention the divisions within the ruling Gaullist party.

How Italy survives is one of the world's wonders, though Orson Welles had as good an explanation as any. Italy, he said, is the home of 50 million actors, and the only bad ones were on the stage or in films. My forebears deceived Mussolini into believing they were grateful to be ruled by him, then, bless their souls, they hung him upside down. Today, the Red Brigades shoot people in the knees and kidnap and kill former prime ministers. The Italian inflation rate reads like a football score. As it does in Israel, where inflation hovered at 40 percent for two years. In Sweden, once hailed for its economic miracle, and its "middle way" between capitalism and socialism, the GNP declined 2.4 percent in 1977 and consumer spending dropped for the first time since 1931. Canada was lashed by 9 percent inflation and 8.3 percent unemployment in early 1978, and a major province—Quebec, which is larger than France—threatened to secede. Most Western European nations are sagging under the weight of decreased industrial investment, unemployment of 4 to 7 percent, soaring inflation, and a looming shortage of credit. Other nations, like Argentina, experienced an inflation rate of 160 percent in 1977.

With the exception of Germany and Japan, the non-oil-producing nations were punished by balance-of-payment trade deficits. The International Monetary Fund projected that this imbalance would grow throughout the eighties. As deficits, devaluation, unemployment and inflation continue, the fever of protectionism spreads, making cooperative solutions less likely. To keep afloat, many smaller nations—and their bankers—follow New York City's example and borrow or lend excessively. The debt of underdeveloped nations is variously estimated to be between $150 and $250 billion. Much of that mushrooming obligation—as New York's was prior to the 1975 market collapse—is short-term debt. The Fourth World, like many older American cities, cannot compete and has nowhere to turn. Bangladesh does not have the luxury of worrying about inflation. Each year, 70 million people, according to the World Bank, face starvation; one-quarter of the earth's population—1.1 billion human beings—live in countries where annual incomes are less than the $265 weekly earnings of a U.S. auto worker.

An international economy, like a city bond market, is largely predicated on confidence. By 1978, many worried about the "global crisis syndrome," as the Club of Rome dubbed it, about the American dollar, about trade deficits, loan defaults, war in the Middle East or Zaire, the arms race, post-Tito Yugoslavia, inflation, unemployment—about the collapse of confidence in the world economy. Perhaps this explains why Paul Erdman's novel *The Crash of '79* led bestseller lists in 1977 and was read by many as a work of non-fiction.

A BLEAK PICTURE? Perhaps too bleak. As I write this, no American soldiers are being killed or maimed in foreign adventures; fewer

Americans are starving; there is at least more talk about human rights and even evidence of success; England is beginning to tap its North Sea oil riches; Anwar Sadat's peace initiative and Jimmy Carter's spirit of Camp David have inspired people around the world. New York has a new mayor with high expectations; you can actually see citizens bending to shovel the dog shit with their pooper-scoopers, the result of a new law that is being obeyed. And, there is always E. B. White:

> It is a miracle that New York works at all. The whole thing is implausible. Every time the residents brush their teeth, millions of gallons of water must be drawn from the Catskills and the hills of Westchester. . . . The subterranean system of telephone cables, power lines, steam pipes, gas mains, and sewer pipes is reason enough to abandon the island to the gods and the weevils. . . . By rights New York should have destroyed itself long ago, from panic or fire or rioting or failure of some vital supply line in its circulatory system. . . . It should have been wiped out by a plague starting in its slums or carried in by ships' rats. It should have been overwhelmed by the sea that licks at it on every side. The workers in its myriad cells should have succumbed to nerves, from the fearful pall of smoke-fog that drifts over every few days from Jersey, blotting out all light at noon and leaving the high offices suspended, men groping and depressed, and the sense of world's end. It should have been touched in the head by the August heat and gone off its rocker. . . . Mass hysteria is a terrible force, yet New Yorkers seem always to escape it by some tiny margin: they sit in stalled subways without claustrophobia, they extricate themselves from panic situations by some lucky wisecrack, they meet confusion and congestion with patience and grit—a sort of perpetual muddling through.

Despite this book's catalog of depressing facts and its view—expressed jointly by urbanologists George Sternlieb and James W. Hughes, that New York City's "immediate past . . . may be the future"—this pessimist is optimistic enough to live here. In some ways, what I think doesn't square with what I feel.

I love New York. Not just the reality of its museums and neighborhoods and theater and restaurants and architecture, but the idea of New York. The idea of diversity, of the bubbling melting pot, of the special compassion generated by America's Statue of Liberty city, of competition among the best in every occupation. Plays try out on the road before meeting their big test in New York. New York, like Paris, determines next year's fashion. For a journalist, this is the big leagues. Sure, Washington has great journalists, but it's also a small town with one industry (government). In New York, you could spend whole days at newsstands surveying the myriad publications that make their home here. New York is the intellectual battery of America. Yes, greater tranquillity can be found in Plains, Georgia; more of a sense of community, in Peoria, Illinois; more comfort and golf, in suburban Summit, New Jersey, or Houston, Texas. But Sinclair Lewis told us all we need to know about those places.

It's hard not to be arrogant about New York. But it's also hard to ignore that my city's crisis is, in many respects, a metaphor for what is happening socially and economically to America and the world. As we shall see, a generation of city officials sealed their eyes to economic currents; tried to ignore the limits imposed by a budget or bond market; tried to tax too much, seemingly unaware that business did not have to do business in New York. As elsewhere, New York did not—does not—know how to cope with decline. It could not harmonize what it wished to do socially or politically with what it could afford. Good politics and good economics were at war in New York. Even today, when New York knows what has to be done, there is scant evidence that our democratic political system can stretch to do the job.

New York has trouble coping with its fiscal crisis; America, with its energy crisis; the world's nations, with the spread of armaments. But Cassandras are no fun. So most of us, like Prince Prospero, prefer retreating to the comfort of our own castles.

Chapter Two

The Causes
of New York's
Fiscal Crisis

SEPTEMBER 21, 1938, was a special day for one resident of Long Island. A war was about to explode in Europe, but on this morning he was more concerned with a long-awaited package that arrived in the mail. Excitedly, he unwrapped his shiny new barometer, noticing that the needle pointed below 29°, where the dial warned of "Hurricanes and Tornadoes." Ridiculous. It was a sunny day. As recounted by William Manchester in *The Glory and the Dream*: "He shook it and banged it against a wall; the needle wouldn't budge. Indignant, he repacked it, drove to the post office, and mailed it back. While he was gone, his house blew away."

Something like that happened to New York thirty-seven years later. For years, few believed the menacing storm clouds. Since 1898, New York had become America's largest and most important metropolis. Then, in the 1960's, New York stopped growing. Each year, the budget would come up short; each year, officials would devise a temporary solution by taxing a little here, borrowing a little there, fudging everywhere they could. Then, during the year and outside the normal budget review process, they would add a program here or there, and fudge some more. By 1975, city expenditures totaled $12.8 billion, while revenues totaled only $10.9 billion. New York was borrowing to close an annual operating deficit of almost $2 billion. While city and state officials tinkered and wrestled with symptoms, New York was being blown away.

Prophets of fiscal and economic doom were scorned. "New York City is in dire financial condition as a result of mismanagement, extravagance, and political cowardice," cautioned William F. Buckley, Jr., the Conservative party's candidate for mayor in 1965. "New York City must discontinue its present borrowing policies, and learn to live within its income, before it goes bankrupt." Judging the reaction, one would have thought Buckley favored a nuclear war. He was summarily condemned as a "nazi" and a "right-wing kook," as was that other perennial candidate, Vito Battista—who could more easily be called a kook. Similar admonitions were issued by State Senator John Marchi, the Republican/Conservative candidate for mayor in 1969. Marchi was labeled an "extremist" for preaching fiscal responsibility. "They were shooting the messenger," Marchi recalls. His opponents, Liberal/Independent John Lindsay and Democrat Mario Procaccino, pounced on Marchi when he warned that the transit fare would climb to 25¢; they would not allow that to happen. Just weeks after Lindsay was re-elected, the fare climbed to 30¢. There were few voices in opposition. Pithy *Daily News* editorials regularly clanged the alarm, the business-oriented Citizens Budget Commission sometimes issued critiques of city budget gimmicks, but with few allies they were easily dismissed as cranks. When he foreboded that the city was living beyond its means, Democratic gubernatorial contender Howard Samuels was assailed for being "anti–New York."

Such was the temper of the times. Critics were bucking the sixties —the Age of Good Intentions, limitless optimism, when candidates vied to outspend their rivals and promised new ideas, new programs, new solutions. Budgets were not viewed as inflexible boundaries restricting what could be spent. Robert F. Wagner, for twelve years New York's bland mayor, captured the go-go spirit of the times in his final 1965 budget message: "I do not propose to permit our fiscal problems to set the limits of our commitments to meet the essential needs of the people of the city."

Armed with that novel government philosophy, the Statue of Liberty City, home for generations of poor immigrants, commenced an ambitious, politically popular and compassionate effort to care for the less fortunate by taxing the more fortunate. New York undertook its own partial experiment in local socialism and income redistribution, with one clear result being the redistribution of much of its tax base and jobs to other parts of the country as middle-class taxpayers and businessmen fled town.

The city's budget, $2.7 billion in 1961, leaped to $13.6 billion in fiscal 1976. The budget expanded at an annual rate of 8.6 percent from 1961 to 1966, when Wagner was mayor; almost doubled to 15.9 percent annually over John Lindsay's first five years, 1966 to 1971; increased at an average annual rate of 10.2 percent between 1971 and 1975, when the city's economic base was rapidly declining. Of equal significance is how the budget grew. "Between fiscal years 1961 and 1976," concluded the Eighth Interim Report of the Mayor's Temporary Commission on City Finances, "the share of total City expenditures allocated to police, fire, sanitation, and education declined from 46 percent to 30 percent, while the welfare, hospitals and higher education share increased from 22 percent to 37 percent."

From an emphasis on basic services—which are most visible to middle- and upper-income residents—the city's budget shifted to providing more public employee benefits and more services for the poor. "Fifteen years ago," the 1977 report noted, "almost half of every dollar spent for operating the City was allocated to police, fire, sanitation, and education. At present, less than one-third of every dollar goes for these functions." By 1975, the Regional Plan Association said, New York was spending an average of $249 per person in aid to the poor vs. an average of $59 for all other local governments in the state.

As their share of the budget pie diminished, middle-income residents found New York less attractive. And more expensive. By 1975, New York City had as many different taxes (twenty-two) as Howard Johnson's had ice cream flavors. There were personal income and commuter taxes, sales taxes, vault taxes, auto use taxes, stock transfer taxes, cigarette taxes. New York developed another distinction: its middle- and upper-income residents came to shoulder the steepest tax burden in the U.S. Using 1974 data, the Eleventh Interim Report of the Mayor's Temporary Commission disclosed that a city family of four earning $25,000 paid 6.6 percent of its income in local and state taxes—almost three times the national average. (Chicago residents, for instance, paid only 2.1 percent.) And the higher the family's income, the greater the disparity. At the $50,000 level, a city family of four paid 11.1 percent of their income for local and state taxes (double Los Angeles' 5.6 percent and triple the U.S. average of 3.7 percent; a family earning $20,000 in Houston would need $27,071 to have the same disposable income in New York City).

Borrowing also grew. With the cooperation of its banks and financial institutions, the city devised a novel method to print its own money. Because New York was a financial center, and because its banks were underwriting more than they were purchasing city securities for their own accounts, the financial community was performing more a sales than a credit analysis function. They were salesmen, pulling down handsome commissions. So sell they did. Between 1961 and 1975, city debt almost tripled—from $4.3 to $12.3 billion. The city's annual debt service payments jumped from $402 million in 1961 to $2.3 billion in 1976. Excessive borrowing led, inexorably, to excessive budget tricks. What didn't come from Washington, Albany or taxes came from borrowing. An internal memorandum written to Comptroller Goldin in 1975 was appropriately titled "City Debt: The Price of Deception." Sketching past city gimmicks, Goldin's staff concluded that more than 20 percent of all short-term debt ($1.5 billion) was attributed to "gimmicks," as was about 10 percent ($700 million) of all long-term debts. That year alone, the memo said, taxpayers would pay an extra $210 million in interest because of those gimmicks—more than the cumulative total spent annually to maintain city parks, repair streets, run a consumer protection agency, provide public health services, enforce housing codes, administer rent control and provide for the relocation of tenants. By 1976, 56 percent of locally raised tax funds ($3.7 billion) was earmarked not for the delivery of services but for debt service, pension payments and Social Security—consuming 31 percent of the total budget.

As the city's economic base shrank, losing one of every six private-sector jobs between 1969 and 1976, New York pioneered its very own WPA. In 1950, government employees comprised 10.8 percent of the city's work force. By 1975, this number grew to 17.5 percent, most with city jobs. In the sixties, four of every five new jobs were for the government.

All of this took place against a backdrop of massive migration in and out of New York. Though the city's population remained a stable 8 million, between 1950 and 1970 the composition of New York changed dramatically. In those years, the city lost about 25 percent of its white middle-income population (1.6 million) and gained an equal number of (mostly) poor blacks and Hispanics. In 1960, just 4 percent of the city's population—324,000—received public assistance. By 1970, the figure was 14 percent—over 1 million people. The age composition also changed. The city's working-age population, aged twenty-five to fifty-four, dropped from one half of all residents in 1950 to less than two-fifths. At the same time, senior citizens and youths swelled from one-third to two-fifths of the populace. New York lost its "money-providers," as Wallace Sayre and Herbert Kaufman dubbed them in their classic *Governing New York City*, and gained "service demanders."

Thus the city's fiscal crisis, which burst into headlines when New York was no longer able to borrow money in the spring of 1975, was really a symptom of a deeper social and economic malaise. Historically, it is New York's most severe crisis, but not the first. Youth gangs roamed New York streets more freely in the nineteenth century; the stench of horse manure and dead rats hugged the air; children and laborers were exploited; the division between rich and poor was greater; communicable disease and fire were constant perils.

Nor was this New York's first fiscal crisis. The January 12, 1884, issue of *Harper's Weekly* carried this editorial:

> But with the continuance of our present system of government, with an increased appropriation . . . for regular expenses of government— an increase inexcusable in the present depressed condition of business— with vast public works, such as new aqueducts, docks and streets, looming up in the future, it is plain that without a sweeping change the bankruptcy of the city and the decay of its commercial power are only matters of time.

Between 1918 and 1932, the city's budget grew by 250 percent to $631 million; its total debt nearly equaled that of all of the forty-eight states combined; and as a percentage of the city's budget its annual debt service payment was almost twice the 1975 percentage. Expenditures were climbing faster than revenues, leading to a series of budget gimmicks, tax increases, and more borrowing. The payroll was larded with Tammany retainers. In 1930 and 1931, Tammany's docile instrument, Mayor Jimmy Walker, reluctantly fired 11,000 teachers. But, like Abe Beame, his austerity measures were too little and too late. Worried about the city's ability to repay, investors clamped down in 1933. The banks refused to "roll over" (postpone) city short-term debt repayments, prompting a pact between Governor Herbert Lehman, Mayor John O'Brien, who had by then succeeded Walker, and the banks. This "Bankers Agreement," as it was called, imposed a strict 7-point fiscal regimen upon

New York, with the government sacrificing some of its democratic prerogatives—as it would, again, forty-two years later.

There are two basic schools of thought regarding the origins of the current crisis. One stresses that New York is the victim of historical or economic forces, federal or bank decisions, beyond its control; the other, that New York is the victim of self-inflicted wounds. There is merit in both arguments.

America's migration patterns were largely beyond the city's control. New technologies led to the mechanization of farms, which freed many poor blacks and others to search for work in the North. The automobile and federally sponsored roads opened up the country. The airplane and modern telecommunications lessened the dependence of businesses on the New York megalopolis, spawning new, easily reached markets and creating regional cities to serve them. Multiple-story factories were no longer required, and space for expansion was more plentiful elsewhere. As incomes rose, people's thirst to own land and a home—to have space—was not satisfied in crowded cities. Air conditioning made warmer climates more attractive. National immigration policies, particularly toward the Commonwealth of Puerto Rico, opened New York's door to many economic refugees. In this sense, New York was the victim of progress.

Unlike many newer cities, such as Houston, New York could not replenish its tax base by annexing its richer suburbs. In effect, that's what Manhattan did in 1898, after a public referendum permitted the consolidation of the City of New York (Manhattan) with the City of Brooklyn and three largely unsettled areas containing just 150,000 people—the Bronx, Queens and Staten Island. The new City of New York, which had been about equal in population to Chicago and Philadelphia, suddenly more than doubled its population to 3.4 million, becoming the nation's undisputed first city.

New York was also the victim of outside economic forces. A healthy national economy or modest inflation eases local economic woes. When the national economy was zipping along in 1969, the country's unemployment was below 4 percent; black unemployment in urban areas, 7.2 percent; black teenage unemployment, 27.9 percent. In 1975, when the economy was in a tailspin, unemployment more than doubled nationally to 8.3 percent and among urban blacks to 17.7 percent; black youths out of work soared to 41.4 percent.

Unavoidably, New York fell prey to what the Marxists call "capitalist accumulation." In their book *The Fiscal Crisis of American Cities,* Roger E. Alcaly and David Mermelstein trace the roots of the crisis to "a system of economic growth dictated by capital's need to seek ever greater profits." It became less economical to do business in New York. Labor was cheaper in other parts of the country, where unions were less strong, taxes and costs lower, the business climate better. In a competitive system, New York lost its edge.

Larger, older cities are uneconomical in still another way: they cost more. Ponder, for a moment, the sheer size of New York City. In 1977, it generated 30,000 tons of garbage and other waste daily —more than the combined total of London, Paris and Tokyo. Each day, its public transportation system, which accounts for 29 percent of all mass transit trips in the U.S., carries 3.4 million passengers. The replacement of this equipment alone would cost $27 billion. The city maintains 25,000 acres of parks; 1,956 miles of reservoirs provide 1.4 million gallons of water a day. There are 6,000 miles of sewers, 6,200 miles of streets, 950 public schools, 223 firehouses.

It costs more to feed an elephant. New York City's population is the size of Sweden's; its budget is almost equal to India's. According to the Bureau of the Census, cities of 100,000 to 200,000 people spent an average of $280 per person for local government in 1972-73. Cities of 1 million or more were two and a half times as expensive, costing $681 per person. Thomas Muller of the Urban Institute has calculated the cost of providing basic services to be three times greater in cities of more than 1 million residents than those with fewer than 50,000. This is not just a function of size. The entrenched politics and mismanagement of older cities also contributes to steeper costs.

Mayors lost control of their government. As state and federal aid grew, their control of city budgets diminished. In 1961, state and federal aid accounted for 23.9 percent of New York City's budget. Ten years later, the figure was up to 44.1 percent. Usually, these aid programs mandated costs on the city; often, they required matching city funds. Since the federal government usually provided 75 percent "free money," there was a natural inclination to seek more—more programs, more grants, more funds. New York got trapped. When the rate of increase in federal and state aid slowed in the early seventies, the city found it difficult to pare its budget because powerful new constituents were loose and because for each dollar the city cut it could usually save only 25–50¢ of its matching local share. Increased state and federal aid also trapped the city into new borrowing. The bulk of this was reimbursable aid, meaning the city had to raise and spend money in order to qualify for reimbursement. To raise the sums, the city issued revenue anticipation notes (RAN's). When processing and other delays ensued, however, the notes were rolled over, backing up from year to year. By 1975, according to Mayor Koch's first budget message, the city had $2.6 billion in RAN's outstanding against federal and state aid—only part of it the result of fabricated city claims.

Mayors also lost political control. It was politically popular to remove education from "politics," to set up independent agencies and authorities outside of direct mayoral control. Ironically, mayors gained too much power over their budgets (particularly the art of revenue estimating) as they lost control of their governments. By the early 1970's, mayors were held responsible for but did not control public and higher education, health care, and transportation; the books of the powerful Port Authority were closed to City Hall review. Social progress led to aroused public expectations and a proliferation of government, community and neighborhood organizations—city, state and federal agencies, local planning boards, community action agencies, neighborhood health councils, PTA's, church groups, civil rights groups, police precinct councils, senior citizens' centers, ethnic societies. The growth of government spending and citizen involvement, as well as the influence of television and mass communications, liberated New Yorkers from the shackles of political party bosses. But there was a price paid for that freedom. Mayors lost the ability to discipline interest groups, to curb new spending demands, to make decisions stick. "Forty years ago a Tammany political boss could give an order to a mayor," Daniel Bell and Virginia Held wrote in 1969.

Today, no such simple action is possible. On each political issue— decentralization or community control, the mix of low income and middle income housing, the proportion of blacks in the city colleges, the location of a cross-Manhattan or cross-Brooklyn expressway, etc.— there are dozens of active, vocal, and conflicting organized opinions. The difficulty in governing New York—and many other cities as well —is not the "lack of voice" of individuals in city affairs, or the "eclipse of local community," but the babel of voices and the multiplication of claimants in the widened political arena.

Even if "the city had had prudent, statesmanlike financial management over the last decade or two," David Stanley wrote in *Cities in Trouble*, "it still would have been in trouble—not so deep or so soon, but clearly in trouble." Probably.

But to blame historical or social and economic forces, everything and everybody, is to blame nobody. We run the risk of learning nothing from what happened to New York. That's where the other school of thought comes in. In my view, New York is much more the victim of self-inflicted wounds than it likes to admit. After a searching analysis of the city's economy and budget, the Mayor's Temporary Commission on City Finances issued a June 1977 final report which debunked what its authors called the "captive-of-events" theory of the fiscal crisis: the belief that the city had "little or no control over the events leading to the fiscal crisis." Such a theory was "popular," according to the report, because "it tends to absolve local political leaders of responsibility for the fiscal crisis and buttresses the also-popular view that the solution to the City's financial problems lies in increased Federal and State aid rather than local political reform. The 'captive-of-events' theory thus has political as well as theoretical underpinnings that provide a justification for previous City policies and a rationale for not changing them in the future." Pretty strong stuff, particularly when you consider that those signing the report include former Mayor Wagner, Governor Rockefeller's former Chief of Staff, Alton Marshall, former City Corporation Counsel Leo Larkin, and the head of the Central Labor Council, Harry Van Arsdale.

The following pages attempt to isolate some of the key events and city, state and federal decisions which helped cripple New York. Some of these decisions were bad; some were good, some neither. All had profound consequences. At the risk of overdramatization, they might be called the "original sins."

Growth of the Suburbs

Americans were shocked in the mid-1970's when the Marxist government of Cambodia harshly ordered the resettlement of a nation. Millions were forced out of cities and into the countryside. The intention of the ruling claque, backed by a murderous militia, was to yank Cambodia back into an agrarian, preindustrial society. An entire people was uprooted at gunpoint.

America experienced a voluntary but no less massive migration, as poor blacks and Hispanics moved north and middle- and upper-income whites fled to the suburbs. The causes of the fiscal crisis cannot be fully comprehended without charting this exodus of wealth and flood of poor people. Admittedly, population shifts were inevitable. They result from "progress"—air conditioning and superhighways and the airplane helped open the South. People's natural desires for newness and space and property are not easily satisfied in aging, congested cities.

But a good deal of this population shift was foreordained by city, state and federal policies promoting highways and low-interest government-sponsored home loans. Such policies did not originate with masterbuilder Robert Moses or the federal government, as is commonly assumed. In a fascinating piece of research, Cornell's Robert Finch unearthed the original 1929 plan of the New York Regional Plan Association. Today, the Association is dedicated to mass transportation and controlled growth; fifty years ago, it was dedicated to and controlled by Manhattan real-estate interests whose aim was to replace the sprawling, low-rise lofts and tenements with high-rise buildings. The Association's twelve-volume plan urged a "highway system, designed like a sculptor's armature to serve as infrastructural support for the desired suburbanization and decentralization of the region. . . ." The plan proposed to shift Manhattan's economic base from light industry to office towers. It was silent about the subway system and largely ignored the issue of mass transportation. It was this plan that was later followed and supplemented by Robert Moses. Manhattan real-estate values soared, and roads cut wide swathes through neighborhoods.

There was business logic to the plan. From a profit-making point of view, the crowded lofts and tenements and small factories were inefficient. Greater profits could be generated from high-rise buildings housing many more rent-paying tenants and businesses. The highways made for cheaper truck transportation. In a free economy, it was not surprising to see landlords and developers act in their own interest. Perhaps a socialist system, intent on development, would have made similar decisions—with the buildings even uglier, a tomb to proletarian solidarity rather than an ice-skating rink in Rockefeller Center. But the demands of profits and growth inevitably clashed with neighborhoods and a sense of community.

Public officials, spurred on by a plethora of developers, construction unions, lawyers, insurance agents and patronage-hungry political leaders, plunged ahead. In the 1930's, the federal government financed private homes by creating the Federal Housing Administration to stimulate the flow of money into home mortgages. This effort was interrupted by World War II, but then on June 22, 1944, President Roosevelt signed into law the GI Bill of Rights. The federal government now offered 4 percent home loans to veterans, with no down payment required. Thus the American dream to own a home led to massive federal assistance to fulfill that dream. Implicitly, government was saying: *We invite you to the suburbs.*

Millions took advantage of that offer and of subsequent home and education loan gifts. Statistics on file with the federal Veterans Administration in Washington reveal the impact of these loans. According to Robert C. Coon, the VA Director of Home Loans, the suburban New York county of Nassau has received more home loans (162,669) since 1944 than all of New York City combined (146,691). Over thirty-three years, Manhattan received 351 home loans; suburban Suffolk County, 76,543. The Bronx received 9,927; its northern neighbor, suburban Westchester, three times that number (29,660). The city government had no plan to retain middle- and upper-income residents; the federal government had no plan to cope with the consequences of its policies.

Government also made it possible for people to get to their new homes. On January 16, 1955, the Triboro Bridge and Tunnel Authority and the Port Authority agreed to a $1.2 billion scheme to construct a second deck on the George Washington Bridge and miles of new bridge approaches and roads that would bulldoze neighborhoods. The architect of this scheme was Robert Moses, who borrowed from the first regional plan. As Robert Caro observes in *The Power Broker*, his masterful biography of Moses, the pact "sealed, perhaps for centuries, the future of New York and its suburbs." It stimulated new road construction. Visions of sugarplums danced before the eyes of the establishment. The banks thought of the bonds to be sold; the construction unions, of the jobs to be created; the law firms and politicians, of the legal fees and insurance premiums; the real-estate interests, of the enhanced value of their Manhattan properties.

Had that money been spent on mass transit, New York might today be a very different place. Caro calculates that the same $1.2 billion could have completely modernized the city's subway system and the Long Island Railroad (purchasing land along the Long Island Expressway to allow trains to speed in and out of the city at speeds of 80 miles per hour), which would have lessened the city's dependence on the automobile.

But the automobile was the wave of the future. On June 29, 1956, the Federal Highway Trust Fund was created. Over the next twenty-one years, $90 billion was raised and $80 billion spent on 38,000 miles of new federal highways, with $2.2 billion of that total spent in New York State to construct 1,246 miles of road. In the program's first ten years, notes Caro, 439 miles of federal highways were constructed in the city—but not one mile of new subway.

America was transformed. People poured out of cities, creating new markets. Businesses followed. A 1977 study prepared by the Academy for Contemporary Problems for the federal Commerce Department describes why:

In earlier stages of our national development, firms and individuals were willing to pay the higher costs of living and doing business in the Northeast's centers of high population and economic concentration because the more primitive transportation and communications of an earlier day made such proximity of suppliers, producers, clients and supporting businesses essential. The benefits of close proximity outweighed the costs. But modern transportation, together with electronic communications, have eroded the once-premium advantage of concentration. Instead, they are underwriting a decentralization of our national economy and population.

By 1970, the average household income of the New York City suburbs ($17,062) was more than 50 percent greater than that inside the city ($11,269). In *Breach of Faith*, Theodore H. White sketches the profound impact of highways on America and New York:

. . . the nation, invited by the new highways to become guzzlers of gasoline, had learned to drive five miles for a six-pack of beer or a pound of butter. Twenty years later, their appetite for driving had become the Energy Crisis. . . . One can follow the thread of this single Highway Act on to politics: the reasoning behind the Federal Highway Act was so seductive as to melt resistance. It ran thus: the entries to and exits from big cities were so congested that a way had to be created for people to move into and out of such cities easily and to go wherever they wanted to. But where more and more Americans wanted to go was the suburbs; and suburbia was to change American politics just as much as the opening of the West a century before. The new highways became not simply holiday routes for Fourth of July and Labor Day weekends, or highball expressways to bring food and supplies into the hearts of the cities. They were arteries of a new way of American life.

Rent Control

"Rent control is metaphysical," sighs George Sternlieb, who has studied it for years. "The subject stops all thinking." There are many who believe it stopped construction and invited the abandonment of apartments in New York City.

On November 1, 1943, every apartment in America was rent-controlled. To dampen inflation and provide housing for returning veterans, on that day the federal government put a ceiling on rents. It was a temporary act and was rescinded in 1948. For the purpose of preventing speculation and what it called unwarranted and abnormal "increases in rents and evictions during a period of housing emergency," the State of New York passed its own stringent rent control law in 1950. Meant to be temporary, the law was administered by the *Temporary* State Housing Rent Commission. In 1962, the state granted the city the option to enact its own statute. In February of that year, the city passed a stricter law of its own, stabilizing rent controls and making it more difficult for landlords to raise rents. This law, declared Mayor Wagner, would create a "slumless city." The government, not the free market, would determine the rent any landlord of a pre-1947 building could charge. For 5 million apartment dwellers, the city was declaring housing an inalienable right. The trouble was that government didn't subsidize that right; landlords did. Throughout the 1950's and 1960's, one across-the-board rent increase was permitted per landlord unless the apartment was vacated or the landlord was willing to claim a hardship and muddle through a bureaucratic maze to win an increase. Being citizens of a free country, landlords were also free to abandon buildings when they became unprofitable.

Rent control, though it protected many poor people, soon became another ripoff for the privileged. Taxpayers, for instance, help subsidize Mayor Koch's $250-a-month, three-room Greenwich Village apartment; its fair market value, says a spokesman for Koch's landlord, New York University, would be $400 to $450. If Koch and some of his neighbors paid a market rent, the building would be assessed at a higher rate, which would mean more revenues to the landlord and a reduction in Mayor Koch's budget deficit.

Arthur Levitt, Jr., president of the American Stock Exchange and son of the tight-fisted state comptroller, also benefits from rent control. He pays $661 a month for an eight-room, high-ceilinged apartment, with a wood-burning fireplace, on East 86th Street. A fair market rental, says his landlord, would be $850 to $1,200 a month. The Stock Exchange president, who is active in the chorus demanding business tax reductions, stumbled when I asked him to justify his cozy rent. "Let me think about that a moment, and exactly how I want to answer it," he said. "I hate to give you a 'no comment.' " Then, after a long pause: "I pay more rent than half the tenants in the building." He admitted that the rent was low but said it was "close to market value." Three times in the last fifteen years, he said, he had voluntarily agreed to hike the rent above the sum required, as his landlord concedes. But he admitted, "It's not unfair to say that the building is underassessed."

Dean Alfange, a former American Labor party candidate for governor in 1942 (now a benefactor of horse racing and the state Liberal party), keeps a five-room apartment with a sweeping view on Central Park West in the Sixties. He pays $373 a month. The same apartment, one floor below, rents for $650. It is not controlled. The good doctor on Alfange's floor also has a controlled apartment. He pays $418 for six rooms overlooking the park, complete with a nice 14½-by-23-foot living room.

Former opera singer and actress Dorothy Sarnoff (she appeared in the original *King and I*) doesn't have a view, but for the last twenty-four years she has had a rent-controlled apartment on plush Central Park South. Mrs. Sarnoff now operates a thriving speech instruction clinic, charging $1,500 for six hours and $2,500 per lecture. Her rent is $470 a month for an apartment said to be worth $750. Reached in Wasington, where she was instructing State Department officials, Mrs. Sarnoff claimed she was paying "a fair rent." Besides, she wondered, "If rents go higher and higher, where does the middle class go?" When pressed, she admitted she was not a member of that class.

Nor is Nat Sherman. His Fifth Avenue tobacco store rents for $210,000 a year and produces hand-rolled cigars and gold-tipped cigarettes; custom-made pipes sell for as much as $800. The monthly rent for his six-room Central Park West apartment is $355. For thirty-five years he has enjoyed the same apartment, though he admits to spending five or six months each year basking in Florida's sunshine. Is this a fair rent? His response: "It happens to be used so little that I think it's fair. I paid my dues in the early days. If my landlord doesn't make money, I'll be glad to pay the difference . . . I wish you wouldn't quote me in that area."

For the last thirty-three years, Mrs. Otto Fuerst has lived in the same Central Park South building as Mrs. Sarnoff. Her two-bedroom apartment rents for $440. The rent control law requires that an apartment serve as a "primary" residence, but that doesn't bother Mrs. Fuerst, just as it doesn't bother Mr. Sherman. Mrs. Fuerst admits to spending most of the year alternating between Palm Beach and California. Why? "I think a person of wealth should get anything they can get," she says. "I'm a parasite. I just spend money." Then she hung up.

At swank 1085 Park Avenue, an eight-room rent-controlled apartment goes for $640 a month. A six-room apartment rents for $473. At 40 Central Park South, where room service is provided by the St. Moritz Hotel and sleek Rolls-Royces parade in front of the long white canopy, 44 of the 143 apartments are rent-controlled. Ms. Carol Hausamen, the owner, says that if those who could afford it paid a fair rent, the building's $4.6 million assessment would rise 10 percent. A means test, she guesses, would remove 90 percent of these tenants from rent-control privileges. But the only way to get them off, she jokes, is to "shoot 'em. They go out feet first."

A lot of shooting would be required to remove all the comfortable people enjoying rent-control privileges in buildings along Central Park West and South, up and down West End Avenue and Riverside Drive, up the East Side, down lower Fifth and upper Park avenues, and across the river in Brooklyn Heights. According to Frank Kristof, vice president of the state Urban Development Corporation and a student of rent control, approximately 15 percent of the current 500,000 rent-control families could afford to pay more. That's 75,000 families. Daniel Joy, a supporter of rent control and the city's Commissioner of Rent and Housing Maintenance, agreed: "Whether it's 14 or 15 percent, that's the ball park."

The citizens of New York City pay for rent control. If rich men like Nat Sherman were not in rent-controlled apartments, perhaps more upwardly mobile black families would live on Central Park West rather than move to Scarsdale. In 1975, 1.7 million of the city's 2.1 million rental units were subjected to some form of rent regulation (either rent control or what is called rent stabilization).

If there were a means test and those in controlled apartments paid a fair rent, the Temporary Commission on City Finances concluded after long study, city real-estate tax coffers would be enriched by $100 million per year. The federal General Accounting Office has said the figure would be twice that. The Commission also calculated that since the inception of rent control landlords have subsidized tenants to the tune of $20 billion. Small wonder that landlords, who felt they were not getting a return on their investment, often abandoned their buildings, removing them from the tax rolls. Between 1960 and 1976, 300,000 housing units were abandoned. And, currently, real-estate tax delinquencies reach almost $1 billion. According to Congressional testimony by Koch's Housing Commissioner, Nathan Leventhal, "*Only* 12 percent of the buildings in arrears showed up on the rent control rosters." Nevertheless, with rent control a persistent local issue—over the years, city candidates charged their opponents with being soft on landlords as national candidates charged theirs with being soft on communism—it is not surprising that the climate was deemed unsuitable for private housing construction. And the public pays, since financially pressed landlords often cut back on building maintenance, giving many middle-income residents another excuse to leave New York.

The issue of rent control received little attention in the 1977 mayoral campaign. Each of the candidates was too busy promising to forge a new, pro-business climate. The candidates never made the connection between this stance and their sworn opposition to even a means test for rent control. Certainly, Mayor Ed Koch never understood the contradiction. Like many legislators and judges who pass on rent legislation, this foe of special privilege knew a good thing when he didn't have to pay for it. "I'm not going to let it go," he declared a month before he was sworn in as mayor. The "it" was his cheap apartment, which he promised to keep while living in his official residence, Gracie Mansion.

Privately, many politicians concede that rent control protects some people who need no protection. Publicly, most perform like seals, squeaking their undying devotion to tenants. Since there are more tenants than landlords—75 percent of city residents are renters—it's a politically safe pose. Which explains why all the studies urging reform remain parked on shelves in the municipal library.

New York is different, says Commissioner Joy, because "75 percent of our population are renters." In Detroit and Philadelphia, only 40 percent are renters; in Houston, 47 percent. New York is different, says Kristoff, thinking of rent control and subsidized middle-income housing, because "There's an unbelievable psychology that you find nowhere else. Tenants here believe they have a right to be protected against high rents." It's a problem shared, for instance, with Washington, D.C., where they also have controls.

In fact, much of the city's population cannot afford to pay an economic rent. The median income of rent-controlled tenants, says Leventhal, was $7,057 in 1974; in 1975, half the controlled "female-headed households" paid 36 percent of their income for rent, while the majority of senior citizen households paid more than 40 percent. Rent control is not just "metaphysical," as Sternlieb said, but may well be an insoluble problem. Most tenants simply cannot afford to pay the rent landlords need to cover costs or earn a profit. Thus smaller landlords frequently reduced services, failed to make building improvements, abandoned their buildings or refused to invest in new housing. The logical solution: a subsidy program to pay the difference between what the tenant can afford and the landlord needs. The question: Who should pay? The city can't afford it. Nor can the state. The federal government, which has a small Section 8 subsidy program under the Housing and Urban Development agency, is not likely to institute a massive new program. A means test for those living in rent-controlled apartments would help. But even if it removed 20 percent of the tenants from controls, the poorer landlord's problem would remain unsolved since most of these tenants live in the larger buildings of wealthier landlords. Solving one problem would create another, since the absence of controls would, no doubt, prompt desperately needed middle- and upper-income residents to flee the city. The city is damned if it does, damned if it doesn't.

In the absence of government subsidies, it's unfair but probably unavoidable that landlords will be stuck with the subsidy. In the short run, they pay. In the long run, the city will continue to pay dearly for politicized housing decisions.

The Introduction of Collective Bargaining

What came to be known as the "Little Wagner Act" was in fact the Big Wagner Act for municipal labor unions. On March 31, 1958, Mayor Robert F. Wagner signed an executive order granting

100,000 employees the right to join the union of their choice and to bargain collectively, which implied the right to strike. In retrospect, one would think this an easy decision.

It was not. The Mayor's advisers were strongly divided. One group argued that unions were just another special interest and that granting them too much power would whet their appetites, encourage inflated settlements and give unions too much sway over elected officials; the opposition countered that collective bargaining would impose an orderly machinery for the settlement of disputes, bring stability, promote efficiency, do justice to workers. As was his custom, Wagner agonized quietly, exhausting everyone. When he finally decided to sign the order, political considerations played a part. As would become the case in subsequent negotiations, the Mayor did not want to give up too much immediate money so he gave up something else. ". . . the Mayor's decision to act now was influenced by a desire to conciliate major union groups on the eve of the publication of the executive budget," wrote Abe Raskin, the respected labor reporter, on the front page of the *Times*.

Jerry Wurf, then Regional Director (now national President) of the American Federation of State, County and Municipal Employees, was more than conciliated. A week before, Wurf had threatened a strike of his 25,000 members. When the executive order was signed, he hailed it as "a monumental forward step," predicting that his membership would double within a year.

Within seventeen years, Wurf's membership swelled to 125,000. By 1977, all but 4,500 city employees—less than 2 percent—were represented by unions. With this growth in membership came new power. The city came to collect and turn over to the unions the dues of their members, including a political action fund to support union-backed candidates. With city support, in 1977 the state approved an agency shop law requiring all employees to pay union dues, increasing the political action kitty. The city came to fully fund the health and welfare benefits of its employees, allowing the unions to administer these funds and hire small armies for that purpose. By 1977, the city was paying the salaries but releasing 126 employees for full-time union activity; another 96 were released with the union paying their salary and the city their pension, health and welfare contributions; still another 41 union organizers were released on a part-time basis.

The union's growing strength is gauged by glancing at the budget of the Office of Labor Relations, the city agency responsible for representing 7.5 million taxpayers in contract negotiations. In the last year of the Beame administration, this office had fifty employees and a puny budget of $800,000. That same year, one union —Wurf's D.C. 37—had fifty-one members released by the city for union work. The dues of all city unions were $32 million, and, in early 1978, one—the PBA—lavished $750,000 to retain an attorney, Richard Hartman.

In addition to their ability to paralyze the city with a strike, as the transit union proved in 1966 and the bridge tenders in 1971, over the years the unions gained management powers and became partners in the city's governance. Executive Order No. 52, signed by Mayor Lindsay on September 29, 1967, allowed such previous management prerogatives as "workload and manning" to be placed on the collective bargaining table. Everything became negotiable. "Collective bargaining has become a means not only for determining the wages and conditions of employment of public employees," writes former city Personnel Director Sol Hoberman, "but also for modifying the nature of public service and the role, authority and responsibilities of the Mayor, the City Council, and agency heads." Union contracts now determine class size and welfare caseloads. The Transit Authority was not permitted to hire part-timers, ensuring that work patterns conformed to employee, not rider habits. The sanitation union successfully insists that three men are required on a truck, though most cities and private carters employ two and even one. Unionization reaches almost to the top. Mayor Koch complains that all but 2,000 of his managers don't belong to a union. He says he can't properly manage since most supervisors have divided loyalties because they belong to a union—often the same one as the people reporting to them—and discipline breaks down.

With the weakening of the political party machine, unions filled a political vacuum. "We have the ability, in a sense, to elect our own boss," conceded Victor Gotbaum, who succeeded Wurf in 1965. Unions also now have the ability to be the city's chief banker. The employee pension funds they control are today New York's foremost lender, pumping a scheduled $3.8 billion into city securities. With such political and governmental power, it has often been difficult for public officials to distinguish between their personal and the public's interest, between the danger of a crippling strike and the danger of giving away the public purse.

The people in the middle—the public—got squeezed. Between 1960 and 1975, the Bureau of the Budget reports, wages and salaries jumped 316 percent, faster than the rate of inflation or comparable wage gains in the private sector. But city services did not rise with wages. In the 1971 to 1975 period, the Temporary Commission on City Finances spotted what they called "some startling trends":

Per employee compensation, despite the increasing severity of the City's financial problems, rose 51 percent in four years, higher than in either previous four-year period; at the same time, the number of police officers dropped 2.1 percent, and total hours worked fell 3.7 percent. Thus in the course of four years, local taxes for police services rose $270 million, almost 50 percent; the compensation of police officers increased over 50 percent; and the number of police officers, and hours of police service delivered, actually declined.

A decision that seemed just and sensible in 1958, which was to promote efficiency and stability, greatly altered power in New York. Before he died, Liberal party and United Hatters union chief Alex Rose, one of the advisers who urged Wagner to sign the order, told me he thought it was "a mistake." He observed that city workers were not like the trade unionists he led because "the city is not an employer in the traditional sense. Profits do not exist. Workers are not extracting a share of the profits but rather a share of taxes. Unlike bargaining in the private sector, municipal collective bargaining is part of the political rather than the adversary process. Therefore, municipal unions are really a pressure group, a special-interest group." Unlike the private sector, governments usually have no real competitors for the services they provide. Short of moving from the city, taxpayers cannot take their business elsewhere. When labor exercises its traditional right to withhold its labor, the public, unlike the private sector, cannot exercise its traditional right to withhold its business.

Asked if he thought his executive order was a mistake, former Mayor Wagner said, "No. Just like anyone else, these people have a right to bargain collectively." But, of course, everyone does not have that right. Welfare recipients don't. Unemployed youths don't. Taxpayers don't have recourse to binding arbitration if dissatisfied with a tax hike. Later, Wagner added, "There's no question it gave the unions muscle. . . . It was a significant decision; but I still say it was the right thing to do. If we didn't do it, it would have happened eventually anyway. . . . Even with collective bargaining, we were able to hold down settlements."

Wagner's successors fared less well. After the fiscal crisis struck, Mayor Beame and the union leadership agreed they were "partners" in saving and running the city. At one of his first City Hall meetings in 1978, Mayor Koch told me early in his term, "The union leaders kept saying we were 'partners' and had to work together on everything. After a half-hour, I felt compelled to say, 'Wait a minute. We share many of the same goals, but we're not partners. You represent one hunded ninety thousand people. I represent seven and a half million. We don't sit side by side at that desk.' "

The Growth of Pensions

Former Mayor Wagner vividly recalls a Loyalty Day parade in 1960. On March 23 of that year, Governor Nelson Rockefeller signed into law a bill increasing by 5 percent the state's contribution to its employee pensions. The Mayor and Governor were, in Wagner's words, "heading up the parade. The policemen and firemen were shouting as they went by, 'Atta boy, Rocky!' " The Governor had become a hero to public employees, and the Mayor didn't like it: "So I turned to Nelson and I said, 'You son of a gun, taking all the credit.' He just laughed."

The bill Rockefeller signed appropriated few dollars. In the long run, however, it opened the door to other pension sweeteners and was the first salvo in a political competition between the city and state and its various unions, each seeking to outdo the other. For the first time, this legislation made pensions part of the collective bargaining process.

City politicians jumped in feet first. Following the state's action, Beame, who was then city Budget Director, announced that the Wagner administration was seeking state permission to "increase the take-home pay of city employees" by increasing the city's share. Not to be outdone, Rockefeller, over the objections of Wagner, signed a bill in 1963 compelling the city to compute police and firemen's retirement benefits on the basis of their final year's pay rather than the average salary of their last five years. Soon other unions would clamor for and win this benefit—inflating overtime and pension costs. In fact, this practice became so abused that the Transit Authority's 1978 contract demands called on the union to agree to limit pensions to 120 percent of the final year's salary. (The union refused.)

The twenty-year retirement at half pay—granted to police in 1857 and firemen in 1894—became part of the collective bargaining demands of every other union. In 1963, sanitation men were permitted to retire after twenty-five years. In 1964, twenty-year retirements were extended to corrections officers and Transit and Housing Authority police; teachers were granted earlier retirement at age fifty-five after twenty-five years' service. In 1966, police were given full-pay pensions after thirty-five years' service. In 1967, sanitation men won twenty-year pensions—an agreement labor attorney Theodore Kheel says was due to labor consultant Jack Bigel, adviser to sanitation union chief John DeLury and many of the city's municipal unions: "Bigel convinced Lindsay that sanitation workers faced the same physical dangers—hernias and that sort of thing—as cops." Also in 1967, firemen kept pace with police and won full-pay pensions after thirty-five years. In 1968, transit employees snared twenty-year retirement at the age of fifty; District Council 37 members got to retire at age fifty-five after twenty-five years, as did many Board of Education employees. In 1969, higher education workers also got twenty-five-year pensions. In 1970, corrections and housing officers won twenty-year pensions; most transit employees were no longer required to contribute to their pensions; and the teachers' union—which helped Governor Rockefeller by remaining "neutral" in that year's gubernatorial race—captured a twenty-year retirement plan at age fifty-five. Teachers also won a pension sweetener, forcing the city to pay more of their pension costs. A study by former city Budget Director Fred Hayes and then Professor Donna Shalala called this sweetener "the largest unconditional commitment of city funds in the history of American city government." The city, they said, was forced to assume $1.2 billion of liabilities and up their annual teachers' pension contribution by $55 million. Sweeteners for other unions followed.

In all, according to the business-dominated Committee for Economic Development, between 1960 and 1970 the state enacted (usually at the city's urging) fifty-four city pension bills. Between 1961 and 1976, the Temporary Commission on City Finances found, retirement costs rose 469 percent—from $260 million to $1.48 billion. Retirement benefits began to hog the city's budget. From 1971 to 1976, for instance, the Commission calculated that the city's budget rose 66 percent while its retirement costs rose 99.7 percent. The growth of these costs, like the growth of debt service, meant there was less to spend on the delivery of services. It meant that pensions, which were supposed to protect people when they grew old, when the kids were grown and they presumably needed less, came to rival their work salary. The city also came to ignore their Social Security pension, which was on top of their city pension.

It also meant the introduction of another gimmick. Since public officials didn't have to pay for pension settlements right away, they successfully hid expensive labor agreements from the press and public, bequeathing the true costs to future generations. The SEC staff report on city finances cited one such gimmick. By claiming "excess interest" on pension fund earnings, they said, the city reduced its annual pension contribution by $361.6 million between 1972 and 1975. By 1977, the city's unfunded pension liability— money owed future retirees but not provided for—was over $8 billion. "The results of such gimmickry are almost tragic," observed a New York State Pension Commission study. "They deceive the public employee and the taxpayers into believing that pension costs (and costs of government in general) have been met. In fact, such costs have not been met—they simply have not been paid. Therefore, next year's taxpayer not only must shoulder his proper share of government costs, but also the costs which have not been paid in prior years and which unfairly have been shifted to him."

The deception was not just the fault of short-sighted "politicians." Union leaders, anxious to show results at the bargaining table, also acted like politicians. They, too, run for office. They, too, winked and went along with the game. It was a problem their successors would have to worry about.

Worrying that pensions were out of control, in 1973 the state legislature voted to cap future sweeteners—in time to block a move by the Patrolmen's Benevolent Association for half-pay pensions after fifteen years' service. But since the state constitution has a special provision preventing a rollback in pension benefits already won, pensions became an untouchable item when it came time for New York to cut its budget. City services would have to go instead.

"Moral Obligation" Bonds

Most politicians like to build things. It's a simple way to quantify a record in office. After all, how do you quantify judgment or saying

no? A dam is a tangible achievement. So is a road, a bridge, the
Albany Mall, the World Trade Center. Or Westway. Whatever social
or economic good these projects were designed to serve, they also
provided monuments to their benefactor.

Nelson Rockefeller, particularly, liked to build things. But he
had a problem. The state constitution required that all bonds carry
"the full faith and credit" of the state and be approved by the
voters. This was a time-consuming process and risked voter disapproval of many worthwhile projects, particularly new housing.
There was another problem. All new Authority projects were expected to be self-sustaining, as they had been since the creation of
the tri-state Port Authority in 1921.

But the Governor was nothing if not inventive. Drawing on the
counsel of a then little-known bond lawyer, John Mitchell, and a
housing task force consisting of such luminaries as the City Club's
I. D. Robbins, now Congressman James Schuer, and labor leader
Harry Van Arsdale, Rockefeller persuaded the legislature to break
tradition. A new agency would be created. It would build nothing.
It would have broad authority to raise money by creating a new
"moral obligation" bond, which would not require voter approval.
Nor would the buildings have to prove they were self-sustaining.

On April 18, 1960, the Governor signed a bill creating the State
Housing Finance Agency. The intent was noble: to build more
housing; to help solve social problems by freeing the state from the
cumbersome strait jacket of voter approval. The "moral obligation"
device was hailed as an innovation. But without the check of rigorous management and voter approval, the new power would come
to be abused. Rockefeller wanted to build now. He would figure out
later how to pay for it. To explain his innovation, the Governor was
not above dissembling.

"How can they [the State Housing Finance Agency] get the
money if the builder can't get it at lower interest rates?" Rockefeller asked state Housing Commissioner James Gaynor in a March
2, 1960, televised colloquy.

"Well, it's a state agency," said Gaynor. "It's a public agency."

"That's a major factor in being able to sell the bonds at a low
rate," the Governor prompted.

"Oh, yes," responded the Commissioner. "There is a reserve
fund which would ensure the payment of principle and interest."

"Which the state would stand in back of," said Rockefeller, "so that if anything happened the state would be able to help out, *but it would not be taxpayers' money.*"

"This would eliminate the need of the voters approving a bond and having to bond the State of New York for fifty years," explained Gaynor.

"That's exactly it!" thumped Rockefeller.

The Governor was having it both ways. On the one hand, the public was being told it would cost taxpayers nothing. On the other, investors were being told that if revenues were insufficient the taxpayers would pay for them. "The decision on moral obligation bonds," later observed Donna Shalala, the Treasurer of the Municipal Assistance Corporation, "reinforced and led to the era of avoiding constitutional requirements. It was difficult for the state to say to the city, 'Look, you're avoiding statutory or constitutional requirements in preparing your budget' when the state ignored the constitution by not going to the voters on bond issues. In a sense, the state was violating the law. The state said to local governments, 'When your structure doesn't work for you, don't stop. Go around it and we'll help you—like we're doing.' "

The city took the cue. Beginning in the 1960's, to cite one example, the city tried to save money by rolling over middle-income Mitchell-Lama housing mortgage notes rather than selling bonds which would have carried higher, but fixed, rates of interest. Later, when interest rates soared from 4 to 8 percent, the city was cornered and forced to borrow just to meet annual interest payments on this public housing. The consequences were seen in Brooklyn's Cadman Towers. In 1973, according to then Deputy Housing Commissioner Ruth Lerner, this project was paying 3.8 percent interest and rents averaged $65.30 per room. Mortgage repayments consumed 57 percent of the rent money. But by early 1977, interest more then doubled to 8.01 percent and rents rose to $83.20 a room. Mortgage payments now made up 79.1 percent of the rent. Later that year, the city felt compelled to sell many of its Mitchell-Lama mortgages, at a considerable loss, in order to repay noteholders.

The state paid dearly for its "trick." In early 1975, the "moral obligation" debt of state public authorities reached $7.4 billion. Public authorities proliferated across the state. In February 1975, the state Urban Development Corporation—an offspring of the Housing Finance Agency—defaulted on its "moral obligations." Within a month, the city found itself unable to borrow money.

A New City Charter

Another "good government" decision was made on November 7, 1961. On that day, voters reelected Robert Wagner as mayor. One may debate whether this was a clear victory for good government. Voter approval of a new city charter was.

With the active support of such good government groups as the City Club and the League of Women Voters, the charter passed by a margin of two to one. For the first time in twenty-five years, the procedures and structure of city government were overhauled. Among the charter changes were several amendments granting the mayor unprecedented powers. One allowed the mayor alone to estimate revenues, a power formerly shared with the comptroller, Board of Estimate and City Council. A second change allowed the mayor to estimate the maximum debt the city could incur for capital projects, also a power formerly shared with the comptroller, Board of Estimate and City Council. The charter strengthened as well the mayor's control of his own Budget Bureau, no longer requiring that the budget director clear any line item budget change with the Board of Estimate.

The new charter was consistent with the prevalent view in New York and Washington that strong chief executives were required. New York strengthened the mayor's office, as John Kennedy sought to strengthen the Presidency from Congressional restraints. But by removing an institutional check of the mayor's powers, later budget abuses were invited.

The charter took effect on January 1, 1963. Three months later, city officials proclaimed a "budget crisis" and Mayor Wagner proposed to balance the city's $3 billion budget by waiving, for one year, payment of $15 million to the Stabilization Reserve Fund. The City Council dutifully rubber-stamped this gimmick, as did the state legislature. But Comptroller Abe Beame was unhappy. The man who years later would tell the SEC that he never got involved in revenue projections, called on Mayor Wagner to employ other tricks. The Mayor now had the power, he said, to unilaterally increase his revenue estimates. Beame's proposal called for the creation of $13.75 million by inflating revenue estimates and changing the payment dates on state aid from one fiscal year to the next. Wagner, saying little, skillfully allowed the idea to germinate. "A way must be found to replace a $40 million loss from the out-of-city sales tax," he solemnized on May 7, still offering no answer. Eight days later, he invented one. Foreseeing a "brighter economic outlook," he announced that the city was increasing its revenue estimates by $26.3 million.

Alarmed, the Citizens Budget Commission and the state Chamber of Commerce accused the Mayor, in October 1963, of using the new charter as "an iron curtain to conceal manipulation of the budget." Comptroller Beame joined in the condemnation, charging that Wagner overestimated general fund revenues by $38.4 million. Beame's solution? The city would have to borrow $69.3 million from the Stabilization Reserve Fund, a kind of rainy day resource. Wagner was silent for a time, finally conceding later in the year that general fund revenues were overstated by $68.4 million.

"The significance of the charter change," says Herb Ranchburg, Research Director of the Citizens Budget Commission, "was that when you had a mayor operating with a Budget Bureau which was creative, the sky was the limit. There were no checks. You had creative budget officials playing the fifth violin, the piccolo and the kettle drum all by themselves."

Expense Dollars in the Capital Budget

A repair truck carrying asphalt lumbered south along the elevated West Side Highway on December 15, 1973, its frame groaning as it bounced over the bumpy, battered pavement. Suddenly, the highway roadbed—which the city government had banned to trucks and said it had no money to repair—collapsed. Not a chunk at a time, not by sagging. As if a trap door had opened, the truck plunged through the gaping hole and crashed onto the street below, injuring fifteen persons.

That hole is a symbol of many critical capital budget decisions tracing back to April 3, 1964, when Governor Rockefeller signed into law an amendment to the New York State Local Finance Law, Chapter 284, Section 11. The amendment permitted city officials to hide expense items in the capital budget. This was significant because, unlike the expense budget, which is financed through tax revenues, capital budgets are financed through the sale of bonds. A capital budget is used to repair and build facilities whose probable usefulness exceeds one year. Thus the benefit—and the costs—will be shared by future taxpayers.

There had always been a barrier between the capital and expense budgets, but in 1964 Mayor Wagner had difficulty balancing his expense budget. His friend, Nelson Rockefeller, wanted to be helpful without supplying more state aid. Solution? It was proposed that the Mayor charge the costs of administering a special census against the capital budget. The Governor's Budget Bureau objected, warning in a memo to the Governor: "It would not seem that a nontangible service such as this should be classified . . . as a capital expenditure." Rockefeller ignored the advice, and Mayor Wagner sneaked $26 million into his capital budget.

This broke the barrier. In 1967, for example, Governor Rockefeller approved a bill (Chapter 634 of the Laws of 1967) permitting "the costs of codification of laws and the fees paid to experts [lawyers], consultants, advertising and costs of printing and dissemination" to be called capital expenses because they had a "three year period of possible usefulness." Expense money in the capital budget went from $26 million to $84 million in 1968. The following year, when Mayor Lindsay was seeking reelection, it almost doubled to $151 million. Four years later, in Lindsay's final year, it more than tripled to $564 million. By 1975, $835 million—more than half Mayor Beame's entire capital budget—was earmarked for expenses. Over the course of eleven years, an estimated $2.4 billion of expense items was shifted to the capital budget.

Reasonable people can debate what is and is not a capital expense. Obviously, some expenses—textbooks, for instance—have a longer-than-one-year life. But if the textbook or salary has a life of only one year, then each year you are borrowing—and paying interest. Costs multiply. The public paid in several ways. First, it cost more; taxpayers were required to pay interest for expenses normally paid from current revenues. Second, as interest costs mounted, fewer dollars were available to provide city services. Third, this trick—like others—contributed to a relaxation of budget discipline; city officials were given a cushion under which they could hide expenditures. Fourth, it robbed the capital budget of funds for needed capital improvements.

The shrinking capital budget drew public notice in the cold winter of 1978. During the first heavy snowfall, one of every three aged sanitation trucks was out of commission; half the 450 street sweepers were also out, as were half the snow blowers. More than 1 million axle-breaking potholes made city streets look like the surface of the moon; fifty-year-old streets that are supposed to be repaved every twenty-five years were scheduled to be repaved every 200 years. Many of the city's 51 water-spanning bridges were literally crumbling, warned a Twentieth Century Fund study prepared by former Budget Director David Grossman. There was concern that the city's water supply system, dependent on just two water tunnels, could be endangered. "We really don't know how serious the problems really are," Water Resources Commissioner Charles Samowitz told Arthur Browne of the *Daily News* in February 1978. "What we should really do is drag [clean] the entire system. Then we'd know how well the system actually works. We haven't dragged the entire system in a decade. It might cost $1 million. We don't have the money now, but it could be worth 20 to 40 times that amount." During the past three years, a 1978 City Planning Commission report lamented, the city spent an average of "only $200 million a year on legitimate capital projects."

And, finally, the public paid when investors became alarmed at the glut of city paper crowding the securities market. One day, investor confidence would collapse—just as the West Side Highway had done.

Mushrooming Short-Term Debt

Mayor Wagner had planned to present his final budget message before the full Board of Estimate and live television cameras in May 1965. Then word leaked out that he had schemed to close a $255.8 million budget gap by issuing short-term notes, payable within one year. All hell broke loose. Newspaper editorials screeched about "fiscal irresponsibility." Comptroller Beame, normally a close Wagner ally, blasted the plan. "This borrowing proposal," he warned, "is akin to a family man who lacks the will to earn a living, but prefers first to clean out his bank account to pay for his regular living expenses and then to continue to avoid working by borrowing to live in the same manner. Finally, he faces the day of reckoning. This will be the city's blight under the proposal to borrow for current expenses."

Wagner scratched the live-TV plans. Instead, on May 13, 1965, the same day John Lindsay announced his candidacy for mayor, he trotted out Deputy Mayor Edward F. Cavanagh, Jr., who meekly recited a six-minute message for the benefit of two Board of Estimate members. Wagner still proposed to close the gap by issuing short-term notes. It amounted, he said, to "borrow now, repay later." The Mayor's message echoed the boundless optimism and rhetoric of the day: "I intend that we shall press ahead with the war on crime, the war on poverty, the war on narcotics addiction, the war on slums, the war on disease and the war on civil ugliness."

Such "wars" cost money, and the Mayor presented a record $3.87 billion budget—up $514,299,699—plus a first-time fiscal trick to pay for it. Unlike subsequent mayors, Wagner did not hide his tricks. It was debated on the floor of the legislature, where State Senator John Marchi called it "bad budget practice" and proph-esied, "We can do it next year, we can do it ten years from now, this is the effect of the proposal." Candidate Lindsay exploded: "New York has tried to climb to prosperity on the Indian rope trick and, when the whole fantastic illusion threatens to crumble, it is propped up with the fiscal magic of borrowing $256 million against nonexistent collateral—a reckless gamble on the future to pay for mistakes in the past." *The New York Times* scolded Wagner, Rockefeller and city and state legislators: "What we have here is an election-year refusal to impose unpleasant taxes to balance the city budget."

Ignoring the criticism, Republican Governor Rockefeller joined with Democrat Wagner and rounded up sufficient Republican votes to pass the borrowing plan in June by a narrow margin. The Local Finance Law was amended. Instead of requiring that all revenue anticipation notes (RAN's) be pegged to the previous year's actual receipts, from now on they would be pegged to the mayor's own estimate of the next year's revenues.

With this decision, mayors were granted a new budget weapon. In addition to using the capital budget to hide borrowing for ex-penses, they could now use the expense budget to borrow. But short-term borrowing is fraught with danger. Unlike bonds, notes are repayable within a year. If revenues grow slowly, or if growing expenditures are not moderated, money must be borrowed again the following year to repay earlier borrowing. Soon the client is borrowing to repay not principal but interest, and is trapped like most loan-shark clients.

This is what happened to New York. In 1965, the city's short-term debt was $526 million, or 10 percent of the total debt; its annual debt service costs were $470 million. By 1975, its short-term debt was $4.5 billion, or 36.9 percent of the total debt, and annual debt service costs were $2 billion. Almost one-third of the city's entire budget was set aside not for the delivery of services but to pay for borrowing and pensions.

Mayor-elect Lindsay foresaw the problem. On December 21, 1965, he declared, "I face a budget gap of almost a billion dollars for the first fifteen months of my administration." Four and a half years after, Lindsay prepared to close his own budget gap by borrowing. Reminded of his earlier criticism by Martin Tolchin of the *Times*, Lindsay said, "It's a lot easier to criticize when you're not there. . . . You find out things aren't as simple as you thought."

The Transit Strike

John Lindsay was a tall, handsome prince who swept much of New York off its feet. "He's fresh and everyone else is tired," Murray Kempton wrote during the 1965 campaign. "He's *gorgeous*," women shrieked. After twelve years of Wagner, the city was ready for change. And change is what the idealistic Republican/Liberal candidate promised. An end to "cozy deals" with labor unions and "party bosses." A return to "fiscal responsibility." A regeneration of spirit—"Fun City."

But not everyone was in love with the Mayor-elect, as his narrow election proved. Labor unions, for instance, fumed that he was "anti-union." Concerned with the approaching January 1 deadline for the transit talks, Lindsay sought to cool tempers by journeying to the Americana Hotel on December 27, 1965, to meet with representatives of the Transit Workers Union and the Transit Authority. In a conciliatory gesture, he mildly requested that both sides negotiate a "fair settlement." Then, with unaccustomed humility, he conceded, "I am not an expert on labor matters."

Over the next sixteen days he proved this. On January 1, 1966, 34,400 transit workers struck, immobilizing New York. It was the first time the transit workers had gone on strike, and it was the most damaging strike in the city's history. Until then, labor negotiations had involved a carefully scripted scenario. The unions would bluster and threaten a strike, the Mayor would say the cupboard was bare, then both sides would retreat to a quiet, smoke-filled room—much to the chagrin of *Times* editorial writers—and work out a settlement. The previous transit agreement, in 1963, added $32 million to the budget.

This time, the Transit Authority offered an additional $25 million; the union countered with demands for a four-day, thirty-two-hour work week, a 30 percent pay boost, and seventy-six contract improvements. Lindsay was outraged and determined to stand fast. It was war, and the young Mayor acted like a general commanding the public's army. He denounced the "power brokers," inspired the populace by stubbornly striding almost six miles each morning to City Hall and went on television to plead for, and win, public support—though he did perplex his troops by requesting that "non-essential" workers stay home.

The hysteria grew. Fiery union leader Michael Quill was ordered to jail. The *Times*, apparently on the verge of a nervous break-down, editorially thundered at the judge for *only* throwing Quill in the slammer. Quill, his Irish brogue thickening, railed at "Mayor Lindsley," dismissing him as a "pipsqueak," called the *Times* "a meddler" and huffed, "The judge can drop dead in his black robes."

Both sides stood eyeball to eyeball for twelve days—until Lind-say, and a weary public, blinked. On January 12, a suddenly subdued Mayor capitulated, announcing that the strike had been settled at a cost of $52 million. Privately, others said the cost would be at least $70 million—almost three times what one of the three mediators, Theodore Kheel, told me should have been the price.

"The cost of the settlement is high," read the next morning's *Times* editorial, "but not so high that it violates Mayor Lindsay's pledge never to 'capitulate before the lawless demands of a single power group.'" In *Pravda*-like fashion, the *Times*—whose editorial-page writers were members of the new mayor's kitchen cabinet—conceded that the settlement violated the federal government's 3.2 percent wage guidelines. But, scrambling to defend their mayor, they added, "the breach will not be significant unless other civil service unions misread the pact as a sign that the way to get more from the city is to match the Transit Workers Union in irresponsible disregard of the principle that public employees have no legal right to strike."

Aside from the immediate $70 or so million price tag, the strike's costs were steep. The city's economy lost millions of dollars in sales and other taxes, and employees sacrificed an estimated 6 million workdays. The transit fare rose from 15 to 20¢; future deficits were guaranteed when the transit system lost 2.1 percent of its riders.

There was another price, harder to quantify. The transit strike was John Lindsay's Bay of Pigs, his first real test. He flunked it, and in so doing set a pattern for future labor negotiations. "They went on strike—a violation of the law," says former Mayor Wagner, "and yet as part of the settlement they were forgiven, with no penalties to any extent." Instead, penalties were leveled against the taxpayers. Lindsay's 1967 budget mushroomed by 24.3 percent—the largest budget increase of any year between 1960 and 1975. Appetites expanded, and over the next four years so did city budgets. According to the Temporary Commission, they grew at an average rate of 15.9 percent—almost twice the 8.6 percent of Wagner's last term. Labor costs zoomed 89.9 percent—a full 60 percent above Wagner's final four years. The public failed the test, too. At the end of twelve days, New Yorkers were exhausted and clamoring for a settlement. Lindsay was a general without an army, a point not lost on other union leaders. In a sense, as would be proven in later teacher and police strikes, New York didn't have a government.

Also, Lindsay didn't know what he was doing. Five years later, while digging through the transit pact, Richard Oliver of the *Daily News* made an important archaeological discovery: "Eight thousand retired transit employees receive not only their half-pay pensions, but an annual $500 bonus to boot—the result of a little-publicized concession to the Transport Workers Union by an inexperienced city official during the costly 12-day subway and bus strike of 1966." Oliver found that similar bonus arrangements had since been demanded, and won, by almost all city workers, costing millions.

Oliver's report reveals just how "inexperienced" the Lindsay team was. He learned that the three members of the Transit Authority never participated in the $500 bonus decision. "They tried to get this benefit from us for years," complained John H. Gilhooley, one of the members. "We said ridiculous. You'd break the bank. We said no, no, no. But then these wise guys got into the negotiations. . . . Mastermind Price [Deputy Mayor Robert Price] left us out entirely and during the course of the evening gave away the store. Price gave it away. And when they came out of the room one of the labor guys came over to me and said, 'Geez, you know what happened?' I said no, what happened? He said, 'We got the $500 pensions.' I said, go on, you're kidding. 'No, no kidding,' he said. When we raised it, Price said, 'What's wrong with that?' . . . Price's exact words were: 'I'm for pensions.' After that, it was on the table and it couldn't be taken off. It was that kind of naivete and stupidity that contributed to the whole bungle. . . . This naive jerk walked in and tried to settle it. Once in, he increased the total cost of the package by 54%. This was the focal point of the problem New York faces today with the talk of the 50-cent fare."

When Oliver talked to him in 1971, investment banker Price declared, "I can't believe that, but if I did it, I did it. If they say I did it. I'm amazed that I had such authority. I was not experienced. Where was the Mayor?"

The Mayor could have been in a helicopter. Which is where he was on January 3, 1966, bringing tragic reports to a beleaguered city. "I'm over the Queensborough Bridge and it looks good," the dashing Mayor announced. "Traffic is moving easily." Standing on a nearby roof, the city traffic commissioner gently corrected his boss. The Mayor was viewing the wrong bridge. Traffic on the Williamsburg was moving easily. The Queensborough, several miles uptown, was backed up.

Medicaid

Nelson Rockefeller was seeking reelection in 1966. His TV commercials featured animated fish talking to each other about the clean water their governor had made possible. Polls were showing that his Irish-Catholic opponent, Frank O'Connor, was weak among Jewish and progressive voters, so Rockefeller donned his "liberal" mask. He hugged, kissed, poked and winked his charming way through an International Brotherhood of Electrical Workers union meeting in Queens. There, with a well-publicized stroke of his pen, on April 30, 1966, he dramatically signed a state Medicaid bill into law, hailing it as "the most significant social legislation in three decades."

For poor and moderate-income people, Medicaid provided a range of free medicine not envisioned in the original federal legislation. Most New York politicians tried to steal the credit. Senator Robert Kennedy applauded the bill, as did labor leaders, newspaper editorials, Republicans, Democrats, Liberals—and both houses of the state legislature, which passed it. One of the few progressives to oppose the bill was Howard Samuels, then mounting one of his four unsuccessful quests for the governorship. Samuels warned that the true cost could be $2 billion, a sum easily calculated by multiplying those eligible by the average annual medical costs. He also cautioned that free medicine was not provided by money alone, and that a management plan and more doctors, more nurses, more beds, more hospitals, more auditors, would be needed as well. Without providing these, the state was promising "free" medicine without the means to deliver on that promise.

Inflated costs was one result; too many people chasing too few doctors and facilities made medical care prohibitively expensive. Corruption was another; it was invited by a system with too few auditors and cost-plus contracts for unscrupulous nursing home profiteers. Medicaid was the compassionate thing to do, but it was a classic case of good intentions subverted by ill-considered legislation.

It was also to prove very expensive. Rockefeller said it would cost the state only "$90 million," and on May 22, 1966, he declared it would "save money for New York City." By 1977, over 2 million state residents received Medicaid benefits, 70 percent of them residing in New York City. Even after tightening eligibility standards, the city, which was to "save" money, spent $573.7 million for Medicaid in fiscal 1979—more than it expends on welfare. When counting the state's share, the cost in the city is over $1 billion. If we count the cost to the federal, state and all local governments in New York, the cost is $3 billion.

Taxes

Time-Life Books closed its Rockefeller Center offices on October 1, 1976, and said goodbye to New York. The company, employing 312 people, spent $2 million to move to Alexandria, Virginia. Despite this expense, company officials estimated that they would save a total of $4 million in reduced taxes and space rental costs in the first year alone. In contrast to city and state business taxes amounting to 22 percent, their Virginia taxes were 6.5 percent.

The "bottom line" dictated the move, Vice President Nicholas Benton told the Washington *Star*. Benton conceded that Alexandria was not New York—he missed the theater, the shops, the restaurants. But there were other compensations. In New York, he spent forty-five minutes on two buses to travel one mile to his office. Today, he has a big house in McLean and drives to work in twenty-nine minutes, including time out to deposit his daughter at school.

Time-Life was not alone. Many businesses fled—or went out of business—and taxes had a lot to do with it. In 1965, according to the Tax Foundation, New York ranked tenth in local and state taxes, averaging $372 per person. By 1975, it ranked first, averaging $1,025 per person. In those years, New York's taxes multiplied thirteen times faster than the national average, expanding by 178 percent. It was no surprise, then, that the Fantus Company, the world's largest business location consultant, concluded in 1975 that New York had the worst business climate of the fifty states.

Sometimes, increased taxation was perceived by New York officials as a less painful, more expedient short-term solution to cutting the budget. "It never was recognized (or, if recognized, never was accepted politically)," observed the final report of the Temporary Commission, "that the City's taxpayers, its revenue providers, represented a long-term asset of the City that had to be maintained rather than a short-term asset that could be exploited."

This exploitation was on view during the city's tax fight of 1966. Early that year, Mayor Lindsay proposed a $520 million tax package, including a first-time city income tax, new business taxes, and a stock transfer tax. The stock exchange let out a scream, threatening to move. They're bluffing, declared City Comptroller Mario Procaccino, speaking for most city officials. Business leaders protested, prompting an attack from the Mayor and newspaper editorials about their "selfishness." It was presumed that business needed New York and that passive acceptance of new taxes was part of their civic duty.

Needing state approval, the Mayor took his tax package to Albany. State legislative leaders declared that Lindsay was asking for more taxes than were needed to balance the budget. At first, the Mayor heatedly denied this. By March, he conceded that the package would leave $130 million for new expenditures. Not wanting to accept responsibility, the City Council joined Lindsay in demanding that the state legislature mandate these taxes upon the city. Not wanting to accept responsibility, the state insisted that the city request permissive legislation and then mandate the taxes itself. The feud was not about whether to tax but about who would get blamed. On July 13, 1966, after a series of feints and jabs, including Lindsay's first public brawl with Governor Rockefeller, the Mayor signed the new tax package into law, declaring that city taxes were now "at their upper limit."

By December, as city officials were laboring on the next year's budget, word was leaked of the "strong possibility" of new taxes. New taxes is what the city got. The commercial rent occupancy tax went up, as did the utility tax, the insurance corporation tax, the unincorporated income tax, the commuter tax, the sales tax, and an array of nuisance taxes. The corporate income tax was raised in 1971 from 5.5 to 6.7 percent, and again in 1975 to 10.05 percent. The city's personal income tax more than doubled. Real-estate taxes zoomed 33 percent between 1970 and 1975.

In the early sixties, many of the city's industries began to suffer job losses, though these were camouflaged by the growth of government jobs. Not until 1969, however, did the city overall suffer a massive employment decline, eventually losing one of every six private sector jobs. Taxation was a chief culprit. "High levels of taxation have been a major contributing factor in causing job loss," said the 1976 report of Governor Carey's Special Task Force on Taxation, which found that in 1974 New York's taxes were 55 percent above the national average. A 1974 study by the city's Budget Bureau estimated that between 1966 and 1971 the city lost 44,500 factory jobs that it would not have lost if its tax burden had been less severe. The Temporary Commission estimated that by 1981 the city's 10.05 percent business income tax would result in the loss of an additional 149,000 manufacturing jobs. Reducing this tax, they said, would mean the immediate loss of $90 million of city revenues. But, if the city failed to act, an equal amount of revenue would be lost by 1981 because of lost jobs.

The flight of fifty-five of the Fortune 500 companies attracted publicity, but the city's job loss cannot be traced to large firms moving to the Sunbelt or Connecticut. According to the Special Task Force, of the 660,000 jobs lost from 1969 to 1976, only 27,000 resulted from the exodus of large headquarter corporations. Most of the lost jobs came from smaller firms quietly going out of business. New York is the nation's premier beer market. Once the home of 121 breweries, today New York has none. Schaefer, Rheingold, Schlitz, Piels—they moved because it was too expensive to do business here.

Taxes also help to explain the flight of middle- and upper-income taxpayers. In 1974, according to a survey by Nicholas Kisburg of Teamsters Joint Council 16, 20.9 percent of the average resident's income was drained by local and state taxes—nearly double the 1959 rate. "The tax collector, rather than the employer—at least in New York—is the worker's major adversary," said local Teamsters President Joseph Trerotola in 1977.

"Past policies have led to the dissipation of our economic assets,"

Governor Carey's 1977 budget message declared. "We have diverted too much of our resources to the public sector. Over 80 percent of the employment growth between 1970 and 1975 was in government—only 20 percent was in the private sector. We failed to recognize that in the long run only growth in the private sector would enable us to pay for our public programs. This left us particularly vulnerable to economic recession."

With that year's budget in mind, that year's election, that week's crisis, city and state officials adopted a soak-the-rich—soak-everybody—tax policy. Politically, this was better politics than cutting the rate at which expenditures were rising. Besides, officials sincerely believed the rich should pay more. They should, but they don't have to stay in New York, not when there are forty-nine other states.

Pay Parity and
Buck Passing to Arbitrators

Passing the buck is mother's milk to politicians. One way to view the city's strange fiscal behavior is as a history of buck passing—first to the state, then to the capital budget, then to next year's budget, future taxpayers, the federal government, or some third party. The rules of the game are simple: take credit and avoid blame.

The police/fire pay parity dispute is a classic case of buck passing. For years, police sergeants complained that fire lieutenants —who they believed did comparable work—should not be paid more. On January 4, 1967, Mayor Lindsay's Office of Collective Bargaining (OCB) passed the dispute on to an impasse panel for study. The panel recommended a compromise, one which rewarded police sergeants less than fire lieutenants but widened the gap between a sergeant's and a patrolman's pay. Lindsay accepted their recommendations. The result was a truce.

A brief one. Two years later, sergeants again complained that they should be equal to fire lieutenants; patrolmen complained that the gap between their pay and sergeants' pay was too wide. The patrolmen's union, the PBA, threatened to strike. Their timing could not have been better. Lindsay was seeking reelection, and the last thing he wanted was another strike. On April 29, 1969, Herbert L. Haber, Lindsay's Director of the Office of Collective Bargaining, quietly initialed an agreement with the PBA granting patrolmen what they wanted, including a $2,700 retroactive bonus.

In an attempt to keep the sergeants happy, Lindsay appointed another impasse panel, this one chaired by Theodore Kheel, one of the "power brokers" Lindsay denounced in 1966. The panel waited until after the mayoral election before recommending that the ratio determined by the first panel be raised. "The Lindsay administration accepted the second OCB recommendation as well," wrote Columbia Professor Raymond Horton in a book on municipal labor relations, "despite the fact that it clearly conflicted with the PBA agreement reached in February."

After the election, the city had second thoughts and reinterpreted their February 1969 agreement with the PBA. Gone were the $2,700 bonus and the higher pay ratio of patrolmen to sergeants. The PBA immediately took the initialed agreement to court and eventually won. The city appealed. Understandably irate that the city broke its word, patrolmen went on strike for six days in January 1971. Shortly thereafter, the city lost its case in court.

But the city lost more. Since the pay of all the uniformed services is pegged to the parity principle, an increase for sergeants or patrolmen ensures an increase for everyone else. Sanitation men, for instance, are supposed to be paid 90 percent of what a patrolman gets—when patrolmen's pay goes up, so does that of sanitation men. "By the time other groups, like firemen and sanitation men, came forward with their related demands," Horton wrote, "the cost to the city was considerable—variously estimated from $150 million to $215 million." That is the additional cost *each* year.

The dispute helped convince elected officials to free themselves from responsibility for ticklish labor disputes. Soon, under the state Taylor law, compulsory arbitration of public disputes was called for. The buck was passed to nonelected mediators, who in the future would command even more generous settlements.

And the city paid another price for the pay parity debacle. New York had suffered strikes from its transit workers, its teachers, its sanitation men, its hospital and welfare workers. Some of these strikes, particularly the 1968 teachers' strike, savagely polarized the city and reminded citizens that their government did not necessarily represent their interests. But until 1971, it had been almost unthinkable that those responsible for public safety would strike. Police are our last bastion against lawlessness. Hell, it was against the law to strike. But cops struck anyway, and with that strike went another piece of the city's social fabric. *What's happening to New York?* was a question everyone asked. *How could cops strike? Who will protect us? Where's the government? Do I want my kids to grow up in a place like this? If my business has a future, and this place doesn't, why should I stay?* As people asked these questions, they picked away at that intangible sense of confidence and faith which is as important to a city's life and stability as "investor confidence" is to its bonds.

Voters Reject
a New State Constitution

It's easy to condemn politicians for the fiscal crisis—and Lord knows, they deserve blame. But it would be a form of buck passing to assume that a handful of individuals partook in a giant conspiracy. It would also be misleading to excuse the public from blame. Many bad decisions were popular. Some good policies were vetoed by the public.

On November 7, 1967, the voters of New York State rejected a new state constitution by the lopsided margin of 3,487,513 to 1,327,999. The reasons were varied. The Convention was a partisan affair, composed of traditional politicians who created a hodgepodge of amendments designed to protect various interests. A key factor, however, was the proposed repeal of the Blaine Amendment, which strictly prohibited state aid to church-related facilities.

The 1967 constitutional convention was the first in twenty-nine years and likely the last for quite some time. But for the city of New York—which cast 56 percent of its ballots against the constitution —passage would have meant dramatic budget savings. New York City pays much more for services than do other cities partly because New York State—unlike other states—does not assume a larger share of city costs. The constitution would have corrected much of that.

No other state, for instance, requires its cities to swallow 25 percent of welfare costs. The closest state is New Jersey, which requires cities like Newark to pay 12 percent. *Article X, Section 16* of the proposed constitution would have required the state to assume the full local costs of welfare over a ten-year period. In fiscal

1979, the city would have been relieved of more than $500 million, or half its cumulative deficit.

Most states assume the full cost of their court systems. Not New York—at least not until 1977 legislation agreed to phase these costs into the state budget over three years. *Article V, Section 25B* of the proposed constitution required state assumption over ten years. In fiscal 1976, the city spent $94.2 million for its courts.

Over many years, the city Board of Education has complained that the state school aid formula discriminated against densely populated areas. Because the formula was pegged to attendance rather than registration, large cities with high absenteeism receive proportionately less aid than suburban school districts. *Article IX, Second 1d* would have switched the formula to school registration, generating hundreds of millions of additional dollars for the city.

Admittedly, nothing is free. Since city taxpayers are also state taxpayers, additional state costs would have entailed some additional city costs. But those costs would have been spread over the broader tax base of the state, resulting in significant city budget savings.

Redlining

Jean Loretto lives on a lovely Manhattan block. So lovely that West 105th Street, between Riverside Drive and West End Avenue, was declared a city landmark in 1973. But when Jean Loretto sought refinancing for her five-story brownstone, she found that the banks thought her block an unlovely investment area. It was considered too far uptown, too near *them*. "I was turned down cold," she told Tom Rosenthal of the weekly *Westsider*. "One banker told me I had invested in the *Titanic*. Another banker said that a person who lives in the city must have a summer home, and must send their kids to private schools. These bankers all have suburban mentalities. They all live in the suburbs and take the train in and never see an area like 105th Street. They all think we're crazy to live here."

Though her building generated ample rents, Ms. Loretto was turned down by three neighborhood banks. Her travail is common. Beginning in the late sixties, neighborhood residents throughout the city—particularly in Brooklyn and the Bronx—encountered difficulty wrangling mortgage money for homes and stores or new insurance policies. Financial institutions, including the Federal Housing Administration–sponsored loans, were saying no or making the terms prohibitively expensive. As money dried up, the process of neighborhood decay quickened; more residents fled to the suburbs, poor people moved in, stores closed, buildings burned.

This denial of mortgage and insurance money is called redlining, a process whereby a financial institution is said to draw a red line or quarantine around a neighborhood, declaring that neighborhood unworthy of investment. Community groups complain that financial institutions are not using economic criteria—Jean Loretto's building is a sound investment—but instead rely on arbitrary geographic and social criteria. Lending institutions deny this, claiming that as profit-making institutions their decisions are economic, whereas many neighborhood loans are not.

Whether or not a conspiracy exists, it is clear that city neighborhoods have been devastated by disinvestment. A thick 1977 report from the state Banking Department to the legislature offered compelling evidence. Surveying the entire state, they dryly reported: savings bank assets rose by $21.5 billion between 1970 and 1975, yet only $3.9 billion of this sum was earmarked for residential mortgages within the state. During the same period, residential mortgages on out-of-state properties *increased* by $4.8 billion. Within the city, mortgage loans as a percentage of local savings bank deposits was just 15 percent. In Nassau County, it was 62 percent. A case study revealed that between 1970 and 1976 fourteen Brooklyn savings banks increased their deposits from $10.1 billion to $16.8 billion. Yet in 1976: "Brooklyn mortgages were 11.2% of Brooklyn deposits." The Brooklyn banks studied had 23.5 percent of their total residential mortgages in Brooklyn—and 51.7 percent in the surrounding suburbs. Money, like people and jobs, was fleeing. "Redlining is happening in New York, not only in the bombed-out areas, but in areas where there seems no rhyme or reason for it," J. Robert Hunter, acting Chief of the Federal Insurance Administration told a city public hearing in early 1978.

There are many reasons for disinvestment. Banks and insurance companies are not charitable institutions. They are in business to earn a profit. In many blighted or declining neighborhoods, profits are precarious and losses are great. One of five FHA multi-family insured mortgages in the New York metropolitan area was in default in 1978, and the city number was higher. The state banking study showed that between 1970 and 1975 savings bank home mortgage delinquencies in the city rose 400-fold to 2.37 percent. The maze of city rent control, housing and mortgage regulations is also to blame. Because of tight city and state regulations on rents and conversions to tenant-owned cooperatives, smaller landlords often do not generate sufficient revenues to justify secure loans. Insurance companies do not start fires or rob stores, and as vandalism grows so will insurance rates. The state arbitrarily set the mortgage interest rate at 8.5 percent—below the prime rate of 9 or so percent—so banks could make more money out of state. The bottom line for financial institutions is profit.

The bottom line for New Yorkers is declining neighborhoods. The economic price of disinvestment is no greater than the psychological. In fact, they go together. When residents sense that a neighborhood is slipping, when investment money dries up, decline becomes self-fulfilling. The result is abandonment. Middle-income homeowners are replaced by poor renters, with welfare often paying the rent. Because landlords can usually collect higher rents from welfare than from the free market, the result is blockbusting. More poor people means more youth gangs. More youth gangs means more arson—often subsidized by landlords to collect on an old insurance policy and get out; sometimes encouraged by welfare recipients to collect a relocation allowance and get out. Bushwick is the result. Or Coney Island. Brownsville. East New York. Harlem. The South Bronx. Maybe Corona?

How redlining starts is hard to trace; the results are highly visible. No doubt, this issue, like so many others in New York, underscores how uneconomic it is to do business in the city. Storekeepers can't afford the insurance premiums; profit-making companies can't afford the risks. Savings banks, however, are nonprofit institutions, and in many neighborhoods with ample local deposits, they are still not making loans. Curiously, Citibank—very much a profit-making commercial enterprise—announced on November 21, 1977, that it intended to make more liberal home mortgages in three Brooklyn neighborhoods, with down payments of 10 rather than 25 percent required. Asked why, a vice president of Citibank, who requested that his name not be used, said, "We think that in the short run there will be some opportunity cost for the bank [a loss or lower profits]. We think this loss is relatively modest compared to the ultimate social gain." Well, was this a public relations decision? "I would quantify it as being 20 percent public relations," was the answer. "Ten percent good intentions, and 70 percent a belief that, in the long run, there will be a return on the investment."

Presumably, in years past, Citibank and others could have made the same decisions, accommodating both their bottom line and neighborhood mortgages. They didn't. And Jean Loretto was not the only one to pay.

Nixon's the One

There were two sets of posters in the 1968 and 1972 Presidential campaigns. The first—"Nixon's the One"—was paraded by his supporters to extol his record. The second—"Nixon's the One!"—was paraded by his opponents and featured a pregnant woman pointing mockingly to her stomach. Nixon will, no doubt, be remembered as "The One" who gave us Watergate, Cambodia, Chile, the saturation bombing of Vietnamese villages and a spate of awful books, including his own.

But New Yorkers should also remember him as the President who, in historian Richard Wade's words, "abandoned the notion of compensatory spending for our cities and instead switched to per capita aid, which favored the burgeoning suburbs." The heart of the Republican party is suburban, and that's where the Republican President redirected federal aid. Richard P. Nathan and Paul R. Dommel of the Brookings Institution show how:

In 1968, 62.2 percent of all federal grants for cities went to cities over 500,000 population; the corresponding figure for 1975 was 44.3 percent. On the other hand, the shares for cities of under 500,000 population rose. Cities of 100,000–499,999 population received 17.5 percent of all federal grants to cities in 1968 and 22.9 percent in 1975; the shares for cities under 100,000 rose even more, from 20.3 percent in 1968 to 32.8 percent in 1975.

Under Nixon, the federal government refused to spend funds approved by the Congress and declared a moratorium on Section 236 housing subsidies.

During the Kennedy and Johnson administrations, the federal share of city budgets jumped from 4.5 percent in 1961 to 14.6 percent in 1969. In 1967, federal aid to New York City leaped by 87.3 percent. Contrary to popular New York mythology, during most of the Nixon and Ford administrations federal aid continued to grow. But much more slowly. When taking inflation into account, the Temporary Commission on City Finances found, for instance, that the "overall adjusted growth rate of 12 percent for the 1971–1976 fiscal period was about one-tenth the real rate of increase experienced during each of the two previous five-year periods." The federal government's share of the city's budget actually declined in fiscal 1974 and again in Ford's last year. (The state's did, too.)

Federal aid, ironically, contributed to the city's own downfall. As aid multiplied in the sixties, and as the local economy was expanding, the city could come up with the matching funds required. But when federal aid slowed and the local economy nosedived, New York was trapped. "A critical series of decisions was the acceptance of federal programs forced on us during the Johnson years," observes former Deputy Richard Aurelio (1969–71). "In the liberal euphoria over these programs, little attention was paid to their long-term costs." A 1976 letter to Congressman Edward Koch, then Secretary of the New York delegation, from Deputy Mayor John Zuccotti explained just how the city was trapped:

Federal matching and maintenance requirements were designed to assure expansion of total outlays for specific programs. When applied to the City at this time, the requirements often have a counterproductive effect. In many cases, the lack of necessary local matching funds means that federal funds and the projects that they support must be forsaken. In other instances, the City is often forced to make painful cuts in other worthy locally supported programs to satisfy matching and maintenance of effort requirements for federally-aided programs. In these cases, the allocation of our dwindling resources is seriously skewed by federal policies contrary to local needs.

Obviously, it's not just Nixon's fault. The mood of the country shifted—Nixon did, after all, carry every state but one in 1972. Much of the federal spending was wasteful, and the public wised up. And, one suspects, federal spending could have soared and New York would still be in trouble because local spending would have tried to keep pace. Parkinson's law—work expands to fill available space—has its home in New York. In this sense, New York, not just Nixon, is to blame. New York refused to adjust to the new no-growth federal reality. And, as we will see, it did not adjust to the reality of its own declining economy.

Ignoring the City's Economy

"How would you like to be remembered?" I once asked Alfred Eisenpreis, Mayor Beame's first Economic Development Administrator, and a genuinely dense man.

"I don't know," he said. "I'd probably want to be remembered as something 'In Progress.' That's very corny, maybe. But, in many ways, that's not untrue."

"But how could you have 'In Progress' on your tombstone?"

"And why not?"

"Because you're dead!"

"How do you know?" he said, a satisfied look settling over his otherwise impassive face.

For years, the city government acted as if it did not know it was bleeding to death. Beginning with John Lindsay, the city government ignored the hemorrhaging of its economy. The nation's economy rebounded from a recession in 1969, but the city's did not. For the first time in history, its economic performance did not mirror the nation's. As the country gained jobs, the city lost them—more in the next five years than it had gained in the previous fifteen. As America's population grew, for the first time the city's total population declined, with 300,000 mostly middle-income residents fleeing between 1970 and 1975. As the nation's median family income went up, the real median income of city families went down by 6.1 percent between 1970 to 1973—among blacks it fell 17.4 percent. Yet as Nixon put his foot on the federal spending brake, the city pressed down on the accelerator.

It's not as if there were no warnings. As early as 1962, the Bureau of Labor Statistics was reporting job losses in four of the city's major industrial sectors. By 1970, their reports showed an absolute decline in employment. On July 20, 1969, the Citizens Budget Commission issued a study—*The Financial Outlook for New York City*—describing "a picture of gloom" and warning that the city faced "choices between what is wanted and what can be afforded." Bureau of Labor Statistics chief Herb Bienstock summed up those years: "No one paid any attention."

One thing John Lindsay paid attention to was dedication ceremonies, like the one to christen the new McGraw-Hill building in March 1973. Before the clicking cameras, the Mayor took to his side a Columbia University professor, Eli Ginzberg, who had just published a book with the silly title *New York Is Very Much Alive*. Holding the book aloft, Lindsay boomed that it put the lie to those who claimed New York was declining. No, the Big Apple was alive and well and this book proved it. The press feasted on the good news.

While Lindsay played Candide, that same day a brief *Times* story carried this headline: JOBS IN CITY DOWN 3RD YEAR IN A ROW. The story noted that the Bureau of Labor Statistics reported the city lost 68,000 jobs in 1972 and 252,000 jobs since 1969. Questioned about this three days later, Lindsay told the *Times* he had "some hope" the job market would expand in 1973 because there was a slight gain in the closing months of 1972. But in 1973 the city lost an additional 95,000 jobs.

The city's spending did not reflect what was happening to its revenue base. Lindsay's expense budget rose 16.6 percent from 1970 to 1971. Overall, the city's budget expanded by 10.2 percent from 1971 to 1975, exceeding the growth rate from 1961 to 1966, when the economy was on the rise. During Lindsay's second term and Beame's first two years, the number of city employees increased by 30,000. Their wages also jumped between 1970 and 1976, when Lindsay and Beame presided. The Temporary Commission disclosed that the pay of policemen went up at the same rate in those years as it did between 1965 and 1970. Lavish pension agreements were conferred, including twenty-year retirement plans for city clerks. (The state legislature embarrassed Lindsay by turning down this agreement in the early 1970's).

Of all John Lindsay's bad and good decisions, perhaps history will judge that this non-decision to recognize economic reality was his most important. His thoughts were elsewhere—on running for President in 1972. But the Mayor was hardly alone. His Budget Bureau, for instance, also chose to ignore reality. The budget grew even though Budget Director Edward K. Hamilton told the *Times* on April 15, 1971, "there's no natural growth of revenues." It grew because, as a former Lindsay budget aide explains, "Our budgets were calculated based on what we expected to spend, not the revenues we expected to receive."

This ostrich-like behavior was sometimes innocent. Many public officials didn't follow the "numbers," might not have understood them, and probably wouldn't believe them if they did. New York, after all, was the Big Apple. There was a genuinely optimistic belief that the turnaround in the national economy would reach New

York—it had always been thus. Besides, for years it had been more or less assumed that New York's economy was a reflection of government, not private, spending.

Abe Beame promised to change that. His 1973 mayoral campaign vowed to beef up the city's Economic Development Administration, to appoint a council of economic advisers, to devise a plan. By 1975, the city had a plan—a twenty-four-page document labeled *Agenda for Economic Development.* The centerpiece of the strategy was the development of twelve industrial parks, eight wholesale markets, and the "revitalization" of 575 miles of city waterfront. If the strategy worked, city officials said, 25,000 jobs would be created—the same number the city was losing every sixteen weeks. That year the Council of Economic Advisors stopped meeting. The "beefed-up" agency relied on one staff member and a secretary to attract and retain businesses. A considerable task, since there were then 172,090 businesses in the city. Unlike its counterparts in other localities and states, this agency was given only $1 million of flexible capital funds to buy and lease land for faltering firms. In 1975, 80 percent of this budget was used to assist just one firm, the Elmhurst Dairy—saving 300 jobs. Without flexible tax incentives or training funds, the head of the agency, Alfred Eisenpreis, was really like a waiter in a restaurant without a kitchen. Not that he could have been anything more. The former marketing executive, who never forgot that he had the opportunity to immigrate here from his native Europe, was so grateful for his new job that he was afraid of losing it. In the spring of 1975, this keeper of the city's economy—who wondered whether you would know when you were dead—peered at me through his Coca-Cola thick eyeglasses and declared, "We are not losing our economic base. Our economic base is shifting."

"New York City has had a total, planless economic development," complained Herb Bienstock. "In 1965, John Lindsay put together a group which proposed that a Council of Economic Advisors be set up. Nothing ever came of it. When Beame came in he set up a Council. The only thing is that after he announced the appointees they discovered it didn't have an economist on it. . . . I was asked to serve on Governor Carey's Economic Development Task Force. I attended one meeting. It was a waste of time. . . . No one has ever put together a group of economists to work on New York City. Really put them to work—with resources and dollars—and said, 'Here, don't come out with a study, come out with a set of policy recommendations.' All that comes out now is bullshit."

Which is precisely what came out of John Lindsay in 1977. Talking about the city's 1975 fiscal crisis, the former Mayor broke a long silence and told writer Harry Stein, "As long as I live I will insist I wouldn't have let it happen. We would have acted quick! Decisively!" Pounding his desk twice with an open hand, he continued: "That was our way, to confront problems head-on, to do anything that had to be done."

Budget Notes

Faced with an emergency cash shortage, in 1942 the State of New York for the first time issued budget notes. Such notes require repayment within a year, and, in this case, were promptly repaid. In fact, to underline the emergency nature, the 1942 legislation said notes were permissible in times of "epidemics, riot, flood, storm, earthquake or other unusual peril."

Looking at the city's recent history, it appears that epidemics, earthquakes and floods were annual events. A truly "unusual peril" confronted John Lindsay in 1971. To balance the budget, city officials ballooned their forecast of federal aid—a device pioneered by Governor Rockefeller, who used it to balance the state budget. When Congress failed to pass revenue sharing, the city was caught short by several hundred million dollars. No problem, soothed Rockefeller, cracking the whip on the legislature to permit issuance of city budget notes. On June 17, 1971, the Governor signed an amendment to the Local Finance Law allowing the city to patch its deficit. If the city couldn't meet yearly installment repayments by 1974, the legislation said it could return to Albany and the state "will make a first instance appropriation."

That month, Lindsay issued more than $300 million of budget notes to cover inflated revenue estimates. The following April, he asked for permission to issue $400 million more. Instead of repaying a part of the original notes each year, as the legislation stipulated, the city merely rolled over this debt, folding it into new borrowing. No heed was paid to the warnings of the Citizens Budget Commission. On April 16, 1972, the Commission issued a study that criticized the issuance of budget notes because it "enables the city to live beyond its means in a given fiscal year" and creates a "double burden" for future taxpayers who must both repay the debt and maintain the spending programs the debt made possible. Asked to comment, Budget Director David A. Grossman said the borrowing was "legal" and "taxpayers would be concerned if we had to raise anything like the $400 million from taxation. It was because of his feelings that the taxpayer was already too heavily burdened that the Mayor instructed me to prepare a plan that would not involve extra taxation."

By 1974, when the original notes were due, the city was saved by a state election. Malcolm Wilson, the conservative Republican who was Rockefeller's Lieutenant Governor and automatically became Governor when Rockefeller resigned, wanted to prove he was a friend of the city's. At Mayor Beame's request, he signed into law, on May 30, 1974, a bill creating the New York City Stabilization Reserve Corporation. It's purpose: to issue new notes.

Had the investors read the legislation, perhaps the credit market would have closed in 1974, not 1975. The legislation states:

The Legislature finds and declares that the City of New York is faced with a grave and unprecedented fiscal crisis which threatens the City's ability to provide essential services and thereby endangers the welfare of all the inhabitants of such City. . . . Accordingly, the Legislature finds and declares that it is necessary for a corporation to be created to assist such City . . . to provide essential services during 1973–74, 1974–75 fiscal years on a sound financial basis.

After this legislation sailed through, the city did not act as if there were a "crisis." Expenditures continued to swell. And the city continued to borrow. The Stabilization Corp. merely allowed the city to borrow to repay borrowing, to pay interest on interest. These notes helped turn New York into a short-term note junkie. The city's short-term debt pyramided 350 percent between 1970 and 1975, from $1.3 to $4.5 billion. By the spring of 1975, the city faced a true "peril." New York City accounted for almost 30 percent of all the municipal notes sold in the country—and within less than a year, needed a $7 billion fix of new securities.

The 1973-74 City Budget

1973 was a pretty good year for wine and a lousy year for city budgets. City budgets always suffer in mayoral election years. But this year was special in two respects. First, its deceit was to the art of budget ballet what Baryshnikov is to Lincoln Center. Second, the budget was unusual in that it was jointly crafted by two artists, outgoing Mayor Lindsay and incoming Mayor Beame.

The gimmicks pirouette across its pages and include: (1) the invention of $148.5 million of "increased revenues," achieved primarily by postponing—with City Council support—the statutory repayment of $96 million to the "rainy day" fund; (2) a one-year rollover of the $308 million of budget notes issued in 1971; (3) the placement of $564 million of expenses in the capital budget, a $290 million jump from the previous year; (4) $100 million of "special" funds suddenly discovered by Comptroller Beame; (5) the assumption that the anticipated tax revenues meant the city's economy was expanding, though it had not for the past four years; (6) the elimination of $17 million set aside for wage increases, though it was commonly assumed the increases would far exceed this; (7) at midyear, the city's arbitrary termination of existing transit subsidies for schoolchildren and the elderly, pretending (a) that the need or the recipients would disappear or (b) that the state and/or federal government would spring to the rescue; (8) the budget's authorization, to match a Beame campaign pledge, of the hiring of 3,000 more cops, though there were 2,250 police vacancies; and (9) the city's outright declaration of a deficit of $211 million, summoning the state legislature, or God, to close it.

It is this 1973-74 budget that Mayor Beame blamed for his later difficulties, protesting that he "inherited a $1.5 billion budget gap." His logic will be of greater interest to psychologists than historians. Since Beame had been the City Comptroller the preceding four years, his fingerprints were all over the document. He attended breakfast meetings with Lindsay on June 11 and 15, 1973, hoping to agree to what they announced would be "a balanced budget." Beame was considered a budget expert, and since he was the clear favorite to become the next mayor, members of the Board of Estimate and the City Council deferred to his leadership. On June 18, a joint statement was issued: "Agreement has been reached on a proposed 1973-74 Expense Budget by the Mayor, the Comptroller, the Board of Estimate and City Council leaders." Everyone was smiling, or, as the New York *Post* accurately reported, "This was the first year in the past four that Lindsay and Beame practiced budget politics of consensus instead of confrontation." The next day, Lindsay issued another press release: "Like all budgets, it contains compromises. It includes a number of items and the use of some financial techniques which I would not have preferred." He went on to thank Beame for his "cooperation."

Looking back on this budget, a prominent official in the present City Comptroller's office said, simply, it was "outright fraud." Looking back on it in a June 1975 memo to private citizen Lindsay, David Grossman, his last Budget Director, used different words to achieve a similar conclusion:

It was not until recently—from June 30, 1973 to March, 1975—that the really sharp increase in short-term borrowing occurred and the market began to ask what was going on. In those two years, short-term debt went up by an astounding 138%. . . . During the same two years, the expense budget went up 19% while the state and federal aid component rose by only 7%. Small wonder, then, that the city ran into a crisis of confidence in March, 1975 and ceased to be able to sell its short-term debt. What accounts for the very rapid growth in short-term borrowing in only two years? It would appear that the answer lies mostly in the way in which the last two City budgets were constructed— built on hoped-for revenues that never arrived, on budgetary techniques that anticipated future revenues by borrowing cash in the present, and on a continuing rollover of past deficits from year to year. . . . The current cash crisis is, in budgetary terms, the end result of a political process that saw the city adopt two successive budgets in which the hard issue of budget balance were avoided.

Abe Beame Sinks to the Occasion

Hair still wet from a morning shower, Mayor Abraham Beame rushed to Manhattan's garment district in July 1975 to proclaim a new traffic control program. The Mayor couldn't stand to be late; he was as proud to be punctual as he was to be called a fiscal wizard. And yet this morning Beame was both late and humiliated. To restore investor confidence and avoid bankruptcy, just days before a state agency had been created to police the city's fiscal affairs.

The five-foot two-inch, sixty-nine-year-old patriot swallowed hard and took it, all to save his city from bankruptcy. But it hurt, and today he had his mind set on proving that neither he nor his government had been crippled by the fiscal crisis. Standing on a street corner, all but hidden by a forest of microphones, he read a prepared statement. The blare of truck horns drowned his voice, as did two local merchants who interrupted to scold their mayor, denouncing his program as "a publicity stunt."

Determined to proceed, Beame sauntered across Seventh Avenue to inspect a new low street curb which would permit the easy movement of clothing carts. Suddenly, he halted. Befuddled, he gestured toward a large automobile blocking the city's new low curb. "Yes, Mr. Mayor," sighed the guide, Transportation Administrator Michael Lazar. "It's an illegal park taking place right before your eyes."

The fiscal crisis of 1975 also took place right before Abe Beame's eyes. The new mayor was as blind to the gathering fiscal storm as Lindsay had been to the city's economic decline. It was supposed to be different. "This time let's elect a mayor who can do the job!" chimed Beame's campaign commercials. "Let this day, the first day of our administration, mark the rebirth of faith in our city and confidence in our city government," concluded the new mayor's January 1, 1974 inaugural address. The torch had been passed from the promiscuous Lindsay to the frugal Beame, the man who "knows the buck"—or so voters thought.

What Beame (and the voters) didn't know was that times had changed. And Abe Beame didn't know how to change with them. He was the victim of cautious instincts nurtured by years of inching up the civil service ladder—from accountant to budget examiner to assistant deputy budget director to budget director (ten years) to comptroller (eight years), finally, to cap a dream, becoming New York's 104th mayor. Beame followed the same route within his beloved Democratic party, rising from doorbell ringer to district captain to esteemed party leader. When others were turning their back on the Democratic organization, Beame remained a party man, rewarding the faithful as he had once been rewarded himself. Proudly, he described himself as a "conciliator," a "negotiator," a man searching for the middle ground. Abe Beame was a survivor, not a shaper of events.

Beame was also a victim of a lifetime of personal habits. He was a kind but also a guarded man. He held his emotions under strict control. He stiffened in the presence of most reporters and strangers. He tended to work alone. The one official he relied on in 1974 and 1975, First Deputy Mayor James Cavanagh, was in many respects a carbon copy of his boss—a career civil servant who had served in the Budget Bureau and who played his cards close to the vest. "There aren't regular strategy meetings," said an aide. "Most of it is done on the phone. That's how Beame operates." By direct phone contact with all his commissioners, by notes on long legal pads and scraps of paper stuffed into his pockets. Each day, Beame made lists of things to do, staring at his pad and crossing off items while munching on a daily tuna fish sandwich. When he returned from a public appearance, he would empty his suit pockets and pile the scraps of paper on the desk. Immediately, a flurry of terse phone calls would commence: no *How are ya*'s, no *This is Abe*— just twenty, thirty seconds' worth of business so the scrap of paper could be discarded. Because Beame did not pause to sort the scraps, preferring to follow the accidental order in which they appeared on the desk, sometimes a commissioner would receive four or five separate calls in a matter of minutes.

That's how the Mayor kept in touch. He was a slave to routine. At the end of the day, most of the items on the legal pad had been checked off, his calls returned, the scraps of paper exhausted. But by immersing himself in such detail, Beame, like the accountant he was trained to be, often lost sight of the larger picture.

Perhaps the most revealing question of the 1977 mayoral campaign was asked not by a reporter but by Ed Koch. In a public TV debate, each of the candidates was allowed to ask the other a question. Beame asked Koch about one of his votes in Congress. Koch surprised Beame with a more general question: What, Mr. Beame, do you regard as the greatest accomplishments during your four years as mayor? Beame took a moment to reflect. Then the Mayor of New York, unbelievably, said his greatest accomplishments were getting the 1976 Democratic convention and the Fourth of July Op Sail celebration.

As the city slipped further into debt and investors grew wary, Beame acted as if nothing had changed. His first budget (1974-75) was business as usual. Instead of making painful cuts to cope with the $1.5 billion deficit he said he inherited, he raised taxes by $44 million; smuggled $722 million of expenses into the capital budget; borrowed $520 million in notes by creating the Stabilization Reserve Corp., a vehicle to float new borrowings; discovered $280 million by advancing the date of sewer rent collections and siphoning what he called "excess" pension earnings.

"What led to Beame and Cavanagh's undoing was the fact that these two guys were unable to adjust to changes in the new intergovernmental ball game we have," says Herb Ranchburg of the

Citizens Budget Commission. "The city came to depend for 40 to 45 percent of its budget on state and federal funds. They could not shuffle these funds. It used to be that the hallmark of a good budget director was when the mayor called and said, 'I need $7 million,' the budget director could do that. As budget director, Beame could do that. He was dealing with small amounts. What happened in the Lindsay administration was that the technically balanced budget became an end in itself. The figures were much larger and there was less control.

"City Hall did not adjust to the situation. He still continued to claim 'savings' based on expenditures not made, and which never would have been made to begin with. The city claimed hundreds of millions in savings for people they could not have hired. It was as if my washing machine broke and my wife got it repaired for $50. Abe Beame would claim a $250 saving since he didn't have to go out and buy a new washing machine."

In addition to his budget habits, Beame's political performance in late 1974 and early 1975 undermined confidence in his—and, therefore, the city's—credibility. He appeared more interested in avoiding blame than solving problems. When a huge budget gap loomed, he acted as if he were a stranger to city government, blaming the $1.5 billion deficit he "inherited" from Lindsay—"If it weren't for that, we would be in good shape now." When City Comptroller Harrison Goldin said his budget deficit figure was too low, on December 2, 1974, Beame blamed Goldin for the city's 9.5 percent interest rate. To reduce the gap, over the next two months Beame separately announced Phase One, Phase Two, and Phase Three of city layoffs. On February 1, he proudly announced that the layoffs had been averted. It almost appeared as if the crisis were over. Two weeks later, Beame projected a $1.7 billion budget gap for the following year. The financial community warned of the need for cuts. In March, Beame said, "Very frankly, I think I've done all that can be done without crippling services." Pressure mounted to cut the budget. Beame responded by blaming callous Republicans in Washington. Then he blamed Albany. Then the banks. Finally, on May 29, before live-TV cameras in the City Council Chamber, he denounced the "conspiracy" fostered by the banks and "editorial columns" to create "an atmosphere of doubt and uncertainty about New York's securities." The answer, he declared, was "an immediate Congressional inquiry" into "who started the whispering campaign to denigrate our fiscal integrity. . . ." His speech was greeted by thunderous applause. Congressman Ben Rosenthal said he would proceed immediately. "Anyone who doesn't stand by the Mayor in his struggle to avoid these massive layoffs," intoned Council Majority Leader Thomas Cuite, "I would consider a traitor, in the classical sense."

Beame and his city cohorts treated the crisis as a public relations problem, as they had always done. On July 7, 1975, after the city had been shut out of the credit market, after the state Municipal Assistance Corporation (MAC) was formed to police city finances, as the city teetered near bankruptcy, Abe Beame sat calmly behind his City Hall desk and told a roomful of reporters that the fiscal crisis was "behind us." Over the summer, Governor Carey briefly pondered removing Beame from office; by September, the state legislature formed the Emergency Financial Control Board to declare fiscal martial law and advertise to investors that Abe Beame reigned but no longer ruled New York.

The Mayor retained iron control of his emotions, courageously resisting the wounded importunings of his son Buddy that bankruptcy was preferable to humiliation. But the personal pain rankled. The new state overseers sniped at him, disdained him, thought he was in the way. Even after the events of the past year, Beame didn't understand. He saw himself as working hard, holding late-night meetings at Gracie Mansion, trying his best. He still rose early, made his lists of things to do. He followed through on phone calls and correspondence. He didn't understand what *those people*, as he called them, expected of him. Didn't they know he was working hard? Wasn't he sacrificing? Didn't he cut more employees from the city's payroll than any other mayor in history—and without strikes? Didn't he sacrifice his old friend Jim Cavanagh when the state and the banks insisted that he be fired? Didn't he bring in Deputy Mayor John Zuccotti and other capable executives? He was too controlled to say so, but it drove him crazy. The city's new fiscal rulers expected him to be something he was not. They expected him to be a leader when all his life he had been a survivor, a match for Ambrose Bierce's definition of perseverance: "A lowly virtue whereby mediocrity achieves an inglorious success."

"Abe Beame could have done much more much earlier and paid much less," state Budget Director Peter Goldmark told me in 1975. "In fact, if the city were willing to get honest with its figures last winter and presented a two- or three-year fiscal plan and agreed to limit its borrowing, there could have been an agreement with the financial community and there would have been no need for Big MAC." Or the Control Board. Or some of the pain of the fiscal crisis.

Repeal of the Port Authority's Bond Covenant

One of the biggest trades in New York history did not involve George Steinbrenner's Yankees. In 1962, the tristate Port Authority, architect and toll collector on many a bridge, tunnel and road, made a swap with the governors of New York and New Jersey. In exchange for its agreement to take over and modernize the Hudson River commuter rail link between the two states, the Port Authority received permission to build a world trade center in lower Manhattan. The legislatures of the two states also passed covenants solemnly pledging that the Authority and its bondholders would never again be asked to take over a deficit-plagued mass transit system. Since such systems chronically lose money, the covenant effectively prevented the rich and powerful Authority from investing in mass transportation. It also reassured bondholders that their investments would continue to be secured by revenue-generating projects.

Years passed. The Authority's surpluses grew. Mass transit revenues shrank. Slowly, a chorus of critics also grew—lashing out at the Authority's refusal to invest in mass transit, at the $850 million lavished on the World Trade Center, at the miles of "profitable" concrete ribbons strangling New York. The leading critic was labor attorney Theodore Kheel. He filed suit in federal court, challenging the covenant as unconstitutional. He organized citizens' committees to support the worthwhile goal of improved mass transit.

By 1973 and 1974, political support for repeal of the covenant was widespread. Before turning over the reigns of state government to Malcolm Wilson in late 1973, Governor Rockefeller extracted a pledge that he would repeal the covenant. On April 30, 1974, Governor Brendan Byrne of New Jersey signed the repeal. The legislature of the State of New York also voted repeal. But Governor Wilson hesitated. He worried, he said later, that repeal would "overturn a solemn pledge of the state." Kheel responded: "Repeal of the 1962 statutory covenant will in no way impair the security of Port Authority bondholders." Wilson was attacked by fellow Republicans, who warned that failure to repeal would lead to failure in the November elections. Hugh Carey and Howard Samuels, the two Democratic challengers for governor, blasted Wilson, as did the City Bar Association, *The New York Times,* and just about everyone in politics, including me. As Samuels' campaign manager, I gleefully encouraged the attack on Wilson, even helped write it. Meanwhile, a handful of bankers prattled about the loss of something called "investor confidence," whatever that meant.

Just moments before the June 15 veto deadline, Governor Wilson relented and signed the repeal. After an agonizing appraisal, he said, it was determined to his satisfaction that the repeal was constitutional. The courts disagreed, deciding in 1977 that repeal of the covenant was unconstitutional.

But the damage had been done. This strange term "investor confidence"—which couldn't be tasted, smelled, measured or quantified because, like air, it is invisible—suddenly took center stage. According to former state Banking Superintendent John Heimann, repeal was "a critical first step" and had a "profound effect on investor confidence" in government securities. "The abrogation of this covenant without consent or compensation, I believe, is not only illegal, but shortsighted," wrote Staats M. Pellet, Jr., of the Firemen's Fund American Insurance Companies to Paul Belica of the state HFA. "You are aware that credit rests not only on covenants between borrower and issuer, but also importantly on trust. With this action, the bond holder's faith in New York State has been shaken. . . ."

Repeal came at a bad time. Following the Arab oil boycott, energy costs were soaring, the national economy was in a recession, there was an international crisis, the financial community was suffering losses and had less cash to invest in tax-exempt bonds. And since a credit market is tissued together by faith as well as facts, repeal signaled to investors that what the state giveth, the state can taketh away. Investors took this as a sign that the governments'—or, more precisely, the politicians'—word was no good. Since the State of New York's "moral obligation" bonds were predicated on the *word* of politicians, repeal of the covenant contained enormous psychological implications, as the state would learn in February 1975.

The UDC Defaults

The sixty-four-page annual report of the state Urban Development Corporation (UDC), the powerful housing construction agency, began: "1975 can be a banner year. . . ." It was, of sorts.

On January 1 of that year, Governor Carey captured banner headlines by blasting the housing agency's "mismanagement." Fifteen days later, UDC President Edward J. Logue—sounding like Abe Beame would a few months later—charged that his agency's inability to borrow was due not to mismanagement or revenues that did not equal expenditures, but to a refusal to "knuckle under" to the dictates of the banks. State Comptroller Arthur Levitt, sounding like a broken record, again deplored the UDC's reliance on "moral obligation" bonds, claiming that they avoided the constitutional requirement for voter approval of all state bonds. Levitt also castigated the banks for "cooperating with a vengeance" to reap handsome profits from the UDC over the years.

The UDC was in trouble. The moral obligation debt of the state had grown by about $8 billion between 1964 and 1974, with the UDC as the largest benefactor. By 1974, the state had almost one-quarter of all the outstanding nonguaranteed long-term debt in the nation. Rushed through the legislature in 1968 by Governor Rockefeller, ostensibly as a memorial to the slain Martin Luther King, the UDC had extraordinary powers to slice through red tape and build housing. The UDC was a national model. But its revenues fell short of its debt service payment needs because most of its projects were not self-sustaining. By late 1974, the most powerful housing agency in the nation was enfeebled, and the incoming governor, Hugh Carey, ordered a task force to seek ways to prevent its collapse.

Since UDC Bonds were backed only by the state's "moral obligation," investors were naturally nervous. After a series of frantic meetings and touch-and-go negotiations with the banks, on February 26 Governor Carey shaped a bipartisan plan to provide the UDC with continuous financing and stave off its collapse. There was statesmanship on all sides, and the plan was duly saluted. Largely overlooked, however, was the fact that the UDC defaulted on the repayment of $104.5 million of notes due on February 25 when the state legislature refused to appropriate the monies. Governor Carey double-talked: since these were short-term notes, he said, they "do not carry the moral obligation of the state."

Four weeks later, the state made good on the money. But the psychological damage was done. The UDC became the first major government agency to default since the Depression. The message communicated to investors was clear: state "moral obligations" were not legal obligations—the state could unilaterally break a contract. "People did business with the UDC—small businessmen, architects, civil rights organizations—thinking they were doing business with the state of New York," explained Richard Ravitch, the man Carey installed as the dollar-a-year UDC chairman after replacing the discredited Logue. "The fact that they technically were not doesn't matter now."

The consequences were swift. Out-of-town investors, the key to the banks' underwriting function, got cold feet about all New York securities. "Why should I buy the moral obligations of immoral politicians?" screamed one Wall Street bond trader. That same day, *The Wall Street Journal* reported, "Public authority bonds fell an average of $15 for each 1,000 face amount." Michigan's Housing Department Authority couldn't sell some of its bonds. The New Jersey Housing Finance Agency complained of paying almost 2 percent more in interest than they should have and blamed the UDC default. Within days, New York City was compelled to accept a then-astronomical 8.69 percent interest rate on $537 million of bond-anticipation notes—up from 7 percent two weeks before.

The financial community was experiencing its own problems, and the UDC default hardened resistance to government securities. "The Nation was just recovering from the most severe recession of the post-war period," Lynn E. Browne and Richard F. Syron observed in a 1977 issue of *The New England Economic Review*.

Memories of double-digit inflation were still fresh and the performance of the wholesale price index over the summer and fall was not reassuring. Bank loan losses were at record levels and the collapse of real estate investment trusts had affected the profits of many financial institutions. Prophets of doom abounded. A natural result of these developments was a significant increase in investors' caution.

Coincident with this overall increase in caution was a major decrease in the demand for municipals by traditional purchasers. Commercial banks have traditionally been the single most important purchaser of municipal bonds and as late as 1972 bought 50 percent of all new issues. The tax-exempt feature of municipals has made them an attractive vehicle for sheltering commercial banks' income. In the last several years, however, banks have developed alternative ways of sheltering income. Also, loan losses of banks in 1975 placed many of them in a position where they had little income to shelter and thus no real need for tax exemptions. As a result, commercial bank acquisitions of state and local obligations fell by 70 percent from 1974 to 1975. Property and casualty insurance companies, the second largest group of institutional buyers, also had a poor profit year in 1975 and reduced their purchases of municipals by 30 percent from 1974.

The spillover from the UDC default hit New York City in another way. For the first time, a bank bond counsel refused to automatically sign off on the issuance of city notes without confirming to its satisfaction that there were sufficient revenues to support repayment. This happened when lawyers for White & Case, who represented a Bankers Trust syndicate of underwriters, told Comptroller Goldin in a February 27, 1975, meeting that they wished to inspect the city's tax receipts. "The Comptroller and the City Corporation Counsel stated that this request for more current information by White & Case was unprecedented," the SEC staff report would later recall. "In response, concern was expressed that, in view of the recent default of the Urban Development Corporation ('UDC') on its debt securities, underwriters should be reviewing new and different types of information than had been previously requested." The meeting in the Comptroller's office dragged on into the wee hours, with the city finally consenting to permit the inspection of its tax receipts.

After studying these receipts on the morning of February 28, White & Case firmly decided not to issue an opinion approving the sale. In response, Comptroller Goldin issued a dissembling press release: "Contrary to inaccurate reports which have been circulated, there is no question concerning the sufficiency of City tax revenues to meet all obligations including the February 19th offering. The certainty of repayment is in no way an issue in the deliberations now taking place." A joint statement from the Mayor and Comptroller chimed: "The recent default by the state Urban Development Corporation" has created an "unwarranted climate of suspicion in the marketplace." New York City taxpayers, they said, should not be forced to pay for the mistakes of "another jurisdiction."

The state Housing and Finance agency was forced to postpone a scheduled note sale. Construction on more than $1 billion in nursing homes, hospitals, facilities for the handicapped and other projects was halted for lack of investors. New York City's market would have collapsed without a UDC default or the repeal of the Port Authority bond covenant. But these two psychological blows accelerated the crisis, prompted the investment community to take a closer look at the city's books. When they did, in the winter and spring of 1975, the game was up.

IN MARCH AND APRIL 1975, the market slammed shut to New York City securities. To save New York from bankruptcy, the state advanced the city $800 million. As default—the inability of the city to pay its creditors, including its workers, on time—again loomed, in June Governor Carey shepherded the creation of the Municipal Assistance Corporation (MAC) to monitor city finances and to create "investor confidence in the soundness of the obligations of the City." In August, all agreed the city's cumulative deficit was over $3 billion. MAC was authorized to borrow $3 billion for the city, pledging specific revenues as security, and it was assumed that in September the city would be back on its feet and in the bond market.

It didn't work that way. Investors remained wary. So, in September 1975, the state created the Emergency Financial Control Board, consisting of four elected officials—the governor, mayor, city and state comptrollers—and three nonelected business executives. The Board was granted tougher "emergency" powers to police the city's budget, to approve or reject city contracts, and to order the preparation of a three-year city fiscal plan. Still, the Control Board did not succeed in restoring investor confidence.

Regular cash deadlines neared, and nerve-ending dramas were played out as all the participants marched to the brink of bankruptcy—each time pulling back at the point of no return. Usually, employee pension fund trustees would relent at the last minute and agree to invest more of their members' money. Sometimes the banks agreed to roll over due dates on securities. With notes coming due in November, the state legislature, at the instigation of city officials, declared a moratorium on the repayment of $2.4 billion of outstanding city notes. Next, the federal government came to the rescue, narrowly approving a $2.3 billion annual seasonal loan to the city (to be repaid with interest) after assurances that this loan would put New York back on its feet. Without it, MAC Chairman

Rohatyn warned, the Western world's economy might collapse. Without it, warned former Under Secretary of State George Ball, communism would achieve a great victory.

For the next three years, the city limped along, again barely escaping bankruptcy when the New York State Court of Appeals declared the Moratorium Act unconstitutional in November 1976. By the winter of 1978, the city once again admitted a huge deficit, once again returned to the Congress, once again issued dire warnings that without new federal loans New York—perhaps the country, perhaps the world—would go bust.

Chapter Three

Is Anyone Responsible?

THE FRANKLIN NATIONAL BANK retains the distinction of being the largest bankruptcy case in American banking history. In October 1974, the bank went broke. And in August 1975, eight Franklin National officers were indicted by a federal grand jury. The indictments charged them with trading in foreign currency without adequate collateral; filing fraudulent financial statements claiming profits of $79,000 at a time when losses were totaling $30 million; defrauding investors and creditors by issuing false financial statements to obtain a $35 million credit extension from Manufacturers Hanover Trust Company. Several laws were broken, including: Title 18, U.S. Code, Sections 1001 and 1014; and Section 32 and Rule 10b-5 of the Securities and Exchange Act of 1934. Most of the defendants received stiff fines and prison sentences.

The City of New York has the distinction of being the largest potential municipal bankruptcy in American history. In August 1977, the Securities and Exchange Commission issued an 800-page staff report accusing past and present officials of fraud. "The city," they concluded, "employed budgetary, accounting and financial practices which it knew distorted its true financial condition." As in the Franklin National Bank case, city officials were judged guilty of defrauding investors, of claiming nonexistent revenues and filing false and misleading financial statements in order to obtain more credit. Unlike the Franklin case, no one who participated in the city's swindle has been indicted or gone to jail.

And yet some of the same laws could apply to past city financial practices:

(1) Federal laws pertaining to fraud—the filing of false statements and failing to make full disclosure. The Securities Exchange Act of 1934, particularly Rule 10b-5, makes it a potential crime—fraud—to fail to "disclose any material fact" in the sale of notes or bonds. Section 1001 of the U.S. Code, Title 18, makes it a crime to file false statements where the federal government is directly or indirectly involved, as they are in the sale of all securities; Section 1014 makes it a crime to file a false document with a bank insured by the federal government.

(2) The New York State penal laws pertaining to fraud. Sections 175.30 and 175.45 define the differing degrees of crime committed when a person files "a false instrument . . . with intent to defraud."

(3) The New York State Blue Sky Law, Chapter 20, Section 352. This law permits the state attorney general to investigate any fraudulent "advertisement [or] investment advice" in connection with the sale or transfer of any securities.

(4) The New York State larceny laws. According to Article 155, it is a crime to "deprive" someone of his property. Section 155.40 says it is a crime for someone to "use or abuse his position as a public servant by engaging in conduct within or related to his official duties, or by failing or refusing to perform an official duty in such manner, as to affect some person adversely."

Violations of these laws entail severe penalties. Sentences range from one to ten years; fines, from $500 to $10,000. For federal and state felonies, the statute of limitations expires after five years; for a state misdemeanor, after two years. The statute of limitations for violations of state law by public officials, however, is extended to "within five years after the termination of such service." Thus for a state felony the statute of limitations extends up to ten years; for a misdemeanor, up to seven.

Fraud laws can be pretty stern. In a 1925 case involving the city of Long Beach, New York (*People* v. *Reynolds*), a state court convicted municipal officials of fraud for making false entries in the city's books, even though they did not personally benefit from their acts. In the 1967 *Walston* case, underwriters of municipal bonds were found guilty for failing "to make diligent inquiry" to ensure that "all material facts" presented to investors were correct. In the 1974 *Ferguson* case, a bond counsel was judged guilty and censured because "he should have known" that a securities prospectus omitted important facts. And one does not have to commit a "willful" or knowing act to become vulnerable to prosecution. "If you are so negligent, at some point you become criminally liable," explains a prominent attorney who advises MAC and is an expert on securities laws. "It's like an engineer on a train who falls asleep and the train crashes and kills fifty. He did not intend to kill those people, but he is criminally liable."

If these laws and precedents were applied to persons involved in "balancing" and financing city budgets during the last twenty years, a stadium would be needed to house the defendants. The roll call of those implicated would read like a *Who's Who* of government and banking: Wagner, Lindsay, Beame, Nelson and David Rockefeller, former Treasury Secretary William Simon (in the late sixties and early seventies, he was the chief municipal bond dealer for the Wall Street banking firm of Salomon Bros. and served on the City Comptroller's Technical Debt Advisory Committee), Harrison Goldin, former Deputy Mayors James Cavanagh and Edward Hamilton, former Budget Directors Melvin Lechner and David Grossman, former speakers of the state assembly, majority leaders of the state senate, City Council and Board of Estimate members, partners in the blue-chip Wall Street law firms, prominent bankers and underwriters— to name a few.

They are Democrats and Republicans, Liberals and Conservatives. They had different personal viewpoints and political backgrounds, supported opposing candidates, feigned outrage in public debate and whispered disdain for each other in private. But they shared a community of interest, the same life preserver. When in a jam, public officials had a friend at Chase Manhattan and other banks. Everyone benefited. The public avoided unpleasant service cuts. Taxes were frozen—in election years. City officials could continue to expand services to their constituents. State officials could hold down state aid payments to the city. The financial community continued to reap handsome profits on tax-free municipals. Bond counselors collected huge fees. Unions received new pay and fringe benefits. The public got the promise of more services. There was little danger of exposure since there was little opposition. Most politicians went along. The press—usually more interested in politics than in government—would briefly note the tricks for a day, then forget them. Besides, these shenanigans were so complicated, the public wouldn't understand—if they cared.

Because of this community of interest, New York, among its

other distinctions, boasts the biggest securities swindle in U.S. history. Bigger than Ponzi. Bigger than Billie Sol Estes. Bigger perhaps, if you count the prominent citizens involved, than even Teapot Dome or Watergate.

And though the city's "crimes" do not rival those of a President who tried to subvert the constitution, they were not victimless. New York City lost its self-government. The public lost services and gained new taxes. Workers lost their jobs. Businesses closed their doors. Interest rates soared. Annual city debt service payments climbed from $402 million in 1961 to $2.3 billion in 1976, depriving the budget of money that could have paid for more services. Retired and current city workers saw their pension funds jeopardized to save the city from bankruptcy. The investments of more than 160,000 note and bondholders—many retirees who invested their life savings—were endangered. Taxpayers in other jurisdictions were forced in 1975 to pay higher interest rates. In all, according to then Deputy Comptroller Steve Clifford, fraudulent budgets robbed city taxpayers of over $4 billion. Clifford arrived at this astounding sum by noting that the city's cumulative deficit was agreed to be $3.5 billion in 1975. Assuming this deficit was financed through the sale of fifteen-year bonds at an average 9 percent interest rate (a modest assumption), he calculated that the annual debt service costs would be $525 million, or a princely sum of $7.875 billion over fifteen years. Subtract the $3.5 billion already spent—assuming taxpayers received its full value in services —and the excess cost to taxpayers is $4.375 billion. According to the *Fiscal Observer*, in fiscal 1979 44 percent of the city's debt service costs—$875 million—was earmarked to cover old deficits.

Actually, this cost is considerably understated. The cumulative deficit figure agreed to by Mayor Beame and MAC in 1975 did not include almost $3 billion of expense items hidden, over the years, in the capital budget. Since the city borrowed these funds, they entailed a substantial additional cost to the taxpayers. These interest charges were, in effect, hidden, as is the city's true cumulative deficit. The originally advertised figure—$3.5 million—is wrong. It excluded not just the almost $3 billion of expense monies, but, according to Clifford, the two-year lag in pension contributions of $2 billion for which no borrowing was necessary but which was money the city owed. In sum, the city's true cumulative deficit was about $8 billion, or more than twice the figure certified by the city's fiscal watchdogs in 1975.

While it is true that city officials were not lining their pockets with this money, and that bad decisions were often made with good intentions, it is not true that these were "crimes" without profit. Money is not the only currency in politics. Power and reelection are profit enough. In addition, huge profits were earned by a lot of banks, underwriters and bond counselors. Some say the question of culpability is now meaningless; that the past is, well, the past. But if people are not responsible for their acts, then democracy—the voters' ability to reward or punish public officials—is a charade.

The previous chapter attempted to show how the city was victimized. Now let's briefly probe the motives.

How and Why

A common denominator for past city budget decisions was *politics*. The actors worried about the next election, not the next generation. "There is a common theme running through all of these trends," Comptroller Goldin, ignoring his own role, told the Treasurers Club in 1975, "the short-sighted approach of fiscal finagling which takes us one year at a time toward the day of reckoning." The public and investors were told the city's budget was balanced when it wasn't. It was made to appear balanced through an array of Houdini-like tricks. This artistic energy inevitably resulted in snowballing but hidden deficits. To cloak them, the city, with the support of its banks, invented money by borrowing it. "Wall Street is only ten blocks from City Hall," observes Senator Daniel Patrick Moynihan of the world's financial capital. "From Wagner's third term to Beame's second year, the city was, in effect, printing money."

The philosophy behind this stratagem was once succinctly stated by James Cavanagh: "It is better to borrow than to tax." "For a number of years," said the SEC staff report, "the City was incurring increasing deficits in its operations. In order to finance these deficits and to appear to comply with the legal requirement that it balance its operating budget, the City, among other things, increasingly resorted to the sale of 'short-term' debt securities." It didn't take long before the city was borrowing to repay borrowing. The note addiction became so acute that by 1975 the city needed to borrow $800 million in notes each month—all repayable within a year. A January 21, 1975, memorandum from Clifford to Comptroller Goldin warned of the "massive increase" of $5 billion in short-term debt since 1970 and said that $2.4 billion of this was due solely to "budget gimmicks (i.e. disguised deficit financing) and recognized deficits."

Most of these gimmicks were sanctioned by the state. The *how* and *why* is contained in—of all places—the voluminous legal briefs prepared by Mayor Beame and Comptroller Goldin's two law firms (at a cost to taxpayers of more than $1 million in legal fees) to challenge the SEC's charges:

> The budget experts of both the legislative and executive branches of the state government analyze the City's proposed budget and make their own estimates as to projected revenues and expenditures. Their concern is obvious: any gap must be filled by aid—which the state must then fund—or by taxes—which the state must authorize. Estimates made by state officials often differ substantially from those of the City, generally expressing an expectation that the City's revenues will be higher and its expenditures lower than the City has foreseen. The result is an "agreement" as to the size of the budget gap. Ultimately, at meetings involving the Governor, legislative leaders, the Mayor, and often members of the Board of Estimate, decisions are made as to how that gap is to be filled . . . the State's judgment is invariably to minimize its obligations to provide aid and its need to authorize taxes.
>
> The reluctance by the State to provide aid or taxing authority creates the need to develop alternative means of financing the gap. These alternative mechanisms include what (in the Staff's view) are "gimmicks." Yet these "gimmicks" are State-created: the State passes upon and has the final word as to whether they are adopted. They are enacted as State statutes set forth in the New York Local Finance Law and other related State laws.

Using the Local Finance Law, the state permitted the city to squirrel expense items into the capital budget, as it permitted the city to issue budget notes to balance the budget. The Local Finance Law, for instance, once set a ceiling of 2 percent of the average assessed five-year value of taxable real estate against which the city could borrow for housing construction. But in 1968, the legislature passed, and Governor Rockefeller signed, an amendment allowing the city to raise the ceiling on housing debt from 2 to 10 percent. The Governor's Office of Local Government protested, dispatching a confidential letter warning that the amendment "would be clearly unconstitutional." No matter. The state proceeded to help the city print money.

Not that the city needed much coaxing. Two 1975 audits by state Comptroller Arthur Levitt disclosed that in fiscal 1973, city officials borrowed money by claiming as collateral $324 million in fictitious state and federal aid. The audits revealed that by June 30, 1975, the city had overstated—by a staggering $408.3 million—its real-estate taxes. The city accomplished this feat by including in its tax base properties that paid no taxes: "diplomatic properties . . . vacant land, city-occupied office buildings, an urban-renewal land site, Carnegie Hall, and even a public park and high school." The audit showed that these "receivables" were then knowingly pledged to repay $380 million of tax anticipation notes issued on June 11, 1975.

To borrow, the city claimed revenues it did not have and had no hope of getting. An October 1, 1974, memo from Clifford to Comptroller Goldin stated: "to balance the expense budget, the City employs a series of unsound budgeting and accounting practices including carrying forward bogus receivables . . . [and] overestimation of revenues. . . . In New York City, we create a receivable not when we bill for services, not when we deliver reimburseable services, but when we estimate revenues. . . . In this method overestimations of state and federal aid need never be recognized, they can simply be rolled over. . . . The total amount of bad receivables which may have been rolled forward may exceed $500 million."

Some years ago the government of Czechoslovakia issued a decree:

Because Christmas Eve falls on a Thursday, the day has been designated a Saturday for work purposes. Factories will close all day, with stores open a half-day only. Friday, December 25, has been designated a Sunday, with both factories and stores open all day. Monday, December 28, will be a Wednesday for work purposes. Wednesday, December 30, will be a business Friday. Saturday, January 2, will be a Sunday, January 3 will be a Monday.

The city of New York did something like that—sometimes arbitrarily lengthening its year, sometimes shortening it. The SEC report marveled at how the city "changed billing dates on water charges and sewer rates to recognize 18 months of revenue in a 12 month period" and "used a 364 day year in computing payroll liability"—postponing "recognition of one additional day of payroll (or two in leap years) each year." This last gimmick, they said, led to an accrued city liability of $130 million as of June 30, 1975.

Abe Beame even took credit for inventing the 364-day year. During his successful 1973 campaign for mayor, Beame ran full-page newspaper ads proclaiming *Abe Beame. He Doesn't Need Lessons in How to Be Mayor.* Beame reminded voters: "Then there was the time the schools almost closed. We needed 25 million dollars to keep them open. I found it. 6,500 teachers kept their jobs. And your children stayed in school." Beame didn't mention that he "found it" by charging the salaries of this year's teachers to next year's budget. At the time, he was hailed for doing it.

I vividly recall another gimmick. In 1971, I served as executive director of the independent New York City Off-Track Betting Corporation. That spring, my boss, OTB President Howard Samuels, presented to Mayor Lindsay for city budget planning purposes a detailed projection for the next year of the number of offices, betting volume, types of bets, costs, tracks to be used, computer difficulties to be encountered. Based on these calculations, profits for fiscal 1972 were pegged at $25 million. A meeting was held in the Mayor's office between Samuels and Lindsay and their staffs. Lindsay explained that Comptroller Beame and the Board of Estimate and City Council were unwilling to impose new taxes or slice the budget, and were insistent that revenue estimates be increased. OTB, they arbitrarily concluded, would earn $50 million the next year. Over Samuels' and Lindsay's objections, the $50 million figure was placed in the revenue column. Plagued by computer breakdowns, that next year OTB earned only $14 million for the city.

A similar scene took place the following spring. Samuels again visited City Hall and on the basis of detailed analysis forecast profits of $43 million for fiscal 1973. Attending a public hearing of the City Council's Finance Committee, the OTB President backed this estimate by noting that OTB was new and "still in the growing stage." Finance Chairman Mario Merola, with no support other than a lively imagination, responded: "I can't see why we can't go to $70 million next year." This warm, intelligent man then smiled and added, "I've got that much confidence in your operation." Over OTB's public protest, the $70 million was incorporated into the budget. That year, OTB earned half that amount—$34.3 million. In both years, OTB's original forecasts were high. Since a budget, like a weather forecast, is based on educated guesses, the law permits mistakes—as long as they are backed by reasonably detailed projections. Such projections were absent from the calculations of City Council and Board of Estimate leaders.

When city leaders forecast revenues on the basis of nonexistent evidence, how different are they from Anthony DeAngelis, the great salad oil swindler? You remember DeAngelis. In the early sixties, he claimed as collateral for his loans 161,111,881 pounds of soybean oil, which he said filled 100 tanks in Bayonne, New Jersey. Almost all the tanks were empty. But no one knew it because De-Angelis would sneak into the warehouse to steal blank receipts, forge signatures, and produce these as proof that there was oil in the tanks.

The city's budget-balancing process worked somewhat the same way. Mayor Lindsay, for instance, began the 1973 fiscal year budget process by predicting in the winter of 1972 that the city would face a $1 billion budget gap. Then he disappeared to run for President. In April, Deputy Mayor Edward Hamilton speculated that "temporary fiscal mechanisms" would be needed to close the gap. The next day, they invented one, with Lindsay proposing that the city count as "revenue" $400 million in federal revenue-sharing and welfare-reform funds—though Congress had approved neither and there was no realistic prospect that it would. Lindsay said he was merely copying the same device used by the state to balance its budget.

In May, the Board of Estimate made its contribution, suggesting Lindsay increase general fund revenues by $50 million. Good. Then the Mayor found there would be $120 million in projected "welfare inefficiencies"—a sum he would soon increase to $162 million. By June 3, the $1 billion gap vanished. Deputy Mayor Hamilton announced that since the PBA had rejected a retroactive wage offer going back to 1971, $49 million could now be applied to close the gap. But, he was asked, wouldn't the city eventually have to reach a retroactive pay settlement with patrolmen? In that case, he said, the city could borrow the money. "The effect," he stated, "is to spread the cost over five years." Council Majority Leader Cuite objected, holding that the "savings" should be used to allow the Council to avoid raising city real-estate taxes by $65 million. "An additional $16 million," Council sources told Maurice Carroll of the *Times*, "would be 'found' perhaps simply by restating a revenue projection somewhere and worrying about raising the money at the end of the fiscal year." With the deadline for approving a budget near, negotiations reached an impasse. The Board of

Estimate refused to take responsibility for raising water taxes by $35 million. Everyone refused to cut the budget. The Council refused to take responsibility for raising real-estate taxes. Councilman Matthew Troy pledged to go to jail rather than approve such an increase. His Council colleagues might have eagerly obliged Troy, but there was no way to punish him without punishing themselves. Finally, a compromise was reached: revenue estimates were raised. On paper, the $9.4 billion budget was balanced. A year later, the budgeted revenues fell short—the city, for instance, received only half the $400 million from revenue sharing and welfare reform (which never passed).

In New York, budget balancing was seen as a game—an annual rite of spring. And the best and the brightest people played the game. City Hall has probably never had a desk occupied by a more brilliant man than Edward Hamilton. Governor Rockefeller was so taken by his brilliance that after one Albany negotiation he enthusiastically offered him the post of state budget director. Hamilton said no. After serving fourteen months as city budget director, he was elevated in late 1971 to the position of first deputy mayor. Hamilton, however, had one glaring defect. "He was very sensitive to the charge that he wasn't known as a 'political animal,' " says a former colleague, "so he tried to swing more."

The first deputy's office had recently been occupied by skilled politicians, and Hamilton was determined to prove to Lindsay that he was not just a numbers man, that he was flexible, sensitive, could help his boss out of a political jam. So he became a pol, though he wasn't treated like one. Because of an instinctive bias against people who work in political campaigns—and because of Hamilton's brains and glittering academic background—the press and good government groups paraded this thirty-one-year-old "expert" as if he were an astronaut. Naturally, it went unnoticed that when it came to budget tricks, Hamilton was no boy scout. Like just about everybody, Hamilton conformed—proved he was one of the boys.

The game went on because there was little opposition. But also because there were no rules. If New York followed standard accounting procedures and retained an outside auditor, as most corporations do, perhaps the game would have been played with an umpire. "The city's accounting 'principles' were virtually incomprehensible," said the SEC. Yet there was a method to this madness. In May 1976, Comptroller Goldin explained it before the Annual Conference of Municipal Finance Officers: "There was a broad feeling, I believe, that even though the City's accounting and budgeting had been revealed as a kind of Rube Goldberg conception—a system which defied understanding or control—it was better to leave it alone as long as it churned out enough money to meet the bills and pay the debts."

While the game was divorced from rules, it was not divorced from the political ethos of the time. The public was demanding, expecting, more. In truth, it would have been difficult, even if New York had enjoyed strong leadership, to have cut the city's budget. The sixties saw Mayor Wagner pledge a local war on poverty. President Kennedy promised Camelot. President Johnson promised both guns and butter. Mayor Lindsay promised Fun City. Martin Luther King had a dream. The Great Society was going to transform slums into Scarsdales, Vietnam into Ohio. Public expectations rose. Cities seethed with rage when the inflated promises of the Great Society and New Frontier were not met, and City Hall tried to step into the breach. The sixties were a decade of optimism. People recognized few limits to what could be done. It naturally followed that the limits of a budget or bond market went largely unrecognized. Beame and Goldin's SEC brief inadvertently makes this point: "If blame for the resulting fiscal effects is to be cast at all, then it is clear that the lion's share must go to the Governors, to the State Legislatures and to their policy of encouraging borrowing— a policy which implements *the decision to place needed social services ahead of fiscal conservatism*." [italics added] Since "fiscal conservatism" was presumed to be at odds with the public good, it follows that lies, gimmicks, high interest rates, whatever, were necessary to escape this dreaded evil.

The Financial Community

New York got away with it because—like national governments— it printed money. And it printed money because the investment community permitted it. Looking at the period just prior to the spring of 1975, the SEC staff report concluded that the banks and other underwriters of city securities had "knowledge of the crisis and the City's related problems" and did not disclose these, thus failing "to fulfill their responsibilities to the investing public." Cited were some of the largest and most powerful banks in America— Chase Manhattan, First National City, Morgan Guaranty Trust

Company of New York, Manufacturers Hanover Trust Company, Chemical Bank and the underwriting firm of Merrill Lynch Pierce Fenner & Smith. The SEC also charged the two major bond-rating agencies—Moody's Investor Services and Standard & Poor's—with having "failed, in a number of respects, to make either diligent inquiry which called for further investigation, or to adjust their ratings of the City's securities based on known data in a manner consistent with standards upon which prior ratings had been based." Also named were the blue-chip law firms retained as bond counsel —Hawkins, Delafield & Wood, White & Case, Wood Dawson Love & Sabatine, Sykes, Galloway & Dikeman—which "should have conducted additional investigation" and disclosed "material facts" to the public before allowing the sales to proceed.

The underwriters were as important to New York's Ponzi scheme as public officials. All governments or businesses rely on banks. They go to the bond market to finance their long-term or capital budget needs. They go to the note market to meet short-term cash needs because expenditures usually must be made before revenues are received (i.e., taxes or intergovernmental aid usually don't arrive when expenditures must be made).

It is the underwriter's or creditor's responsibility to check that the debtor has, or is likely to have, sufficient resources to repay the loan. When revenues don't match yearly expenditures, a default— and usually a declaration of bankruptcy—results.

But New York City defied the rules followed by most governments, businesses and individuals. When its income chronically did not match its spending, the financial community printed more money. Soon the city was borrowing not to retire principal on old debt but to repay interest. The city's total debt and interest costs were rising. Imagine a family earning $22,000 a year but spending $25,000. To close this gap, the parents visit the local bank to ask for a loan. The bank officer asks for collateral and proof that the loan can be repaid. The parents fib and certify that their combined earnings are $35,000. The bank fails to check and grants the loan. The family fails to cut back on their food, rent and other spending. Their income remains fixed, while their expenditures rise. Pretty soon, they realize a choice must be made between paying the food bill or paying back the loan. They don't make that choice. Instead, they visit another bank in search of still another loan, pledging as collateral a summer home that doesn't exist.

Carry this analogy out and you have a fair approximation of

what happened to New York. With one difference. In the case of most loans, banks will check to certify that the person or business is credit-worthy, has sufficient collateral. That didn't happen with New York City loans. The obvious question is, Why?

One reason is that the banks had a good thing. They were earning handsome underwriting fees and high rates of interest. The interest on all municipal securities is tax-free. And financial institutions and wealthy individuals were the sole suppliers. It's also true that the banks were taxed and regulated by government, and one is less likely to question the word of a would-be borrower who happens to have a gun in his hand. Besides, the banks—and the market in general—probably suffered from the same optimism as city officials. They didn't check the arithmetic. After all, not many believed that a city like New York—the financial capital of the world, the Big Apple—could default or go bankrupt.

There is no question that the financial community should have known the city's true financial condition. But did they know? The SEC was certain they did. "Long before October 1974," declared their chapter on the role of the underwriters, "the financial community realized that the City's fundamental problem was the insufficiency of revenues to meet expenses, resulting in a chronic and ever-increasing budget gap. The financial community had also come to understand the consequences of using short-term debt issues to close its budget gap and questionable budgetary practices to conceal the gap."

Among the evidence produced by the SEC: a November 8, 1974, memorandum to Alfred Brittain, III, chairman of Bankers Trust. The internal document revealed that in the previous fiscal year the city had an "excess of expenditures over revenues by nearly $2 billion, with less than half of the difference to be made up eventually by planned state and federal payments." The memo noted that expense items consumed 53 percent of the city's capital budget and that in the first half of 1974 New York City accounted for an alarming 27 percent of all the nation's tax-exempt short-term borrowing. Yet Bankers Trust and the other underwriters continued to extend credit to New York. The SEC also observed that on December 13, 1974, Comptroller Goldin, with the approval of the banking community, permitted the lowering of note sales from denominations of $25,000 to $10,000—spreading the risk to smaller investors.

For these reasons, the SEC staff report charged underwriters with a failure to make full disclosure to investors. Though their report covered only the brief period from late 1974 to mid-1975, they said: "The underwriters continued to offer and sell City notes to the public as safe and secure investments without disclosure of significant risks." Between October 1974 and March 1975, the underwriters marketed $4 billion of city notes. Instead of sharing their private concerns about the city, said the SEC, the banks "reached out for the smaller investor"—thus "shifting the risk for financing the City from the City's major banks and large institutional investors to individual investors."

In doing this, the banks were charged with another breach: ridding their portfolios of city securities and dumping these on an unsuspecting market. The SEC concluded, "Certain of the underwriters were in the process of reducing or eliminating their holdings of the notes. Moreover, certain underwriters determined not to purchase additional city notes for their own accounts and for their fiduciary accounts." This charge has been made more dramatically by others. In the early stages of the city's fiscal crisis, municipal labor leader Victor Gotbaum led a delegation picketing in front of Citibank and carrying placards that charged the banks with precipitating the crisis by "dumping" massive amounts of city paper. In their book *The Abuse of Power*, Jack Newfield and Paul Dubrul claim that between the summer of 1974 and March 1975 "the big New York City banks as well as other major banks across the nation, quietly dumped approximately $2.3 billion in New York City securities." Therefore, they concluded: "It is our judgment that the banks . . . are largely to blame for the last year and a half of pain in New York." Others have made similar charges, citing as evidence the SEC staff report.

A close reading of the SEC report, however, shows they never used the word "dumping." Nor does the SEC make a case for massive disinvestment in city paper. Instead, the SEC charges that of the six major city banks, all but Chemical Bank "followed a policy of trying to reduce or eliminate their own holdings in city notes. . . ." The word "dumping" implies a massive disinvestment. In fact, the SEC report revealed that: between September 30, 1974, and April 30, 1975, Bankers Trust reduced its city note holdings from $118.7 million to $58 million; Chase Manhattan, from $165 to $58 million; Manufacturers Hanover Trust, from $180 to $163 million. Citibank actually increased its "total position" in city notes from $24 to $30 million but purchased no new securities for its investment account. Figures for Morgan Guaranty were incomplete, but the SEC said it "made no additional purchases of City Notes for its investment account." Chemical increased its investment account from $187 to $224 million. On the basis of this evidence, add and subtract and you'll find that in the critical months leading up to the fiscal crisis the six large city banks "dumped" a total of just $141 million—a figure later confirmed by a series of phone calls to the SEC. Thus the six banks "dumped" not $2.3 billion but a relatively modest $141 million. Which suggests that the banks' and financial community's failure to make full disclosure to investors is a more serious charge.

The Defense

The 800-page SEC staff report was published thirteen days before the 1977 Democratic mayoral primary, striking Abe Beame with the force of a bazooka. The charges dominated the news. Stunned and shaking with rage, Beame counterattacked, denouncing the report as "a shameless, vicious political document" and claiming, "The record shows that I was leading, and not misleading, the City during this period." In a vain attempt to rescue his candidacy, the Mayor took to the streets. An outside organization, he said, had "injected itself into the political campaign at the eleventh hour with malicious abandon." Clearly, the SEC had, as Beame complained, "rushed to judgment." An inquiry begun eighteen months before need not have been released days prior to an important primary.

But the report's timing was the least of Beame's complaints. *Why pick on me?* was the attitude adopted by Beame and Goldin, the two city officials singled out in the report. Didn't the Governor and the state legislature approve most of these so-called "gimmicks"? Didn't the City Council and Board of Estimate? And didn't the banks make the loans? Hadn't this practice been going on for some time, not just the brief period studied by the SEC? Everyone was guilty, not just them. This view was echoed in the city's first legal brief, submitted nine months before the SEC staff report appeared, and was intended to refute the anticipated SEC judgment: "The staff's criticism, therefore, cannot be leveled at the City or its officials. It must rather be aimed (if at all) at the very touchstones of our democratic political process." The city's second brief, following the SEC report, reminded the federal agency of the state's role: "If, with the benefit of hindsight, the means adopted to finance these services appear to have been unwise, the fault does not lie with the City or with its officials alone."

Why pick on Beame and Goldin and a narrow time period? "The answer is simple," says William D. Moran, Administrator of the SEC's New York Regional Office and the person who supervised the staff report. "We didn't have unlimited manpower. We took what appeared to be the most critical period—November 1974 to March 1975. To go back to the Lindsay and Wagner period—we'd still be working on it!" Adds an important SEC official, "I'm confident that Wagner and Lindsay engaged in the same kind of shenanigans."

The city's defense (really Beame and Goldin's) also pleaded that the staff report was unduly legalistic and narrow—ignoring not just the other actors but the larger social forces and responsibilities influencing public figures. Dripping with sarcasm, the city's brief states:

From a reading of the Staff Report one would believe that the City operated in a social, economic and political vacuum. One would assume that its social welfare programs and the means for financing them were enacted by its own City Council; that it was unaffected by the national inflation, recession, tight monetary policy and oil embargo; that it was divorced from the federal and state governments and existed as a politically autonomous entity, with inherent powers of taxation. Indeed, one would conclude that the City was subject to no national or state policy and was governed by no national or state law, with one exception—the federal securities laws. It is perhaps understandable that a specialized agency would take such a parochial view of the laws it administers. . . .

Their earlier brief made the point a different way: "To the extent that this investigation has been directed to the City and its officials, it is not truly a securities investigation. It is an inquiry into the political, social and economic forces which have shaped the City of New York. It is an inquiry into the nature and operations of the governmental process. As such, it is beyond the competence and authority of the SEC. . . ."

"Hell, five years ago all the so-called 'budgetary gimmicks' were being called genius," Lindsay's former chief of staff, Jay Kriegel, told writer Harry Stein. "It wasn't Lindsay, it was the times." And the times were optimistic. John Kennedy kicked off the decade of the sixties promising to "get this country moving again." Lyndon

Johnson's first State of the Union message, in 1964, announced "a national war on poverty. Our objective: total victory." Vietnam was to preserve the world for democracy. When John Lindsay captured the mayoralty in 1965, *Newsweek*'s cover story rhapsodized that his campaign was "the most important political operation in America today. . . ."

In addition to optimism, the sixties featured social upheaval. A new wave of immigrants—from Puerto Rico and the South—came to New York seeking opportunity. The anti-poverty effort spawned new community-based organizations. There were civil rights, welfare rights, and antiwar demonstrations. There were near-riots in New York streets, and city officials lived in constant dread of racial polarization and even warfare. The peaceable techniques of the civil rights movement were adopted by community groups demanding greater government services. Thus, the city's brief argued, "Mayors, Comptrollers, City Councilmen, Governors, and State Legislators were constantly called upon to make what was in essence the same choice—whether to provide services or exercise draconian fiscal restraint."

It would not have been easy to cut city spending. When cuts were proposed in the projected 1972 budget, City Council Finance Chairman Mario Merola, reflecting the consensus of the time, said, "I don't believe that the City of New York could close hospitals, libraries or schools. . . ." Mayor Lindsay used to prepare annual scare scenarios, outlining the cuts and "payless furloughs" that would be necessary if no new aid or taxes were granted. They were usually not taken seriously—probably even by the Mayor himself—as they were not taken seriously when Beame repeated them in 1974 and 1975.

The SEC staff's parochial concerns, in the city's view, led them to confuse political rhetoric with a bond prospectus. The staff report charges, for instance, that Beame and Goldin's press releases and public statements "did not provide investors with accurate and balanced information as to the City's finances and its securities." In their defense, city leaders replied that in the critical months before the shutoff of credit, these reassurances were

no different from President Roosevelt's assurances, during the depths of the Depression in 1933, that "the only thing we have to fear is fear itself." Under the standards by which the staff seeks to judge the City this statement would be deemed to be misleading and an "unwarranted reassurance." Was President Roosevelt faulted for seeking to reassure the nation? The answer, of course, is no—he was praised for his leadership. A President—or a Mayor—in making a speech to his constituency has far greater leadership obligations than does a corporate officer discussing a corporate balance sheet. The responsibility of an elected official to his electorate does not include a prerogative to engender fear or panic when he does not believe that the cause for fear or panic exists.

There was also a difference between the SEC and the city as to what constitutes disclosure. The SEC said the city failed to disclose *all* the material facts, including "gimmicks" used to balance the budget. Yet Beame's testimony before the SEC reminded them that government operates in "a fishbowl," and as his legal brief stated, "One cannot find any material facts about the city's fiscal condition which were not fully disclosed." As proof, the city submitted a "Disclosure Appendix," consisting of sixteen volumes containing 2,000 separate documents—speeches, press releases, newspaper and magazine accounts—published between December 1973 and April 1975. The SEC chastised the city for omitting negative information from their bond prospectus. The city chastised the SEC for ignoring negative reports in the press. The SEC said investors were not warned. The city responded: "It is difficult to conceive how the staff of a financially sophisticated agency can look at the difference between an interest rate of 3.73% on a State BAN, and an interest rate on a City BAN at about the same time of 8.1–8.75%, and conclude that the market and investors were not aware of the City's financial plight." (A BAN, incidentally, is a bond anticipation note. That the city was permitted to borrow so excessively against borrowing—like a compulsive gambler borrowing in anticipation of a loan-shark loan—tells something about its finances.)

A similar perceptual chasm separated the SEC staff and Comptroller Goldin. The SEC charged that the Comptroller, like the Mayor, "misled public investors." Yet Goldin—after waiting two days to let the dust from the SEC charges settle (and candidate Beame take all the heat)—summoned the press to his office in the Municipal Building to release 448 pages of his SEC testimony and a collection of press releases, newspaper reports and other items. "On more than 50 major occasions," he declared, "in increasingly grave and urgent language, I warned the public about the city's worsening fiscal condition and budget practices. To say I did not disclose the city's fiscal condition is like saying Ralph Nader did not warn consumers about unsafe cars because people continued to get killed in auto crashes, or Gen. Billy Mitchell did not warn the Navy about air power."

And, finally, city officials didn't understand why the SEC berated them for failing to heed the admonitions of bankers that the credit market would close. To city officers, such warnings were not new. On March 23, 1975, as the crisis was nearing a climax, Beame told the public, "You have to realize that I've been dealing with some of these bankers for a long time, since I was Comptroller." He told the press he was calm, despite harsh criticism and growing bankruptcy threats. As the SEC notes, the banks were demanding that Beame impose new austerity measures. But Beame was demanding that the banks and other underwriters do what they had always done: support the city. Beame, like most city officials, saw the banks as salesmen, not policemen. "I think the banks have to exercise the responsibility to let the public know that New York securities are good investments, to restore confidence in their investors," he said then. Also, like many others, Beame assumed that the underwriters and "the market" were one and the same—a handful of individuals who talked to each other and treated David Rockefeller as if he were the Pope.

Besides, people hear what they want to hear, not always deliberately. Through March 1975, for instance, the Mayor and Comptroller met regularly with top bankers who served on the Financial Liaison Committee and with their staffs, who composed what was called the Working Group. "In a sense," retorted the city's brief, "the fact that these meetings were even taking place can be said to evidence the shared feeling of the City and the financial community that the securities markets had not yet closed to the City. This was certainly the City's view." City officials were also not unmindful of 1974, when similar warnings were issued that the UDC was about to default. But the banks, to help their friend Nelson Rockefeller and his candidate for governor, Malcolm Wilson, extended the due dates on their loans until after the election.

The financial community's defense against the SEC staff report charges is remarkably similar to the city's. Regarding the first charge—failure to disclose—they, too, responded that the SEC was guilty of nitpicking legalisms, ignoring the larger reality of what was going on at the time, that is, how they were trying to keep the city afloat, trying to avoid panic. How could they have secret, inside information not shared with investors, they ask, when the danger signals were "generally known"?

"The SEC staff offers the explanation that naive investors were deliberately misled by unscrupulous underwriters," said Walter B. Wriston, chairman of Citicorp, ridiculing the SEC report:

As proof, they submit a survey of individual investors, 90 percent of whom now deny that they had any awareness of potential risk when they bought City notes. I suppose, in theory, it is possible to imagine a person at that time who had at least $10,000 to invest, who never read a newspaper, who never saw a fiscal crisis headline, who never heard a high-decibel debate on radio or television, and who invested without the least inkling that there might be a worm in the apple. It is possible to imagine *one*. Two is extremely doubtful. And 90 percent is ridiculous on the face of it.

There is a more believable explanation. New York City had a credibility problem in reverse. Rather than too *little* investment credibility, it had too *much*.

Wriston's testimony, which was given to the State Assembly Committee on Banking in October 1977, went on to note that these were anticipation notes and city officials were offering assurance they would be paid promptly. Who could believe that a city of 8 million people—the Big Apple—couldn't come up with the funds?

In his book *A Time for Truth*, former Treasury Secretary William Simon has a chapter on New York in which, for half a page, he stops pointing his finger at others and elaborates on his own role:

No one—whether the New York politicians or the unions or the most prominent bankers of New York or the New York press—has ever given a coherent explanation of why a collapse that had been building for a decade had not been anticipated. I cannot point the finger in this respect, for I hadn't expected it either. It was particularly ironic in my case, for in the late sixties and early seventies, when I worked at Salomon Brothers, I had been a member of the Technical Debt Advisory Committee set up by Abraham Beame when he was Comptroller of New York. We supplied the city market advice on its financial transactions, but at no point during any of these sessions did any one of us seriously question the underlying fiscal condition of New York. We all worked with the numbers given us by the city itself, just as do the advisory committees to the federal government. It never occurred to us to disbelieve those figures, which always indicated that New York would be able to repay its debt.

Twenty-seven pages later he accused the banks of "cowardice" for not standing up to the city.

"Even with the benefit of hindsight, it is difficult to see what more the underwriters could have done," claimed Wriston, the city's foremost banker. They had no authority to compel city officials to disclose new information, nor, he declared, in the crisis-wrenched atmosphere, was there time to prepare such a prospectus. "To state it flatly," he said, "there were more urgent problems to solve at the time. When the house is on fire, you don't sit on the curb drafting new safety regulations." A vice president of Wriston's bank put it another way: "We were cowards." Rather than risk the political heat and blame for a city default—vituperative charges, vengeful legislation, Congressional investigations—the banking community played ball.

The banks' defense against the charge of dumping revolves around facts as well as perceptions. Again, the SEC is accused of molelike vision, of failing to consider the larger picture of what was happening to the banking world during the time of the city's travail. This larger picture was sketched by the city in their November 1976 brief to the SEC. Offering a defense of their own actions, the city also, perhaps inadvertently, offered a defense of the banks:

The problem for the City in this period of increasing capital scarcity, was compounded by the growing inability of its principal supplier of credit—the banking community—to purchase its securities. This difficulty was not necessarily related to any particular City problem. Rather, it reflected difficulties which the banks themselves were having—difficulties largely the product of a serious depletion of their available capital caused, among other things, by losses in Real Estate Investment Trusts (REITs), major bankruptcies (such as W. T. Grant) and foreign loans. And at the same time as their capital base was shrinking, banks began to view alternative tax shelters as more beneficial to them than municipal investments.

Such tax shelters as the leasing of equipment and foreign loans were competing with municipal securities. According to the Comptroller of the Currency's figures, 259 banks leased $412 million worth of equipment in 1967. By 1975, 691 banks invested $3 billion in such equipment. Not only was the leasing of this equipment tax-free, but the banks could deduct the depreciation of this asset against their ordinary income. A similiar boom took place in foreign loans. According to the Federal Reserve Board, between 1965 and 1976 the number of American bank branches overseas exploded from 13 to 126; their assets, from $8.9 billion to $229 billion

In 1972, commercial banks were purchasing half of all municipal securities in the U.S. But, according to a study by Lynn E. Browne and Richard F. Syron, in 1974–75 these purchases plunged 70 percent nationally, and insurance company purchases declined by one-third. Disinvestment wasn't happening just to New York. The Congressional Budget Office has released figures showing that nationally banks purchased $3.4 billion less of *all* municipal securities from 1974 through the first quarter of 1975. But also—contradicting the conspiracy view—their investment in municipals rose by $6.7 billion in the next quarter of 1975.

In addition to tunnel vision, the banks accused the SEC of being blind to the facts. William Haddad, the Assembly Banking Committee's chief staff interrogator charged: "The city's major banks quietly and quickly divested themselves" of $2 to $2.5 billion of city securities between the fall of 1974 and the spring of 1975. In testimony before the Committee, five of the six major city banks came armed with refutations. Of the six, only Chase was shown to have reduced its city note holdings in the period prior to the market's closing on New York (by $93 million). Morgan Guaranty said its holdings almost tripled, from $51 to $148 million. Bankers Trust went from $38.5 to $50 million; Citicorp's own investments remained zero throughout, but its dealer account grew from $24 to $30 million; Manufacturers' holdings remained constant at $164 million; and Chemical, as the SEC reported, expanded its holdings.

To buttress their case, the banks point to a September 7, 1977, letter from SEC Chairman Harold Williams. The letter to the banks acknowledged that his staff's "interpretations and conclusions" of certain facts were contestable. "Naturally," he wrote, "others may reach conclusions different from those of our staff." The "key question," he said, was not whether the banks dumped but whether, in effect, they *should* have "in the face of increasingly adverse information—unavailable to the public in an understandable form—which cast severe doubt on the city's financial capabilities."

Confronted with this evidence, Haddad told *The New York Times* that his use of the words "dumping or divestiture" was not meant to apply just to the banks' portfolios: "He said that by 'dumping' he was referring to all notes that the banks sold to individuals in that six-month period in their capacity as underwriters of city securities." The banks countered that Haddad and critics are stretching the English language beyond recognition. How can the banks be blamed when investors refuse to purchase securities that the banks, themselves, are underwriting? After all, didn't the SEC produce evidence showing that the banks repeatedly warned city officials that the market was closing? Critics, say the banks, are trying to have it both ways: first charging them with "dumping" city paper on unsuspecting investors, then, when that doesn't stick, charging the banks with failure to sell city paper to suspicious investors.

A Personal Verdict

The SEC staff report is both important and somewhat irrelevant. Important, because it tried to hold public figures accountable for their acts. Somewhat irrelevant, because it focused on a narrow one-year period and, primarily, on the harm done investors. One needs no legal brief, no delineation of the securities laws, to understand the harm done taxpayers. It is worth remembering that the City Charter—passed by the voters—requires a balanced budget. Robert Wagner, John Lindsay and Abe Beame are guilty of knowingly failing to honestly balance city budgets. By not disclosing the truth, they burdened future taxpayers with costs they were never given an opportunity to reject—taxation without representation. But mayors were not alone. Also guilty were Governors Rockefeller and Wilson, state legislators, City Council members, comptrollers, City Council presidents, borough presidents and platoons of appointed and career civil servants.

They—the entire political system—failed. "The Mayor and the Comptroller—not just this Mayor and this Comptroller—were at fault for twenty years," says Bernard Nussbaum. Since Mr. Nussbaum is a partner in one of the two law firms defending Beame and Goldin, his candid testimony is important. Over a long lunch early in 1978, Nussbaum reflected on what he learned preparing the defense: "Politicians see it as in their interest to make bad long-run decisions if they will look good in the short run. They're competent at getting themselves elected, not in running the city."

Incompetence was clearly a factor—the city's books were a

mess. Marty Lipton, Nussbaum's senior partner at Wachtell, Lipton, Rosen & Katz, recalls: "They were all wrong on the size of the deficit. Not out of stupidity but out of an inability to cope with the technology. When we came in to act as bond counsel, there was this Czechoslovakian with a green eyeshade sitting on a ledger stand in the Municipal Building with his own ledger book. It was right out of Dickens! That ledger book was the only record we could find to justify the bonding."

But there was also a reason for ignorance. It was safer. It allowed city officials to lie while believing, sometimes sincerely, that they might be telling the truth.

Which brings us to the question of disclosure. In their formal briefs to the SEC, Beame and Goldin say they made full public disclosure. As proof, they offer hundreds of press reports and warnings from organizations like the Citizens Budget Commission. Their definition of "disclosure" would please Orwell. One of the city's defense briefs, for instance, quotes the Staten Island *Advance* of March 15, 1974. The *Advance* reported that Councilman Biondolillo voted against the 1974-75 capital budget "because of the inclusion of approximately $500 million in funds which he asserted belonged in the expense budget." This constitutes disclosure, the city says, though it doesn't say that the city and the Council approved the budget—with the gimmicks. Another example of "disclosure" is a 1974 *Times* editorial which warned, "This city is sliding into bankruptcy with dismaying speed." What remains unsaid in the city's brief is that this same editorial prompted an angry letter from Beame and Goldin, published on November 11, 1974. After presenting their facts, they concluded, "This picture [of the city's fiscal condition and debt] should be very reassuring to all city investors." Still another example of "disclosure": the SEC is reminded that David M. Breen, an analyst for Weeden & Company, issued a similar warning in January 1975. But it is not reminded that Beame and Goldin, in a joint press release, denounced Breen as "irresponsible."

The logic is comical. It asks us to assume that an attack on Beame equals a disclosure by Beame, that a press disclosure— usually buried in paragraph 20 and refuted at the time—constitutes full public disclosure by the mayor of New York. Here, the city's defense is as narrowly legalistic as it claims the SEC's charge to be. Even if one concludes that investors who could read had reason to worry about the city's finances, that is not the same as saying taxpayers were told the truth by their elected officials. Thus the city pleads innocent to a lesser charge (failure to disclose) while, implicitly, pleading guilty to a far more serious one (fraud).

The financial community's disclosure defense parrots the city's. Investors, they are saying, should have known. But banks did not disclose to investors the devastating information contained in their own memorandums, which were published by the SEC. They kept this information private. The same can be said for the rating services and bank bond counsels. If they had done their job, White & Case's tardy but courageous refusal to sign off on a note offering would have occurred sooner. A *Wall Street Journal* editorial the day after the SEC report sliced through the pretense: "Surely the prescription for rose-colored glasses does not extend to underwriters, bond counsel or the like. These gentlemen knew their duty well enough back in 1975. If they had done it, if they had found the courage to voice the truth, a lot of small investors would have been spared their savings, and New York would be a lot further on the road to recovery today." Because the investment community is more aware of the rules and securities laws, their culpability is greater. For many years these people eagerly placed the city's bonds, in effect printing the city's money and collecting huge profits. When the bubble—which they helped puff—burst, investors were not the only victims.

The lies come at you like machine-gun bullets. Beame, for instance, blamed his budget difficulties on the $1.5 billion deficit he said he "inherited" from Lindsay. Yet as comptroller, he approved each of Lindsay's last four budgets. Lindsay says it wouldn't have happened if he had been mayor. Yet it was happening while he was mayor. Sometimes the lies came under oath. Testifying before the SEC on September 1, 1976, the official transcript contains the following exchange with Beame:

Q. Mr. Mayor, in addition to the one shot revenues, it has been stated that the City would from time to time overestimate its revenues at the commencement of a fiscal year for purposes of producing a balanced budget.

A. Not in my time. I certainly wouldn't permit it. I know of no such instance where anything like that occurred.

Asked by the SEC attorney whether he agreed that state and federal aid was sometimes overestimated, Mayor Beame responded:

"Based on the information given to me by my staff, I disagree with the statement. . . . You have to remember, of course, that—as I want to stress—that I don't get into that estimating area. I am sure you understand the Mayor has got enough things to do besides sitting down with a pencil and estimating revenues for the city."

After Beame, unbelievably, released this testimony in August 1977, the *Daily News* socked him good: "To hear His Honor tell it, he was nothing but an innocent bystander, a detached observer. . . ." Candidate Ed Koch was no less direct: "In taking great pains to avoid any implication of wrongdoing, Mr. Beame has made a lie out of his campaign for re-election, in which he is telling us that 'he made the tough decisions,' and of his campaign for election in 1973 when he assured us that he 'knew the buck.' His testimony to the SEC is a catalogue of all the ways Abe Beame failed to get involved in the important decisions affecting city finances." But, of course, Beame was involved. Before becoming mayor in 1974, he had been comptroller for eight of the twelve previous years and budget director from 1952 to 1962. On June 15, 1971, to cite one instance, Comptroller Beame issued a press release charging that Mayor Lindsay "underestimated" revenues by $330 million. His colleagues cheered. Beame had found $330 million. Beame had saved them from the perils of voting on higher taxes or cutting the budget.

Another commonly accepted falsehood is that there were only two choices open to city officials in 1974-75: do what they did or go bankrupt. The city's brief responding to the SEC charges explicitly states that the federal agency seems to have expected the city to say "there was no hope for its future." The sub-headline of a *Times* story after the report was released probably reflected the common view: DECEPTION MAY HAVE KEPT THE CITY SOLVENT. A few days later, Beame elevated his lack of leadership to a patriotic virtue: "I'd have done the same thing over again. I could do it no better than I did." (Goldin made the same preposterous claim.) This is the same mayor who confessed, in a September 10, 1975, address to the people of New York, "I accept the responsibility, along with officials past and present," of using what he called "fiscal gymnastics."

Straining to be fair, a mushy editorial in the *Times* outlined the terrible choice between the Mayor's "financial and political responsibilities," asserting there was "no easy answer." The editorial then climbs to Olympian detachment: "Hence the final judgment on the wisdom of the Mayor's asserted deceptions in 1974-75 must turn on whether the city was better off defaulting early or defaulting late. We don't think there is a clear answer to that question. Nor, for that matter, do we think the answer is very important. The critical issue is whether Abe Beame or any prospective Mayor will have sufficient incentive to avoid taking similar short cuts in the future."

That is not, I think, the "critical issue." How do we draw lessons from the past unless we understand it? In effect, the *Times* was saying let bygones be bygones. To assume city officials had only two choices—what they did (fraud) or bankruptcy—is to ignore a third option: tell the truth, really cut the budget and drastically improve the city's management. This is the option pressed in a series of 1974-75 memorandums to Comptroller Goldin from staff members Steve Clifford and Jonathan Weiner. The memos are quoted extensively in the SEC report. They were not acted upon. Certainly not by the Mayor. Instead, Beame contented himself with the traditional warnings, phony layoff figures and the pretense that he was cutting the budget while in fact it was growing. Comptroller Goldin, who is unfairly lumped with Beame in the SEC report, did make a decision late in 1974—after Beame blamed him for high interest rates—that caution was the better part of political valor. So this young, ambitious public official who intended to run for state comptroller in 1978 stopped criticizing Beame, swallowed the memos, denounced White & Case's suggestion that the city did not have income to cover borrowing and joined the Mayor in a united front.

What would have happened if the city had fully disclosed the bleak facts in 1974-75? "The answer, in the view of everyone interviewed yesterday," concluded a front-page *Times* story, "was simple: The City would have gone bankrupt." Why? Because, the story ended, it was "likely" that "the political climate in late 1974 and early 1975" was not right for disclosure. Perhaps that is true. But city officials failed to test that climate. Instead of rising to a difficult challenge, they collapsed. They never gave the public a chance.

Nor, frequently, did the press give the public a chance. As Kriegel said, "all the so-called 'budgetary gimmicks' were being called genius"—particularly by the press. Because of his ability to invent funds, when James Cavanagh was assistant budget director, he sported the nickname "Cash Cavanagh." When Beame devised the 364-day year, front-page headlines heralded his "solution" to the budget crisis. Lindsay's threats of budget cuts were seen as a clever political ploy to put the state on the defensive and extract more state aid. After Mayor Beame's first ninety days in office, the *Times* printed a news analysis in the form of a report card. "The budget is the most important document a Mayor deals with," the story said. "Mr. Beame understands it thoroughly." So the Mayor was awarded an A for "Arithmetic."

"I'll tell you who's really at fault," blurted Bernard Nussbaum, the city's SEC attorney. "It's the media. They treated the people who created the gimmicks as if they were geniuses. If the press treats you like a genius it increases your chances of reelection, and so it encourages more gimmickry. The problem with the press is, one, it's incompetent. Two, it doesn't work hard. And three, it's sensationalist."

Ultimately, all the excuses fit quite nicely with the city's official defense. Underlying that defense is the unspoken assumption that no one is responsible. We are all victims. Leaders are not supposed to lead. Telling the truth can be harmful. The political system won't allow it. A variation of the no one—is—responsible thesis was expounded by Lindsay's former corporation counsel, Norman Redlich, now dean of NYU's School of Law. "The fiscal crisis was not created by Robert Wagner, John Lindsay or Abe Beame, either individually or collectively," he wrote on the Op-Ed page of the *Times*, "and it is grossly unfair to our former Mayors to make them the villains of our urban tragedy." The "tragedy" was caused, he said, not by city officials but by such historical forces as the movement of poor people into New York and the exodus of middle-income residents; other levels of government were to blame for not picking up more city costs. Could the budget have been cut? No, he implied, because New York had "hallowed institutions (such as the City University and the municipal hospital system) that imposed financial burdens vastly greater than those faced by any other city." And what about high taxes? Not so, implies Redlich: "Every year, the body politic of this city, led by some state and local elected officials, insisted that the taxes were not needed. . . ." Redlich ends Lindsay's defense (and his own) with a familiar refrain: "It is time, however, that we cast a true light on his past. And by doing so, we might be better able to deal with the problems of the present."

It is unfair to make Lindsay *the* culprit; to ignore the many good things he did as mayor, including keeping the streets cool during a very difficult period, bringing zest and idealism to City Hall, introducing the concept of "productivity" and management reform, renewing interests in our parks and architecture. But, like a lot of other city and state officials, he made some dreadful mistakes, told some whopping lies. And, like a lot of other people, he and his mulish apologists should at least exhibit the grace of contrition.

Looking back, one sees that the reality gap almost equaled the budget gap. Redlich, I think, suffers it now, as does his pouting former boss who refuses interviews. And Abe Beame suffered it in 1974–75. One reason Beame failed to make the tough decisions is that he and others honestly did not believe the market would close, honestly did not believe this crisis couldn't be handled just as previous ones had been. "Beame was warned of the fiscal dangers," says one of his attorneys, Marty Lipton. "I don't think he understood it." Beame treated the fiscal crisis as if it were a public relations crisis. The city's "failure to make meaningful disclosure," said the SEC report, "prolonged the agony of the City's fiscal crisis, and delayed major necessary corrective efforts."

It was a swindle. To date, no one has been punished. Perhaps no one should be. Perhaps Beame's loss in the primary is a sufficient punishment. He and Lindsay and others have been humiliated. Rockefeller is retired from politics. The city's bookkeeping methods have been improved. But, as usual, the public pays. As I write, the snow is falling heavily and the city sanitation commissioner is complaining that 40 percent of his snow removal equipment has broken down. The city cannot borrow money and is again pleading with Washington that without federal assistance bankruptcy is inevitable. People have been laid off and the round-trip $1 subway fare can cost more than lunch. City workers' pension funds are dangerously overextended. The debt is growing and debt service costs consume more of the city's locally raised revenues than welfare and Medicaid combined.

And, as I write this, Abe Beame is appearing on WNBC-TV as a well-paid urban affairs commentator and has become chairman of the federal Commission on Intergovernmental Relations. John Lindsay is plotting to run for the U.S. Senate in 1980. The banks have escaped—freed of their city notes, most of their city securities converted to more secure MAC bonds, and the statute of limitations for bondholder suits or federal fraud charges is quietly expiring. Harrison Goldin won reelection and is the frontrunner as the Democratic candidate for state comptroller in 1978. Robert Wagner is a venerated political name, an intimate of governors, the new U.S.

ambassador to the Vatican. James Cavanagh is employed by a foundation, draws a $29,000 city pension and has been consulted by Mayor Koch. Nelson Rockefeller is writing art books and advising the Saudi Arabian government. William Simon has written a book blasting the city and is scheming to run for President in 1980. Edward Hamilton is California Governor Jerry Brown's new budget guru and runs a lucrative consulting business.

Neither the SEC nor the U.S. Attorney for the Southern District has pushed the prosecution of former officials. Like the *Times* editorial, the SEC has focused on the future, quietly summoning all the officials named in their staff report to determine how they have improved their bookkeeping and disclosure techniques. Why had the SEC sought no indictments? According to Andrew Rothman, their Washington spokesman, "The Department of Justice and the U.S. Attorney have all the information. We referred everything to the appropriate federal agency." There it has remained, buried. *Why no indictments?* A major SEC official thought a long time, began several sentences, then stopped. "We probably could have sought indictments," he said finally. "Why were there no indictments? There is a thing called the *scienter*. It means that someone must do something viciously and willfully. Applying that test to Mayor Beame and Goldin and others, I think that in their heart and soul they really believed the city couldn't collapse, even though the evidence was there. You don't indict people for that."

Perhaps. But many people have gone to jail for less.

Chapter Four

Is Washington to Blame?

IN THE JAPANESE movie classic *Rashomon,* there are four eye-witnesses to a killing. Each observed the same crime, the same weapon, the same victim. Yet the witnesses offer four very different versions of what they saw.

That is an approximation of what's happened throughout New York's marathon fiscal and economic crisis. In this case, the victim is New York City. There are multiple eyewitnesses. There is no dispute that the victim is bleeding. Where witnesses differ, however, is in whether they observed an attempted murder or suicide.

New York officials claim that Washington is committing murder. The city's economic ills, Senator Daniel Patrick Moynihan exclaimed on July 15, 1977, "are in substantial measure . . . the consequence of policies of the national government." The "true cause of the urban fiscal and economic crisis," Richard Morris writes in his book *Bum Rap on American Cities*, is the fact that New York and the Northeast do not get their fair share of federal assistance. This is a familiar refrain, sounded by most city officials and, according to polls, by a majority of New York residents.

A very different view is heard in Washington and around the country. New York, they say, has been committing suicide. They can point to a Treasury Department study revealing that in 1977 New York ranked first among the fifty states in federal dollar aid and enjoyed the largest increase—$1 billion—of any state; a National Tax Foundation study showing that in 1977 New York State paid 82¢ for each dollar it got back from Washington. "We think it makes sense for New York City to do more for itself rather than spinning new schemes for federal help," warns Elinor Bachrach, a key aide to Senator William Proxmire, Chairman of the Banking Committee, which must pass on most city aid legislation.

"We don't seem to be talking the same language," worries MAC Chairman Felix Rohatyn. "It's scary." The gap between New York and Washington is wider than the city's budget gap. New York officials claimed long-term federal loans would end its need to return to Congress for yearly fixes; many in Congress claimed it would worsen New York's addiction. City unions complained they had made too many sacrifices; Washington complained they had not made enough. The state and the banks said they were overextended; Washington said they were underextended. New York bleated that bankruptcy could topple our federal system; Washington cried back that deepening involvement in local affairs could topple it sooner.

Murder or suicide?

To probe the question, Senator Moynihan and I agreed to lunch in early 1978. The former Harvard professor chose to meet in the Edwardian Room of the Plaza Hotel. His costume, appropriately, was Ivy League—slate-gray suit, pale yellow button-down shirt, simple polka dot bow tie. I asked a simple question and was dragged on a detour through Keynesian economics, past the fascinating rubble of differing academic methodologies, to a lengthy discourse on how New York State had actually "recovered" from the 1969, but not the 1973, national recession.

After a time, I was reminded what an engaging man Moynihan can be. But also that there has always coexisted within the junior Senator from New York two parts academic and one part ham. In the contest between the two, sometimes the ham wins. The contest —and the question of murder or suicide—is crystallized vividly in Moynihan's current search-and-destroy mission. "My hypothesis," he argues, "is that the federal government is systematically deflating the economy of New York State." The state, he charges, sends about $36 million to Washington and gets back only $29 million, leaving "a deficit" of over $7 billion. Others have arrived at a higher number. The Northeast governors forged a coalition to lobby for their fair share. "There are no sufficient reasons for the absolute decline of our state, not even our own considerable mismanagement of our affairs," Moynihan told the Senate on June 27, 1977. "To the contrary, I have reached the conclusion that our decline has come about as the largely unintended, but nonetheless direct and palpable consequence of the policies of the Federal government." The "deficit," he said then, was $10.6 billion.

That was the ham speaking. Shortly thereafter, the Temporary Commission on City Finances issued its 398-page final report, documenting some of the city's self-inflicted wounds. In what could have been viewed as a direct challenge to Moynihan's thesis, the Commission said, "The 'captive-of-events' theory is also popular because it tends to absolve the local political process of responsibility for the fiscal crisis and buttresses the also popular view that the solution to the City's financial problems lies in increased State and Federal aid rather than local political reform." The Commission noted, for instance, that federal aid to New York City has increased twenty-three-fold since 1961.

On July 15, 1977, Moynihan cited the same sentence in a "revised edition" of his speech, with a new five-page introduction. "What the Commission says is true," he declared, "and it is vastly important that it be said . . . many perceive a conflict between what we say and what the Commission says. I believe there is no such conflict. . . ." Acrobatically, the Senator who on June 27 said the federal government was "largely" to blame now described that speech as setting forth "the proposition that the exceptional economic difficulties we have faced in recent years are in substantial measure—not altogether, not even in greatest measure, but in substantial measure—the consequences of policies of the national government." He also pronounced, "We now calculate a 'gap' of $17.1 billion"—up $6.5 billion in eighteen days.

Caught between common sense and his constituency, Moynihan tried to please both. To common sense, he blew the Commission a five-page kiss and continued to make compelling points about past city and federal mistakes. To his constituency, he railed and thundered and vowed never to rest until the federal government surrendered. The press ignored the five-page revision and headlined Moynihan's charge of murder, as they had once headlined his UN attacks on Uganda's murderous Idi Amin. Moynihan now had what every politician craves—a torch issue—generating attention but not criticism from constituents. New Yorkers stood up and cheered as their righteous Senator marched off to slay the federal dragon.

Immediately, he dispatched his speech and arithmetic to the

White House, requesting that Jimmy Carter stand up and declare himself. Three months later, and somewhat vaguely, Carter did so. "Your statement on the impact of federal programs on the economy of New York," he wrote Moynihan in September, "has raised a number of important issues that will receive the full attention of this Administration." With considerable glee, the Senator released this letter, as he later released a string of "Dear Pat" letters from Treasury Secretary Blumenthal, Commerce Secretary Kreps, Chairman of the Council of Economic Advisors Schultze and domestic policy chief Eizenstat.

The Senator was pleased but not placated. The President's advisers conceded the need to know more about the impact of federal policies on states, conceded that federal aid formulas did not take into account New York's higher cost of living. But they specifically did not concede Moynihan's "gap." No matter. Moynihan pressed on. "I would contend," he said on September 27, "that the more we learn about this issue, the more it will emerge that the 'balance of payments' is indeed a good rough measure of the federal impact on a state." He insisted that in calculating what New York received from the federal government the feds were arbitrarily apportioning and crediting $14.3 billion of foreign aid and interest on the national debt to New York State. If this sum were subtracted, rather than a surplus, the state's "balance of payments" would show a $7.4 billion "gap"—down $9.7 billion in seventy-four days.

Moynihan did not relent. He continued to flail away at the bookkeepers in the Carter administration. Finally, perceiving it as an academic point, on January 11, 1978, the federal government hoisted the white flag. They would, wrote the Director of the Community Services Administration, no longer credit the $14.3 billion to New York. The title of their reports would be changed from *Federal Outlays* to *Geographic Distribution of Federal Funds*. Viewing this as a major victory, Moynihan summoned the press. The front page of the next day's *Times* celebrated the victory, somehow ballooning the $7.4 billion "deficit" to $10 billion. The *Post* and the *Daily News* applauded, boasting that their gladiator had emerged with proof that New York was being murdered. Senator Moynihan had made his political point.

But did Professor Moynihan? As he sipped his fourth Guinness stout and awaited the arrival of his pea soup, I asked him to explain why his "deficit" figure changed as often as Abe Beame's. What was the real gap? "The first thing to say," he surprisingly admitted, "is that it's not certain how significant this all is." The Professor had spoken.

Then Senator Moynihan took over, reminding me that the gap was real and important. But he came to it, I countered, by making two contradictory assumptions. First, he assumed that *none* of the $14.3 billion of interest on the national debt and foreign aid payments should be credited to New York. Second, he assumed that *all* of the $6.8 billion paid by New York in corporate taxes should be credited to the state. Both assumptions rest on weak legs. An analysis for the Lehrman Institute by Columbia University's Dr. Charles Brecher and Kurt Katzmar suggests that 15 percent of the interest on the national debt is probably spent here—meaning a roughly $2 billion benefit to New York. And a good part of the corporate taxes paid by New York are collected from national corporations that merely funnel their tax payments through New York.

Professor Moynihan looked up from his plate of sliced British beef and admitted, "Maybe, if we evened it out, the number would be $4 or $4.5 billion, but that's still a lot." It is, but it's incomplete. The "deficit" shrinks further when you consider commuters who pay New York taxes but live in other states; count not just the primary federal contracts won by other states but also the subcontracts won by New York; make allowances for New York's disproportionate number of not-for-profit institutions (which attract federal aid). And Moynihan's "deficit" calculation fails to measure what he calls the "hidden policies of government"—regulations, tariffs, imported oil policies, paperwork—which entail costs but defy easy quantification. Printed in the *Federal Register*, for instance, are 60,000 pages of government regulations which *Business Week* has estimated tax national consumers $60 to $130 billion annually.

Trying to pin down a "balance of payments gap" is like trying to catch eels with your hands. It is also illusory. It attacks the progressive income tax, which presupposes that the rich are to pay more than the poor—and New York is considered a rich state, or at least its median income is high. "The logical fallacy of Moynihan's argument," Senator Proxmire says, "is that if you want the states to get the same back from the federal government that they send to Washington, why have an expensive federal government?"

But doesn't the federal government murder New York by shortchanging the city on federal aid? Professor Moynihan has been careful not to make that accusation. "This is indeed an old established New York charge," he says. "The trouble is that in the main it is false." How false is documented in the Brecher/Katzmar analysis. The best measure of federal assistance, they explain, is to use two criteria: tax collections and need. New York City, for instance, in 1977 had 3.6 percent of the nation's population, collected 4.4 percent of all federal revenues, and accounted for 4.3 percent of the nation's poor; yet the city received 5.4 percent of all federal outlays. The state, the Treasury reported, ranked 1st in federal dollar aid, 1st in the growth of aid, and 6th in per capita aid.

One could make the argument that Washington should do more, but that's different from arguing that New York does not receive its fair share of federal grants. Lester Thurow, a very good and very liberal M.I.T. economist, has written that in 1975 New York City's per capita federal aid totaled $314, compared to a national average of $228. "While the average city," he wrote, "gets 36 percent of its revenue from state and federal grants, New York gets 43 percent of its revenue from the same source." The Temporary Commission's conclusion: the federal government treats New York "comparatively well" and "reasonably equitably."

President Carter may not be the friend candidate Carter promised to be, but he—and Gerald Ford—helped New York nonetheless. Assistant Secretary of the Treasury Roger Altman reminded the Association for a Better New York on December 1, 1977: "During this city fiscal year, total grants to New York will total $3.67 billion, a 33 percent increase over the $2.75 billion provided during fiscal 1976, the last full year of the Ford Administration." Making allowance for some puffing on Altman's part, Beame administration officials conceded that Carter, relying heavily on Ford's last budget, increased aid by $500 million. In early 1977, the Brookings Institution released a government-sponsored study warning that if federal aid formulas were not changed by 1980, the chief beneficiaries would not be the older cities of the north but small towns, suburbs, and Western and Southern cities. But their projections showed New York to be an exception. Even under the old formulas, New York would receive more than its fair share. Within months, and after skillful coaxing from Senator Moynihan, among others, these formulas were amended to tilt toward older cities. New York was a big winner. Federal monies to New York State increased by $7.7 billion in fiscal 1977, the largest gain made by any of the fifty states. Mr. Moynihan made this announcement in July 1978, presumably to show how effective Senator Moynihan had been. By releasing these numbers, however, he was inadvertently undermining his "gap" argument.

"I think there's a solid indication that New York is being helped and not scalped by the federal government," Senator Proxmire told me, attacking both the balance of payments argument and New York's self-image as an orphan. That hurts, coming from the chairman of a committee which reviews most federal urban aid programs. As Professor Moynihan once declared, "It's all very well to get a speech printed in a New York newspaper saying New York is being short-changed on this or that program. But it has absolutely no effect if the director of the Office of Management and Budget tells the President that the charge is false."

When it comes to certain federal policies and programs, the charge is not always false. Yes, the federal government sometimes does commit, or permit, murder. Moynihan can be eloquent on the subject: "There is a fundamental bias against New York State in the way the federal government collects its taxes and distributes its revenues. Tax rates accelerate as money income goes up. Benefits accelerate as money income goes down. The Scythians could not have bred two wild horses better equipped to pull New York State apart. Incomes are higher in New York in the way they are higher in Alaska—because the cost of living is higher." (One reason it is higher, Moynihan notes with the force of a whisper, is because local and state taxes are higher.)

By not accounting for differences in the cost of living, the same federal dollar is worth more in Texas than New York. But a word of caution is in order: cost-of-living differences among poor people —for whom most aid is earmarked—are only about 8 percent higher in New York, compared to between 16 and 25 percent for intermediate and high-income families. Therefore, if the formulas were changed, New York would receive less of a bonanza than is commonly assumed. The First Bank of Boston found, for instance, that if cost-of-living escalators were added to the revenue sharing formula, the entire Northeast's share would have risen only $109 million in one year.

As a candidate, Jimmy Carter recognized this and other inequities. In August 1976, in a long interview aboard his campaign plane as it streaked from Seattle, Washington, to Des Moines, Iowa, Carter focused on urban concerns. Invited to the front of the 727, I slid into the wide first-class seat facing the bulkhead. Carter, in

the next seat, paid no notice, continuing to read a two-page memorandum, glancing up at aide Greg Schneiders to impart instructions,
glancing again at the memo. When he finished, Schneiders lingered
and briefed the candidate on the purpose of the interview, requesting forty-five minutes of his time. No, a still-seated Carter admonished him. The campaign had a strict rule: no more than thirty
minutes per interview. Then Carter removed, folded, and placed
his glasses in a shirt pocket. He had yet to address or even look at
me. Perhaps five minutes after I took the adjoining seat, Carter
turned for the first time to offer a warm greeting. My tape recorder
clicked on. For the next fifty minutes the candidate's steel-blue eyes
remained fixed on the interviewer.

Did he favor federal aid formulas which took into account differences in the cost of living? "In some categories of assistance,
yes," he said softly. "Welfare would be one example."

Q. The Northeast is in a sort of depression, with unemployment
rates 2 percent above the national average and the growth rate
lagging behind the nation's. In terms of federal aid formulas, you've
talked about having some national criteria, such as poverty or
unemployment levels, to give extra aid to areas that need it most.
Would you also favor special federal aid to depressed regions, such
as the federal government gave to Appalachia during the sixties?

A. I would rather allot special federal aid to much narrower targets than the entire eleven or twelve or fifteen state regions of the
country, as was the case with Appalachia. We also need, under
existing federal programs regarding pollution control, housing, law
enforcement, and so forth, to concentrate those allocations of funds
where they are most needed, which would fall within the inner-city
areas. In the past, when we passed a housing program, quite often it
was the Congress's intention that that money go to the people who
needed it the most. But because of the intelligence and educational
level and the political influence and good organizations, say, in the
suburbs, they sapped away a great deal of the available federal
assistance for housing and other programs, to the detriment of the
inner cities, where the concerted grantsmanship was not so well
developed. Those two forces would be what I would pursue: immediately to let existing aid go where it is needed the most; and,
secondly, to have regional aid designed but focused on much narrower targets than the one you described.

Q. Could you define a narrower target?

A. A city, or it might even be a particular industry, or it might be a particular age group. But let me add one thing. My own economic advisers say that if we do this targeting of job opportunities, we can reach at least one-half percent lower unemployment without increasing the inflationary pressures by targeting. If you do something nationwide, you get high inflation pressures. If you target it, the inflation pressures are much less for a given level of unemployment.

New York also suffers the accident of geography, something Carter and the federal government have chosen to ignore. The Northeast region is forced to import roughly 85 percent of its oil from foreign sources; the rest of the country relies on only 65 percent foreign oil. Thus the 1973 OPEC oil embargo was much more devastating to New York and the Northeast. According to Neal R. Peirce, a contributing editor of the *National Journal* and now a syndicated columnist who covers government, not politics, for the Washington *Post*, in 1972 the Northeast states expended $7 billion on imported fuel; by 1975, that sum tripled to $20.7 billion. This drove up New York's costs and reduced its ability to compete economically. In 1975, for instance, the average New York resident paid $37.33 for 500 kilowatt-hours of electricity; the Boston resident, $24.86; the Chicago resident, $20.60; the Seattle resident, $6.97; the Houston resident, $15.02. Admittedly, New York's steep utility taxes drove up these costs, but its fuel costs are still higher. As are its natural gas costs. Because of the accident of geography, the Sunbelt is blessed with ample natural gas resources. A Southern industry can rely on less expensive natural gas for 50 to 70 percent of its energy supply; an industry in the Northeast uses on the average about 20 percent natural gas—and it's twice as expensive here.

Most federal grant programs benefit New York, but some do not. Section 5 of the Urban Mass Transportation Act, for example. Under this act, transit aid is pegged to population rather than riders. And as Senator Moynihan and others have complained, by ignoring transit ridership and transit vehicle miles covered, New York City—with over 30 percent of the nation's mass transit riders—receives just over 10 percent of these funds. Moynihan figures federal assistance to average 3¢ per rider in New York and 20¢ in

Los Angeles, 19¢ in Houston, 12¢ in Dallas. The average aid per rider in cities of more than 1 million people is double New York's.* The New York Regional Plan Association calculated that if this formula were changed, in 1976 New York City would have received an additional $110 million in mass transit aid. New York is only one of thirteen states to receive the minimum 50 percent federal reimbursement for welfare. Poor states, like Arkansas, receive 75 percent. Yet if New York garnered the same 60 percent as Proxmire's Wisconsin, according to the *Fiscal Observer,* an independent and respected publication, the city would save $195 million in welfare and Medicaid. New York, as another instance, has 30 percent of the nation's known addicts, yet receives less than 1 percent of the $296 million in available federal funds.

Where New York gets murdered is in its share of "hard" federal dollars—defense expenditures, federal installations and jobs, dams, roads, public works. In 1977, a bipartisan coalition of sixteen governors and 204 members of Congress from the Northeast and Middle West released a study showing how defense dollars neglected their regions. Their sixteen states accounted for 45 percent of the country's population and almost half its taxes, yet received 20 percent or less of all defense expenditures. The number of defense employees mushroomed 35 percent between 1950 and 1976, yet the number of defense employees declined 3 percent in their states—39 percent in New York. The military construction budget for fiscal 1978 earmarked just 9 percent to their states. Of the 761 defense facilities closed between 1961 and 1975, 43 percent were in the sixteen states—fifty-three in New York. "The decline in defense expenditures," lamented Republican Congressman Donald J. Mitchell of Herkimer, New York, "has increased unemployment in the region, exacerbating economic problems, while the shift of expenditures to other areas has helped fuel those areas' economic boom." If military wages and salaries had been allocated "equally" to all states between 1940 and 1976, a study by Bernard Gifford of the Russell Sage Foundation reported, "New York State would have 'received' more than $21 billion (in current 1940–1976 dollars) above the amount that it actually received. And Georgia would have 'lost' $5 billion."

* The same pattern does not hold for federal mass transit capital construction funds. Over the last ten years, the New York region has received more federal construction dollars—$2 billion—than any other and ranks 6th in per capita aid.

Of course, these disparities can be as misleading as Moynihan's balance of payments "gap." Defense expenditures cannot be "equal." Strategic considerations often dictate where defense dollars are spent, a prime reason Alaska, Hawaii and California rank so high. Climate also plays a role—inclement weather impedes military training and operations, and cold weather costs more (heavy coats, boots, electricity costs, etc.). I hated every goddamn minute of my winter basic training, but I thank the Lord it was in warm San Antonio, Texas, rather than frigid Watertown, New York. Political climate also plays a part. The Northeast states have traditionally been less politically hospitable to the military than have Southern states. Ours, thankfully, is a tradition rich in social protest. A pass is needed to build here, plus several years of public hearings. We wouldn't even give the President a pass—by 1968, the only places where Lyndon Johnson could escape demonstrations and speak were out-of-the-way military bases.

But geography and climate played only a part. Congressional barons like Mendel Rivers of South Carolina and Richard Russell of Georgia, by controlling the important Appropriations and Defense committees, delivered the pork for their districts, as Sam Rayburn and Lyndon Johnson delivered space facilities for Texas or Robert Kerr delivered dams and public works for Oklahoma. While members of New York's delegation tended to deliver speeches on the suffering in Bangladesh, the killing in Northern Ireland.

A similar tilt shows up in federal employment. Between 1960 and 1970, for example, the number of federal civilian employees grew but 3.5 percent in New England and 1.3 percent in the Mid-Atlantic region; at the same time, federal civilian employment jumped 30.7 percent in the South Atlantic region and about 20 percent in the rest of the South and West, where the unemployment rate was lower. In those ten years, New York City lost 9,900 federal civilian jobs. Since 1970, the city has lost another 19,200 federal jobs. But a word of caution is in order: federal employment usually matches population and economic activity. As New York declined, and other areas grew, federal jobs followed.

Because it is a special city—America's true capital—New York merits special aid. No other city in the world is as much a national treasure or resource. New York is not only the home of the United Nations, but also the world's center of commerce, communications, finance, fashion, ideas. As New York is diminished, so is the resource. And unlike other nations—England, France, Italy,

which subsidize London, Paris and Rome as national resources—
the federal government does not provide special support to New
York.

Murder or suicide?

One has to be careful to distinguish between *soft* federal dollars
—direct grants, CETA funds, countercyclical aid, community development funds—which tilt toward New York, and *hard* federal
dollars—highways, home loans, military and space expenditures,
dams, water projects—which tilt toward the Sunbelt. One also has
to slice through some thick local gibberish, portraying New York as
a victim of a federal conspiracy (like conservatives who blame
communists, liberals enjoy scapegoating). The social legislation of
the past forty years, we sometimes forget, was promoted by the
Northeast, often over the objections of Southern legislators. Some
of those bills, including minimum wage laws, liberalized immigration and tariff policies, inadvertently aided the Sunbelt.

For years, a succession of New York officials charged that
the United Nations drained New York's budget and that the federal
government should reimburse the city for upwards of $20 million.
Along comes a study in late 1977—co-sponsored by the Consular
Corps, a city agency—revealing that the 22,000-member diplomatic community pumped about $450 million annually into the
city's economy. We measured the cost of policing the U.N.—but
not the tourism it attracted, the sales and other taxes its employees
paid. There's a lesson in this. We need more information and less
rhetorical posturing. "We do agree," the Chairman of the Council
of Economic Advisors and President Carter's chief domestic aide
wrote to Moynihan in September 1977, "that the federal government needs more systematic information on the overall impact of
all its programs, collectively, on regional economies."

There's also a political lesson for New York. New York officials,
if they don't want to be laughed at, need to determine how they can
logically complain about those federal policies which hurt New
York while ignoring those which help. They also need worry about
a political civil war. "Not since the Southern Governors Conference
was formed over 40 years ago has there been such a concerted
effort against our region," Oklahoma's Governor David L. Boren
warned the 43rd annual Southern Governors Conference in 1977.
"Last year, the Northeast received $300 per person in federal
grants while the South averaged $250. This happened even though
the South and Southwest remain 10 percent below the national

average in per capita income." The Sunbelt was marshaling its forces, as the Northeast had earlier done. Emotions ran high. So high that in late 1977 Governor Hugh Carey journeyed to Austin, Texas, to warn, "Our larger society is in danger of splintering badly from a host of real but reconcilable differences. Our Congress of caucuses is in danger of turning into a cacophony of caucuses. . . ."

Unlike the first Civil War, this time the North couldn't win. With the loss of population comes a loss of Congressional representation. The 1980 Census is expected to result in New York's Congressional delegation shrinking by another four members, to thirty-five. Just a few years ago, forty-five members represented New York in Congress, and that bunch, like this one, was not known for its effectiveness. When New York's representatives are not running for mayor, senator, or governor, they're usually maneuvering to join a foreign relations committee. Like the Dallas Cowboy cheerleaders, they look pretty but don't know how to block. Even if they did, the country's disposition in the mid- and late seventies had soured to the kind of spending favored by most Northeast representatives. "The mood of the Congress will not be particularly receptive to massive new federal spending," Tennessee's Senator James R. Sasser told Detroit Mayor Coleman Young while chairing urban hearings in February 1978. "So, if you had to choose the most important things for an urban policy, what would your priorities be?" Young replied, "That would be difficult to answer. We came here to give up nothing. We came here to ask for everything." New York, thank God, is not Peoria. We often forget, Peoria thanks God it is not New York. And the city needs Peoria's votes in Congress.

It is simpler to make a speech than to change policy. New Yorkers have to get used to the idea that the country and its problems are just as interdependent as progressives used to say the world is. There is a consequence for everything. Amending federal aid formulas to give the North more means giving the South less. Permitting European flights to originate from Southern cities, as President Carter has done, is more convenient for citizens and fair to the South, but it lessens the nation's dependence on cities like New York. Allowing the two-martini lunch to be tax-deductible is a ripoff for business executives—yet New York's restaurateurs and their unions plead that their business depends on it. In addition, some things government can't change, particularly in a democratic society. Part of the Northeast's decline had nothing to do with government policies and a lot to do with people's preferences. Many citizens simply want to live in a warmer climate, seek space, grass, new schools, lower taxes, a two-car garage—all plentiful in the Sunbelt. In a free society, how do we order people not to vote with their feet?

Instead of platitudes and shrieks about the need for a new national urban policy, says Professor Moynihan (now conveniently ignoring Senator Moynihan's shrieks for "economic justice"), "The whole point of an urban policy should be that New York does not go bankrupt." Sipping coffee, Moynihan leaned back and recalled returning from Hubert Humphrey's funeral with President Carter on *Air Force One*: "I almost said to him, 'Herbert Hoover wasn't responsible for the great Depression. Yet it's called Hooverism.' "

In early 1978, Moynihan and most other New York officials were warning that without new federal loan guarantees the city would be forced to declare bankruptcy. The consequences, they said, would be swift. Under this domino theory, the market would close to New York State; then local school boards who depend on state financing would default; then other states and municipalities would follow; then a massive crisis of confidence would likely engulf the nation and the world. The city would become a ward of the federal government. And how would the world react to the spectacle of the United States government callously standing by as the world's premier city declared bankruptcy? That would be murder. Right?

Yes, and no. There would be no evidence to charge the federal government with discrimination had the Congress rejected loan guarantees since no other city receives them. New York also rightly suffered a credibility problem. City and state officials sold the $2.3 billion annual seasonal loan program in 1975 on the basis that it was a one-time-only request. That was untrue, and officials knew it. Or, as Moynihan candidly told the White House Conference on Balanced Growth and Economic Development in January 1978, "The persons who put the emergency arrangements together assumed that in three years' time—in 1978—there would be a Democratic administration in office and that it would take care of the problem with a massive infusion of Federal funds." City labor leaders in the audience exploded. "We were really angry with Pat," a prominent union leader told me later that night. Was Moynihan wrong? "No," he said. "Don't quote me, but he's absolutely right. but why did he have to say it?"

New York's case before the Congress was also weakened because, contrary to 1975 promises, by 1978 the city had not balanced its budget. It is comforting to portray those opposing loans to New York as neanderthals and bigots. Some are. But there was also a legitimate concern—expressed most eloquently by Proxmire—that if Congress made an exception for New York, another domino theory would unfold: other cities would clamor for similar loans; would fail to balance their budgets if there's a federal Santa Claus to protect them; the federal structure, which defines cities as creatures of states, would be altered. Congress, which can't manage itself, would be asked to manage local budgets, to pass judgment on local labor settlements and policies.

New York's best case for federal loan guarantees was predicated on practicality, not principle. The consequences of a bankruptcy are matters of judgment, not fact. If New York's dire scenario is wrong, a catastrophe is avoided. If opponents of federal assistance are wrong, a catastrophe is ensured. Practically speaking, the worst possible consequences come if the opponents are wrong. A bankruptcy will also cost the federal government money. As Senator William Proxmire, in urging President Ford to support seasonal loans, declared on November 10, 1975, "A New York City default would cost the federal government $6.5 billion in loan guarantees by 1980, whereas loan guarantees *before* default would lead to a maximum of $2.4 billion in guaranteed bonds, in 1977." Though federal loans or loan guarantees may help drive up federal interest rates, they otherwise don't cost federal taxpayers a dime—unless the city defaults on the loans guaranteed by the federal government. In fact, over the three years of the seasonal loan program, the federal government, by charging a 1 percent premium above the normal interest rate on these Treasury notes, earned an extra $30 million in interest. And because these notes were taxable—unlike municipal securities—MAC Chairman Rohatyn estimates the federal government was awarded an extra $200 million in taxes.

While it is true that no other city receives federal loan guarantees, many citizens, businesses and countries do. By the end of fiscal 1978, the federal government was expected to have $324 billion outstanding in loan guarantees—contrasted with the $2 billion asked by New York. Senator John Tower of Texas once sat behind a large desk in his Capitol office inveighing against federal loan guarantees for New York. Yet, just moments before, he had kept this reporter waiting while he concluded a session with Texas farmers demanding federal support for their "unprofitable" farms. Tower said he saw no inconsistency between pledging to support loan guarantees for these farmers and opposing them for New York. Nor does Senator Proxmire see any inconsistency between his vote for the New Communities Loan Guarantee Program (1970) and his strenuous opposition to city guarantees. The Congress of the United States has voted loan guarantees to bankrupt corporations (Lockheed), foreign dictatorships, college students (with a one-third default rate), small businesses, tenants, even for the construction of RFK Stadium in Washington. After performing these tricks, members of Congress warned that as a matter of principle they wouldn't go to bed with the City of New York! In August 1978, the federal government went to bed with the city, approving $1.65 billion of loan guarantees. The loan question—at least for the next four years—seemed settled.

But beyond the loan question lurks another: What, if anything, should the federal government do for depressed areas like New York? Faced with a similar question in 1938, President Franklin Delano Roosevelt declared: "It is my conviction that the South represents right now the nation's No. 1 economic problem—the nation's problem, not merely the South's. It is an imbalance that can and must be righted, for the sake of the South and of the nation. . . ."

Today, the Northeast, and particularly New York, is like the Old South. Its living costs, taxes, climate and aging physical structure are no longer competitive. Its tax base has shrunk as its service needs have expanded. New York, like many small farmers, can no longer compete. Left alone—through a policy of "benign neglect" advocated by laissez-faire professor and occasional *Wall Street Journal* columnist Irving Kristol—the "economic imbalance in the nation" will probably tip further. The nation's real per capita income grew 6.5 percent between 1970 and 1975, reported Bernard Gifford for the Russell Sage Foundation. Yet in the same period New York City's income dropped 1.4 percent. "Had the city grown in tandem [roughly parallel] with the national economy," Gifford writes, "as it had for more than 20 years, its per capita personal income would have increased by 3.9 percent between 1970 and 1975. . . ."

Stating the problem is not the same as stating the solution. The era of massive 15-point programs, of neat panaceas, of soaring optimism, seems to have ended. Like many, I have learned there is a difference between what *should* and what *can be* done, between what's *needed* and what's *possible*. "If the President called me in tomorrow and asked what the solution is for the nation's aging cities," Assistant Secretary of Housing and Urban Development Donna Shalala told me in late 1977, "I wouldn't know. Nor does anyone else."

As a Presidential candidate, Jimmy Carter seemed to be struggling to redefine liberalism, to approach problems with a fresh sense of humility; to marry a desire to right wrongs with a sense of fiscal responsibility. He took care, in a May 25, 1976, letter to Mayor Beame promising the federal assumption of local welfare costs, to strike the promise of a "prompt" takeover from a draft and substitute the phrase "as soon as possible." Mindful that promises cost money, he toned down a staff-drafted speech on national health insurance, as well as language committing his Presidency to a sweeping Humphrey-Hawkins full employment bill. He seemed to understand that declaring health care or a job a right was different from telling people how to pay for that right, or how to set up a system to deliver that right. Many ADA liberals took this as a clue that Carter was not one of them. As a reporter covering Carter, I took it as a clue that he had a realistic sense of limits, an engineer's concern with how things worked, not just how they sounded. The first nineteen months of his Presidency suggest that I may have been wrong. Carter may not have known what he was doing, may just have been struggling not to offend moderate and conservative voters.

In the campaign, Carter's letters to Mayor Beame promised: "As soon as possible the federal assumption of the local government's share" of welfare would be picked up. Pressed to explain, Carter told me (and a roomful of reporters), "The local government should pay no part of the costs . . . and over a period of time the federal government should pay an increasing proportion of the cost, which would mean the state would pay a lesser amount of the cost." Almost exactly one year later, Presidential press secretary Jody Powell declared that Jimmy Carter never promised a federal assumption of local welfare costs and instead had said the state should assume these costs. At about the same time, the President promised his long-delayed welfare reform proposals would entail "no additional cost above and beyond what we presently spend on welfare. . . ." That August, after a torrent of criticism from the Urban League's Vernon Jordan and others reminding him of his campaign pledges, he suddenly added $6.2 billion to his welfare reform proposal. By 1978, that sum had mysteriously ballooned to over $20 billion more, though it was hardly a Presidential priority.

In the campaign, Carter blasted President Ford: "Our country has no urban policy or defined goals," he said, "and so we have floundered from one ineffectual and uncoordinated program to another." Yet, fifteen months into his Presidency, Carter was floundering and had yet to announce his own urban policy.

None of this should suggest there are simple answers. According to Moynihan, if President Carter's welfare reform bill had been passed, it would, for example, relieve New York City of just $60 million of the $560 million it expended on welfare in fiscal 1978. Even the federal government's assumption of costs would be no panacea. City taxpayers are also federal taxpayers. And even if the Congress agreed to a national welfare standard, it would never be set as high as New York's current standard. New York would then have two alternatives: *cut* welfare payments or *continue* to spend many millions to subsidize welfare.

An even greater danger is ignorance—both national and local. Committed to showing he cared, Carter decided to visit another planet in October 1977. The President had been severely criticized for neglecting urban areas, so he stepped aboard his *Air Force One* capsule and was deposited in Manhattan. From there, he journeyed north to the South Bronx.

Nothing had prepared the man from Plains for what he would encounter. Stretching before his eyes were more than 3,000 vacant lots, 43,000 newly abandoned apartments, a welfare caseload bearing one of three residents. The average inhabitant, he learned, earned $2,340—60 percent less than the average in his nation.

Stunned, and ever mindful of the cameras, Carter decided to deposit his flag on this strange land, vowing a special program to "salvage" the South Bronx and "turn it around." The President got what he wanted—a headline. The natives got what they wanted—his purse. The mad scramble was on. The President, who didn't know what he was doing, had company.

"Slum tourism" is how the Urban League's Vernon Jordan dubbed the President's trip. *Why pick the vast South Bronx for a test program?* "I think it's partly because the President came here," conceded the local federal coordinator, Alan Weiner. *Why the South Bronx?* "He came there," admitted Mayor Koch's original co-ordinator, Lloyd Kaplan. "Tolstoy's *War and Peace* is about events and what flows from them. Jimmy Carter came to Charlotte Street. What else flows from that? That's what I'm going to live out."

The city lived it out by submitting, in December 1977, "A Plan for Revitalization" of the South Bronx. The price tag, considering the task, was modest: about $800 million. The "plan" called for economic development incentives, new housing and parks. A flurry of meetings followed. By April 1978, the city and federal government announced agreement on a joint seven-year plan to "save the South Bronx." The city hoped that the total federal dollar commitment would reach $520 million and that this would trigger perhaps another $1 billion of public and private spending.

Do their schemes match their dreams? Will it work? The obstacles are forbidding. The South Bronx's "Dresden-like quality is in no way typical of America's urban problems," Roger Wilkins of the *Times* has written. "To take the moonscape of the South Bronx as the metaphor for the nation's urban needs is to inflate an already horrendous problem to a scale that would defy even the most ambitious political imaginations." Carter's entire national urban program, announced in late March 1978, totaled just $4 billion of new money. In the first year, the Carter plan called for the federal government to spend $55.6 million in the South Bronx. Yet one of Carter's Washington urban strategists guesses, "To turn the South Bronx around would take maybe $10 billion." The President is stalking a rhino with a pea shooter.

A good argument could be made that the President should be stalking smaller prey. "If I had to pick the area to put those resources in, it wouldn't be the South Bronx," said City Planning Commission Chairman Robert F. Wagner, Jr. "It might be a Bushwick or a South Jamaica"—smaller, more viable neighborhoods where limited resources and concentrated effort might make a real difference. If Carter wanted an urban test case to prove government could work, why pick the worst possible case? Why risk granting ammunition to those who say government can't work?

Carter's impulsiveness was again matched by the city's. As has been proven time and again, city officials will do anything for a federal buck, even if they believe it makes no sense. Take, for instance, the proposed $1.1 billion Westway project, which would replace the dilapidated West Side Highway along Manhattan's waterfront with a modern highway and park land. In his campaign for mayor, Koch called the scheme "a disaster" and vowed, "It will never be built." Yet, six months after he was inaugurated, Koch failed to alter Governor Carey's support for the project and agreed to support the "disaster" rather than risk losing federal dollars. His Parks Commissioner, Gordon Davis, supported a $750,000 federal grant to build a new park and ball field in Brooklyn's Canarsie section—until the local planning board said it didn't need a new park and ball field. What they really needed, they said, was $250,000 to maintain the two parks and ball fields they already had. Commissioner Davis tried vainly to convince them they were "sacrificing" a federal gift. But the local board knew a "disaster" when they saw one coming.

Which, I fear, cannot be said for the city's South Bronx plan. Privately, many city officials think the plan will fail.

"Why did you have to tell a reporter you wouldn't have picked the South Bronx for a federal experiment?" Deputy Mayor Basil Patterson is said to have scolded Planning Chairman Wagner at a Koch cabinet meeting.

"Do you disagree?" Wagner asked. "No," said Patterson. "But did you have to say it?"

Parts of the city's plan "are a joke," groused a city official. "What good does it do to build a beautiful new park when you need a machine gun to walk through it?" says Denis Alee, then the First Deputy Administrator of the Economic Development Agency. He was referring to the deeper economic and social problems of places like the South Bronx which are blithely ignored by new parks or buildings. A danger in rebuilding the South Bronx is that the same underclass will burn it down again.

We can't deal with this problem until we talk about it. One of the few local politicians who does talk is Herman Badillo, born in Puerto Rico and once a representative of the South Bronx in the Congress. Today, Badillo is a deputy mayor of New York, and one of his responsibilities is coordinating the South Bronx plan. He speaks of youth gang members and the hard-core unemployed "who have no superego," no sense of right or wrong. New business tax incentives, new housing, new parks—as called for in the federal/ city South Bronx plan—don't address this problem. Nor, necessarily, do conventional counseling techniques, more schools, more hope, more concern. It's a tough problem they don't have in Plains, Georgia, and we fear talking about in New York.

Unfortunately, Badillo's concern does not seem to loom large in the South Bronx plan he shaped. Badillo prefers talking, quite impressively, about the consequences of continuing to neglect places like the South Bronx. "Planned shrinkage," or "encouraging abandonment," as he also calls it, "is a good theory for making New York a poor city. If we don't build in places like the Bronx, the poor will move to middle-class areas and the middle class will leave. Soon there will be nothing but the South Bronx. . . . Parts of New York still look like they've been in a war. They represent indifference. We can't allow them to stand." The South Bronx is not a total wasteland. There are 750,000 real people living there, hundreds of community organizations—dedicated citizens struggling to salvage their neighborhood and lives.

But saying *why* something must be done is not the same as saying *how* it will be done. Sadly, resources are limited. There is no way to achieve a balanced federal budget and eradicate the spreading blight of the South Bronx. Spending money for urban ills—like spending money for defense—does not guarantee success. Ten years ago, the Mott Haven Development Fund Project was formed to rehabilitate twenty decayed buildings on East 139th and 140th streets in the South Bronx. The federal government guaranteed $4 million of bank loans, community-based organizations pitched in. Five- and six-story brick buildings rose from ashes, creating two gleaming new blocks. Today, six years after the rehabilitation was completed, half the twenty buildings are totally abandoned and the rest are slipping fast. The Mott Haven Development Fund Project was not the answer, as earlier high-rise public housing or the Cross Bronx Expressway which tore up neighborhoods was not the answer. Sometimes we just don't have answers. Or, as the city's original South Bronx plan admits, "We cannot say with any confidence that practical solutions exist."

In the early seventies, it was thought that the new Yankee Stadium would transform the surrounding Bronx neighborhood. It hasn't—though it cost four times the original projections. The New Orleans Superdome cost nine times what it was supposed to, and in 1977 lost $13 million. In 1975, Renzo Zingone, a Milanese builder, was to lead a flock of Italian manufacturers to construct a vast industrial park in the South Bronx. It was, then city EDA Administrator Alfred Eisenpreis announced at the time, "a vote of confidence in New York." Mr. Zingone has not been heard from since.

There is reason to worry that the South Bronx plan will become another false promise. A gap exists between the almost infinitely difficult task and the finite resources Carter will make available; between abstract plans and real people and problems. Beyond this is the inevitable clash between the *desirable* and *do-able*—the same clash witnessed throughout the city's last twenty or so years. Wishing to do good for people, New York often tried to do too much. Enthusiasm, or desperation, overcame our sense of limits. We forgot there were limits to what a city could spend, tax or borrow. Just as the city, and Jimmy Carter, may be ignoring a sense of limits in the South Bronx—trying to do too much with too little on the wrong battlefield.

New York's demands for massive national assistance may also be ignoring federal budget and political limits. Washington should further tilt toward its declining cities. It should target jobs, low-interest loans, incentives for business expansion, relief for high welfare and energy costs; further help stretch the city's enormous debt to permit the easing of choking debt service payments; offer incentives to state and local governments to improve their productivity. New York, like other older cities, is afflicted with too many poor people and too few resources. Alone, sometimes all New York can do is imitate, in Brian Berry's words, "the man with the garbage can following the elephant into the ring, just cleaning up the awful mess that's there."

But after saying this, honesty compels recognition that most federal aid programs already tilt toward New York. President Carter's proposed urban policy would tilt even more toward older cities. Yet his proposed tilt aroused potent political opposition. The Sunbelt is angry, as are the suburbs. Everyone wants a piece of the action, and everyone doesn't have the same generosity of spirit exhibited by liberal New Yorkers in the thirties. In addition, the President is committed to balancing the federal budget and has already announced his intention to reduce the percentage of the GNP spent by the federal government. Many in Congress and the nation already blame government spending and the huge federal deficit for raging inflation. As of June 1978, twenty-three state legislatures—two-thirds the required number—had approved an amendment to the Constitution banning federal deficits.

In short, there is not likely to be a federal Santa Claus. That is why Senator Moynihan's putative $7.4 billion "gap" is so harmful. It is a narcotic. Washington will not believe it; and the greater danger is that New Yorkers will. And if they do, they'll be off on a crusade to right an economic wrong that may not exist—in the process, ignoring the harsh, unpleasant decisions New York has yet to make for itself.

Chapter Five

Mismanaged
New York

THE DOOMED LOBBY of the Municipal Building, across from City
Hall, is still as a snapshot. The sixteen elevators stand at attention;
except for the solitary guard leaning against a wall and two newsstand employees frozen in thought, the lobby's marbled surface is as
smooth and clear as a lake of ice. It stays this way from the end of
the lunch hour until about 4 P.M., when the snapshot explodes
into a motion picture. The elevators, like giant LCV's, spring open,
spilling wave after wave of city employees—clerks and computer
programmers, secretaries and accountants, office boys in shirt
sleeves and office managers lugging briefcases. Some pause to buy
the afternoon paper. Most don't have time, darting directly for one
of the four gold spinning doors leading to the street. At 4:40
P.M. the doors stop spinning, the newsstand begins to close.
Within five minutes, they are done. "Most people who work here
have left by four-thirty," explains the woman who works at the
stand.

City employees, except those few who work staggered hours, are
supposed to work until 5 P.M. Even in the Municipal Building,
where they do stagger hours, many don't work a full day. That they
don't can be blamed on employees for disobeying orders, or on
their bosses for not enforcing them. Or both. No matter who's
blamed, New York City's government—with an almost $14 billion
budget matched by only one of the fifty states (California) and
few nations, and a work force of 300,000, which is considerably

larger than the combined populations of the state capitals of New York and New Jersey—is a model of mismanagement. People may argue over what government should do. But those functions it does perform should be done as cheaply and efficiently as possible. That is the management challenge the city is flunking. New York is spending more and getting less, as the following suggests:

■ City taxpayers spend three times more than they did ten years ago to receive the *same* level of police, fire, sanitation and education services, according to the Mayor's Temporary Commission on City Finances.

■ It costs about as much to educate a child in public as in private schools. The sum has risen from $500 per student in 1960 to $2,600—a jump four times greater than the consumer price index. Yet today there are only 10 percent more students, class sizes have expanded, reading scores have declined—and the number of school employees has doubled.

■ Between 1968 and 1977, the city's transit system lost 22 percent of its riders but gained 384 employees, according to the business-oriented Economic Development Council.

■ The city has 2,000 more policemen than it had in 1961—yet in 1977 policemen worked 1 million fewer hours than they did in 1961, according to a study by Mary McCormick, former research director of the Temporary Commission.

■ In 1970, there was one sergeant for every eleven cops. In 1977, there were 25 percent fewer patrolmen and one sergeant for every seven cops.

■ Hospital services declined at the same time expenditures and the number of hospital employees multiplied. Between 1961 and 1971, the municipal-hospital system's patient services dropped 20 percent while 4,000 new employees were hired, a study by Charles Brecher of Columbia University's Conservation of Human Resources Project found. In the decade through 1976, the city's health expenditures tripled, averaging $226 a day in a city hospital in 1976—70 percent above the national average.

■ The growth of the city's budget has not meant a corresponding growth in taxpayers' services. Between 1961 and 1975—after discounting inflation—city labor costs jumped three times faster than the number of employees. More city employees are working fewer hours for a lot more money. If all city employees worked the same forty-hour week as federal or most private employees do, the Koch administration calculated, taxpayers could potentially receive 20 million extra hours of service—the equivalent of adding more than 10,000 new employees.

When set against the backdrop of New York's fiscal crisis and economic decline, these facts seem to add up to a disaster. But they also add up to an opportunity. Since no one can deny the city is engaged in a struggle for survival, New York has the rare opportunity to alter dramatically the way government—which accounts for about one quarter of the nation's GNP—delivers services. While it is commonly assumed that the federal government is *the* giant bureaucracy, in fact four of every five civilian government workers—12 million—are employed by state and local governments. And one of every seven American workers is on the payroll of a local government. Local government is not only our largest industry, says the National Council on Municipal Performance, it is "our least efficient." In this sense, New York can again be a pioneer: closing its performance as well as its budget gap; figuring out how to do more for less.

Today, New York is a pioneer of another sort. Its basic management and personnel system, like a huge, immovable rock, has so far weathered the fiscal storm. Imagine beneath that unscathed rock lurks a rabbit sporting a watch in its waistcoat pocket. Follow him down the rabbit hole and enter New York City's very own Wonderland, where you find:

City employees enjoy a 4-day work week. According to a 1976 report from the Temporary Commission, most city employees work 210 out of a possible 261 workdays. They average 25 days' vacation, 12 sick days, 11 holidays, half a day for death in the family, and over two days' terminal leave. City teachers receive about 75 days off, including summer, Christmas and Easter vacations. City University professors receive about 80 days off, and a full professor, reports the Commission, is paid $33,475 for less than 11 hours a week in the classroom. Beginning sanitation men get 5 weeks' paid vacation (private carters in the Teamsters Union get 2 weeks the first year and 5 weeks only after 15 years). The average policeman or fireman is off about 55 days a year. After three years, all uniformed employees—police, fire, sanitation, corrections officers,

Housing and Transit police—receive 27 days vacation. In addition, cops, corrections officers, Housing and Transit police get another 8 chart days off in return for an extra 15 minutes spent each workday on paperwork and checking in and out. (They won an additional 6 chart days in the 1978 labor negotiations.) Sergeants do even better, receiving 18 to 28 chart days off. The Emergency Financial Control Board has reported that the reduction of sergeants' chart days off to 8 would be equivalent to adding 256 sergeants to the police force. If there were no chart days for patrolmen, the Police Department has said, the extra coverage would be equivalent to adding 900 cops. If the city followed the same annual leave policies as the state, noted the Temporary Commission, over the next 25 years it could save almost $2 billion.

City managers, who are supposed to check time clocks, not punch them, receive overtime pay. In most cases, this overtime is called compensatory time and requires that managers fill out time sheets. If they earn more than $22,500 and work more than 40 hours in a week, these hours can be used as additional vacation days; or they can be banked and paid in a lump sum at the termination of city service. Until January 1978, managers were allowed to collect up to one year of accumulated overtime, sick leave and vacation pay. When First Deputy Mayor James Cavanagh retired after 37 years with the city, for instance, he received a lump sum equal to his final year's salary—$49,849. The average departing city executive, a 1977 survey by Comptroller Goldin disclosed, was paid for 36 overtime days—not counting the overtime days already taken off, the unused vacation and sick days, and terminal leave pay. In the first week of the new Koch administration, after executives from the outgoing Beame administration submitted claims for $5.5 million of overtime and severance pay, Koch concurred with a Goldin directive limiting severance pay to 54 days.

Some city managers receive straight overtime pay. The former executive assistant to the Fire Commissioner accumulated almost $11,000 in one recent 9-month period. Police lieutenants and fire marshals also receive overtime pay. The potential harm of overtime pay for managerial personnel is suggested by looking at detectives. They used to work round the clock until a case was broken. It was a matter of professional pride. The reward: promotions, or just getting to keep their gold shields. When promotion opportunities were reduced in the early seventies, the Detectives Endowment Association demanded, and won, cash overtime. Paid overtime was limited to 100 hours. Anything above the ceiling could be taken as time off. With the fiscal crisis, city officials push to hold down overtime costs and detectives resist working extra hours unless they're paid overtime. One result: solved homicide cases have slipped dramatically.

Police and firemen who donate blood are given a bonus day off. Thus charity is rewarded—4,938 days' worth to police in 1977. "No one should get those days off," says city Director of Labor Relations Anthony Russo. "They're men with good constitutions. Civilians don't get them."

Uniformed employees—including police, fire, corrections officers, Transit and Housing police—are granted one personal leave day each year "for whatever reason." Sanitation men agreed to temporarily sacrifice this privilege during the fiscal crisis. In urging repeal of this contract provision, the Koch administration calculated the city could save $2.4 million annually, adding 45,000 workdays.

Police or firemen who are veterans and whose chart requires them to work on Veterans or Memorial Day, must receive compensatory time off, according to state law.

Election Day is declared a special paid holiday, though state law requires only that voting not be hindered. Since voting hours are from 6 a.m. to 9 p.m., there is no conflict with the workday. In proposing to eliminate this holiday from employee contracts, the Koch administration estimated the city would save $5 million.

All uniformed employees are allowed unlimited non-line-of-duty sick leave. In the last 6 months of 1977, police averaged 16.5 sick days—about 1,000 cops out sick each day. Sanitation men averaged 14 sick days. This permissive policy contrasts with that of the Soviet Union, which rigidly monitors sick leave, or with Teamster workers in the private carting industry who aren't paid if they're out sick. The city's sick leave policy can lead to abuse. "They have a buddy system," explains Commissioner Russo. " 'Say, Joe, you take tomorrow off, and I'll get time and a half to take your place.' You see, the guy who takes Joe's place has to be paid time and a half. Then the next time they reverse, and Joe gets time and a half." In proposing to replace unlimited with 12 sick days annually, the Koch administration calculated a savings of $3.4 million over 2 years. If workers were not paid for the first half-day out sick, as is customary in private industry, Koch said the city would save $13 million over 2 years.

All other city employees receive 10 to 20 sick days, and are allowed to accumulate these from year to year. Sick days, which were designed to ensure that workers would not be penalized for legitimate illnesses, thus become additional vacation days. When the worker leaves government, he or she is paid on the basis of 1 day's pay for every 2 sick days not taken, up to a maximum of 120 days. Unlike many city workers, teachers aren't required to submit even a friendly doctor's note. They have what is called "10 self-treated days." Instead of overtime costs, this leads to substitute teacher costs—$19.6 million in 1976-77. Sick days are granted to the bosses as well. The average departing city executive is reimbursed for 29 unused sick days, according to Comptroller Goldin.

The Transit Authority's union contract prohibits part-time employees, ballooning overtime costs. A November 1977 audit by Sidney Schwartz, the Control Board's Special Deputy Comptroller, sketched how this requirement for a minimum 8-hour day invites abuse: A Staten Island–to–Manhattan express bus driver leaves his depot at 7 A.M., completing his morning run by 8:30. His next run is not until 5:30 P.M. and is completed by 7. In between the two runs, the driver may go home. For 3 hours of actual work, the driver receives 10½ hours' pay, including 7 hours of what is called "swing time" and one-half hour of "penalty" time. If permitted to hire part-timers—to conform to rider habits rather than worker convenience —the Authority would pay for only 3 hours' work. Schwartz's audit disclosed: in 1976, 1,000 of nearly 9,000 bus drivers earned overtime 40 percent above their base pay of $14,800. Built-in overtime is standard for most of the Authority's 33,000 employees and explains why the Authority's overtime bill was $54.7 million in 1976-77—more than was spent by all mayoral agencies combined—and more than half the cost of the new 2-year contract negotiated by the transit workers in April 1978. This built-in overtime is used to determine vacation pay and pensions, which is why most transit pensions exceed 120 percent of the employee's base salary for his final year. The Authority's new contract with its workers, megotiated on April 1, 1978, allows the hiring of up to 200 part-timers, but since they are prohibited from performing the tasks of full-timers the ban on part-timers continues.

The city follows what's called "minimum manning" practices in the sanitation, police and fire departments. All sanitation pickup trucks must carry 3 men, though most cities and private carters use 2, sometimes 1. The city would like to employ 2 men in less dense residential areas—in effect, expanding the work force—but the union won't permit it. Most cities use 1-man patrol cars in low-crime districts. For years, the city required 2, and is only now gingerly experimenting with 1-man cars. The fire department once had a contract requiring 5 men to a fire engine company and 6 to a truck company. An arbitrator recently waived that requirement, reducing the number to 4 and 5, respectively. However, because of "minimum manning," if 1 man is absent the department is required to pay overtime to a fireman from the previous shift. "The number of men on a truck doesn't matter," says Commissioner Russo. "What matters is the number of men at a fire." In proposing the elimination of minimum manning, the Koch administration said the city could save $45 million in reduced overtime over 2 years.

The firemen's contract contains what is called a "mutual," allowing some firefighters to commute to work but once a week. Instituted some years ago to "boost morale," a "mutual" permits a fireman to work at least a 9-hour tour of duty for a friend who wants to take off. The friend has 15 days to return the favor. Since firemen have living quarters in the firehouse, by exchanging several "mutuals" a fireman can compress his work week into three consecutive exhausting days. Thus a fair number of firemen moonlight on a second job—and, fatigued, risk their own and the public's lives.

Many "managers" hold "seldom-show" jobs. The Board of Water Supply sports two commissioners at $20,000 and a chairman who earns $25,000. Each is rewarded a limousine for this lifetime appointment. Yet each is required to attend but one meeting a week and is permitted a full-time job outside government.* The City Council retains a huge staff, including people who make guest appearances to collect checks. Gerald Esposito, a former Bronx Democratic district leader, receives $18,700 for part-time work on "special research projects"; Murray Lewinter, secretary to the Bronx Democratic organization, garners $31,975 to "supervise" the Council's staff. Two councilmen, Eugene Mastropieri and Theodore Silverman, employ their wives under their maiden names. A 1977 audit by Comptroller Goldin spotlighted physicians paid with city funds who signed in but did not show up for work. In one hospital, Bellevue, taxpayers were cheated out of $8 million an-

---

* The state legislature, at Mayor Koch's urging, abolished the 3 commissioners in mid-1978.

nually by doctors who "were not on the job when they were supposed to be." Supreme Court judges, a study by the Economic Development Council found, often did not work a full day. They averaged but 3½ hours a day on the bench hearing felony cases. Supreme Court judges working a full day, they concluded, would equal 3 dozen new courtrooms, worth $20 million.

"Summer hours"—a 30-hour week—are granted clerical and other workers in non-air-conditioned offices. This does not apply to workers hired after 1976, when their union, D.C. 37, sacrificed this benefit for all new employees.* They also sacrificed "summer hours" for all employees working in air-conditioned offices. Still, a union leader muses, "When we gave back summer hours the city couldn't account for $5 in savings. Call up your friends at 4 P.M. on a Friday in the summer and see how many you find."

Three "heat days" off are granted certain workers in non-air-conditioned settings. This benefit applies only to those who've worked at least 1 year and, usually, only when the temperature reaches 90°. In the summer of 1977, 14,000 hospital workers received either this benefit or shorter summer hours.

Employees are paid for special time off, including "administrative," "maintenance," "wash-up" and "check-cashing" time, "rest periods," "preparation periods," coffee breaks and lunch hours. Officers in the fire department daily receive a half-hour of "administrative time" to wash up and write reports. Firemen get a half-hour a day for "maintenance of personal firefighting gear." Sanitation men end their work day 15 minutes early for paid "wash-up time" and receive 2 daily "rest periods" totaling 25 minutes. Transit workers get "wash-up" and "check-cashing" time. High school and junior high school teachers receive five 45-minute "preparation periods" a week—eight if they work in the 50 percent of city schools that have a majority of "disadvantaged" students. The average academic high school teacher, according to a 1978 audit by Comptroller Goldin, spends 64 percent of his or her work day in the classroom; a vocational high school teacher, 66 percent; a junior high school teacher, 67 percent. An additional 27,000 periods of classroom instruction could be provided each week, concluded the audit, by having non-teachers perform the administrative and other "in lieu of instruction" activities currently performed by teachers. "This would have the same effect," they found, "as in-

---

* This benefit was won back by the unions in the 1978 contract negotiations.

creasing the instruction budget by 1,080 teachers, or $23.1 million." All police and housing patrolmen, plus all transit workers, enjoy a paid lunch hour each day. Sanitation men have a half-hour paid lunch. All other city workers are not paid for lunch. If police received the same half-hour as sanitation men, the city would gain 2,600,000 additional hours of police coverage a year—the equivalent of hiring 1,500 police officers.

Social service employees are excused for 480 minutes of lateness before being penalized. Commissioner Russo's office calculates that a policy of "cash docking for lateness" could save the city about $10 million.

The civil service and collective bargaining system effectively guarantees a city job as a right. Termination procedures are so difficult that employees often feel independent of their "boss." According to the city's personnel manual, "the employee attains permanent status" after a brief probationary period (usually 6 months). He or she may "be discharged only after a formal hearing," and the grievance procedure invokes 6 to 8 steps and consumes about 9 months (21 months in the federal government). If an employee is promoted and fails in the new position, it is required that "he must be restored to a position in his former title." This almost fail-safe system explains why the city demoted only 4 and fired only 235 employees for unsatisfactory performance in 1977. That's a better percentage than the federal government, which terminated 200 out of 2.9 million civil service employees (down from 226 in 1976).

Managers, or bosses, are a privileged class, almost immune from layoffs. Under civil service seniority requirements, a laid-off employee has the right to bump any non–civil service worker (provisional) or any civil service worker in their agency with less seniority. Since workers usually get to be managers by inching up the civil service ladder, they become untouchables. The city's Director of Operations, Lee Oberst, identified 3,000 surplus city managers and supervisors. If they were terminated, Oberst said in early 1978, taxpayers would save about $90 million. Yet the mayor can't fire them. Because of state civil service law and seniority requirements, workers must be laid off on the basis of seniority—last hired, first fired. Suppose, then, that in New York's Wonderland the mayor or commissioner decides to terminate an administrative manager. They probably can't. Because the administrative manager invariably inched up the seniority ladder, he or she has seniority. So the person below is bumped—a senior administrative assistant bumps an administrative associate, who bumps a supervisory clerk, who bumps a senior clerk, who bumps the most junior employee, a clerk. Result: The mayor aims to fire an incompetent or surplus boss and winds up hitting an innocent clerk. The city doesn't save the $90 million because clerks earn less than bosses. Which is why, with the exception of a few civil service managers in the Sanitation Department, no civil service managers were laid off during a 3-year period (1975–78) when 25,000 city workers were severed. "It's crazy," complains Russo. "You end up with more Chiefs than Indians."

Teachers are granted paid sabbaticals. The Board of Education unilaterally rescinded sabbaticals early in the fiscal crisis, but an arbitrator ruled that this was in violation of the teachers' union contract. The sabbatical policy once offered 70 percent pay for 1 year off after 14 years' teaching. Today, after 7 years, all teachers receive 6 months off at 60 percent of salary. In February 1978, 1,225 teachers won this benefit. The cost, according to the Board's Personnel Director, Frank Arricale, was $3 million (which does not include the cost of substitute teachers).

Secretaries who work in schools and are members of the teachers' union also receive paid sabbaticals. For the winter-spring 1978 semester, 45 secretaries were off on sabbaticals.

THE PUBLIC PAYS for these work rules in two ways. They impede productivity—reducing the delivery of city services. As we've seen, the Koch administration estimated, for instance, that if all city employees worked a forty-hour week—as federal or California state employees do—taxpayers would potentially receive 20 million extra hours of service. The public also pays because these work practices cost money.

But that's not all the public pays for. According to the Temporary Commission on City Finances, in 1976 the average annual cost of employee fringe benefits (including leave benefits) was $4,640—almost three times the average cost of other municipalities and private corporations. Municipal union consultant Jack Bigel disputes this conclusion, contending that health insurance benefits are more generous in three or four other cities and that, unlike New York, other governments often provide cost-of-living escalators in their pension plans. Comparative pay and benefit analysis among governments is primitive—the Urban Institute, in 1978, was in the process of wrestling with this monster. The nonpartisan Congressional Budget Office has said city wages were "not particularly out of line" but "what little reliable evidence there is seems to indicate that New York City provides its employees with considerably more in the way of fringe benefits—pensions, health insurance, etc.—than is offered the employees of other large cities."

In New York's Wonderland, almost $2 is spent on pensions, leave and fringe benefits for every $3 spent on salaries. These benefits include:

Pensions: After debt service, pension benefits are the largest non-service delivery item in the city's budget ($1.2 billion in fiscal 1979). Taxpayers contribute approximately 90 percent of the total cost of funding these pensions, which offer half-pay retirement after a specified period to all city employees. Workers were supposed to contribute 25 to 33 percent of the cost, but as seen in Chapter 2, special legislation (ITHP) increased the city's share while pension underfunding reduced the employees' share. Some city employees contribute less than others—transit employees hired prior to 1976 contribute nothing. Most public and private retirement plans compute retirement benefits as a percentage of the retiree's 3 to 5 highest paid years. New York does it differently, allowing employees to retire on their final year's pay—leading to overtime abuses and quickie promotions. One of management's contract demands—rejected by the Transport Workers Union in their 1978 negotiations with the Transit Authority—would have limited retirements to 120 percent of pay. New York also excuses retirees from paying city and state income taxes on their pensions. However, not all retirees have it so good. Approximately 3,000 widows of police and fire officers subsist on frozen pensions of $106.66 a month—less than $1,300 a year. Unlike many cities and states, New York does not have cost-of-living escalators built into its pensions.

Social Security: Like other employers, the city pays half the cost of its employees' Social Security contribution ($234 million in fiscal 1979).

Health Insurance: The city pays the full cost of health and hospital insurance for each employee and his or her family ($183 million in fiscal 1978). Health insurance coverage is also extended to all retirees and their families, including retirees in their forties who hold other jobs. Unlike New York, the federal and most state governments require employees to contribute half the cost.

Welfare funds: The city supplements health costs with what are called "union welfare funds" ($127 million in fiscal 1978). These are solely administered by the unions, though the city pays the full costs. Among the benefits offered: free prescription drugs, free eyeglasses and dental care for all employees and their families, free legal services, free psychiatric counseling, education and "training" reimbursement, free tax and pension counseling. Partial welfare benefits are granted to part-time employees after 6 months. The city pays between $350 and $420 per full-time employee, yet these funds are called "union welfare funds." Workers often come to believe the benefit is provided by their union, not the city.

A special annuity retirement fund is provided all uniformed employees, transit workers, and teachers (about $36 million). Beginning with sanitation men in 1967, the city agreed that for each day the employee was on the payroll—including vacation, sick leave and paid holidays up to a maximum of 261 days a year—the city would pay $1 to an interest-bearing account. When the sanitation worker retires, he can draw regular annuity payments or collect one lump sum payment of principal and interest. The sanitation union's annuity booklet advertised that a worker, after 30 years, could receive $30,750. Once sanitation workers captured this benefit, all other uniformed employees demanded and won it. In 1970—an election year—the governor and state legislature gave it to teachers. Annuity benefits extend to chiefs as well as indians, and are not always limited to $261. Certain police officials, for instance, receive more, as do teachers with at least 8 years' service (who get $400 annually) and many transit workers (who receive $500 annually).

Though Gracie Mansion is provided as a free residence, a mayor's pension base includes the $30,000 "cost" of the Mansion. This practice, begun years ago, allows a mayor to peg his pension to $90,000 rather than the $60,000 salary. When he retired in 1978, Mayor Beame was eligible for a $76,000-a-year pension. Over the years, he chose to contribute less, so his annual pension is $55,000.

Police and firemen are eligible for special tax-free pensions under the so-called "Heart Bill" (about $17 million). First passed by the state legislature in 1970, and annually since, this bill presumes that any heart disability is work-related, allowing retirement at three-quarters of the final year's salary. As an added bonus, this pension is tax-free. And one need not be disabled to receive it. The Police Department's Chief Inspector, George McManus, got a $28,465 tax-free disability pension when he retired in 1971 (he currently earns $25,000 as an executive with the National Auto Theft Bureau). Chief of Detectives Albert Seedman retired with a tax-free $25,904 pension (he currently earns $35,000 as vice president for security of Alexander's department stores). Police Commissioner Michael Codd, who left office on the final day of the Beame administration, applied for a $46,000 disability pension— $493 less than his salary. "I am suffering far greater physical limitations that I did four years ago," he told the *Daily News*, explaining that doctors discovered his heart problem when he was admitted to a hospital in September 1977. That's odd, since at the time the Commissioner said his problems were due to "exhaustion." (After it became a public issue, the Police Pension Board turned down Codd's request.)

Special tax-free disability pensions are available for all city workers. An "ordinary" disability pension is available to any city worker who is the victim of a non-work-related injury—getting hit in the head with a golf ball, for instance. Those with less than 10 years' city service can retire on one-third pay; those with more than 10 years receive half pay. A "line-of-duty" injury entitles the worker to a three-quarter pay pension. Again, one need not be disabled to qualify. August Gary Muhrcke, claiming a back injury, retired from the fire department 4 years ago. He receives a tax-free $11,822.04 pension. Yet his "disability" did not prevent him from winning the First Annual Empire State Building Runup—covering 85 flights of stairs in 12 minutes, 32 seconds. Commissioner John T. O'Hagan energetically ran the Fire Department for 5 years. Upon retiring in early 1978, he claimed a "hearing loss" disability and requested a $41,000 disability pension. (Like Codd, he was turned down.) Since 1970, according to the *News*, 55 percent of all retired police officials with the rank of captain or above received disability pensions.

Police, firemen, teachers and professors at the vast City University receive what is called "longevity" pay. Police, firemen and corrections officers get a bonus of $100 every five years. Teachers receive a bonus of $750 after 10 years and another $750 after 15.*

Certain city employees receive what are called "pay increments." These are automatic promotions, divorced from performance. Teachers, for example, receive two $500 increments a year, for a

* The teachers' bonuses were enlarged in 1978.

total of 16 over 8 years. These cost $10 million annually. (They were increased in 1978). Like other employees, they also receive cost-of-living increases of almost $1,200 annually. All uniformed employees, including sanitation men, also receive yearly increments. Police and firemen receive an increment of $2,443 after the first year, an additional $675 after the second year and $671 after the third. The Koch administration calculated a 2-year budget saving of $43 million if all increments and longevity payments could be eliminated.

Many city employees receive what is called "terminal pay." All uniformed employees and sanitation men are entitled to 1 month paid leave for every 10 years worked, prorated for those with less than 10 years. Civilian workers, after 15 years' service, are eligible for 1 month for every 10 years worked (or, like all civilians, they can choose to take 1 day's pay for each 2 sick days not taken). The Koch administration, for its 1978 labor negotiations, estimated that elimination of terminal leave would have saved $5.4 million in fiscal 1978.

Many uniformed employees receive special holiday pay, even when they don't work holidays. Commissioner Russo, an outspoken opponent of bloated benefits, complains: "An inordinate number of policemen do office work. A patrolman works from a chart, which defines the number of days he works and the number of days he's off. In addition to his salary, every year he is paid for 11 holidays— let's say $80 a day, or $880 a year—whether he works the holiday or not. The guys in the office rarely work holidays because they're not on a chart. Yet they still get extra holiday pay for 11 holidays. Thus they get paid twice for the holiday." The Koch administration calculates that taxpayers could save $10 million a year if this benefit went only to those who actually worked holidays. They also claim that holiday pay adds 4 percent to the salary of uniformed employees.

The city provides uniform allowances to those in 190 different job titles, including many who don't wear uniforms. In 1976, more than 93,000 employees received allowances of from $25 to $265. Detectives, for instance, don't wear uniforms—yet they receive annual uniform allowances of $265. Koch claimed that $700,000 a year is distributed to workers who don't wear uniforms.

Transit employees receive special "birthday pay."

Through a special arrangement, city maintenance workers receive the same prevailing wage as skilled construction workers. "If we employ a carpenter, even though he's doing maintenance, not construction, we have to pay prevailing construction wages," says Russo. Mayor Beame's Management Advisory Board recommended that this practice be terminated (Beame ignored this recommendation, as he did others). Russo says a change would allow the city to pay 25 to 40 percent less for new maintenance workers.

Sanitation men receive "out of town" work allowances for working in town. Translated: A sanitation worker receives 4 hours' extra pay, at time-and-a-half rates, if he is asked to work outside his normal sanitation district—even if asked to work in the same borough.

Sanitation men are paid overtime for 2 of the hours worked on Saturdays, though Saturday is a regular workday for many. They are also the only city employees paid double-time rates for Sunday work.

City employees who work nights are paid a special night-differential rate. This is standard in private industry. What's different is that the city defines days as nights for certain employees. For most city workers, "night" begins at 6 P.M. For transit workers, it also begins at 6 P.M., in the middle of rush hour, when they receive 10 percent more. For police and corrections workers, "night" begins at 4 P.M. For sanitation men, it can begin as early as 3 P.M. Commissioner Russo in 1977 estimated that if "night" were standardized at 6 P.M., the city would save at least $150 per uniformed worker a year.

The city also provides for pay differentials based on assignments or educational degrees. In addition to shift differentials, these cover workers in 44 city agencies and are budgeted at $53 million in fiscal 1979.

Free lunches are granted certain city employees. Corrections workers, who are not permitted to journey outside, receive free lunches. The city pays half the cost of meals for municipal hospital workers and those employed at Social Services Department institutions.

EXCESSIVE BENEFITS cost a considerable amount of money. But they generate, or represent, attitudes that may cost even more: that one is in public service not to serve but to grab as much as possible; that a government job is a right, not a privilege; that one's benefits are paid by "the city," not the taxpayers. *Me* replaces we—*me* too, *me* wants, *me* demands, it doesn't concern *me*.

We don't always see it because our attention focuses on how government looks rather than how it works. Because management is a cold abstraction, and the people who run government are too often judged by how well they run for office—by what they say, not what they do. Because we live in a self-indulgent society. And also because many of us retain vivid memories of the class conflict and abuse of an earlier era when all workers—like today's migrant workers and coal miners—were victims of callous indifference. We remember the sweat shops, the union-busting goons, the conscripted children slaving fourteen hours a day. We remember Upton Sinclair's poignant portrait of assembly line cruelty; John Steinbeck's *Grapes of Wrath*. If you grew up in a working-class home, as I did, your natural instinct is to side with the worker against the boss and robber barons, to draw lines between *the people* and the privileged few. Government was a friend, labor unions represented the people against management.

Today, government is not always a friend; is often wasteful, rigid, a tax-eating bureaucracy as immune to competition as any business monopoly. Today, public unions don't necessarily represent the public. Our world is turned upside down. What happens when management (i.e., government) and the public are one? When public unions become powerful special interests, demanding *more* when taxpayers want to pay less? Why is a falsely labeled budget or union contract not as much a consumer issue as the contents of a jar of baby food? Does the public get what it pays for? Is a union ripoff different from a landlord's? What happens when ordinary workers become a privileged class—what Milovan Djilas called the "new class"?

New York Is Not Alone

New York suffers an advanced case of self-indulgence. But the disease is contagious. Burton W. Johnson, former fire chief in the nation's capital, sprained his back at home lifting a carton of Coca-Cola. He filed for—and won—a $33,250 disability pension. In Washington, D.C., there are four "disabled" for every one regular retirement. In New York City, there are thirteen regular retirements for every one disabled. The Congress of the United States, which enjoys lecturing New York, created D.C.'s tax-free, two-thirds pay disability pension system, which Senator Thomas Eagleton calls "far and away the premier ripoff system in the United States, second to none." Congress also approved twenty-year military retirement plans, allowing 141,000 retirees to collect pensions and fat federal civilian salaries as well. Of these double-dippers, 161 earn more than the $66,000 paid members of the President's Cabinet. The head of the Social Security Administration, James B. Cardwell, "retired" in November 1977 to take a $53,000 post in private industry. At the age of fifty-five, this former guardian of the people is also drawing a $24,000 government pension; in ten years, his Social Security checks will come too, though since he was a federal employee only now does Cardwell begin contributing to this system. In 1978, eighteen members of Congress were collecting monthly disability pay from the military, and another fourteen were cashing monthly military pensions or Veterans Administration benefits.

Nassau County cops are not only better paid than New York's but receive fatter longevity bonuses—$450 after six years, $1,400 after twenty. Actors Equity members collect a $25 "meal penalty" if an afternoon's shooting exceeds six hours, even by one minute. Members of the New York Newspaper Guild receive triple pay for working holidays. Members of Congress receive free medical treatment, free prescriptions, free annual physical exams, free parking, free books, free plants, free telephone service, free use of members-only swimming pools, gyms, and steam rooms with masseurs; they enjoy bargain basement prices on haircuts and beauty shop care, eat tax-free and inexpensive meals in special dining rooms, pay no Social Security taxes and only $46.14 a month for a $60,000 life insurance policy. Newspaper and railroad union contracts provide for featherbedding—the publishers of New York's three daily newspapers precipitated a strike in 1978, complaining that their pressman union's contract forced them to employ 50 percent more workers than are needed.

Featherbedding and bloated benefits are taken in stride not just because they are more common or workers are insecure, but because the benefactors are so big that it is assumed cost is of no consequence. Unlike members of a family, a small community or a small business, people feel little responsibility toward strangers. As government, businesses, assembly lines, unions, cities and suburbs get bigger, the sense of responsibility breaks down. The work ethic erodes. People clamor for and get what they can.

The problem is widespread. Big business comes to think big government will protect them. Lockheed seeks and wins a government bailout. The airlines prefer the security of government regulation and a guaranteed market to competition. Naturally, the public pays through cost overruns and steeper fares. Just as they pay steeper consumer bills to artificially support crop prices and subsidize farmers not to farm land. Each year, Congressman Charles A. Vanik of Ohio compiles figures on the tax payments of major corporations. In 1976, seventeen major American corporations, with combined earnings of $2.6 billion, paid no U.S. income taxes. Admittedly, many of these corporations paid taxes abroad. But of the 168 companies surveyed, 41 paid to the U.S. government less than 10 percent of their worldwide earnings. The corporate tax rate prescribed by law is 48 percent—yet the average effective U.S. tax rate for all 168 companies was 13.04 percent. American Airlines, U.S. Steel, General Dynamics and Chase Manhattan Corp. paid no taxes; Exxon, just 8 percent on earnings of $7.5 billion. To pay less than 13 percent of their income in taxes, the average American family would have to earn less than $20,500. Not that beating the government on taxes is alien to John Q. Citizen. The government estimates, for example, that it loses billions in uncollected taxes from people who work off the books and comprise what they call a "subterranean economy." The state reports 5,000 New Yorkers are illegally drawing unemployment insurance—$400,000 a week—while basking in Florida's sunshine. Ten percent of all National Student Loans to New York State residents—$55 million—have not been repaid.

In March 1978, coal miners received a three-year 39 percent wage and benefit hike. The Teamsters Union reflexively demanded the same. According to the White House Council on Wage and Price Stability, since 1950 doctors' fees multiplied 80 percent faster than inflation, and in 1977 zoomed 9.3 percent, or 50 percent more than consumer prices. The pay of Edgar Griffiths, head of RCA, jumped 26 percent in 1977, to $475,000. Chairman David Rockefeller, according to a 1976 Chase prospectus, was compensated $279,168 annually (exclusive of his dividend payments) and was eligible for a $125,904 annual pension upon retirement. When he was chairman of Bendix Corporation, Treasury Secretary Michael Blumenthal received a free box at Forest Hills tennis stadium and 200 free tickets for all Notre Dame games. Johnny Carson, in addition to an annual salary of $2.5 million, receives fifteen weeks' vacation, works only three afternoons for twenty-five weeks a year, owns free RCA stock and reportedly snares a free $1 million life insurance policy. Professional sports, which is supposed to be competitive, features athletes demanding no-cut contracts. No-cut contracts already exist for most civil servants. Also for members of the New York Newspaper Guild, who, except in extreme cases, cannot be fired after fifteen years' service; or for the nation's 500,000 postal workers who have a no-layoff clause in their contract. Also for longshoremen, who last year muscled guarantees for 2,080 hours of work a year, even if there was no work. In New York, there was no work in 1977 for 3,000 longshoremen. But shipping companies were compelled to pay them up to $16,640 anyway. Of course, the cost is passed along to the consumer. Demands for lifetime job security are becoming more common. "Why should steelworkers have lifetime security?" a union official said to the *Times*. "I'll answer with another question. Why should a teacher have lifetime tenure? Why should government workers be protected for life by the Civil Service?" *Me* too.

We come to produce what the Washington *Post* aptly calls "the Gross Nothing Product." George Plimpton, a talented writer and raconteur, is paid $2,000 simply to attend a Washington cocktail party. The Commission on Federal Paperwork found that the federal government pours over $100 billion annually into paperwork, much of it make-work. Chic Parisian fashion houses merchandize their name rather than their own products. "Saint-Laurent recently drew the line at putting its label on automobile tires," deadpanned the *Post*.

Lagging productivity and mismanagement—a kind of Gross Nothing Product—knows no borders. Try talking, simultaneously, to four duplicate hotel managers when the air conditioning breaks down in Dubrovnik, Yugoslavia. Or visit downtown, where stores close all afternoon for five-hour siesta breaks.

"We still have many, too many, cases of absenteeism, latecomings and forced idleness. This is a great evil entailing the loss of millions of man-days." The speaker? Soviet party Chief Leonid Brezhnev, complaining to the 1976 Central Committee Plenum about their failure to meet the goals of the five-year plan. Communist and Socialist nations—where work is guaranteed, but often at slave pay and with strikes prohibited—have difficulty motivating workers with the promise of a line in the plant newspapers or snappy new titles such as *Shock Worker of Communist Labor*.

Chinese workers in 1977 received their first pay increase since the late fifties—one reason for their factory slowdowns and productivity woes. They, too, suffer from government monopoly. Sensing that their nonincentive system offered insufficient rewards—ours tend to offer insufficient punishment—China's post-Mao leadership is less a slave to ideology. "It doesn't matter whether a cat is black or white as long as it catches mice and is a good cat," party Vice Chairman and Deputy Prime Minister Teng Hsiao-ping has said.

As government becomes more important in our lives—directly employing 15 million people, consuming one-quarter of America's GNP—its management and work practices command attention. No, require it. Members of the Senate Appropriations Committee were shocked, for instance, when Joseph Califano, Secretary of Health, Education and Welfare, revealed that his agency employed an additional 980,217 people the Senators did not know about. The Senators were just counting the agency's 144,256 regular employees. Califano was counting, as well, all those who receive government contracts, research grants and federal salaries while working for state or local governments. "My God, we are over one million!" exclaimed Senator Ernest F. Hollings of South Carolina. Yep, and that's just for HEW. A survey by the Washington *Post* found that the federal civilian work force, alleged to be 2.9 million, is actually more than twice that when you include those supported by federal dollars. The Defense Department, as another example, has 1 million civilian employees—and another 2,050,000 "outside the walls" who receive their paychecks from Defense. Another 50 million Americans are supported by welfare, Social Security, pensions or public service job programs. Government pervades our lives. At some point, when costs are rising faster than tax receipts and productivity, the economy is retarded. Inflation runs out of control. And everyone pays.

Times have changed. During more perilous crises, the Depression and World War II, New York City policemen suffered fourteen years without a pay raise; city workers, led by fiery Fiorello LaGuardia, accepted an extension of the work week from forty to forty-eight hours. Labor Commissioner Anthony Russo well remembers the Depression. He began working for the city as a $840 a year clerk in 1935. In 1977, at the age of fifty-nine, he was eligible to retire on a pension exceeding his $47,093 salary. But this man who had risen to the top of the civil service to become the city's chief labor negotiator, who lives in a nice house in Flushing,

Queens, who was honored as Vice President of the National Public Employee Labor Relations Association, was unhappy. Gazing out the dirty windows of a cluttered downtown office overlooking the Brooklyn Bridge, Russo recalled the old days: "Working for the city has totally deteriorated. When I came in, there was a great deal of respect for authority. There were no unions. People worked hard because they felt good. It was a steady job, an opportunity for advancement. There was respect for commissioners. Everyone worked as hard as they could. Everyone was afraid of getting fired. We were residents of the city. This was our town. . . . Today, to some degree, city employees are mercenaries. They work for a wage. They fear their surroundings, for their safety. . . . Today, workers want uniformed guards and petitions. They don't want to go into the field. People spend the day here and go home to the suburbs. There's no identification with the city, no sense of mission."

This affliction, and others, are not unique to New York. But New York helps crystallize many of the questions confronting America. Can we inspire worker job satisfaction for routine jobs? How do we win consent for long-term decisions which violate the short-term interests of constituent groups? Do we know how to cope with economic decline? With resources that expand more slowly than our expectations? Will waste and inefficiency rob government of its public support? Do we know how to manage a sprawling government octopus? In this sense, the New York fiscal crisis places democracy on trial.

How do you satisfy constituent groups when there is no *more* to offer, when the money well is dry? Private industry covers higher costs by passing them on to consumers. New York, already the most heavily taxed city in the nation, cannot pass on taxes without losing more of its tax base. It cannot freely borrow. It can no longer offer *more* by hiding deficits. Like Israel, it can seek help from the U.S. government but, ultimately, it can only rely on itself. If there is an escape, it can only come from different and better management of scarce resources. To accomplish this task, four broad subjects require attention: *management, productivity, civil service,* and *collective bargaining.*

Management

Lee Oberst supposedly knows something about management. When the telephone company was in hot water with consumers in the late sixties, it summoned Oberst to become V.P. of the New York region. *Fix it*, they told the fifty-one-year-old executive. *Fix* the lousy service. *Stop* those protests and investigations. *Stop* those damn newspaper attacks.

Lee Oberst did. Relying on the street smarts of a kid from the South Bronx who didn't go by the book because he didn't go to college, Oberst knew how to fix it. He and other executives neatly divided the management problem into two parts, one dealing with reality, the other with appearance.

Appearance came first. Oberst figured that if pay phones suddenly worked, the public would notice. So he spared no effort to fix them. At the same time, he figured that if journalists were pleased with their own service, they would assume everyone else was. So he pinpointed where key editors and writers lived—mostly in Manhattan—and rushed to improve service in those selected areas. The strategy worked. The protests subsided. The phone company purchased precious time, permitting it to plan to improve its management and the public's phone service.

Since February 1977, Lee Oberst has been trying to fix the city's primitive management system. The phone company continues to pay his $120,000 salary, but he's on loan (till November 1, 1978) and serves as the city's first director of operations. From their fourteenth-floor, barracks-blue Broadway offices, across from City Hall, Oberst and a staff of thirty on-loan business executives and fifteen civil servants struggle with reality.

And the reality is pretty grim. Everyone has his favorite villains, but the chief culprit of New York's fiscal crisis is mismanagement. If previous mayors, beginning with Wagner, had not resorted to deficit financing, the city would not be crushed with $2 billion a year in debt service charges, consuming about 30 percent of all locally raised taxes. The federal government didn't force the city to agree to an unbelievable array of work rules and costly benefits. The municipal unions didn't force the hiring of political hacks to manage the city agencies. The banks didn't raise taxes.

The final report of the Temporary Commission on City Finances, issued in June, 1977, sums up the import of past mismanagement:

The City's relations with its organized employees were symptomatic of the increasingly near-sighted character of local political and managerial decision-making. Organized City workers began to make major gains at the collective bargaining table, particularly—though certainly not exclusively—in the area of retirement benefits. Because pension improvements, unlike salary increases, do not have to be funded immediately, officials were able to defer payments into the future while reaping short-term political benefits such as municipal union support in electoral politics. The more than $8 billion in unfunded pension liabilities that exist today, much of it resulting from negotiated pension improvements in the post-1965 period, represents a not-frequently mentioned form of debt that New Yorkers are carrying above and beyond the $13.4 billion that currently is owed for outstanding notes and bonds.

The growth of debt in the decade prior to 1975, particularly after 1969, also bears witness to the increasing propensity of local political decisions to reflect short term political needs rather than long-term economic needs. . . . The short-run orientation of local political decision-making also was evident in the City's tax policy. New taxes were introduced and existing taxes increased to the point where the City's taxes contributed to the wasting of another important long term asset: businesses and individuals of means who were a major source of local revenues. . . . Essential services were consciously reduced in the early 1970's when the City chose to limit its expenditures by reducing the number of police, fire, and sanitation employees rather than moderating salary and other benefit increases. . . . In short, the City's political management was exacerbating rather than easing the City's problems. . . .

The financial implications of the City's management failures were enormous. During the 1961–1975 fiscal period, the average annual increase in labor costs was 10.65 percent. If through a combination of *slightly* better collective bargaining and *slightly* more efficient management, the City somehow had been able to hold the average annual increase in labor costs to just *one-half* of *one percent less* than actually occurred, the City would have saved $1.9 billion cumulatively.

The city's management, while improved since 1975, was by its own testimony pretty primitive in 1975. A Productivity Council report, approved by First Deputy Mayor Cavanagh, concluded, "The writers of this report consider the most crucial deterrent to effective service to be management. Adequate management—at the top as well as in the middle-level positions—is lacking in almost every City agency. . . . The staff of the Productivity Council has found that for all intents and purposes middle-level management does not exist."

One reason it didn't exist is because mayors carved out or gave jobs to people whose political connections exceeded their abilities. It was forever thus. Under the office of Superintendent of Streets, for instance, there were once six manure inspectors. That was in 1840. Throughout 1975, the first year of the fiscal crisis, it was an open secret that Sanitation Commissioner Robert Groh and Transportation Administrator Michael Lazar were inadequate managers, to put it kindly. Yet Groh clung to his job until September 1975, and Lazar until early 1976, because Mayor Beame felt an obligation to both—to Groh because he was backed by Donald Manes, the Queens borough president and Democratic county leader, and to Lazar because he was a major Beame fund raiser. Beame's first budget director, Melvin Lechner, was appointed budget director because Beame and Cavanagh didn't want a budget director, figuring they could handle it themselves. And also because Lechner was a nephew of Beame's longtime friend Bernard Greidinger. Lechner was a nice man, in addition to being incompetent. He was openly laughed at by reporters as he struggled to brief them on the budget. He kept his good cheer—and job—until late 1975 when the joke became public and the state and financial community pressured the Mayor to replace him. Reluctantly, Beame did—but not before lining up two city consulting contracts paying Lechner almost $60,000.

Abe Beame, like previous mayors, was loyal to his friends. Jerome Hornblass, his Addiction Services commissioner, worked for Comptroller Beame. As a rabbi, he was also a political asset in the Orthodox Jewish community. He was not considered an asset as a commissioner. His staff openly protested that he was "unstable." The federal government severed the agency's funding because it said Hornblass couldn't manage money. Finally, in March 1976, Beame announced that the agency, and Hornblass's job, would be folded into the Health Department. A year later, in March 1977, Hornblass was still commissioner. At the time, First Deputy Mayor John Zuccotti frankly told me, "I do not think Hornblass is a good manager." But Beame waited until Hornblass's name finally cleared the Bar Association screening committee. The thirty-five-year-old Hornblass was made a criminal court judge.

John Burnell, Director of the Office of Labor Relations during Beame's first three years as mayor, was thought ineffectual by everyone, probably including Beame. But he retained his post because he had a powerful friend, Harry Van Arsdale, Jr., head of the Central Labor Council. In early 1977, Beame replaced Burnell with Anthony Russo. But he did not fire him. Instead, he created a new sinecure—director of the Office of Labor Management Relations—at the same $47,093 salary. Burnell was supposed to serve as "liaison" with private sector unions.

These were just a few of the politically connected people responsible for managing the city. After discovering that the city had never prepared a detailed organization chart, Oberst said that if he had a free hand he could identify up to 3,000 excess managers and supervisors on the city payroll, at a cost of $90 million. The problem wasn't just political favoritism. Mayors also didn't know how to manage. Robert Wagner knew how to manage political conflict, to put out fires, but he had little executive experience or inclination. John Lindsay had even less. Lindsay, like Koch, was a lawyer and legislator. Beame was an accountant and auditor. Obviously, some legislators make good executives—Mayor LaGuardia and Governor Alfred E. Smith spring to mind. But that owed to luck, not training.

The problem only begins at the top. "The current system by which the City's managers are appointed is inadequate in many ways," reported Mayor Beame's Management Advisory Board in March 1977. The report, prepared under the direction of business executives, savaged the city's management. It got the sort of reception such critiques tend to get: Mayor Beame released it late one Friday afternoon, a terse press announcement stated the Mayor would appoint still another committee to study its findings. Such reports were not new. As far back as 1963, a Brookings Institution study concluded: "The Brookings staff rarely interviewed an official who indicated satisfaction with the quality of the professional, technical, or managerial personnel the City was getting." This study was ignored, as were others. By the late sixties, Mayor Lindsay was relying on outside consultants to cope with what he called "a middle-management crisis."

Administrations changed, but the management problems lingered. "The City has failed to develop a strong identity for its managers," said the Management Advisory Board. Former Deputy Mayor Edward Hamilton spoke of this when interviewed by the State Charter Revision Commission: "The problem in most governments is that the challenge to middle management is greater than other places, because they have to deal with employees over whom they don't have the usual levers—they can't fire them, they can't lower their salaries, they can't usually do much about their promotion, they can't do any of the things that a middle manager expects to use as his stock in trade. . . . Public managers on the whole have to be superb people to really motivate people in a situation like that. Despite this, middle managers in the city have virtually nothing on the other side. . . . They had no training, they had no sense of being part of a management cadre which was somehow looking over the shoulder of people who did what they did for a long time, and so forth. There is no equivalent to the key to the executive washroom; there is no recognition, no feeling of peer-group identification, none of the things that help turn a person into a manager."

One reason the management ethos is missing is that many managers identify not with the city but with the union they belong to. Of all the city's managers and supervisors, only 2,000 don't belong to a union. In the Fire Department, deputy chiefs, who earn about $40,000 and supervise three to five battalions consisting of five to twelve companies, belong to a union. In all the uniformed services, less than 100 managers don't belong to a union. In the Housing Authority, housing project managers belong to the same union as the people they are supposed to manage. In the City Comptroller's Office, the auditors of District Council 37's Health and Security Plan are members of D.C. 37. In the Offices of Labor Relations and Collective Bargaining, which are supposed to represent management and the public, only nine of ninety-two employees do not belong to a union. "In the Parks Department," complains Russo, "the only men we have who aren't union members are the borough park managers. The assistant park manager in each borough—the person responsible for discipline—belongs to Victor Gotbaum's union, District Council 37. In case of a strike, who opens the door to let in workers who want to work? Who represents us—the people? In Parks, if the borough manager tells his deputy to do something, there is a conflict. He might do it. But he also has in the back of his mind the union identification." And loyalty.

Managers not only develop conflicting loyalties, they naturally come to view the union as their source of protection, their vehicle to muscle higher salaries, their source of health and welfare benefits. The necessary adversary system between boss and worker breaks down. Union leaders concede, usually privately, that too many managers belong to unions. Publicly, union leaders are more circumscribed. They, too, must worry about the next election.

"Union leaders won't let us sensibly define who is a manager," says Jack Ukeles, former executive director of the Management Advisory Board. "Ask any private company and they'll tell you 10 to 15 percent of their employees are managers."

But it's too simplistic to blame the unions. In late 1977, many nonunionized managers were clamoring to join a union. "I don't want them," declared Victor Gotbaum, understanding both their frustrations and the city's dismal management. But Gotbaum may have no choice. For years, elected officials feared political reprisal if they raised management salaries. So they did nothing, allowing the salaries of many workers to surpass those of their boss. Managers have no grievance procedure, no weekend premiums, no increments, no night-shift differentials, no shared sense of community and management ethos. This is an invitation for bosses to seek protection by joining unions. When he assumed office, Mayor Koch courageously decided to risk the political heat and grant raises to 2,000 managers. His timing was awful, coming on the eve of citywide labor negotiations. Worse, he granted raises the way Beame cut budgets—across the board. Everyone got a raise, irrespective of whether it was deserved. Or, as Councilman Henry Stern observed, "The flat rates imposed under this plan reward the office rather than the person."

Good management requires a clear, carefully defined structure. Is the manager given authority as well as responsibility? Does he know whom to report to? To fix responsibility, Mayor Lindsay grouped agencies into a superagency structure. Commissioners complained that they lost authority. Mayor Beame promised to return power to the sixty agency heads, with each reporting directly to the mayor. This tended to confuse responsibility. Mayor Koch came in vowing to have not one preeminent first deputy but seven co-equal deputy mayors. This risks deluging the mayor with both too much authority and responsibility, forcing the mayor to mediate minor disputes and get bogged down in minutiae.

Good management requires good employee morale, something that is clearly absent. "If you're in a war," says teachers' union leader Albert Shanker, "you need a goal, a terminal point, some overall plan . . . a sense of shared sacrifice. There is poor morale because people don't know there is a plan. And they don't know there is a plan because there isn't one." That requires sensitivity and leadership, and not just from commissioners and middle managers. If New York is in a wartime-like crisis, only the chief executive can inspire people to "shared sacrifice." Only the mayor can command people's attention, define the challenges, set the goals. Only the mayor can hire and fire commissioners. Only the mayor receives a mandate from the electorate.

Good management also requires a system of measuring managers. Goaded by the Emergency Financial Control Board and the Management Advisory Board—not to mention the new City Charter passed in 1975—the city initiated a management-by-objectives program. Each agency was to commit to paper its yearly and monthly goals, and be measured by their results. This is the program Lee Oberst was asked to direct and monitor in 1977. Such a program represented a dramatic departure for government. "There were bright guys in previous administrations," says Ukeles. "Why were they not successful, and why do I believe we will be? Historically, the criterion for success in the public sector was not performance. It was not how much we're getting for how much. It was responsiveness. In other words, if I had a pothole in front of my house and I called the department and it was fixed the next day, I felt government was succeeding. There was no balance sheet." That was political management.

Bad management costs money. Comptroller Goldin has reported, for instance, that "940 dead New Yorkers are continuing to be issued Supplemental Security Income checks four or more months after their deaths" at an annual cost of $1.7 million. The Board of Education, his auditors found, spent 59 percent of its $2.8 billion budget on administration; the national average was 43 percent. The city's welfare fraud rate was 13.6 percent, compared to a national average of 8.6 percent and California's 3.5 percent. Approximately $60 million could be saved, says the State Department of Social Services, by eliminating double billing on Medicaid claims. The federal government says almost 25¢ of each Medicaid dollar is misspent due to fraud, waste or mismanagement. In early 1978, the Inspector General's office reported that the federal Department of Health, Education and Welfare misspent $6.3 to $7.4 billion—largely through waste and mismanagement—in fiscal 1977. One small federal agency, the General Services Administration, admitted to Congress that it wasted more than $100 million of its $5 billion budget. In his first four-year financial plan, Mayor Koch said "management improvements to reduce costs" would save city taxpayers $174 million in fiscal 1979, $337 million in 1980, $452 million in 1981, and $544 million in 1982. These are annual savings, and when pressed by Treasury Secretary Michael Blumenthal, Koch conceded the city could do even more.

The value of good management can be seen by comparing the police and fire departments. Both cops and firemen, for instance, receive unlimited sick days. Yet in 1977 cops were averaging 16.5 days sick and firemen only 7. Why the difference? Because, unlike Police Commissioner Codd, Fire Commissioner O'Hagan—the same man who asked for a disability pension—personally monitored the performance of his department's fourteen doctors. If reports showed they were permitting too many "sick days," the good doctors were summoned to the Commissioner's office. "He's not loved," said Oberst. "But, boy, is he good." If all commissioners were as demanding, he said, the city could save $30 million in reduced absenteeism and overtime costs.

Good management could also help to save neighborhoods. After the blackout looting in Bushwick, I visited Bushwick Avenue in Brooklyn. A solid row of attached wooden houses, with neat gardens in front, stretched for a whole block. Except for three burned-out hulks on the corner. This was a black working-class block, and worried members of the Granite Block Association complained that despite their fervent protests the hulks remained. They could get no one in the city government to tear them down or cement them shut. Neglected, they remained invitations to arson. In a flash, their dream of owning a home could vanish. Because the city did not act, members stayed home from work, took turns patrolling their block night and day. But how long would they persist before deciding, as so many others had, to flee Bushwick?

Good management is critical to the city's economic development efforts and its hopes of squeezing savings to close budget gaps and provide raises for workers. Businesses and people look not just at city taxes but at its schools and sanitation and other services before deciding whether to move. "I agree with the unions," declares Oberst—thinking of the 3,426,000 tons of garbage to be collected, the 6,000 miles of city streets to be policed and repaired, the 437,600 yearly false fire alarms, the 395,000 housing code violations. "The biggest problem we have is bad management. A good manager sets standards. If you play golf, par is a standard. If you have no standard, you don't tax people to the limit of what they're capable of doing."

But Oberst has few illusions. He is a very neat man—three times in the course of a two-hour interview, he got up and walked the length of his gym-size office to discard, first, an empty pack of cigarettes, then a mint wrapper, then a Styrofoam coffee cup. Democratic government is never as neat. "My greatest frustration," says this round-faced executive who looks like a construction worker, "is the inability to make things happen as fast in government as in industry. Business is much more autocratic. The President asks you to jump and you say, 'How high?' Government is much more democratic. There are so many constituents. There are 100 bureaucracies issuing orders in the federal government. The state has fifty bureaucracies. Then there's the City Council, the State Legislature, the Board of Estimate, fifty-nine community planning boards—each constituency must be served."

Managing a business and a government, the late Wallace Sayre, coauthor of *Governing New York City*, observed, "are alike in all unimportant respects." Were they alike, there are limits to how far good management can take you. Even a good captain on the *Titanic* could not have kept the decks dry. But perhaps the captain could have steered clear of the iceberg.

Productivity

A business measures its success (or failure) by the bottom line— profits. A politician measures success by winning elections. The attempt to find a comparable bottom line by which to measure a government's efficiency (or inefficiency) in delivering services is what productivity is supposed to mean. But productivity is a word of many meanings and nuances. In February 1977, for instance, Abe Beame didn't seem to agree with Abe Beame about what productivity meant.

The city's first biannual management report carried a signed introduction from the Mayor proclaiming, "In the next fiscal year it will be possible to deliver *better* [emphasis added] services at lower costs." Yet page 1 of the same report reads, "The basic management goal for the City of New York is to *maintain* [emphasis added] the quality and quantity of essential municipal services." District Council 37's research director, Alan Viani, said the Beame administration was confused: "Productivity could mean savings. It could mean better quality work. It could mean increased revenues. It could mean decreased staff over a period of time. The current productivity program gives no credit for improving service. They're looking for dollars. They're not dealing with productivity. They're dealing with savings."

At first, there was a sharp difference between the city's and the Emergency Financial Control Board's definition of productivity. The city's 1976 agreement with the municipal unions provided new cost-of-living pay adjustments, called COLA II, if funded by productivity savings. The unions objected, saying productivity was often impossible to measure. "I teach a course on it," said labor leader Victor Gotbaum, "and I can't define it." The city agreed, and prodded the Control Board to amend its COLA policy to allow funding from one of three sources: "productivity," "other savings" or "other revenues." The Board relented, permitting cost-of-living increases when the city corralled new state or federal aid, or cut the budget. In March 30, 1978, when I asked Basil Paterson, Koch's Deputy Mayor for Labor Relations, to define productivity, he responded, "In the fiscal four-year plan that's been projected by this administration, you're talking about a 10 percent attrition rate. . . . That is increased productivity." By that definition, if the city encouraged its entire work force to retire or resign, there would be improved productivity.

The city's definition of productivity was—and is—both confused and political. Strictly speaking, productivity is improved, says Raymond Horton, former staff director of the Temporary Commission, if one of three conditions is met: (1) services are increased while costs are held level; (2) services are maintained while costs are reduced; (3) services are increased while costs decline.

The city, however, devised its own definition, increasing costs while simultaneously decreasing services. Though the city said it decreased its work force by 61,000 or just over 22 percent in the first three years of the fiscal crisis, its total labor costs decreased by only less than 1 percent. Fewer workers were earning more money and providing fewer services. The city's budget continued to expand, admittedly more slowly than in the past. The workers got more money. City officials got peace and continued cooperation. The public got reduced services.

Former First Deputy Mayor John Zuccotti, in March 1977, defended the city's efforts. "First, we have introduced—and we haven't invented the wheel—a systematic approach that allows an ongoing review of an agency's performance," he said, pacing to and fro across his City Hall office. "We have been able to minimize reductions in personnel in the delivery of services." He ticked off areas in which he felt the city received improved services: the Fire Department had a 25 percent greater work load and 2,500 fewer men—yet maintained the same level of service. (A spokesman for the Department said the Commissioner refused to claim the same level of services, preferring to say service was "adequate.") "And take the police," said Zuccotti. "They're down 6,000 cops—yet this year there are more men on patrol than in the previous year." Day care: "We have defunded seventy-five day-care centers—yet we are serving roughly the same number of children."

Few deny that the city had improved its management. But the degree of progress depends on where one is standing. If you were John Zuccotti, a talented, hard-driving man struggling to push the rock 200 feet, 20 feet of progress was reason to be grateful—particularly since you knew the obstacles only too well, especially the five-foot two-inch obstacle in the adjoining office. But for someone with a greater distance, the emphasis would probably be on the 180 feet remaining. Take Zuccotti's police illustration. Granted, the city was doing better—but compared with what? In the spring of 1977, the city employed 25,355 police. Mayoral candidate Ed Koch charged that there was only an average of 1,500 patrol officers on the street during each of a day's three shifts. Commissioner Codd disputed Koch, asserting that each shift averaged 2,100 officers. If you accept Codd's figures, only one-quarter (6,436) of the force was on patrol on any given day. By August 1977, the Department reported that the daily average was down to 6,049—842 fewer than the Department's management plan called for.

"There is yet no measure of what each department should be doing," complained a former Lindsay administration official who worked for Beame in 1977. The city's productivity program measures the total tonnage of garbage collected, says former Sanitation Commissioner Martin Lang, "but what counts is the per-man tonnage." What also counts is whether the streets are clean. The Productivity Council offered one grievous example of the city's propensity to quantify rather than qualify results: the Office of Code Enforcement, they found, claimed its productivity improved because building inspections per inspector were up from six to eight per day. "Yet the statistic itself is meaningless—the question is what happens as a result of these inspections? Is there a follow-up visit to see if violations have been corrected? If they have not been attended to, is the landlord properly punished? When a landlord cannot immediately be located, are efforts made to track him down? In other words, how many of the inspectorial visits actually result in building improvements?"

There are other obstacles facing the city's productivity efforts, some self-imposed, others inherent. To win peace and forge a partnership with its municipal unions, the Beame administration agreed to forgo selective layoffs and substitute a policy of encouraging people to retire early (attrition). The city and unions were implicitly agreeing the work force was too large but would be reduced randomly, as 25,000 earlier layoffs were randomly made on the basis of seniority—last hired, first fired. (A 1976 report by the City Commission on Human Rights revealed that this layoff policy wiped out half of all Hispanic employees and 35 percent of all black employees; 33 percent of those terminated were female, as opposed to 22 percent white males.) The city's attrition policy was "insidious," said then Parks Commissioner Martin Lang, who nevertheless presided over a declining department. "An organization that has no influx of new people is doomed. An agency can't be preserved like a fly in amber. The average age of my field force is fifty-six. All city departments must be dynamic. The Parks Department is dying."

Productivity efforts raise still other problems. The government's measure of productivity improvement may not be the same as the public's. Lang, for instance, was proud of having introduced "mobile crews" traveling from park to park to clean up, replacing stationary crews who simply remained in one park. More parks got cleaned. But the public complained they were being abandoned because they were more concerned with safety and the presence of a uniformed employee than with cleanliness.

Equipment breakdowns hinder productivity. The Sanitation Department's 1976 management plan predicted that 43 percent of their mechanical sweepers would be out of service at any one time. Actually, 52 percent were. Other unanticipated problems arise. The Medical Examiner's Office found that the attrition policy was too successful—their staff was 30 percent below budget. The Corrections Department exceeded their overtime spending goal by 24 percent, but blamed unanticipated prison riots. Some city agencies even complained that the increased paperwork required by the productivity program reduced productivity. The October 1976 Department of Consumer Affairs report apologized that its Enforcement Division had not performed as many garage and gas station inspections as planned because: "The inspectors spent an additional day in the office so that the productivity figures would be calculated and the report submitted on time."

Improved productivity also assumes worker cooperation. City officials may hatch ambitious schemes and mechanize their flow charts, but workers are not machines. They need to be motivated, to get a sense of satisfaction from their work, to maintain their morale. But workers have reason to be insecure. The job security they expected from a government job is no longer there. For the first time since the Depression, they are being asked to give back benefits won at the bargaining table. They *feel* (inaccurately) that their pay was frozen for the first three years of the fiscal crisis. They *feel* (accurately) that compared to the banks or politicians or managers, workers have born a disproportionate share of what sacrifices were made. Workers know that their pension funds are threatened if the city goes bankrupt. They *feel* the press portrays them as slothful. "Every time they read the press," says labor consultant Jack Bigel, "they see it's the city workers who are overpaid and underworked. They feel they've been held up to ridicule." It's worth noting, in this regard, that one-third of the 36,000 workers lost through attrition resigned rather than retired.

Recognizing the obstacles to productivity is not the same as saying it can't be done, as city and union leaders tend to. A 1977 audit of Martin Lang's Parks Department by State Comptroller Arthur Levitt, for example, highlights what remains to be done. Loafing by Parks employees, Levitt said, cost the city more than $18 million that year. Crews were averaging less than 50 percent of their workdays in productive efforts, routinely taking seventy-five-minute breakfast breaks, arriving at work sites ninety-five minutes late; forestry and maintenance crews were idle 61 percent of the workday; half of the supervisors were assigned to cushy desk jobs. A 50 percent Parks productivity improvement, the Comptroller said, would totally compensate for the personnel cuts imposed by the fiscal crisis. In short, a reduced work force could improve—and at least maintain—services. A similar Levitt audit of city pothole repair crews found that if they "had been fully productive, they could have filled 700,000 more potholes than the 1.2 million which the department reported it had filled" in 1977. The audit concluded that repair crews spent more than one-third of their time not filling potholes. That's the day shift. The night shifts were "unproductive" 52 percent of the time. The average age of the asphalt crewmen was fifty-seven years—a backbreaking job for a man that age.

The major impediment to productivity is not definitional; it's managerial and political. The city lacks both a managerial ethos and management know-how. And it lacks the political will, as Beame demonstrated, or political clout, as Koch was learning, to change union work rules which impede improved services. The minutes of a September 27, 1976, meeting between Deputy Mayor Zuccotti and Sanitation Commissioner Anthony Vaccarello are instructive. The city was pressing the union to allow two rather than three men to work a sanitation truck in certain districts. The union contract is silent on the subject, but the city dared not unilaterally alter a longstanding practice. The minutes simply read: "Union won't negotiate with Department on this issue. . . . Issue to be raised with Office of Labor Relations." Asked whether he had raised this issue, Labor Relations Commissioner Russo replied, "One of the things labor leaders and their people argue is that at the productivity table we should not try to get back their benefits. That, they say, must be reserved for collective bargaining. Yet when we bring it up at collective bargaining, they tell us, 'Go to hell!' "

Not to press that issue was a political decision, as Beame's stance when seeking reelection in 1977 was political. Like most incumbents, Beame boasted of the city's accomplishments, downplaying its problems. He said the city had "turned the corner" because he had "made the tough decisions." His "balanced" $14 billion budget for fiscal 1978 contained money to rehire laid-off workers, stop the attrition clock from running, keep libraries open, provide pay increases and slightly reduce taxes—though he acknowledged the next three budgets would be in the red. It would be left for the next Mayor to play Scrooge. Asked why the Mayor was halting the agreed policy of shrinking the city's work force, Deputy Mayor Zuccotti replied, "That's a good point. I would say to you there probably would have to be additional reductions in city manpower." Beame had made a political decision, and one with productivity consequences. By emphasizing what had been done rather than what remained to be done, by expanding rather than contracting the city's budget and work force, the Mayor was flashing the green light, whetting appetites, blowing an opportunity to win greater public support for change. Why should a worker or resident believe further sacrifices were required when the Mayor's actions suggested otherwise?

The new Koch administration promised to emphasize productivity. As a candidate, Koch opposed "blind attrition" and vowed to improve services. Yet as mayor he enlarged Beame's attrition program. His first management report said "nothing of the quality of performance" of city agencies, complained Queens Councilman Edward Sadowsky. It listed the number of arrests, he said, but not "how many arrests held up in court"; cited the number of square yards of streets repaved, but not the number needing repavement. Koch's four-year financial plan, unlike Beame's, called for major management improvements and savings. But it also contained this little-noticed sentence: "The citizens of New York will continue to encounter reduced services."

Civil Service

On his first full day as mayor—January 2, 1974—Abe Beame issued an executive order requiring all agency heads to select civil service aides strictly on the basis of the highest decimal-point rating on a written civil service examination. The message: there would be no favoritism in the Beame administration. The Lindsay administration's "reform"—permitting a commissioner to pick from one of the three top exam scorers—was banished. Henceforth, the mayor's written permission would be required. Beame, the career civil servant, was hailed by the civil service associations and many good-government forces. It was commonly assumed the Mayor had minimized "politics" in the selection of staff aides.

Fear of "politics" has a long tradition. The civil service system was first introduced in 1883 as a reaction against the spoils system. Washington newspapers once carried political advertisements requesting $5,000 in cash for a $1,500-a-year government job. New York political bosses involuntarily advanced the career of cartoonist Thomas Nast, who immortalized their cigar smoke, corruption, bulging wallets and stomachs. With the introduction of the civil service, government workers were given a necessary sense of security, of protection from political whim and favoritism. "My father was a barber," Arthur Tibaldi once told a reporter. "He said, 'You need security. Work for the City. You got a job for a lifetime.'" That sense of security was important to an immigrant population, and created greater government stability and professionalism.

But over the years the civil service calcified. A system designed to protect the public's interests came to protect the employee's; granting employees what, in effect, is lifetime tenure, is not the best way to keep them on their toes. The merit system became, in the words of a 1972 report from the city's administrator, "a meritless system." This 143-page report, prepared under the guidance of Deputy City Administrator E. S. Savas, went on to plead that good people could not be selected solely on the basis of a written examination (the federal civil service, for instance, permits no written exams above college entrance level). The report also said that strong municipal unions had come to duplicate the protections of the state civil service law.

The report landed on page 1, prompting Mayor Lindsay to disown it. It was bad politics to appear to side with those favoring a return to "politics" and bossism. A similar reception greeted a 1970 report from the National Civil Service League. "Many of the methods by which governments have contrived to assure merit employment and protect the service against past abuses," declared these long time advocates of civil service, "have also served to exclude many well-qualified persons, severely limit the flexibility of responsible public officials, and curtail the overall effectiveness of the public service." Consumer advocate Ralph Nader lent his voice as well. In the introduction to *The Spoiled System* by Robert Vaughn, Nader wrote of the civil service as if it were a basic consumer issue: "These vested interests include the security of tenure, the security of inevitable promotion, the security of habit, the security of sloth, and the unfettered right to stifle dissent within the ranks and block evaluation of performance from outside, whether by the public or by other governmental bodies."

People collect civil service horror stories. The city's Director of Pharmacy, the Productivity Council report said, must be drawn from the principal pharmacists' list. Yet the exam does not test administrative competence—the primary skill required in the job. The first deputy of one city department explained his current predicament: "We are stuck with an accountants' list for an entrance-level accountant which is three years old. Many people are on that list who cannot read English. We have a need for accountants, but we simply cannot use that list." He had the same problem finding auditors: "It's a different skill from accounting, so we're trying to set up a different exam for auditors from that given accountants. I'm going crazy. The Civil Service people's desire is to have the lowest possible number of exams." His desire was to find a good auditor.

His greatest frustration, moans Frank Arricale, then Personnel Director of the Board of Education, is the hiring of teachers. "The overwhelming majority of teachers, perhaps 85 or 90 percent of them, are sent at random to districts on the basis of rank order or seniority," he says. "If a district needs twenty-five teachers, the first twenty-five on the list are sent to that district. The district has no input. A mark on an exam and when you took the exam determine where and when you go. The reason behind the system is to eliminate political and racial patronage. But it takes away from the district superintendent and the principal any input into staff selection. We're wedded to a system where someone with a 98.5 score is hired ahead of someone who scored 98.4. If there were fifteen slots and one of them was for a teacher with a music background but none of the first fifteen teachers on the list had a music background, you couldn't choose a person with such a background even if that person was sixteenth on the list."

The state system's rigidity is demonstrated by the case of Joseph K., a state employee requesting anonymity. In 1975, his agency offered him a higher level supervisory position in Albany, 100 miles from where he lived and worked. It was a promotion, sort of. Joseph's salary was not raised from the $15,500 he was making because no civil service title existed for the new job. And he had to commute 200 miles a day, peeling on and off the heavy leg braces he had worn since a childhood polio attack. Still, Joseph was honored, and happy.

Then the state Civil Service Commission got in the act. Compelled as they are to follow the rules, the Commission told Joseph that he couldn't be promoted two rungs up the ladder, as his new position called for, because those on the rung just below were permitted first crack at the job. Desperate to keep Joseph, his superiors decided to reduce his promotion by one rung. Joseph was still happy. The Commission wasn't. They ruled that Joseph would have to compete in a written examination with all others at that level. If he failed to finish among the top three, he would be forced to return to his old job. It didn't matter that he was doing a good job, that his bosses were pleased with his work. The system had taken over.

"Civil Service makes it difficult for managers to perform," said Jacob Ukeles of the Management Advisory Board. "For example, we have thousands of titles in the Civil Service, so it's difficult to transfer people. The number of steps in the grievance system takes nine or more months. To manage, you need the ability to hire and fire, to redeploy, to change responsibilities. And you don't have those things." Commissioner Russo uses saltier language: "You could have the worst possible banana and still not be able to bring him up on charges."

The Mayor's Management Advisory Board, in 1977, counted more than 3,900 different Civil Service job titles, in 243 occupational groups. The federal government has only 22 occupational groups. The larger number of groups results in more rigid tests, more paperwork, more pigeonholing. If a person has the right test score, title, and group, he or she must be promoted to fill any opening—even if the manager does not think them qualified. The system takes over. Workers are reduced to titles. Salaries are pegged to titles, not performance. Promotions depend on test scores. Or seniority. Pay increments are awarded across the board, rather than individually. It is hard to reward initiative or punish failure. The system, in effect, robotizes workers into a fail-safe system. Sometimes workers feel it. So do their families. "I'm ashamed to tell the neighbors my husband works for the city," a Queens woman writes. "After twelve years, they still don't know."

The so-called "merit system" also becomes a seniority system. As further protection against "politics," civil service workers and others pushed for seniority laws. "In the police department, it took ten years to increase the number of black cops from 5 to 7.5 percent," laments Koch's Deputy Mayor for Labor Relations, Basil Paterson. "That increase was wiped out in six months by the layoffs." Why? Because state law requires that layoffs be based solely on seniority. "Look at the police and fire departments," Patterson says. "The youngest and most active and effective workers were the first to go. Merit should play a role. Opportunity should play a role."

The civil service often discriminates in another way. It requires promotion from within. Which is fine, until you consider what is within. Few blacks, Hispanics or women populate the top or middle rungs of the civil service. Only 16 percent of the jobs near the top of mayoral agencies were held by women, a late 1977 study by Karen Gerard and Mary McCormick found. In the federal government, says Alan Campbell, Chairman of the U.S. Civil Service Commission, of the top 10 percent of civil service jobs only 4 percent of these are held by minorities and 2 percent by women. Of those eligible for promotion to these top slots—grades 13, 14 and 15—less than 6 percent are minority workers or women.

These dismal numbers are partially explained by another encumbrance grafted onto the civil service system—veterans' preference. While the Bakke case and preferential treatment of blacks and other minorities aroused and polarized American opinion, the preferential treatment of veterans wins wide acclaim, or at least silence. In New York, a nondisabled veteran gets 5 percent added to his entrance exam and 2.5 percent to his promotion exam. But he may only invoke this preference once—unless there are layoffs. In the event of layoffs, a veteran gets thirty months' seniority added to his service. The federal laws are more generous. In the case of layoffs, federal employees who are veterans—including those who served in no wars—get absolute bumping privileges (as was true in New York prior to 1973). Thus a veteran with three years on the job bumps a federal worker with twenty years' service. The federal government also grants 5 percent extra on exams, even if the veteran seeks a federal position twenty-five years after completing his military service. Forty-seven states give veterans preferences, and several give preferential treatment to the relatives of veterans.

Civil service contributes to bureaucracy. "The City has two personnel systems, a Civil Service and a labor-relations system," said Mayor Beame's Management Advisory Board. "These provide total redundancy in many areas"—salary scales, employee-grievance procedures, and work rules are set by both systems. Because it is difficult to single out individuals, to judge work as opposed to test performance, the hot breath of competition is minimized. Our government system would qualify as an ideal anti-trust case if government itself did not define a monopoly.

There has recently been some movement to change the system. The amended City Charter repealed Beame's executive order, going back to Lindsay's one-in-three rule to select aides. The Beame administration consolidated some job titles (called "broadbanding"), allowing more flexibility in awarding promotions. Labor leaders say they are receptive to further changes. Albert Shanker, president of the United Federation of Teachers, says he would like to "find some method that would allow managers to proceed against incompetent people." Alan Viani, of D.C. 37, worries about "extreme" reforms but supports more broadbanding, freedom to transfer workers from one department or title to another, and lessening the reliance on written exams. President Carter made civil service reform one of his priorities and labored a modified reform bill through the Congress. Mayor Koch has denounced the system as "an outrage," and introduced legislation to loosen the civil service strait jacket.

But change comes very slowly. For almost three years, Sandy Frucher, Executive Director of the Temporary State Commission on Management and Productivity, has sought to rouse the Governor and state legislature to amend the state Civil Service law. The Commission has conducted hearings, issued mountainous studies, lobbied legislators, comforted civil service unions, wooed the press.

He might as well have been a diseased animal. His reports were quarantined, as was the truckload of reform proposals gathering dust in the Municipal Library. Trying to change the system, wails Frucher, "is like pushing a boulder up a hill." The Chairman of the U.S. Civil Service Commission, Alan Campbell, knows the feeling: "I'm not sure one can make it a sexy issue."

Collective Bargaining

The Civil Service is a toothless tiger compared to the collective bargaining system. "The City's capacity to act as an arm's length employer in bargaining with the municipal unions is not what it should be," mildly concluded the state Charter Revision Commission. The Management Advisory Board put it another way: "A Mayor's ability to relate to municipal unions as chief manager of the City is sharply limited by his need to relate to them as an *elected* official." Labor leader Victor Gotbaum, a disarmingly frank man, came closer to the truth when he said a few years ago, "We have the ability, in a sense, to elect our own boss."

Negotiations are very different in the private and public sectors. The Charter Revision Commission said a public employer differed from a private employer in at least three critical respects: (1) "the Mayor is a political animal who, in many instances, must rely on the support of powerful union forces at election time"; (2) "the City, as employer, is not subject to the same constraints of supply and demand that dictate to the private employer in negotiations"; (3) "the Mayor, because third-party forces outside his control" often arbitrate and order settlements, "cannot say 'no' in negotiations and make it stick." There are other constraints. A government does not generate profits. And a public strike—as the transit workers proved in 1966 and the bridge and toll collectors in 1971—can cripple a city.

Polls suggest public employee unions are not as popular today as they once were. They used to be able to act as a special interest and yet succeed in not being treated as one. That is changing. Their power was a major issue in the 1977 mayoral campaign and the winner, Ed Koch, was probably their most severe critic. But union power remains vast. In addition to the power to strike, they retain political clout. They can provide a treasure chest of money and manpower for local and state candidates, a power enhanced by the passage in 1977 of an agency shop law increasing their dues. Their raw political power was visible in the 1976 Albany fight over the Stavisky-Goodman bill. Though most state legislators privately believed that this bill—ordering the city to increase its educational expenditures—was fiscally irresponsible, they voted to override Governor Carey's veto and Mayor Beame's objections. Democrats and Republicans, liberals and conservatives, joined in the veto override. The reason: intense pressure from the United Federation of Teachers, including midnight phone calls and threats to run candidates in primaries against legislators who voted "wrong." The same muscle surfaced in early 1978 when Mayor Koch, who presumably had won a public mandate, asked the state legislature to free 3,000 more managers from union membership. The unions objected, and by early May the Koch administration could find not a single Democratic sponsor of the bill in the Democrat-controlled state assembly.

In some ways, the fiscal crisis lessens the power of the unions. They must temper their demands, worry about other audiences, including the Congress of the United States, forge a partnership with the city/state/and banks to avoid bankruptcy, perform under the glare of constant publicity. But over the first three years of the crisis they also assumed new powers as the city's chief banker. By June 1978, the municipal employee pension funds were scheduled to have invested $3.8 billion in city and MAC securities—three times the amount invested by the banks. The unions milked this power, using it as leverage in their contract negotiations—no contract, no loan. Another indication of their power is that, strictly speaking, these are not "union" pension funds. Not only did taxpayers contribute roughly 90 percent of these funds, but public officials exercise voting control over three of the five major city pension funds, a power they prefer not to advertise since they traditionally defer to union wishes. In the privacy of their offices, and on condition that they not be quoted by name, some public officials venture that it is wrong for union leaders to control city pension funds, bargaining both as employee and banker.

Municipal unions also exercise management power. Section 1173–4.3 of the New York City Collective Bargaining Law seeks to define "management rights." It has come, however, also to define union rights. The final sentence reads, "Questions concerning the practical impact that decisions on the above matters have on employees, such as questions of work load or manning, are within the scope of collective bargaining." Thus unions are free to bargain with management about almost anything. And they have. As we've seen, a plethora of work rules—including such matters as class size and maximum caseloads permitted welfare workers—are chiseled into contracts.

To change them the city must negotiate, and that raises still another problem: the city is eclipsed at the bargaining table. The city's Office of Labor Relations, for instance, had a budget in 1977 that was five times smaller than the $3.6 million taxpayers spent to release city employees to do union work. "I'm outclassed, outmanned, outgunned," complained Commissioner Russo. "They hire the best lawyers in the country to negotiate for them—firms like Phillips, Nizer or Kaye, Scholer. They can pay a fee of $400,000 for one case. We can't even hire a $25,000-a-year lawyer." To save money, in 1976 the city sacrificed 8,000 square feet of Russo's office space, including five conference rooms. "Because we have no space, we now go to the union offices to negotiate," Russo says. "It puts us at a disadvantage. The other alternative is to go to a hotel, which is very expensive. You're in their home. There have been times when Jack Bigel has threatened to throw us out."

Space is the least of Russo's woes. He concurs with the Management Advisory Board's recommendation that the number of labor bargaining units should be reduced from 122 to 10 or 12. The state bargains with only 6. "It's the biggest problem we have," he says. "Every unit tries to outdo every other." To compound the problem, non-mayoral agencies like the Board of Education and the Transit Authority traditionally bargained separately from Russo's office. Another problem is the absence of a common data base. Thus there can be no agreement between the city and its unions on how well or how badly workers are compensated. In the past, both sides performed as lawyers in a courtroom, making the best possible case, though the city's was usually the worst possible case since a couple of junior assistants did the work. Determined to correct these deficiencies, the Koch administration assigned some budget experts to Deputy Mayor Paterson and Commissioner Russo's office and began to challenge the voluminous briefs prepared by labor consultant Jack Bigel's firm, Program Planners, Inc. Koch also adopted a policy of tandem negotiations with the mayoral and non-mayoral agencies, pledging the same dollar settlement for each. When the transit workers captured a bigger than expected settlement, the Mayor retreated from this "linkage" policy, claim- ing the other unions would have to settle for less. Not unreason- ably, Victor Gotbaum called him "a bald-faced liar." By the end of the citywide negotiations, in June 1978, Koch—desperate to pro- duce a settlement to show Washington—awarded the unions more than they ever expected.

A major problem with collective bargaining is perceptual. Russo and many others begin from the assumption that the municipal unions have too much power; union leaders think they have too little. "To a great extent, the servants have become the masters," says Russo. Bigel, on the other hand, says, "I have a sense of in- equality. I sense that management has more power. It is manage- ment that determines the economic fruits for its employees. We have the right to grievance. They have the right to layoff. They have the right to determine people's lives. A union is a defensive instrument." To say that municipal unions have too much power, argues teachers' union president Shanker, is to forget the time when individual citizens or groups couldn't "sue the sovereign. In a democratic society individuals can sue the government as equals. . . . The issue is one of democratic values in a pluralistic society. In a pluralistic society workers do have the right to strike. The final answer is not the government." Shanker concedes unions are spe- cial interests—"But I don't think public officials necessarily repre- sent the public interest."

New York's fiscal crisis subjects the collective bargaining system to new tests. Traditionally, it is a trading system, a process where workers demand more and city officials, defensively, merely seek to hold down the cost of a settlement. Both sides claimed victories: unions when workers improved their economic condition; City Hall when a strike was avoided. But today there is no *more* to give. For the first time, city officials are publicly striving to regain management prerogatives and reduce fringe benefits. The rules have changed. Yet it's unclear whether the game has. Can govern- ment reconcile taxpayers' desire to pay less and receive more services, and the desire of employees to earn more and work less? Will there be strikes? Can union leaders, with an appreciation of the budget crisis, buck the legitimate thirst of their members to at least keep pace with inflation and be reelected union leaders? Does the fiscal crisis provide an opportunity to carve a new middle ground, one concerned with economic justice for citizens as well as workers? One that permits the introduction of radical changes in the delivery of services, including competition between public and private concerns, worker cooperatives or gainsharing, with savings passed on to the public and workers? Is government, which is labor-intensive, doomed to suffer costs which grow considerably faster than its productivity, setting up an inevitable clash between worker and taxpayer?

If there is a new middle ground, the Beame administration did not find it. The message implicit in his record $14 billion election-year budget was: Relax, the worst is over. The Koch administration came to office with a different message: the worst was yet to come. Yet, despite Koch's view that certain contract provisions were "outrageous" and his demand for "give-backs" at the bargaining table, a settlement was tentatively reached with the Transport Workers Union on April 1, 1978, in which the union proudly announced to its members, "We gave nothing back." This mayor, like others, decided at 3 A.M. that the cost of a devastating transit strike exceeded the approximately 9 percent cost of the new contract. In June, Koch dropped his sixty-one give-back demands and reached a proclaimed 8 percent pay settlement with the citywide Municipal Labor Committee. The Mayor said he felt compelled to settle not so much to avoid a strike as to meet Washington's demand for a settlement before Congress would take up any city loan legislation. Compared to previous settlements, these were modest. Compared to the city's proclaimed four-year budget gap, the contracts were extravagant. The city might not be able to afford the overall $1.1 billion extra cost of a two-year labor settlement for all of its workers; yet it felt it couldn't afford not to settle. At least for a while, Koch's new administration had achieved "peace in our time."

Chapter Six

Is New York Unique?

DR. SAMUEL JOHNSON, according to legend, once absconded with a housemaid for a brief holiday. Mrs. Johnson, ever vigilant, followed. As the Doctor and the maid thrashed under a coverlet, Mrs. Johnson burst into the bedroom and exclaimed, "My dear. I am surprised!"

"No, my dear," corrected her husband. "You are shocked. *I* am surprised!"

In the jockeying between New York and Washington, each side vies for the role of the shocked wife. Each claims the other is cheating. Most New York officials believe there is a national urban crisis and the city's afflictions are common and require national solutions. Many in Washington and around the country believe they are unique to New York and require local solutions. New York views itself as a bellwether city; the country views New York as a bastard child. Who is right is as important a question as whether Washington is to blame.

Is New York unique?

Governor Carey thinks not. Addressing the Congress in 1975, Carey capped his plea for seasonal loans by claiming, "I cannot deny that there is a contagion in New York which is about to sweep across the nation. Don't kill us because we are ill." A similar thought was expressed by Jack Newfield and Paul Dubrul in their book *The Abuse of Power*. It was "a myth," they say, to assume that "New York was different from other cities; it had tried to do too much for its citizens. . . . New York was the Typhoid Mary of cities. . . . If New York alone was the victim of this fiscal malady, it must be quarantined." The polar view is expressed by economist Milton Friedman, who said that "New York is a special case. New York's lavish spending reflects the most welfare state-oriented electorate in the U.S."

Who's right? To unravel this puzzle, let's isolate seven broad indicators of a city's life—its *social* and *economic characteristics, government* and *labor cost, fiscal health, debt* and *politics.*

Social Characteristics

New York's size is unique. No other American city approaches 7.5 million population (Chicago, the next largest, has about 3.5 million people). And New York's official population figures do not include its extraordinary number of illegal aliens, variously estimated at from 500,000 to 1.5 million people. New York's density is also unique. Tokyo, for instance, has more residents (11.7 million) but almost three times as much space—840 square miles—as New York. An average of 26,318 people are packed into each of New York's 300 square miles—67,000 residents per square mile in Manhattan. The average density of the rest of New York State is only 217 people per square mile. According to Thomas Muller of the Urban Institute, the average density of older cities is half that of New York (11,660), and growing American cities average but 4,000 people per square miles. Great size brings special problems. Muller has estimated, for example, that larger cities spend about twice as much per citizen to provide the same services as smaller cities. "Any city that abandons more housing in two years than the entire housing stock of Des Moines is certainly not typical," writes historian Richard Wade of New York.

Large, older cities share a common characteristic: they are losing population. Between 1970 and 1976, the nation's population expanded by 5 percent—63 percent of this increase taking place in the Sunbelt states. In that same period, New York City's population shrank by 442,000 and the Northern states by 2 million people. Central cities, according to George E. Peterson of the Urban Institute, were drained of an average of 345,000 people between 1960 and 1970; from 1960 to 1973, Cleveland, Pittsburgh, St. Louis and

Buffalo—to name a few—lost one-fifth their total populations, suffering a much steeper rate of decline than New York. The suburbanization of America continues, with older cities contributing their middle-income residents to newer city-suburbs like Houston or Greenwich.

Physically, the older cities share a common malady: their aging infrastructure is crumbling. Cursed with an abundance of pre–World War II construction and dwindling resources, New York is not the only city racing physical catastrophe. Boston's leaking water pipes result in the loss of half its fresh water; the antiquated sewers of San Francisco vomit raw sewage into its bay and in 1977 resulted in eighty overflows; a young boy drowned when Philadelphia's clogged storm sewers flooded. Unlike Dallas, aging metropolises don't own computers that pinpoint potential breakdowns of their underground pipes, wires, water mains, tunnels. Like New York, they often paint, rather than repair, their rusting bridges. Surveying the capital facilities and reduced capital expenditures of older cities, a report from the Joint Economic Committee of Congress said neglect "appears to be the single greatest problem facing our nation's cities." Years of neglect spring from a common preoccupation with short-term needs. "Out of sight, out of mind," moans Philadelphia's Water Commissioner, Carmen Guarino.

The proportion of New York households living below the national poverty standard is less than the average for declining cities, as is New York's percentage of black families. In 1974, New York ranked 6th in the percentage of welfare recipients (12.4 percent), behind Boston (16.9 percent), Baltimore (16.3 percent), Philadelphia (16.2 percent), St. Louis (15.8 percent) and Newark (14.4 percent). And New York is not alone in suffering high welfare fraud. A recent city survey concluded that in the first half of 1977 there were seven cities with greater ineligibility rates. Contrasted with New York's 8.4 percent—which seems understated—were Boston (13 percent), Washington (12.1 percent), Chicago (12 percent), Akron, Ohio (11.5 percent), Baltimore (9.7 percent), Kansas City, Missouri (9.5 percent) and Memphis (9 percent). Still, New York was considerably above the proposed federal standard of 3 percent.

The problem of too many poor people ails most older cities, and some new ones. Their economies behave less as satellites, clinging to national growth patterns, than as whirling meteors lost in space. The number of poverty families declined by 2.3 percent in the U.S. between 1970 and 1974. In that same period, the number of poor residents swelled by 8 percent in New York and by more elsewhere. The disparity between relatively rich and poor cities is spreading. George Sternlieb, director of the Center for Urban Policy Research at Rutgers University and one of America's foremost urbanologists, estimates that while the median income of New York City tenants was 8 percent below the national average in 1965, by 1975 the gap had widened to 30 percent. And New York's lagging income growth is unique. "The per capita income growth in the City," Alan Campbell and Roy Bahl of Syracuse University wrote in 1976, "is a full 10 percent lower than that in the nation's ten largest central cities. Using this disparity, the *income potential* of the City can be estimated—if per capita income in New York City had grown at the same rate as that in the ten largest cities over the 1969–73 period, it would have reached $6,254 by 1973, an amount in fact $404 higher than the actual 1973 level."

New York's declining public school enrollment is less unique. Between 1970 and 1975, its public school population slipped 3.8 percent—the smallest drop among the nation's fifteen largest cities. St. Louis and San Francisco, for instance, lost about 22 percent of their enrollment; New Orleans, 14.3 percent; Philadelphia, 10.2 percent; Los Angeles, 6.2 percent. And the flight of white pupils from the public schools is not a New York phenomenon. A survey of twenty-nine cities by Diane Ravitch of Columbia Teachers College reveals that New York's white school population decreased by 29.8 percent in eight years (1968–76). Twenty-four cities experienced sharper losses, including Atlanta (78.3 percent), Detroit (61.6 percent), San Francisco (61.5 percent), Chicago (40.4 percent). Even booming Houston lost 45.2 percent of its white school population. Though few of the twenty-nine cities have a majority non-white population, all but eight had a majority non-white school population. New York no longer calls them "Public Primary Schools for Colored Children" as they did in the 1840's, but they might as well.

New York may rank first in the perception of crime, but not in the actual incidence of crime. In the first nine months of 1977, according to the FBI's *Uniform Crime Report* statistics, eleven other cities had higher crime rates. Three growing cities—Phoenix, Denver and Dallas—were ranked 1, 2 and 3. Boston, San Francisco and Detroit had more crime per capita than did New York. The city ranked 12th in murders, 18th in forcible rape, 3rd in assaults, 21st in larceny, 2nd in robbery, 12th in home burglary. The Police Department reports that in 1977, for the first time since 1973, the number of violent crimes in New York declined. Of course, none of this news is any consolation to, say, senior citizens, who, when they brave the outdoors, clutch their handbags as if they contained uranium. Or to those who recall that in 1830 there were no murders in New York, no cases of arson, one rape, thirty-eight burglaries and four manslaughters.

There is comfort—and discomfort—in the social characteristics of New York's population. New York is not a bastard-child. It shares many of the same social problems—too many poor and too few middle-income people, spreading segregation, a worn-down infrastructure, eroding neighborhoods, slums, youth gangs, haunting fear of crime. But, one might ask, if New York is similar to other cities, why has no other major city confronted bankruptcy?

Economic Characteristics

The economic trauma of New York is on display elsewhere. The percentage of poor people is greater in the South than in the North. Even bustling Houston has a seventy-three-square-mile distress zone —half the size of Washington, D.C.—where one of four residents lives below the poverty line and one of ten lives at half the poverty level. According to David T. Stanley's 1976 monograph *Cities in Trouble*, New York is one of twelve major cities with a declining or static tax base. In 1976, three cities had higher unemployment rates —Detroit (13.1 percent), St. Louis (12.8 percent), Philadelphia (11.3 percent). New York's 11.2 percent unemployment contrasted with the U.S. average of 7.7 percent. The average for all central cities was 9.2 percent. New York's economy brightened some in 1977 and early 1978 (for the first time in eight years there was a small gain in employment). The city's unemployment rate dipped to 9.5 percent, reflecting a surging national economy. That's the good news. The bad news is that New York, from December 1976 to December 1977, ranked 1st in unemployment. Philadelphia's rate dropped from 11.3 to 7.5 percent; Detroit from 13.1 to 6.7 percent; St. Louis from 12.8 to 7.3 percent. New York benefited from national economic growth, but not nearly as much as other cities.

Being somewhat divorced from national economic growth is not new to New York or other cities. When the U.S. entered a recession in 1969, New York followed. When the nation rebounded, for a variety of reasons the city did not. It was drained of 660,000 jobs between 1969 and 1976. The nation gained 8.3 percent more jobs between 1969 and 1975, while the city lost 11 percent of its employment and most older central cities declined or failed to keep pace with the nation's growth. "If employment in New York had grown at the national rate," Campbell and Bahl's 1976 study found, "it would have 1.03 million more jobs than it now has, nearly 25 percent more." A 1977 study of Philadelphia by Sternlieb and the Rutgers Center for Urban Policy Research showed that if the City of Brotherly Love "had kept pace with the nation" between 1970 and 1975, "it would have gained more than 192,000 jobs. In this period, Philadelphia hemorrhaged 11.9 percent of its jobs.

The Northeast is the only region to suffer a net job decline between 1969 and 1975. It is commonly assumed that New York's employment woes are the same as the region's. Not true. If New York City's job growth imitated that of other Northeastern cities between 1965 and 1973, the Campbell/Bahl study found, the city would have generated 451,000 additional jobs. "Thus," the study somberly concluded, "the characteristics of the regional location and central city status explain about 60 percent of the gap between New York City's employment growth and that of the nation as a whole. Still 40 percent of the difference remains unexplained and it is this 40 percent which differentiates New York City from its region, the Northeast, and from other large central cities. To this extent, New York City's economic situation is unique." Of fifty cities studied by the Bureau of Labor Statistics, between June 1975 and June 1977, only two lost jobs—New York and Philadelphia. While New York suffered a loss of 4.4 percent of its jobs and Philadelphia 0.7 percent, Newark gained 3.4 percent, Detroit 8.5 percent, Atlanta 6.6 percent, San Francisco 4.5 percent, Washington 3.7 percent, Cleveland 3 percent, Buffalo 2.2 percent, St. Louis 1.7 percent. And the entire Northeast, though growing at one-third the rate of the next region, still gained 2.1 percent.

Why are New York and Philadelphia today so different from other aging cities? They are not, says George Sternlieb: "In a strange way, New York and Philadelphia's decline has lagged behind other older cities because of their more diverse job base and huge government expenditures. New York and Philadelphia held together better than older industrial cities. They are the rear runners, not the front runners. In the fifties and sixties, they did not lose 35 percent of their population, as places like Cleveland, St. Louis and Detroit did. So, in a sense, New York and Philadelphia were the last ones to lose. Beginning in 1970, they lost about 12 percent of their jobs and began to lose population. When you start losing population, you start losing your mom-and-pop stores and your buying power. It kind of feeds on itself." Many of those mom-and-pop stores—groceries, luncheonettes, dry-cleaning shops—don't show up on the Bureau of Labor Statistics reports because they often paid salaries off the books. Many were victims of "progress." Such major construction projects as the Cross Bronx Expressway, urban renewal, the World Trade Center in downtown Manhattan, uprooted neighborhoods and the satellite businesses that serve them. Perhaps eventually those people and businesses would have left anyway. Older cities like New York suffer from obsolescence. Small garment center lofts were designed to serve neighborhood retail haberdashers, not large discounters like J. C. Penney with more than 1,700 stores.

What was the effect of taxes, which are high in New York and Philadelphia? "Economists look at the total tax burden and say that compared to elsewhere it's not that much worse," answers Sternlieb. "But economists are schmucks. They often ignore the psychology of businessmen"—who see no end to the growth of local taxes —"and the real pocket costs to the decision-maker, who decides whether the business stays or goes. This is controversial, but why is New Hampshire growing as fast as the Sunbelt? It's a Northeastern state. It has a reactionary governor. But it also has no taxes. It's pulling jobs out of Massachusetts and Vermont." Well, does this suggest that if New York drastically reduced its taxes, it could recapture its lost economic base? "I'm afraid not," says Sternlieb. "Once you've busted the egg it's very hard to put it back together again." If that's true—and I'm not sure it is—the argument for special federal help for New York is, ironically (and tragically), strengthened as the city becomes economically weaker. Small comfort. More than likely, New York—like other older cities in the past—will continue to shrink as the nation continues to decentralize.

New York is not an exception in the attention focused on its "resurgent" downtown. Because Fortress Manhattan is alive and well, it's assumed that the rest of New York is, too. Ten years after its devastating race riots—43 killed, 5,000 left homeless, $50 million in property damage—Detroit is also said by the press and its officials to be coming back. They cite the sparkling new shopping centers, town houses and apartments that dot downtown. A modern seventy-story hotel looms over its glittering $337 million Renaissance Center complex. St. Louis has preserved the flat where Scott Joplin composed his ragtime music and persevered to witness a burst of office and hotel construction redefine its skyline. The Boston Plan, as it is called, has pooled $1 billion of private and public money to reinvigorate downtown and face-lift four neighborhoods. Baltimore imported Mies van der Rohe, I. M. Pei and Edward Durell Stone to forge a new downtown silhouette. Pittsburgh and Atlanta have almost totally modernized their central business districts.

But the plague spreads and surrounds these glittering castles. Middle-income people—black and white—continue to ooze from central cities, leaving the poor behind. Building abandonment multiplies. Tax revenues stagnate. Dependence on federal aid grows. As in New York, the national unemployment rate among urban blacks is almost twice that for whites; among black youths, it hovers between 40 and 50 percent. A September 1977 survey of twenty-five cities by the federal Housing and Urban Development agency, reported on six critical indicators of a city's economy—employment, assessed valuation of real estate, loss of population, investment, retail sales and office space. Most of the twenty-five cities, they found, continue to decline, though the erosion has slowed. In 1976, devising what they called a Hardship Index, Richard P. Nathan and Charles Adams of Brookings contrasted New York with thirty metropolitan areas and thirty central cities. Against six criteria—unemployment, dependency, education levels, income level, crowded housing and poverty—New York fared comparatively well, ranking 11th among the metropolitan areas and 29th out of the thirty central cities.

The economic decline of central cities contrasts not just with the new downtown office towers and hotels, but with national growth. According to *Fortune* magazine, non-farm employment in the U.S. increased by 14.3 percent from 1970 to 1976. In those same years, non-farm employment soared 40 percent in Arizona, 34 percent in New Mexico, 29 percent in Florida. Texas alone gained almost 1 million jobs—more than the combined growth of Michigan, Illinois, Ohio and Massachusetts. The Houston job market expands by

4 percent annually, easily providing employment opportunities for the 1,000 families who arrive each week. Since 1960, New York City has experienced the slowest growth in non-farm jobs of any major city in America. While older cities worry about too little growth, newer cities like Houston and San Diego worry about too much. Riverside, California, where a young attorney, Richard Nixon, was married thirty-eight years ago, is struggling to wall off developers and preserve what remains of its orange groves.

To raise revenues to support a more dependent population, most declining cities raised taxes. As they raised taxes, those who could afford to moved elsewhere. The result is not peculiar to New York, though it is the most extreme case. "For more than a decade," concluded Governor Carey's Special Task Force on Taxation, "New York has imposed the highest state and local taxes per capita in the United States. In 1974, the charge was $952.29 per person. This burden was 25 percent higher than the next two states, Hawaii and California, and 55 percent higher than the national average." In 1977, the Temporary Commission on City Finances released a study—*The Effects of Personal Taxes in New York City*—which found: "The average tax burden is greater for New York City residents than for residents of the fourteen next largest cities in the United States. . . . In 1974, the most recent year for which comparative data are available, per capita local taxes averaged $699 in New York City compared to $569 in Boston, the second highest tax-burden city, and $529 in San Francisco, the third highest. Chicago and Los Angeles had local per capita taxes of $213 and $212 respectively." When state taxes are factored in, they discovered, "the average per capita tax for New York City residents increases to $1,186"—a different figure from that of the Governor's Special Tax Force—"almost double the average of $632 for the other fourteen cities." In 1976, according to the U.S. Commerce Department, New York State and local per capita taxes were second to Alaska's, but that was before the Alaskan pipeline bathed that state in oil. The Empire State's taxes rose 56 percent above the U.S. average. Texas was 21 percent below the national average; Arkansas, 38 percent below.

New York's higher taxes mean higher costs. A family of four earning $50,000 a year, said the Commission, ransomed 11.1 percent of its gross income to New York City and State—three times the national average of 3.7 percent. The same family in Los Angeles paid half New York's rate (5.6 percent); in Boston, 4.4

percent; Atlanta, 4.1 percent; Chicago, 2.3 percent. The same family in Houston or Seattle paid zero. A family earning $25,000 ransomed 6.6 percent to the city and state of New York—almost three times the national average. The same family in Los Angeles paid 3 percent; in Boston, 4 percent; Atlanta, 3.1 percent; Chicago, 2.1 percent. A Houston or Seattle family paid zero. Another way to put it: a family of four earning $20,000 in Houston would need to make $27,071 to have the same disposable income in New York. Or: to take home $25,000, a New York resident would have to earn $33,676—10 percent less than the $30,651 a Connecticut or New Jersey resident would have to earn. To lug home $150,000, a city resident would need to earn $294,114, while a business executive in either of the two neighboring states would need only $251,000—20 percent less. In the face of these numbers, it requires a vivid imagination to blame the federal government for the exodus of middle- and upper-income citizens and businesses from New York. Mayor Koch's Task Force on Economic Development found, for instance, that "75% of manufacturing jobs lost between 1960 and 1976" moved not to the Sunbelt but to the tri-state area, where costs were cheaper.

It's also difficult to blame only the federal government for New York's extraordinarily high living costs. Half the excessive living costs of upper-income families here, says Herb Bienstock of the Bureau of Labor Statistics, "is attributed to higher personal income taxes." These are the people who own—and relocate—businesses. The Bureau gathers household living costs for three types of families. In late 1976, a *low-income* family's cost of living in New York was 8 percent above the national average; an *intermediate family*, 16 percent above; an *upper-income family* 25 percent above. Removing the extremes, the intermediate New York family's costs are comparable to those of a family in Boston or Newark, for example, but considerably above those of all other cities. Beginning in 1972, however, this gap began to narrow as New York's living costs have risen more slowly than the nation's.

New York City is also plagued by uniquely high energy bills. Mayor Beame's first five-year economic development plan, offered in December 1976, admitted that energy costs in New York outdistanced those in each of the twenty-three major metropolitan areas. Many New Yorkers blame Con Edison, the giant, inefficient utility company. Yet the city's plan acknowledged that 25 percent of the consumer's bill was attributable to city taxes, though even when taxes are eliminated, Con Ed's costs exceed those of neighboring areas. The city's official bond prospectus, issued in May 1977, shows how much more expensive electricity is in New York. A modest industrial firm with a maximum demand of 75 kilowatts would receive a monthly electricity bill of $1,261 from Con Ed. In Houston, the same firm would pay $455; in Los Angeles, $589; Chicago, $718. New York is also unique within its own region. The same firm would pay the Long Island Lighting Co. $766; in Stamford, Connecticut, the cost would be $756; in Greenwich, $693. A similar pattern prevails for gas prices. According to the Bureau of Labor Statistics, in 1974 the gas bill for 40 therms in the New York metropolitan area was $13.59—almost double the cost of most cities. In Detroit, the same gas costs $7.63; in Cleveland, $6.50; San Francisco, $5.63; Chicago, $7.52; Dallas, $4.31; Pittsburgh, $7.54.

New York's economic climate is also fairly special. Until recently, a succession of mayors and governors paid little heed to economic development, starving their development efforts of tools and resources. While the city reclined, the State of Alabama's development office summoned its own jet plane to fly executives south; Georgia opened development offices in Brussels, Tokyo, Toronto and São Paulo; Indiana retained the national Gallup organization to conduct surveys to determine which firms might want to relocate there. Most states and cities, unlike New York, offered businesses cheap land and tax inducements. In 1975, the city's Economic Development Administration budgeted just $7,400 for surveys and travel expenses. In 1976, New York ranked 17th in the money spent to promote tourism, its second largest industry. The city government earmarked $500,000—one-sixth Las Vegas' tourism budget.

Steep taxes don't make for a good economic climate. *Fortune* condemns Northern states for thickheadedly missing the point behind the Sunbelt's surge: "It's booming in great part because it's pro-business—and Northern cities, by and large, aren't." That's an exaggeration, but it contains the skeleton of truth. The Fantus Company, a business location consulting firm based in New York, regularly ranks the business climate of the fifty states. Using such indices as costs, taxes, regulations, tax breaks, etc., they once found that of the top ten states, seven were in the Sunbelt. The worst state: New York. An April 1977 Fantus memorandum to the Foundation committee for Economic Development in New York

City concluded, "The existing economic environment in New York City is not conducive to the creation of new jobs. . . . At this point in time, New York City cannot offer, to a prospective client, the quality and array of services available in other United States cities."

Four months later, now under contract to the city, Fantus prepared another report, suddenly discovering some of the "locational advantages" of the city: "(1) New York is the cosmopolitan metropolis of the United States; (2) Every service needed by modern, sophisticated business is readily available; and (3) Operating costs are competitive." Comparing all costs, they said a foreign firm would find it less expensive to do business in New York than in Los Angeles. The city's labor costs, for instance, are now more competitive. In 1976, according to the U.S. Department of Labor, city manufacturing workers earned less than the U.S. average. And there are other indications of New York's changing economic climate. The city is phasing out the stock transfer tax, has reduced its occupancy tax and promised to cap real-estate taxes. Governor Carey, in 1978, proposed and won agreement for a $750 million reduction in state taxes. State commerce Commissioner John Dyson, an outspoken business advocate, set aside state monies to promote tourism. The state legislature expanded the tax and land incentives local governments may offer business. The business community is much more visibly involved in the government of the city, as they have traditionally been in other cities. Ironically, the most compelling arguments against Abe Beame's reelection were made not by his opponents but by his own business or establishment–dominated commissions, particularly the Temporary commission on City Finances and his Management Advisory Board.

No doubt, New York's economy and climate are healthier as I write this in 1978 than they have been since 1969. Still, New York remains more aberrant than Big Apple bombast cares to admit. Fortress Manhattan is not New York City.

Government Costs

New York City's government is—and is not—unique. Unlike many growing cities, New York cannot replenish its tax base by annexing its wealthier suburbs. Thomas Muller of the Urban Institute finds: "Among cities experiencing population growth in the 1960's, all but four—Atlanta, Miami, Norfolk, and Yonkers, a suburb of

New York City—annexed sizable areas." And all but three of America's growing cities were located in the South or West. Thirteen of these larger cities, he found, increased their combined boundaries by 46 percent.

Where New York stands alone is in the cost of its government. Not just the total cost—the $14 billion 1978 budget surpasses all states but California—but the average cost per citizen. Quoting 1974 Census figures, the Governor's Special Task Force on Taxation said New York City spent $1,382 per person for local government. The average in the next twenty-six largest cities was $726, or almost half New York's. Neighboring Nassau County spent $330 less per person than New York. Pushing aside its uniquely high debt costs, the city spends more partly because it provides a wider range of services than any other city in America, and also because its state or county government assumes proportionately less of the city's costs, particularly for functions like welfare and Medicaid. In comparing cities, there are two types of functions to consider: *variable functions*, which include welfare, health, housing and higher education supplements, and *common functions*, which cover such basic services as police, fire, sanitation and public school education. New York, over the years, has come to define a variable as a basic service. "New York City's per capita expenditures for variable functions are far out of line compared to other large city governments in the United States," the Eighth Interim Report of the Temporary Commission on City Finances discovered. In the 1974 fiscal year, the city spent $1,076 per person for variable functions. Washington, D.C., actually spent more ($1,326), but that city has no state government to share its costs. Next came Baltimore ($584), Boston ($582) and San Francisco ($506). In sixth place was Denver, spending less than 30 percent ($298) of the New York total.

No other city enjoys its own vast City University and provided its students with free tuition. No other city offered the same poor and middle-income housing subsidies. No other city has such an extensive municipal hospital system. No other city so richly supplements its welfare and Medicaid benefits. According to the Temporary Commission, New York's per-person spending for higher education was $64—three times the $21 average of the twenty-five major cities. San Francisco, in second place, averaged half what New York spent per person for health and hospitals. New York's per-person welfare costs were $338—five times the $67 averaged by local governments in major metropolitan areas.

Many of these costs were not imposed on the city. Rather, the city elected to make them. Some, admittedly, result from the failure of New York State to assume costs that other states or counties do. Cook County assumes much of Chicago's health costs. Many states pay for local court and welfare costs. The Temporary Commission found, for example, that New York City's 25 percent share of Aid to Families with Dependent Children was unique. Ten of twelve cities surveyed paid nothing (New York City paid $270 million in 1975). The only city approaching New York's burden was New-ark, which paid just 12 percent of the cost. Only six other states require any local contribution for public assistance; only 13 require a local contribution for Medicaid. If just these two costs were assumed by the state government, the city would have saved $1 billion in 1978—almost enough to truly balance that year's budget.

New York's welfare costs are fairly unique, though not to the extent they used to be. Between 1964 and 1974, New York's welfare costs multiplied seven times, more rapidly than those of any other city. Through 1975, the city provided the most generous welfare payments in the U.S. Since July 1, 1974, the state has frozen benefits and cracked down on ineligibility. Still, in 1977, New York remained at or near the top in both the level of payments and the percentage of ineligibles, though its ranking would drop if its 8 percent higher cost of living for poor people were taken into account. New York ranked 1st in the nation in June 1977 in Aid to Families with Dependent Children, according to Florence Aitchison, Acting Assistant HEW Regional Commissioner. The state spent an average of $113 per person per month, followed closely by Alaska ($111) and Hawaii ($110). After these three states, the gap widened. The number four state was California ($97). Illinois averaged $78; New Jersey, $81; Texas, $32. The national average per person was $75—60 percent below New York's.

New York's Medicaid payments are also uniquely high. In fiscal 1976, according to Seymour Budoff of HEW's Bureau of Medicaid Assistance, New York's average payment per low-income person was $1,780—more than twice the national average ($730). The second-ranking state was Massachusetts ($1,310), which spent 36 percent less than New York. In the third major welfare category— the Supplementary Security Income (SSI) program for the aged, blind and disabled—New York ranked second. California granted the fattest benefits ($179.89 per person in February 1978). New York's $146.89 exceeded by 70 percent the national average of

$87.48. But only four states require their local governments to pick up part of these costs, and in fiscal 1978 New York City expended $81.4 million for SSI. (New York State agreed in 1978 to assume the city's share if the federal government continued countercyclical aid, but the Congress terminated the program in 1978.)

For the same functions performed by other city governments—called common functions—New York ranks high, but not as consistently high as for variable functions. For the delivery of basic housekeeping services, the Temporary Commission found that in fiscal 1974 New York ranked 4th, spending $232 per person. First was Washington, D.C. ($369), followed by Baltimore ($290) and Seattle ($245). But the Commission warned that these Census figures omitted pension costs, which are high in New York. They also noted that even without pensions New York's costs were 47 percent above the national weighted average of $159 per person.

Labor Costs

New York's labor costs are—and are not—unique. Mostly, they are confusing. There are no meaningful comparative studies. Through the early seventies, there is general agreement that the city's benefits and pay for municipal workers usually led the nation. More recently, this lead has been challenged. Like New York, Los Angeles permits its police and firemen to retire at half pay after twenty years' service (with no minimum age requirement). The federal government offers the same benefit to all military retirees. Elsewhere, this benefit—which allows a worker to retire at about age forty and get another job while receiving a fat pension—is almost unheard of. San Francisco and Chicago allow their non-uniformed employees to retire after twenty years' service (at age fifty in San Francisco, age sixty in Chicago). Few private workers can retire before age sixty-five. In New York, most civilian workers can retire after twenty-five years (at age fifty-five). But unlike federal employees and those in many cities—Chicago, Dallas, Los Angeles, San Francisco—New York employees do not have their pensions adjusted as the cost of living zooms. Like most citizens, they retire on fixed pensions.

In a *City Almanac* article in December 1977, Herb Bienstock said New York's pensions were not "seriously out of line" with those of five major cities—Chicago, Dallas, Atlanta, San Francisco and Los Angeles. His argument was cheered by city labor leaders and paraded in union-sponsored newspaper ads. Yet the two charts Bienstock produced revealed that in 1976-77 New York was the pension leader in most categories. But the disparity was not pronounced, at least in relation to these cities. Comparing New York with twelve major cities, including Chicago, Los Angeles and San Francisco, Mayor Beame's Management Advisory Board in 1977 reached a different conclusion. With rare exceptions, they found that New York "provides the highest benefit." A sixty-two-year-old city employee with thirty-three years' service, for instance, received a retirement benefit (excluding Social Security) equal to 82 percent of his final salary. This was because the city, unlike most governments or businesses, permits pensions to be calculated against the final year's pay, including overtime. In New Orleans, the Advisory Board found, the same employee would receive a pension equal to 68 percent of his final salary; in Boston, 65 percent; in New York State, 60 percent; in the federal government, 56 percent. Federal judges, however, receive 100 percent pensions. Like the retirement plans awarded by most cities and states, the pensions of all government workers in New York State are not taxed by the city or state; the federal government excuses its employees from taxes on Social Security benefits. All of this contrasts starkly with private sector employees who pay taxes and averaged only $2,204 in annual pension payments in 1976.

The amount city workers must contribute to their pensions is unusually low but not unique. The maximum any city worker contributes is 4.5 to 5 percent of salary. Firemen pay 2.5 percent; transit workers hired prior to July 1, 1976, pay nothing. Members of the U.S. military also contribute nothing. Nor do Nassau County, Long Island, police officers. However, most public employees contribute more. Federal workers pay 7 percent of salary and most private industry workers pay an even larger percentage. The federal government, unlike New York and elsewhere, pays the full cost of its employees' Social Security contribution, as it does for members of Congress. Unlike the federal government and most governments or businesses, the city pays 100 percent of the cost of its workers' health and welfare benefits.

Even if New York solves its immediate problems—closing its budget gap, regaining access to the credit market, reducing unemployment, reconstructing the South Bronx—it will be haunted by future pension obligations. In this regard, New York is not alone.

Throughout the public and private sector, unfunded pension liabilities—over $8 billion in New York City—loom just over the horizon. Like New York pols, most leaders prefer making short-term decisions, pushing the pain off to another generation. The largest single program in the federal budget—$133 billion in fiscal 1979—is for Social Security. Yet the Congress has traditionally awarded more benefits without imposing more costs. As the baby-boom children get older, and the birth rate continues to shrink, there will be more retirements and fewer people to pay the required Social Security taxes. As inflation shrinks the value of the dollar, the prospect dawns that an intolerably high burden will be placed on future taxpayers, setting the stage for a kind of class warfare—young vs. old—that America, unlike other societies, has traditionally avoided. The problem afflicts the corporate world as well. According to *Fortune* magazine, "Ten of the top 100 corporations on the Fortune 500 (in 1977) have unfunded pension liabilities equal to a third or more of their net worth, and total uncovered benefits for all corporations exceed $50 billion." In 1977, military pensions cost $8.4 billion. By the year 2000, at current rates they will jump to $34 billion. Over the next decade, a recent federal study found, pension plans covering 1.3 million people could fold, forcing the federal insurance program to make good. "The total unfunded liability of social security, military, and federal, state, and local employee pensions is about $5 trillion," reported my favorite magazine, the iconoclastic *Washington Monthly*. "At current rates, it's a debt equal to the total national budget for the next 20 years."

Comparative government salaries and fringes also invite dispute. The Temporary Commission on City Finances reported in 1977 that New York salaries were way out of line. Jack Bigel's Program Planners, Inc., countered that New York trails most large cities. Bienstock says city wages are becoming more competitive. The Congressional Budget Office claims that wages are not out of line in New York but that fringes are. Candidate Koch asserted that city wages were above comparable public and private jobs. The Office of Labor Relations prepared a report for the Mayor-elect, suggesting he was wrong. After reading it, the Mayor told me, "For my part, I don't believe it."

Confused? You should be. There has never been a comprehensive comparative study of total compensation—including overtime, pay increments, night shift differential, longevity pay, annuity payments, fringe and pension benefits, worker contributions to pensions and health and welfare and Social Security benefits. Nor has any study divided a worker's total compensation by the key measure—actual hours worked. New York municipal workers tend, for instance, to work a shorter week. Most work 35 hours, compared to 37.5 in New York State and 40 in California, the U.S. Government and the manufacturing industry. To compare the salaries of a New York fireman, who averages about 40 hours a week, and a San Diego fireman, who averages 56, is meaningless. It doesn't tell us their hourly rate of pay. Nor does it tell whether they both receive a paid lunch, paid wash-up time, coffee breaks, administrative time, cost-of-living adjustments, built-in overtime. A New York City bus driver is paid an average salary of $15,000. But he also, according to the Economic Development Council, receives at least $3,500 in built-in overtime and $6,500 in fringe benefits. On an annual basis, they found, the driver's hourly pay averaged $24,413.

The Bureau of Labor Statistics, which presumably should collect these figures, does not. Instead, they release skimpy and thus misleading data. For example, the Bureau's comparison table of twenty-five cities as of September 1976 reveals that in five city job categories New York ranked 9th in clerical pay, 7th in skilled maintenance pay, 7th in janitorial pay, 3rd in sanitation pay and 2nd in public safety. Yet the bottom of the page contains a tiny footnote bringing all these comparisons into question: "No adjustments, however, were made for differences in standard workweeks."

Nor do comparisons usually take note of New York's steeper cost of living or higher number of employees. Thomas Muller, who is preparing a comprehensive comparison of labor costs for the Urban Institute, has found that "an average declining city requires 10 percent more workers to maintain the same number of duty hours as in the average growing jurisdiction." He also found that in 1973 many larger growing cities performed the same services as declining cities—yet used half the work force. "In 1972–73," he said, "New York City spent $637 per capita for personnel; declining cities spent $240 or 71 percent more than the growing cities, which spent $141." Boston averages 8.5 cops and firemen for every 1,000 citizens; Houston, only 3.5. In their formal defense to the SEC, Mayor Beame and Comptroller Goldin's brief read, "In 1974, New York City had 517.1 employees for each 10,000 population. This compared with 140 employees for Chicago, 162.2 for Los Angeles and 434.1 for Baltimore. New York's employees statistic was greater than all the major cities surveyed." In April 1977, the federal General Accounting Office reported that New York City "has twice as many municipal workers per capita as its surrounding suburbs. . . ."

In counting employees, like computing pay, comprehensive comparative studies are nonexistent. Those that do exist fail to take into account employees doing city work but paid by some other level of government; they usually also exclude part-timers. In early 1977, for instance, I tried to pin down the number of city employees. According to the Department of Personnel, the number was 232,000. Yet when I went back to the Mayor's press office in February 1978 for a number, they came up with 296,145. The discrepancy owed to the fact that this time the city counted all mayoral and non-mayoral agencies, all capital budget employees, all city workers paid by the federal government. They did not count part-timers. Counting these, Sidney Schwartz of the Emergency Financial Control Board totaled 332,000.

The perquisites, or "perks," offered city workers are also astounding—particularly to the majority of citizens, who don't enjoy them. As we saw with pensions, the trend in public labor negotiations has been to try to hold down salaries and award "hidden" increases. It is true that few public or private workers match the vacation days, chart days off, paid holidays and personal leave days enjoyed by city cops and firemen, though cops in neighboring Nassau and Suffolk counties do. But while New York's perks are extreme, they are not unique. Members of the United Auto Workers receive up to seven and a half paid weeks off. The presidents of many corporations receive interest-free loans, the use of private jets, free medicine, free life insurance, free travel for their spouses on business trips, free limousines. Rock stars have been known to enjoy free cocaine. All of which encourages me-tooism, whetting everyone's appetite for more, driving up costs ultimately passed on to the consumer. The answer to unemployment, many labor leaders and others clamor, is shortening the work week and hiring more employees. But since they usually don't propose to reduce the pay of those who work a shorter week, labor costs would rise as productivity remains about the same. Guess who pays?

Whether New York City's labor costs are unique or comparable may be the wrong question. Whether New York can afford them is more relevant. Comparability tells us what everyone is doing, not whether it should be done.

Fiscal Health

New York is not the first city or state to confront bankruptcy. In the 1930's, 4,000 state and local governments defaulted. Today, like New York, other cities stare at expenditures expanding faster than revenues. A joint study by the National League of Cities and the U.S. Conference of Mayors in 1975 said, "The cost of running cities is now rising at an annual rate of 11 to 14 percent, but the yield of local taxes is up only 8.8 percent." Sternlieb's Philadelphia study projected a cumulative local revenue shortfall of over $400 million through 1980. Even after they made "sacrifices," Detroit budget officials pegged their fiscal 1976 deficit as $44 million, warning it would climb to $207 million by 1980. In recent years, the mayors of Cleveland, Boston, St. Louis, Buffalo, Yonkers, Chicago—to name a few—have wrestled with budget deficits. Cleveland, says Sternlieb, "is going out of business." Like New York, Cleveland and other aging cities have grown more and more dependent on federal aid to balance their budgets, more and more dependent on federal CETA (Comprehensive Employment Training Act) jobs, which now comprise 25 percent of the municipal payroll of many cities. London, Paris and Rome have huge deficits, but these are quickly closed by their national governments. Rome's annual deficit, for instance, is about $1 billion, which the Italian government closes by guaranteeing bank loans.

The city of Tokyo is also teetering. Like New York, Japan's capital lurched toward bankruptcy in early 1978. A $979 million deficit was projected. City officials pleaded with the federal government for help. The federal government responded by scolding the city for not getting its own house in order and crying wolf too often. Chastened, Tokyo's Governor-Mayor, Ryokichi Minobe, a Socialist, slashed city limousines, increased school tuition, abolished some employee pay raises, reduced hiring and sold $221 million worth of city-owned land. "We understand how hard the Tokyo government is trying right now," a spokesman for the Conservative national government told *The New York Times*, "but it is already two years too late. They should have adjusted their spending policies to their revenue realities a long time ago."

Figuratively speaking, New York's budget woes are not unique. Literally speaking, they are. No other major city matches the severity of New York's fiscal crisis. Tokyo, for example, has 60 percent more people, yet its budget in 1978 ($10.9 billion) was almost 30 percent smaller. Tokyo employs 188,000 municipal workers—almost half New York's total. And despite New York's claim that it receives insufficient federal aid, about 22 percent of its budget is tendered by the federal government. Only 10 percent of Tokyo's budget comes from the central government.

New York's budget is unusual in another way. It not only assumes costs other local governments escape, but it also *chooses* to provide more variable services. Mayor Beame and Comptroller Goldin's brief to the SEC, while striving to escape blame, demonstrates the consequences of these broad services: "The per capita cost of functions *common* to all nine cities represented only 18% of the total per capita cost of New York City government in 1972, while common functions consumed 46% of total per capita expenditures in the other nine cities." Thus: after New York has "performed the 'normal' local functions . . . it has expended only 18% of the total it ultimately must spend. Conversely, when the nation's nine other largest cities perform these common functions, they spend nearly half of all that they will be required to spend."

In his 1976 survey, David Stanley found, "Two cities, New York and Yonkers, have been *insolvent*—unable to pay debts as they mature." This contrasts with the surpluses enjoyed by many cities and forty-four states, whose tax base is more progressive and who thus capture more revenues with rising inflation. The aggregate state and local government surplus in 1977 was $14 billion. That year, tax collections by the six largest cities and counties surrounding Washington, D.C., expanded almost twice as fast as government spending. Senator Proxmire's state of Wisconsin rolled up a $437 million surplus in fiscal 1978. Michigan, like New York State, has a surplus. Texas, with no income tax, expects a $3 billion surplus in 1978. California, with high taxes, in 1977 collected $2.9 billion more than it spent and in June 1978 had a cumulative surplus of $5 billion. Aside from New York City, one of the few governments projecting a budget deficit in fiscal 1979 was the federal government—$60 billion, up from $4.8 billion in 1974.

New York's fiscal magic show has played in other cities. Mayor Poelker of St. Louis also invented the longer fiscal year. To save $4.1 million, he slipped his final 1976 payroll into fiscal 1977 and squeezed five quarters of federal revenue sharing funds into four city quarters. Buffalo "rolled over" $1.7 million of its 1975 school payroll into 1976. Cleveland played tricks with its capital budget.

In 1974, Mayor Ralph Perk, a conservative Republican, sold the city's sewers to a new regional authority for $32.2 million, using the proceeds to balance his budget. In a speech that could have been written by Wagner, Lindsay or Beame, Mayor Perk explained, "I realize this is a one-time only receipt and normally should not be used for operating expenditures. However, an examination of the city's needs currently indicate there is no way we can provide the essential city services without these proceeds. . . ." Parroting the Citizens Budget Commission, the Greater Cleveland Growth Association—the local Chamber of Commerce—warned: "Such a policy allows the City to increase its expenditures to a level which becomes increasingly difficult, if not impossible, to maintain once the funds have been spent."

Kafkaesque bookkeeping systems are common in other mismanaged cities. David Stanley describes two Cleveland State University professors who spent a decade deciphering Cleveland's bookkeeping: "The difficulties facing citizens who seek to understand the City's finances are substantial. The authors present numerous examples of potential confusion, double counting, inconsistency between financial figures, misinterpretation, as well as confusion between net and gross figures and between capital and current accounts. . . . Thus, there is no present source from which the individual citizen can secure a comprehensive and coherent picture of the City's financial position." Most city and state governments—which account for two-thirds of all government spending and 75 percent of all government employees—operate on a cash rather than accrual accounting basis. This invites budget manipulations since officials account for money only when it is spent, not obligated. Want a surplus? Governor Carey in 1978 slowed down state income tax refunds, giving him an election-year cushion. Want a deficit? Governor Malcolm Wilson pumped extra school aid into the first quarter of the state fiscal year, also an election year, leaving his successor to pay for it. There is a method to this seeming madness, which is why it is so widespread.

And yet New York has been so extreme as to qualify as unique. As Richard P. Nathan and Paul R. Dommel have written, "Most cities—New York is the major exception—have avoided relying extensively on borrowing for operating expenses." The Congressional Budget Office reached the same conclusion. New York, they said, is "the only major city that has chronically run a large current operating deficit in both good and bad economic years."

"Is New York the 'bellwether' city for America in its financial difficulties?" Terry Nichols Clark and three associates at the University of Chicago asked that question in a paper, *How Many New Yorks?* To find the answer, they monitored the fiscal temperature of fifty-one large cities and counties over eight years. Choosing twenty-nine indicators but relying on four—per capita expenditures for common functions, the ratio of local revenues to local taxable property, per capita long-term debt and per capita short-term debt —they devised what they called a Fiscal Strain Index. Using data from the fiscal 1974 period, they found that New York suffered the greatest fiscal strain. The average (mean) for all cities was 84. New York's was 165.03. Boston was in second place with a score of 128.82, followed by Newark (105.91) and San Francisco (102.97). By their measure, many older cities were quite healthy, including Chicago (55.33), Pittsburgh (48.35), Schenectady, New York (32.68), Gary, Indiana (21.21). Their answer was obvious: New York was not a bellwether. If anything, New York's fiscal strain would be worse today than when Clark took the city's temperature almost two years before the 1975 crisis.

Debt

New York's debt and credit problems are also unique. No other city is shut out of the credit market (though my mid-1978 Cleveland— "the mistake on the lake"—was threatening to join). No other city has petitioned for federal loans. No other city has such a massive debt. And no other city was burdened with so much short-term debt—over $6 billion in the spring of 1975, about 30 percent of all the short-term municipal paper sold in the country that year, up from $1.3 billion in 1970. In the spring of 1975, the city's total debt was $12.3 billion, up from $6.5 billion in 1970. This doubling of the debt contrasts with, say, the 1 percent growth in the city's debt between 1842 and 1845, when the debt reached $12.7 million. And if you count the unfunded pension liability and public authority debt, the city's true debt in 1975 was over $20 billion. In 1970, the city's annual debt service payments were $676 million. Six years later, they nearly quadrupled to $2.3 billion.

Comparing cities in 1974, Thomas Muller discovered that New York's interest payments on its long-term debt were four times greater than that of the average municipality—averaging $66 per resident, compared to $15 for all municipalities and $21 for declining cities. When contrasting total debt per person, Muller found declining cities averaged $351—59 percent more than the norm for growing cities. But New York stood alone, averaging $1,031. A federal Bureau of the Census report for 1976 suggests just how unique New York City's debt portfolio is. New York, with twice Chicago's population, had a total debt almost twelve times that of the Windy City. The Census shows that New York's $12.8 billion debt (it is now considerably higher) came to $2,080.60 for every city resident. The next city was Atlanta, averaging $1,326.23—57 percent below New York. Boston was $887.13; Los Angeles, $869.06; Philadelphia, $806.93; Baltimore, $657.91; Newark, $503.84; Chicago, $449.50; New Orleans, $444.71. Peoria, Richard Nixon's symbol of heartland America, averaged $69.02 per person.

New York's uniqueness was the reason a Treasury official was at first despondent, in early 1978, about chances of winning Congressional support for city loan guarantees. "The real problem," he said, "is that New York is the only city that needs it. Cities like Buffalo, Newark, Detroit, Pittsburgh, Youngstown and St. Louis are able to go to the market and borrow. They have truly balanced their budgets. Those cities are selling tax-free bonds at 2 percent less than if they were taxable Treasury notes." Perhaps New York's prospects would have then appeared brighter if it called itself the Republic of South Korea or some other pro-Western military dictatorship seeking a loan guarantee. Or Lockheed. But they would have initially appeared brighter if the city had, since 1975, truly balanced its budget. MAC Chairman Felix Rohatyn, Governor Carey and other prophets of doom who warn of the collapse of the bond market and of capitalism itself if New York goes broke, conveniently ignore some facts. Despite their scare rhetoric and New York's market collapse, in 1977 the municipal bond market experienced its greatest surge in history—up $44 billion in sales, or 30 percent from the year before. And unlike most cities and states, New York's debt as a percentage of revenues has risen since 1975.

Politics

The nation's largest "Dial-A-Ride" mass transportation system was inaugurated in San Jose, California, in 1974. For 25¢ a ride—10¢

for senior citizens and minors—each of the county's 1.2 million residents could telephone and receive door-to-door chauffeured service within a 200-square-mile radius. Not surprisingly, Dial-A-Ride was successful. Too successful. Six months after the inaugural, reported Robert Lindsey in *The New York Times*, the "county supervisors voted to kill the unusual mass transit system because experience had shown more than twice as many buses—and double the original budget—were necessary to make it work, and the county did not think the cost was worth it."

Imagine a similar experiment in New York. It is practically inconceivable that once in operation the Dial-A-Ride would have been terminated. Attempts to curb the buses would be greeted by outraged protests. Public officials would be condemned for making secret deals with the highway lobby. Or the oil interests. The poor and the public employees, it would be chanted, were sold out by the politicians! The issue would have been not cost but convenience, not what was affordable but what was desirable.

New York's special political culture would not have tolerated it. Why is New York different? Unlike anywhere else in America, New York is a city of renters—75 percent of its residents pay rent. Many receive housing subsidies. A homeowner usually sees a direct connection between government spending and property taxes—as California's 1978 Jarvis Amendment proved—creating popular support to hold down costs. But in New York the property tax leans on unpopular landlords and commercial interests. Residents came to believe that services were "free." They also believed that government was a friend, and it was. New York is the capital of liberal compassion and concern. New York was the entry point and the social laboratory for the country. New York is also blessed with an unusual number of Jews—about 25 percent of its population and half the country's total. The Jewish tradition stresses that government is a friend of the needy; government work, an honor; education, a necessity; compassion, a badge of virtue; voting, an obligation of citizenship. Because Jews overwhelmingly identified with the Democratic party and voted in greater numbers than any other group, until recently the liberal Jewish tradition dominated New York Democratic primaries. Since primary victories were usually tantamount to election, more conservative and numerous Catholic and Protestant voters lacked similar clout.

New York's politics were invested with a moral mission. Not only did we wish to do good, we wanted, as Irving Kristol once wrote, to *feel* good. Immediately. Questions about cost or budget limitations were often equated with the voice of right-wing reaction. *Either you want to help people or you don't.* The question was *whether*, not *how*; whether you were pro or con, good or evil. In New York, a city with four registered Democrats for every Republican, there was no two-party system to constrain the debate, no organized home owners, no coordinated business community. The press, more often than not, focused on the conflicts; on what was said, not what was done. Not surprisingly, people feared being attacked, being called heartless, reactionary, perhaps evil.

"The fundamental causes of the fiscal crisis are shared by many cities," says Donna Shalala, Assistant Secretary of HUD, whose responsibilities include urban research. "But the way New York dealt with its declining economic base was unique. Other cities had declining economic bases. They all raised taxes. They all begged the state and federal government for more money. Or they cut services. New York did all of those things, except it really didn't cut services. We pretended we did. Instead we borrowed and borrowed. That was our unique contribution to the urban crisis."

She continued: "New York has a different political philosophy about what the role of government is. When I was a kid growing up in Cleveland [where there are no Republicans on the thirty-three-member City Council], we didn't expect our garbage to be collected every day. It was, and is, good politics in other cities to have a balanced budget. It wasn't in New York. In New York, we saw the role of government as helping to redistribute income from the rich to the poor. Places like Seattle and San Francisco didn't view their city government that way. New York constantly searched for money and revenues to do the things they wanted to do." Even if it meant printing money.

No other city offered the same range of services. None had a city university bigger than most state universities, with free tuition and open enrollment.* None has a vast municipal hospital system or provides similar housing subsidies. Only one other state—Rhode Island—has a law requiring companies to pay unemployment compensation to their striking workers; if there's a strike, the affected company subsidizes it. No other city pays such high taxes. No other city was allowed to borrow so much. Few states

---

* Since the fiscal crisis, tuition has been imposed and open enrollment curtailed.

have New York's constitutional prohibition against amending employee pensions. Only nineteen offer full collective bargaining rights to public employees. Unlike most cities, New York has operated with less actual state control of its affairs, removing a potent check on fiscal abuse. In neighboring New Jersey, for instance, since 1938 a constitutional ban has forbidden local deficits and required each of the state's 558 counties and municipalities to submit detailed budget estimates to a special state agency. Borrowing is strictly limited and monitored. By law, New York budgets are supposed to be balanced, but unlike New Jersey they had not been carefully checked.

New York's labor relations have been, well, unusual. Like forty-two other states, New York prohibits strikes by public employees. However, when city employees strike, the penalty provisions in the law have rarely been invoked. Unlike Texas, New York has not treated its workers as serfs. New York has a different tradition. Labor is the good guy, the aggrieved party fighting management and bosses. John Lindsay became a hero to the country—but a leper in New York—when he proposed that the National Guard be called in to break a 1968 sanitation strike. Lindsay was forced to cave in. A similar strike in Atlanta in 1977 was handled very differently. Mayor Maynard Jackson acknowledged that fairness would dictate a rise in the average sanitation man's $7,400 salary, but the city couldn't afford it. He pleaded with the 943 sanitation workers, many of them black like their mayor, to return to work. When most refused, he fired them. "I'm not going to be the first mayor since 1937 to take us to the bank," he vowed. "Before I take the city into a deficit position, elephants will roost in the trees."

In New York, to grant teachers a pay raise in 1975, the Board of Education agreed to shorten the school week, sacrificing the children to the demands of organized teachers. New York's municipal workers in 1975 chose layoffs of less senior workers and service cuts over substantial cutbacks in benefits. Some of their members—a disproportionate number being women and minorities—were laid off so that the survivors could continue their benefits and pay increases. Neighboring Yonkers, with its own Control Board, followed New York's example. Sidney Hillman would twist in his grave, as would most true Socialists. In Pittsburgh, former Mayor Peter Flaherty promised voters he would reduce city employment, increase city services and reduce city taxes. He did. Blithely ignoring the fiscal crisis, in early 1978 New York cops demanded 22 percent raises. A few years ago, New York's 4,000-member bricklayers' union agreed to a 14 percent wage cut to save jobs and construction companies from bankruptcy. Why? I asked a major construction union leader. "The difference with my workers and city employees," he said, "is that we know that if the contractor goes under, we lose our jobs. In the city, they think their job is a right."

A perspective on New York's unusual political culture was given by Newark's Mayor Ken Gibson at a 1975 *New York Affairs* symposium. For years, people have worried aloud that New York might become another Newark. A jobless city, a poor city, a black city. Yet Newark—just sixteen miles from New York—has a balanced $220 million budget and a very tough-minded black mayor who doesn't have to prove anything. Newark doesn't have free tuition or open enrollment, extensive housing subsidies, or seventeen municipal hospitals. Gibson would like these, no doubt, but he does not confuse what he would like with what his city can afford. "I firmly believe," he told the symposium, "that the purpose of city government is to provide basic services to people. That has to start with those services that are absolutely necessary in the city and progress to another order of priority, and once you define what those basic, absolutely needed services are in the city and you go to some point where you're going to say, 'At this point we stop,' then you have to decide where you get that money to provide those basic services. There's not much beyond that. . . . Now, New York's budget is near the top when you look at any government structure in this country, about third to the federal government. You're not talking about a big city any more at that level; you're talking about a budget that is larger than most countries in the world. You have to look very carefully at what services the city should be providing, because it is still part of the state and still part of this country."

Reflecting the view prevalent in New York, Peter Salins, Chairman of the Urban Affairs Department of City University's Hunter College, challenged Gibson. The purpose of a city, he said, is not just "the maximization of the economic output of the city"; the city is "an upward mobility machine." A city has "to make sure that all of those activities that contribute to upward mobility are kept intact. Now what that means is that, in some ways, conventional housekeeping is the least important. I'm not saying that I like a city littered with garbage or a city with inadequate fire protection, but in terms of the very essence of the city's responsibilities and the ultimate well-being of its residents, some of the social services

which are considered so expendable are the least expendable."
Presumably, balanced budgets get in the way of this egalitarian
goal. The city becomes a substitute for the national government.
Business comes to be viewed as provider of taxes rather than
jobs; middle-income people have an obligation to stay—despite
reduced services—so that the poor may move upward. Whether it
works matters less than whether you try to make it work.

This philosophy, embedded deep in New York's political culture,
helped break the city's economy. But this breakdown of a political
culture has occurred elsewhere. On the other side of the social and
political scale, states such as Mississippi and Texas choose to ignore
their poor, preferring surpluses, huge profits and low taxes to people
services. Many Southern states ignore the unfair labor practices of
companies such as J. P. Stevens. New York firemen, unlike those
in Dayton, Ohio, never went on strike and watched, callously, as
buildings burned to the ground. Despite the Civil War, segregation
was legally sanctioned by many states into the 1960's. Despite
balanced budgets and labor peace, the poor and other citizens of
Chicago paid a steep price for Mayor Richard Daley's autocratic
rule. Whether in the city of Detroit, where collection boxes are
pilfered, or in the medieval village of Auletta, in southern Italy,
where the crucifix and saints in its tiny hilltop church have been
stolen, our churches are no longer shrines.

In this sense, New York is not unique but is a metaphor for the
nation and the world. Or, as former Treasury Secretary William
Simon argues in his book *A Time for Truth*, "New York is not
disconnected from America. It is America's premier city and its
intellectual headquarters. It is America in microcosm—America in
its most culturally concentrated form. The philosophy, the illusions,
the pretensions, and the rationalizations which guide New York
City are those which guide the entire country. What is happening to
New York, therefore, is overwhelmingly important to all Americans, and it is imperative that they understand it . . . [or] New
York's present must inevitably become America's future." Steep
taxes, huge deficits, burdensome debts, high energy and pension
costs, placating interest groups with public money, industries that
can no longer compete, the declining work ethic—are common
elsewhere. "I find it very unsettling these days," Felix Rohatyn
wrote in a *Business Week* guest column, "to see that many of the
same elements that led New York City close to financial catastrophe exist on the national level, and on a larger scale." Taxpayer

dissatisfaction with government waste and spending is spreading, as is resentment toward government employees and bureaucracy—not just in New York. The average pay of a federal worker in 1977—$16,936—is one-third higher than that of the average American in the private sector ($12,232).

Ironically, many national conservatives and city liberals have a stake in proving that New York is not unique. But despite the self-serving admonitions—Simon's to make a conservative point, Governor Carey's to make a case for federal aid to New York—America is different from New York. "A favorite alibi of those who have presided over the disaster of New York City government over the past decade is that 'all urban America' is in crisis," Senator Moynihan proclaims, in one of his many lucid moments. "This is not true. Indeed, it attains to the condition of a political lie. It may make us feel better to tell this lie to one another, but in the end it is mere self-deception. Our urban problems are not unique, but neither are they general. At most they are Northeastern." And, as we've seen, New York's fiscal and economic ills are more chronic than the Northeast's. "It is important to recognize," Richard P. Nathan and Paul R. Dommel state in their study *The Cities*, "that the United States does not have what can be called a 'national urban crisis.' Many large cities are well off. Moreover, most city dwellers live in suburbs or in relatively small cities. What we face, in short, is a situation in which some—though by no means all—central cities and a few large suburban cities are experiencing what can be called 'urban crisis conditions.' " The Congressional Budget Office buttresses this view. After surveying the city's unique deficits, debt and economy, their study found: "All of these peculiar aspects of New York's situation should make one pause before concluding that the city's crisis is but the forerunner of those that will occur widely elsewhere."

New York City is more unusual than its officials care to concede, and less unusual than the rest of the country enjoys believing. Nevertheless, because of the political shift of power away from older cities to the suburbs and the Sunbelt, because of the burgeoning taxpayer revolt against soaring taxes and spreading government bureaucracy, New York and other cities will likely be forced to become more self-reliant. At a time when the people of California and other states are demanding reduced state and local taxes, it defies common sense to believe they would support steeper federal taxes to help New York clean its streets or care for its poor. As long as

New York remains unusual, it will enjoy neither a substantive claim to common aid nor the political muscle to win special aid. As long as that is true, much of America will undoubtedly continue to act as "shocked" as Mrs. Johnson was when she surprised the good Doctor.

Chapter Seven

The Failure
of Democracy

ON THE SURFACE, New York is suffering a fiscal crisis. Scratch the surface and you find a deeper economic crisis. Scratch further and you discover that the fiscal and economic crises symbolize a profound political crisis. What really failed in New York was democracy.* By the mid-seventies, New York could no longer say what Wallace S. Sayre and Herbert Kaufman said in the final sentence of their 1959 classic, *Governing New York City*: "the City of New York can confidently ask: What other large American city is as democratically and as well governed?"

In New York, the natives proved incapable of self-government, and in 1975 the city was made a ward of the state. To advertise to investors that Mayor Beame now shared power, in June 1975 the state created the business-dominated Municipal Assistance Corporation to monitor Beame's budget and hold hostage certain revenues to repay investors. When that scheme failed to restore investor confidence, three months later the state imposed the Emergency Financial Control Board to hold Abe Beame himself hostage. The

* Democracy, by which I mean representative government, presupposes meaningful competition in elections; elected officials who feel accountable not just to pressure groups but to an electorate, believing there is a broader public interest that is not necessarily determined from bargaining among groups; and a public which believes its government is honestly searching for the broader public interest.

Board, composed of three nonelected businessmen (plus the governor, state comptroller, mayor and city comptroller), was granted sweeping "emergency" police powers. "The people we've been appealing to throughout this crisis," Governor Carey's Chief of Staff, David Burke, said at the time, "are not so much the voters as the investors." When the Control Board also failed to restore investor confidence, the federal government was ceded a voice in the city's governance. The unelected MAC representatives forced the transit fare to be raised 40 percent. The unelected business representatives on the Control Board vetoed city-negotiated contracts. Officials in Washington demanded the abolition of free tuition. Those in Albany compelled the Mayor to replace his closest aide, Deputy Mayor James Cavanagh, and others. Since 1975, the banks and the unions, whose investment in city paper is crucial, were granted a virtual veto power over elected city officials, reviewing their budgets and management. Ironically, democracy was abrogated in order to avoid the failure of democratic government—bankruptcy—where a nonelected judge tells elected officials what to do.

New York's democracy collapsed because New York was, paradoxically, the victim of too much—and too little—democracy: a plethora of special-interest groups combined with short-sighted politicians and a self-centered electorate. The dilemma was anticipated by the Founding Fathers. In Federalist Paper No. 10, Publius—in this essay, James Madison—urged the Constitution's ratification because, he said, the elaborate system of checks and balances would prevent any "faction" or special interest from dominating the common public interest. But Madison did not want to banish "factions." Quite the contrary. He understood that they were as necessary to the functioning of a democracy as air to breathing. "The inference to which we are brought," he wrote, "is that the *causes* of faction cannot be removed and that relief is only to be sought in the means of controlling its *effects*." The *effects* would be controlled by dividing power between the state and federal governments, between the executive, legislative and judicial branches, between a popularly elected House of Representatives and a more elitist Senate, between the right to vote and the Bill of Rights. America was to be both a democracy and a republic. And for a democratic republic to work, said Publius, elected officials need search for the broader public interest and not "sacrifice it to temporary or partial considerations."

In New York, the "factions" went unchecked. City Hall was

bombarded by what Douglas Yates of Yale has aptly called "street-fighting pluralism." Groups vied to get theirs. The party organization demanded patronage. The banks angled to sell their services for interest-free deposits, underwriting fees and extortionate interest rates. The politically connected wanted their day-care center leases; the construction unions, their public works; the builders, their permits. The municipal unions, their lavish benefits. David Rockefeller, his World Trade Center. Tenants, their rent control and subsidized middle-income housing. Blacks, their own community control; Hispanics, their bilingual education. Government did not just protect; it rewarded. Interests inevitably clashed. The federal poverty program pushed for more community participation and local politicians for more control. Cops were pitted against community forces in opposition to a Civilian Review Board. As were teachers in opposition to local school boards. Often, there was "right" on both sides. Community school boards said they wanted the freedom to choose who would educate their children, and teachers said they wanted the protection of seniority and due process. The city administration wanted to further the cause of integration in middle-class Forest Hills, and local residents wanted to protect their community from high-rise, low-income public housing. Northside, Brooklyn, demanded the retention of a firehouse, while City Hall needed to cut the budget. Co-op City residents said they couldn't afford escalating rents, and the state said it couldn't afford the mortgage payments without them. Environmentalists insisted on sulfur-free coal, which Con Edison insisted would lead to higher consumer electricity bills.

There blossomed a multiplicity of organizations dedicated to a specific goal, a specific group, a specific neighborhood. Democratic reform clubs sprang up throughout the city, weakening the ability of the dominant Democratic party to discipline disparate voices. City Hall's power to command was weakened by mushrooming state and federal aid—up from 21 percent of the city's budget in 1961 to 42 percent in 1977, with the federal share jumping from 4.5 to 20.3 percent. Public authorities—the Port Authority, Triboro Bridge and Tunnel Authority, Metropolitan Transportation Authority, Independent Board of Education, and Health and Hospitals Corporation—assumed functions formerly controlled by City Hall. Municipal unions became partners in the city's governance. Mayors were left with less control of their budgets and more demands for a piece of it. More poor people required more services.

Black power demands were followed by community and then ethnic group demands from poor Hispanics, Jews, and Italo-Americans. There surfaced community action centers, police precinct councils, neighborhood health centers, ethnic and racial groups, community planning boards, community task forces, social clubs, block associations.

While these separate voices grew, simultaneously the family, the church, the party, the government were losing their venerated status. The oversized city became a vast sea of hostile elements. The cop on the beat was now often a stranger, no longer living in the neighborhood. The white teacher and the black or Hispanic child couldn't communicate. High-rises plowed through once-stable neighborhoods. Residents in the four boroughs felt Manhattan was favored by City Hall. Blacks shrieked racism; Jews, anti-Semitism. Ugly racial differences replaced milder class conflicts. Parents admonished their kids not to go out at night, not to talk to strangers.

The city atomized, and became more depersonalized. The large supermarket replaced the corner grocer and butcher. Government competed with the family as provider. But it wasn't as if you could talk to the government. No more the party leader with the welcoming turkey or bag of coal for the new family on the block. There were too many officials, too many districts, too many names to remember. Government was a big, impersonal bureaucracy. Lots of forms and surly clerks. Strangers. It wasn't as if government's money was your money. You got what you could. That's what everybody was doing. Weren't those people on welfare doing it? Those rich people in rent-controlled housing? Those landlords with the special tax breaks? Those municipal workers and Mitchell-Lama residents and political big shots?

Size contributed to remoteness, as did television. Television brought the world into our living rooms, made the foreign familiar. Too familiar. Television was the impersonal city of the air. It helped desensitize us. Murder means less after you've watched a President's head get blown off. Vietnam became a nightly war movie. Bull Connors' vicious dogs snapping at civil rights workers were followed by regular clubbings, hosings, church bombings, shotgun murders. After a while, Vietnam and civil rights became a bore. Like last year's *I Love Lucy* show. Television was supposed to entertain. It allowed people who already feared unsafe streets to retreat to their living rooms. They did not to have to go out and meet people. They no longer sat on stoops and, in effect, policed the streets.

Television also changed politics. It permitted candidates and elected officials to speak directly to the people, to go over the heads of party and other intermediaries. But since television was expensive, candidates grew beholden not to local party bosses but to fat-cat contributors, media magicians and unions with few community ties. These new bosses were rarely neighborhood-oriented. They demanded not fixed traffic lights but zoning changes, fees, leases or public works which often transformed neighborhoods. Union leaders insisted on more spending for less work. Television allowed citizens to communicate directly. Instead of visiting or writing party or local officials, citizens learned a much more effective means of being heard. They learned how to make "news." Because the media, particularly television, often defined news as something that was new or entertaining, conflict was at a premium. Citizens came to understand that few paid attention to a civilized press conference or letter. The media paid attention when you "sat in" or dumped your garbage in front of City Hall, joined in a "stall-in" on the Grand Central Parkway, made loud threats. Citizens became actors, vying to make it on the 6:00 news. Actors became broadcasters, mindlessly vying to sharpen the conflict. Voters became fickle critics, determining the ratings.

And elected officials became trapped. Their first principle—political survival—often clashed with their good judgment. Responsiveness to constituents came to be viewed as more important than fiscal responsibility. City Hall was bombarded by demands from constituent groups, each crowding the time and attention of city officials. Mayors and their administration were constantly called upon to extinguish fires, leaving them little time to think, to plan, to exercise calm judgment. Unavoidably, policy makers' present political needs clashed with the city's long-term needs. Former city Housing Administrator Roger Starr, now a *Times* editorial writer, described one such clash: "I must plead guilty to having a sense of panic and to doing what I think all of us do in city government when we feel the ground slipping away beneath us—we do things we cannot afford, and we do them more desperately than ever." So, Starr lamented, an earlier city and state administration approved construction of a vast middle-income housing complex, Co-op City in the Bronx, siphoning middle-income residents from the Bronx's still viable Grand Concourse. And Co-op City was built without due consideration for the need of a transportation system to serve the 65,000 people who would live there. The same short-term considerations were followed in sculpting city budgets. Rather than anger groups by slicing the budget or tempering its growth, City Hall tricked its budget or borrowed. Because it could freely do so, a sense of responsibility broke down. Normal budget and borrowing constraints did not apply. Today's problems were ameliorated, interest groups appeased, by mortgaging the future. Besides, elected officials could rationalize, wasn't it their responsibility to satisfy citizens? To maintain order? To do good things, didn't they have to get reelected?

New York's leaders failed Publius' test. They worried more about the next election than the next generation. Too often, they ignored the common good, the broader public interest. But citizens also failed Publius' test. They were selfish, demanding more for *ME*. Unlike the civil rights movement, which helped legitimize direct citizen action, the goal, too frequently, was not a more just society but a bigger piece of the pie. The larger community—the future, the "dream"—was often overlooked. A neighborhood, a great city, a nation, is not just a collection of competing special interests, all clashing and vying for favor. If there is no sense of community, no shared goals or ties that bind people together, then there is no neighborhood, no city, no nation. As in Salvador Dali's poignant painting "Premonition of Civil War," a body is pulled apart.

The delicate local system of checks and balances also broke apart. Specific demands for more spending by special-interest groups were not countered and checked by a constituency demanding fiscal restraint. As the city commenced to spend more taxpayer dollars on nonbasic services—municipal hospitals, welfare supplements, housing subsidies—demands for more of these services grew. A more dependent population, naturally, came to view nonbasic services as essential. The city's budget began to tilt away from such basic services as police, fire, sanitation and public school education. Thus middle- and upper-income residents found the city less attractive. The very constituents who might have demanded fiscal restraint were fleeing to the suburbs. The city had too few homeowners—less than 25 percent—who meet mortgage payments and pay property taxes, and who might have made a connection between city spending and their taxes. The city had too many commuters, people who worked but did not have roots here. Unlike many cities—Rochester, Pittsburgh, Atlanta—New York did not have a homogeneous business community to effectively protest new business taxes or city management policies. Small businessmen quietly went out of business. Larger firms protested with their feet. The multinational and headquarter companies had other reasons to be here. Besides, they dealt with presidents, not mayors and city council members. "Service demanders," to quote Sayre and Kaufman, replaced "money providers."

Another potential check—the two-party system—also didn't work. In New York, Republicans, like the bald eagle, are an endangered species. There are four Democrats for every one Republican. In the 1977 mayoral contest, the Republican candidate got less than 5 percent of the vote. Out of forty-three members of the City Council, only five were Republicans in 1978; of the sixty-five members of the State Assembly from New York City, four were Republicans; of the twenty-six state senators, eight were Republicans. Were the number greater, it might not have mattered. There was scant ideological difference between the leaders of both parties. Governor Rockefeller, the gray eminence of state Republicans, had an alliance with Democratic Mayor Robert F. Wagner, even offering him the Republican nomination for mayor in 1973. His brother, David Rockefeller, later contributed money to Democrat Abe Beame's 1973 campaign. John Lindsay captured the mayoralty in 1965 as a Republican, but he won with less than 50 percent of the vote in a three-way race in which he was positioned as the most liberal. When such conservatives as William F. Buckley or John Marchi raised their voices to protest city spending, borrowing or tax policies, they were dismissed as loons or reactionaries. In a sense, a nonideological "permanent government," as Jack Newfield christened it, ruled in New York.

"There are classified Pentagon documents that get more press coverage than the Republican party," complained Barry Farber just days before voters sentenced his 1977 mayoral campaign to oblivion. "The disease in New York is a one-party system. Whether it exists in the Soviet Union or New York, it's a disease. I want a party of opposition, like in England and Israel, where the bony finger of indignation is thrust regularly into the face of power. Martin Luther King used to declare, 'I have a dream.' I have never heard of a higher local Republican dream than 'Let's get a judge.' " To get judges and other patronage appointments, the local Republican party often became a wholly owned subsidiary of the local Democratic party.

Whatever two-party system existed in New York was the result of a civil war within the Democratic party. Reformers vs. regulars. Reformers constructively opened the political process and checked the iron power of political bosses, but they didn't serve as a check against the fiscal and economic abuses of New York officials. After defeating the last boss of the Democratic party, Carmine De Sapio, in the early sixties, the attention of reformers remained fixed on procedural party matters rather than government—they continued fighting the last war. When local procedural squabbles didn't drain their energies, ending the war in Vietnam, dumping Lyndon Johnson or impeaching Richard Nixon did. Like most of us, reformers were attracted to the larger issues. Besides, Robert Wagner was against the "bosses," as was John Lindsay. They shared a common liberal philosophy: taxes were good because they redistributed income from rich to poor; spending was good because it helped people; unions were the good guys, business the bad guys. Management was a "conservative" issue.

Ironically, the success of the reform movement—as well as the advent of television—removed the strong party organization as a potential check on the abuse of power. No longer was there a coherent party apparatus through which citizen complaints could be filtered, sorted out, disciplined. In 1959, Sayre and Kaufman observed, "no single ruling elite controls the politics and government system of New York." But as Professor Raymond Horton of Columbia observed in a recent unpublished paper—*Sayre and Kaufman Revisited*—they assumed, as did James Madison, that the many competing special interests would balance each other, creating stability. In theory. In fact, city officials grew politically more dependent for their power and reelection on the very forces they were to regulate, on those who shared a public-profit motive, benefiting from the growth of government. Instead of being dependent on one political machine that practiced the art of political trading, they were now dependent on many smaller machines that got more than they gave. "The result," Francis Fox Piven writes in *The Fiscal Crisis of American Cities*, "was a virtual run upon the city treasury by a host of organized groups in the city, each competing with the other for a larger share of municipal benefits. . . . The cities are unable to raise revenues commensurate with these expenditures; and they are unable to resist the claims that underlie rising expenditures. And that is what the fiscal crisis is all about. . . ."

Of course, the city was profligate under the bosses. In the mid-nineteenth century, during the last four years that Boss Tweed ruled New York, the city's debt tripled. In 1933, after boss-controlled Jimmy Walker was deposed as mayor, Governor Herbert Lehman was forced to step in and submit to a "Bankers Agreement" obliging the city to accept a stern fiscal regimen. It is at least possible that a strong citywide party, immune from Republican or factional attack, could have policed and curbed the demand for more when there was no more to give. Mayor Richard Daley presided over a corrupt party but not a bankrupt Chicago. "He can and does say no to demands for spending," wrote Terry Nichols Clark in 1976, "because he is strong enough to say no." New York's fractured political system made strong leadership difficult.

The mayor had power to say yes. It was harder to say no; easier to gimmick the budget than to cut it. With the passage of a new city charter by a two-to-one margin in 1961, another check was removed by granting the mayor sole power to estimate revenues. No longer would the comptroller, the City Council and the Board of Estimate share this power. Also, unlike many states which check the fiscal abuses of their local governments, New York State did not play cop. To avoid new state aid, the Governor and state legislature preferred to see the city increase its revenue estimates, taxes or borrowing. The permissive state parent, which created "moral obligation bonds" and its own array of budget gimmicks, had little moral authority or inclination to prescribe medicine they themselves abhorred as if it were poison. "Public discussion of state finances," a September 26, 1973, audit by state Comptroller Arthur Levitt declared, "now includes such phrases as 'rollovers,' 'reverse rollovers,' and 'accelerations.' What these terms have in common is that they represent manipulations of the financial reporting process and tend to reduce public understanding and public confidence in government operations." Levitt was one of the few public officials to regularly warn of city and state fiscal practices, but his audits were usually issued a year or two after an event. He rarely mounted public campaigns, seeing his role as a detached referee. A press release sufficed. Levitt, not surprisingly, continued to be invited back to stay at Governor Rockefeller's mansion in Albany. City comptrollers certainly didn't blow the whistle. Abe Beame, who was comptroller for eight critical years, would have had to blow the whistle on himself. For him, like most city officials, it was good politics to play the game.

The banks and bond counsel, which also could have blown the whistle, played the game, too. They belonged to the same community of interest. More borrowing meant more profits, more legal fees. They had a good thing going. And the city had a good thing— access to its own money printing plant. To question city or state officials was to risk government retaliation or public abuse. For what? Their friend Nelson said it was okay. The city certified that its books were balanced. Why make waves when business was thriving?

Society's official whistle blowers—the press—did not do its job, either. *Wall Street Journal* editorials were on target but were read by the wrong audience. On fiscal matters, *Daily News* editorials should have been read but weren't. The paper that thinks of itself as the city's conscience—*The New York Times*—abdicated. Its editorial bleats—claiming that servile acceptance of new business taxes was "a civic responsibility," warning of the dire consequences of budget cuts—would appear even more ridiculous if it were not for fatuous New York *Post* editorials. The editorial page editors of both papers, John Oakes of the *Times* and James Wechsler of the *Post*, were too close to Lindsay, serving as advisers. They were not only politically but ideologically coopted. They supported the city's tax and spending policies. Instead of viewing what the city was doing as harshly as they would Defense Department cost overruns, they permitted their liberal ideology to sway their judgment. Or, as Louis Rukeyser, in a devastating critique of past *Times* and *Post* editorials in *MORE* magazine, once wrote, "New York's editorialists would often have been more astute if they had forgotten about 'liberal' and 'conservative,' and remembered to check their addition."

The reporting press, which would have had more effect on the public and its officials than the editorial writers, paid little attention. The *Times* never assigned an investigative reporter to go through the city's books (nor have they since). The *Herald Tribune,* which might have, folded in the mid-sixties, leaving New York with three citywide dailies—there were six in 1847 and eleven in 1952. With little competition, and less interest, a big story was neglected. Yes, the papers dutifully reported statements from the Citizens Budget Commission, an occasional bleep or dissent— usually on page 63 or down deep in paragraph 26. However, the "pattern" of their coverage, as Martin Mayer once scolded the *Times* in the *Columbia Journalism Review,* was to report what officials said, not what they did; to cover their ass, not the story. Even as late as the winter of 1975, when Mayor Beame claimed the deficit would be $641 million, the press reported this as a fact, with no qualifiers. Any challenge of the figure was usually reported as "an allegation."*

Reporters often filtered the story through their own prism. "No matter how critical we were in the Lindsay years and how we appeared to be in an adversary relationship," says Richard Reeves, former City Hall Bureau Chief of the *Times,* "we allowed him to focus the direction of our coverage. And the directions he chose were: Washington was short-changing the city; Albany was anti-city; and any questioning of Lindsay's actions was somehow connected to racism." Covering the city administration from room 9, the City Hall press room, it is difficult not to allow the mayor "to focus the direction of our coverage." Undermanned, often overworked, a City Hall reporter becomes a fireman—there's a two-alarm fire in the Municipal Building, with the comptroller charging waste and mismanagement, the mayor is holding a two o'clock press briefing, the Board of Estimate a press conference at three. Instead of just printing excerpts from relatively worthless press releases, journalists often allowed their sources to determine what was news. They too often covered fires, not the workings of government. Little time was left to tell the reader what was really going on. Editors, who had the time, often didn't give the direction. They were generalists, and the subject demanded specialists. Besides, city finances and budget intrigue and management were also, well, boring. "The big mistake I made," reflects one former City Hall bureau chief, "was in willingly letting certain reporters cover finances. The reason I didn't was because I was bored." Those who weren't bored —at *The Wall Street Journal* or other specialized publications— were easily ignored. Those who covered City Hall for TV or radio couldn't do the subject justice in two minutes or less—even if they understood it. The academic community, which could have understood it, produced little evidence that they tried.

And, finally, in managing the city, the mayor lost the ability to

---

* The press, particularly the *Times* and *News,* did do a good job exposing Beame's phony layoff figures in 1975. As it should have, this reporting had a profound effect on "investor confidence."

check the burgeoning power of the municipal unions. The adversary relationship that is supposed to exist between boss and employee collapsed. The mayor became a supplicant, seeking political support, with no weapon in his arsenal to equal the atom bomb of a paralyzing strike. Unions exercised a veto over the appointment of certain commissioners. The civil service system insulated workers from political control, but, also, from mayoral control. Unionization reached up into managerial ranks, claiming all but 2,000 managers. Workers and managers were often brothers and sisters in the same union. Mayors come and go; their unions remained and expanded. A mayor, elected by the people to manage the city, could not easily do so.

When the city's revenue base rapidly deteriorated, starting in 1969, first Lindsay and then Beame wouldn't wrestle with the municipal labor tiger. "So resistant to contraints posed by the deteriorating fiscal environment was the labor relations process," Ray Horton wrote in the *City Almanac*, "that real compensation for most City employees increased more rapidly in the 1970–1975 period than in the 1965–1970 period. The political power of organized workers . . . effectively insulated the labor relations process from the effects of resource scarcity." In the 1971–75 period alone, the Temporary Commission found, while police services and hours worked declined, the compensation of cops rose by an average of 51 percent—more than in the prosperous sixties. The city's tax levy budget, according to the Budget Bureau, expanded more rapidly between 1970 and 1975 than during any other five-year period since 1960, soaring 15 percent annually.

The power of organized constituents was on display when the city government, in the spring of 1977, tried to withdraw its contribution to the Medicaid program, which pays the doctor's fees of its retirees. Retirees already receive free medicine under Medicare. Normally, the medical fee is paid by the individual. But for years the city sent an annual check—about $80 in 1977—to each of its 40,000 retirees. The yearly cost was a relatively modest $4.4 million, but with increased retirements city officials worried it would quickly escalate. Acting like the statesman he can be, labor leader Victor Gotbaum agreed to terminate this fringe benefit to help pare the budget. The Beame administration introduced the necessary legislation before the City Council in February. By early March, Brooklyn Councilman Robert Steingut warned Labor Commissioner Anthony Russo that the bill was dead because of pressure from constituents. By March 31, the bill was an orphan. The Mayor, running hard for reelection, pretended defeat was victory and issued a press release, claiming: "We were able to avoid imposing this hardship on retirees." Russo put it differently: "Abe collapsed. There was too much political pressure on him. City Council President Paul O'Dwyer has even introduced a bill to *increase* the reimbursement to match the increase in premiums."

"I do not rule Russia," Czar Nicholas I moaned; "ten thousand clerks do." After just six weeks in office, Mayor Koch learned the same lesson. On February 7, 1978, the Mayor issued his sixth executive order, which abolished the Office of Service Coordination, terminating 186 workers, saving $2.2 million. Koch had good reason to pick on the agency. It was supposed to coordinate neighborhood services; instead, during the Lindsay and Beame years, it protected out-of-work basketball players and between-campaign advancemen. Still shaking his head, James Capalino, the young man Koch chose to command and dismantle the agency, says, "There were forty-five supervisory and assistant Youth Service specialists who were paid to play basketball games."

A month after the Mayor issued his executive order, they were no longer playing basketball on city time—but that's about all that changed. The 186 workers were still being paid. Owing to strict civil service regulations, 125 of them bumped non–civil service provisionals in other agencies, leaving 61 of the original 186 to be fired. But because of the fail-safe duplicative protections of the collective bargaining system, even this number was uncertain. Under state law, the union had two weeks to invent new job titles. If these titles matched other titles of workers with less seniority, the surplus basketball players get to bump other employees with less seniority.

All a mayor elected by the people could do was issue an executive order. All Capalino could do was send 186 individual notes warning people that they would be off the payroll as of March 8. All hard-working junior clerks could do was pray that their number wouldn't be called. "The provisional could be a top guy and yet get bumped by some banana," snorted Commissioner Russo. The system takes over. "After six weeks in office, I've come to the conclusion that Boss Plunkett wasn't all wrong when he talked about the civil service," said Koch of the boss who preferred the spoils system. "One shudders to think what it would be like to take on a big agency," said Capalino.

A leader committed to change must first calculate the political price he has to pay to achieve that change. In a pluralistic trading system of government, Koch might win legislative approval to amend civil service laws—but lose his battle to gain control of the Board of Education.

Political leaders make choices and trade-offs. The system bogs down as the problems spread more quickly than government's ability to cope with them. Entrenched interests or "factions" check the ability of a mayor to represent what the Founding Fathers referred to as the "common good."

The problem is universal. Conrail claims one reason it loses money is because members of Congress—who control the purse strings—insist that trains stop in their little out-of-the-way hamlets. The President determines that thirty-two water projects around the country are wasteful of taxpayers' money, but the outcry from the affected states reaches such a roar that he can cut only nine. One Senator, Russell Long of Louisiana, Chairman of the powerful Finance Committee, can bottle up tax reform or energy legislation. The American Medical Association succeeds in killing a hospital cost containment bill. Wasteful military bases remain open because powerful constituents protect them, including representatives of unhealthy local economies (like New York's) who protest the loss of needed jobs. HEW Secretary Joseph Califano announces plans to discourage unhealthful cigarette smoking, and tobacco-growing states smoke that their economies will be razed. Local governments pay fees to tie into computers which tell them not what programs they need, but what they can get from the federal government.

"It may just be a sign of old, or at least upper middle age," declared Otis G. Pike of New York's Suffolk County after announcing his retirement from Congress, "but people bug me more than they used to. They are asking their government to do more for them and are willing to do less and less for themselves. . . . In our all-consuming effort to get reelected, we kept telling the people we'd do more and more for them, and they've come to expect it."

It gets pretty expensive. In 1965, President Johnson struggled to hold the federal budget at $118.4 billion. By 1978, the budget reached $453.5 billion. Even when there are sound reasons to terminate benefit programs, as was the case with Medicaid reimbursements for city retirees or federal water projects, a public-interest constituency does not exist to counter the organized voices of special interests.

This leads to logrolling. Urban members of Congress, for instance, promise to support inflationary farm support programs in return for pro-city votes. You scratch my back, I'll scratch yours.

"Frank, that speech yo' made wasn't one bit helpful," President Johnson once reportedly said to Senator Frank Church.

"I'm sorry, Mr. President, the headlines exaggerated what I said," Church sheepishly responded.

"The headlines were all Ah read, Frank, and they're all the people read."

"But I didn't go any further than Walter Lippmann."

"Well, Frank," LBJ retorted, feigning sorrow, "the next time you need money to build a dam in your state, you better go to Mr. Lippmann."

That's how the game often works. Ed Koch, like Jimmy Carter, is called a confrontationist if he speaks out and threatens to take his case to the public; if he doesn't heed the counsel of the domestic equivalent of the military/industrial complex—the banks, unions, landlords and other organized-interest groups who profit from government. Government spending grows. Conservatives like Nixon and Ford didn't stop it, and liberals don't try. As spending rises, so do expectations. Parents demand tuition tax credits. Teachers demand more school aid. Farmers demand guaranteed prices. Cities demand more programs. Scientists demand more study grants. The airlines demand more subsidies. Chrysler and gas stations and the steel companies demand federal loan guarantees. Government becomes a giant commissary where free lunch is served. Politics becomes an arena not just where competing interests clash but where gifts are exchanged, often in return for votes. Legalized vote buying. For years, many of us said the federal government could afford this because, unlike cities or states, it could print money. And yet in recent years we have learned federal spending does contribute to inflation, just as local taxes contributed to the flight of people and jobs. We have learned there are limits to growth and what government can do. Newton's law—for every action there is an equal and opposite reaction—applies to government, as well as physics.

There are also political limits to growth. As citizens pay more for government and receive less, a taxpayer revolt becomes inevitable. Taxpayers will simply refuse to pay the bill, turning off to all government, all reforms that cost money, all belief in progress. Government becomes the enemy; politicians and public unions will become scapegoats—they're all a bunch of crooks! Escalating public cynicism thus poses a threat to democratic government because citizens will not trust their elected officials to make decisions. This attitude toward government threatens the "social contract." But it is, we shouldn't forget, a reaction against another kind of cynicism. In New York, politicians lied about their budgets; the police, sworn to uphold the law, break state law by going on strike; Mitchell-Lama tenants lie about their incomes to remain in subsidized housing. Landlords rip off high rents from the city, nursing home owners rip off Medicaid, hustlers rip off welfare. City workers assume expensive perks are really prerequisites for a good life and that a government job is a right. The public becomes an abstraction. Gimme. Gimme. Why not? Everybody in America's doing it. The rich usually don't pay their fair share of taxes. Legislators get rich off lucrative law practices. Politicians buy votes with public money. College students don't repay their National Student Loans. Secretaries ask to be fired to collect unemployment insurance for a year. Farmers get money not to farm.

Democracy in New York—America, the world—is suspended between what it wants to do and what it can do, between its divergent political and economic goals. New York cannot cope with its powerful "factions." America cannot cope with its energy or balance-of-payments woes. Italy cannot cope with terrorism; Japan, with corruption; France, with the rich who don't pay taxes; England and Sweden cannot cope with their unions; Canada, with Quebec. None has learned to cope simultaneously with inflation and unemployment. In addition to not working, the tension between our social goals of equality and our economic systems' ability to pay the bill pulls government in opposite directions. To further social justice, New York City undertook tax, spending and borrowing policies which undermined its economy. The requirements of social democracy and greater equality clashed with the requirements of a free market (capitalism) and the liberty of people to move.

"Liberal democracy's crisis is real," Alan Wolfe, author of *The Limits of Legitimacy: Political Contradictions of Contemporary Capitalism*, has written. "Its roots lie in the fact that in Western societies the economic system is liberal and capitalist while the political system is formally democratic and therefore potentially socialist. This is why some . . . argue that the political system must be revamped to bring it in line with the economy. It is also the reason why others work to transform the economy according to the principles of democracy. The impasse of liberal democracy will not be resolved until óne side or the other has its way."

The clash was obscured as long as there was a growing economy —*more* for everyone. But in New York, as is becoming evident in America and around the world, everyone cannot be satisfied. For many, there is no more *more*. There are limits to what New York can spend, tax or borrow. There are limits to what the federal government can do or spend to reduce unemployment or curb inflation. Coal miners cannot capture 39 percent pay hikes without affecting consumer prices, including the prices that they themselves will have to pay. There are limits to what the growing Sunbelt will spend to rescue the lagging Northeast, to what the middle class will voluntarily pay to help the poor. Private capital expansion may not be possible under a socially just tax system, just as true tax reform might threaten capital formation. Alaska cannot enjoy unrestrained growth and an unspoiled environment. Japan and the Western European democracies cannot reduce America's balance-of-payments gap without harming their own economies, at least in the short run. Someday, we know, the warming of the earth's surface will melt the ice caps, the oil wells and coal mines will lie fallow. Eventually, the light from the sun will be extinguished.

We know all this, and yet even when we know what to do we can't or don't know *how* to do it. Peter Jay, the British Labor government's ambassador to Washington, wrote some years ago, "Democracy has itself by the tail and is eating itself up fast." With the exception of England, New York was one of the first to complete the meal.

Chapter Eight

Politics:
The Melody
of the
Fiscal Crisis

DURING A LONG, weary night in autumn of 1975, when it appeared
the city would plunge into bankruptcy, Mayor Beame's Contingency
Committee on bankruptcy was summoned to Gracie Mansion. The
Mayor, just returned from the Alfred E. Smith dinner, was wearing
white tie. Some of the borough presidents were in sweat shirts. Together, a large contingent waited out the clock to learn whether the
teachers' pension fund would lend the money necessary to meet the
next day's bills. "By 4 A.M. or so, we were all getting a little hys-
terical," recalls Beame's former press secretary, Sidney Frigand.
"Ira Millstein [one of Beame's SEC attorneys] came over to me and
said we should have an announcement of bankruptcy ready. How do
you write a release that the city is going under? It's like saying, 'We
announce today the end of the world.' I said, 'Who the hell will take
the blame for this?' " Those in attendance roared when Frigand
showed them his draft press release. It began: "City Comptroller
Harrison Jay Goldin announced today. . . ."

Goldin, not Beame, would be the messenger of the bad news.
Frigand says it was all a joke, and that they would not have issued a
release in Goldin's name. But, he admits "It's not out of the question." The point—as Alexander the Great's messenger tragically
learned—is to take credit for good news and avoid delivering bad
news. The game among politicians is well understood by Charles
Rosen, the charismatic leader of Co-op City's 60,000 tenants. "Most

politicians want to come out clean," he says, his voice perched between a squawk and a shriek. "They don't care who wins, as long as they come out clean. Everyone wants to be there for the bar mitzvahs, just as everybody wants to avoid the funerals." To take credit and avoid blame.

Avoiding blame has an inglorious tradition in New York politics. Beame obviously cared deeply about avoiding bankruptcy, silently suffering humiliation to avoid it. Yet when it appeared the dreaded announcement had to be made, he preferred not to make it. Hiding behind the slogan "The Second Toughest Job in America," John Lindsay sought reelection in 1969 by suggesting the city was ungovernable. Robert Wagner, his predecessor, won reelection in 1961 by blaming the failures of his first two terms on "the bosses." In early 1975, Beame blamed Lindsay, Goldin, Republicans, the press, and then the banks for the fiscal crisis. When the 1977 SEC report blamed him, the Mayor's remarkable response was that everyone was guilty. Therefore, no one was. Throughout the sixties, New York politicians blamed Vietnam and misplaced national priorities for urban failures. When the war ended, they blamed Richard Nixon, the banks, Washington, Robert Moses, the Sunbelt.

Today, there is a tendency among city politicians and others to suggest that the city is a victim of forces beyond its control. While there is some truth to this claim—no single devil theory explains what happened to New York—New York suffered from a leadership blackout. "I know only two tunes," Ulysses S. Grant declared. "One of them is 'Yankee Doodle,' and the other isn't." The dominant tune—the common denominator for most of the fateful local decisions leading to New York's fiscal crisis—was *politics*. Simply defined, *politics* was the absence of leaders who thought about the long-term public interest. They were always thinking about the next election. It didn't matter whether you sported a Democratic or Republican label, whether you were a liberal or conservative, a banker or union leader—most everyone sang the same tune: Protect your ass. Don't be a martyr. Worry about the next election. Avoid blame. Take credit.

In New York, good politics was at war with good sense. To pay for their short-term election promises, officials raised business taxes —undermining the city's long-term economy. More often, they resorted to inflated revenue estimates and borrowing—socking future generations with the tab. When resources were limited but public and union officials wished to show constituents they had delivered, lavish new pension settlements were publicly announced, while, privately, both sides agreed to underfund them. To escape political attack (and continue receiving handsome tax-free profits), the banks and their bond counsels sealed their eyes to city budget fraud. State officials encouraged puffed-up city revenue estimates and borrowing to avoid increased state taxes or state aid. All this was deemed good politics. Like attending bar mitzvahs.

Yes, as we've seen, the system failed. But New York's leaders failed as well. When it came to long-term decisions, New York was ruled by political midgets. To assist his political ally, Democrat Robert Wagner, Governor Rockefeller approved the first scheme to hide expense items in the capital budget. Amendments to the State Local Finance Law, which were required to approve much of the city's budgetary legerdemain, won bipartisan approval in Albany. As did most pension sweeteners. Conservative members of the legislature, including Senator John Marchi, voted to enrich the pensions of cops and firemen, two groups which tended to support conservative candidates. Governor Malcolm Wilson, a knight in the conservative cause, urged Mayor Beame in 1974 to borrow $800 million to paper over the city's budget hole. He couldn't, he said privately, raise taxes or appear to be helping New York City too much in an election year. His base, you see, was the suburbs and upstate.

Governor Rockefeller manufactured "moral obligation" bonds—sticking future taxpayers with debts he told present taxpayers they wouldn't have to pay for. In 1974, the Republican-controlled legislature approved and Governor Wilson signed a record $307 million school aid increase. To pay for it, they opened what has come to be called "the magic window," frontloading the cost into the first quarter of the state's fiscal year, which begins on April 1—the last quarter of the fiscal year for most local school boards and municipalities like New York. After the November election, Wilson's successor, Hugh Carey, inherited a $250 million deficit because of this trick.

To win favor with their lower- and middle-income constituents, the City Council skewed the property tax system to extract lower rates from homeowners and apartment buildings and higher rates from commercial property in Manhattan. To show they favored education—and the powerful teachers' union—state legislators timidly voted for the Stavisky-Goodman bill mandating increased city educational costs. One of the sponsors of the bill, Republican State Senator Roy Goodman, who would later run for mayor as the "fiscally responsible" candidate, admitted at a *Daily News* editorial luncheon that the bill was "irresponsible." Nevertheless, he meekly told startled editors, it was "good politics."

Among its many distinctions, New York boasts its own foreign policy. Justifiably outraged at the Arab boycott of American firms doing business with Israel, the state legislature in 1975 passed and Governor Carey signed an anti-boycott statute, preventing firms from complying. Proudly, New York politicians proclaimed they were the first to do so. But because the federal government did not pass a similar statute, New York politicians took their bows while New York's port took its lumps. After one year, according to Clifford B. O'Hara, Director of Port Commerce for the Port Authority of New York and New Jersey, the port lost 300,000 tons of export cargo—mostly, he said, because of the anti-boycott law. Much of this business merely shifted to American ports with no such law. The business, he feared, was permanently lost: "Once a shipper and a buyer set up a way of doing business, it's hard to change the pattern."

Similar political posing is fundamental to New York's past housing policies. This reporter once phoned John Heimann—then the state housing czar and now federal Comptroller of the Currency—to solicit his thoughts on the abbreviated housing platform of an unnamed political candidate. The office-seeker promised: (1) "to assure that mortgage assistance loans can be granted to existing Mitchell-Lama housing to keep rents down"; (2) to "change the formula for income limitations for Mitchell-Lama tenants which, because of inflation, are now unrealistically low"; (3) that all Mitchell-Lama tenants could "withhold rents if the apartment is in need of serious repair"; (4) to "promote new building in the state."

The campaign promises, Heimann sneered, were totally "unrealistic." He audibly gulped when informed these were the 1974 campaign promises of his boss, the Governor. Those promises helped Hugh Carey capture the votes of many of the state's 500,000 Mitchell-Lama tenants. Not surprisingly, tenants want to avoid rent increases. Not surprisingly, public officials prefer denouncing rather than acting like landlords and raising rents. The result: rents don't keep pace with costs, thereby threatening foreclosure. Rather than confront this no-win political problem, public officials assumed an ostrich pose—ignoring it, appointing study committees and mediators, appropriating a few million here or there, all with bipartisan support, of course.

The state's middle-income housing program presupposes that Mitchell-Lama projects are at least self-sustaining, though in places like Co-op City they clearly are not. The city, with broad political support, long ago abandoned the legislative intent of the Mitchell-Lama law, financing their projects not from rents but from the issuance of city debt. To hold down rents, and hoping long-term interest rates would decline, the city began rolling over this debt rather than floating new bonds. Interest rates rose. The deficit spread. "As a consequence," UDC Chairman Richard Ravitch wrote Governor Carey, in a confidential January, 1977, report, "the successive Housing and Development Administrators were free, as a practical matter, to impose rent increases in amounts they decided should be imposed regardless of the fact that mortgage debt service defaults had to inevitably result from the low increases. . . . The result in the overall has been that without legislative authorization, the City's program has been transformed into a partial direct subsidy program, although the continuing and increasing shift of costs of the program from the City Mitchell-Lama tenants to City taxpayers has not been publicly acknowledged as deliberate City social policy and is only dimly perceived by the public."

The city altered the program in another significant way. Though state law requires income affidavits to certify that tenants are eligible to move into a middle-income project, or are paying a fair rent once they do, the City Council, with the support of past mayors, prohibited the use of income affidavits as a violation of privacy. The Council, also with mayoral support, regularly rushed through legislation strictly limiting rent increases. After surveying this dismal history, the Housing Committee of the New York City Bar Association concluded, "It is an understatement that the program early on became highly politicized."

The financial consequences were profound. By 1976, according to an audit by State Comptroller Levitt, 98 of the city's 140 projects were delinquent in their mortgage payments. According to Mayor Koch's fiscal 1979 budget message, "By June 30, 1975 the City had outstanding $1.1 billion in BAN's [bond anticipation notes] issued for Mitchell-Lama purposes and another $118 million of BAN's issued for municipal loans to owners of multiple dwellings. And yet another $200 million in debt issuance remained to complete the financing of projects already in construction." In late 1977, after the state Court of Appeals declared the city mora-

torium on the repayment of notes unconstitutional, the city undertook to sell these mortgages, at a considerable loss.

It is good public policy to seek to retain the middle class. But it is
also good politics to promise to hold down rents. In New York, the
politics preceded the policy. During his 1977 campaign, Mayor
Beame made a rare appearance at a Board of Estimate hearing,
and before a large, cheering audience of tenants, voted to exempt
senior citizens from rent increases (for five years) and to offer tax
exemptions to Mitchell-Lama housing companies to suppress rent
increases. The measures passed unanimously. On another occasion,
before 1,100 cheering tenants from Manhattan's Lincoln Towers,
mayoral candidate Ed Koch pledged solidarity in opposing federal
rent increases ordered to meet rising costs. Obviously, many tenants
cannot afford rent increases. Others can. The point, however, is
that in New York this economic question is superseded by political
considerations.

Rent control is a classic case. Privately, most public officials concede that it has hastened the city's property tax base decline, encouraged abandonment, and squeezed many smaller landlords out
of business. But the issue, they whisper, is political dynamite. What
about a means test to ensure that those who could afford to, pay
a fair rent and are not subsidized by other taxpayers? No, they say.
It would be an invasion of privacy to check people's income—something welfare does all the time. Presumably, conservative Republicans would take a different view, seeing it as an ideological
issue—free enterprise, a free market, etc. Instead, they, too, see it
as a political issue. To score political points, in April 1977, Albany
Republicans pushed for and won agreement for a four-year extension of rent control. As reported by Linda Greenhouse of the
Times, "The closed-door Republican conference at which the plan
was adopted yesterday was reportedly an acrimonious one, with
upstate Senators maintaining their philosophical stand against rent
controls for more than an hour. 'But we are practical people,' one
of those Senators said. 'We realize the tremendous political problems.' " The bill sailed through the legislature, was signed by the
Governor, and created still another commission to study the subject.

Nassau and Suffolk County Republicans, who dominate those
counties by parading their fiscal conservatism as if it were man-
hood, also played the game when it suited their purposes. For years,
Nassau and Suffolk Republicans have chided city Democrats for
their profligate ways. Yet their cops, who generally vote Republi-

can, have been gifted more lavish pay and fringe benefits—including more days off, bigger longevity payments, more generous duty charts, noncontributory pensions—than have city cops. Proving that principle in the pursuit of votes is a vice.

Nationally, the most devout conservatives play the game. Senator Strom Thurmond of South Carolina voted against the federal seasonal loan program to assist New York City in 1975. It was, he said, a "give-away" to permissive liberals. No doubt, his constituents cheered, as they do when he supports "give-aways" to farmers. In 1976, for instance, farmers were victims of a severe drought, facing financial ruin without federal help. Congress broadened by $750 million the loan program of the Small Business Administration. With the loans in the pipeline, and the drought ended, the following year harvests were so bountiful that farmers were complaining about falling prices. So they called for new loan assistance and "disaster" aid to speed federal help, some of it necessary. Prodded by conservatives like Thurmond, the SBA overgenerously declared two-thirds of all U.S. farm counties disaster areas. (When New York, after heavy snows, sought such designation, the same members of Congress, and President Carter, said no. Presumably the difference between drought and snow is that one is God's fault, the other New York's.) Under the terms of the "disaster" loans, farmers were allowed to borrow up to $250,000 over twenty years at 3 percent interest (New York City paid more than 7 percent for its seasonal loans).

By early 1978, the farm loan program was expected to cost $4.6 billion. Reminding the Congress of the earlier $750,000 loan limit, Congressman Robert Giamo, Chairman of the House Budget Committee, was quickly outmaneuvered by conservatives who barreled across a $1.4 billion supplemental appropriation. Giamo told *Time* magazine he at least hoped to increase the interest rate to 5 percent—two-thirds the rate banks were charging corporations. But he wasn't hopeful: "The SBA loan fund is set up to help people cope with an unusual disaster—one that happens once in a lifetime. What has happened is that it has turned into a crop insurance program for agriculture." It was also a political insurance program for Thurmond's reelection. He was playing the same game as New York pols who voted hidden housing subsidies for middle-income residents.

In a piece subtitled "The Sweet Smell of Pork," Ward Sinclair of the Washington *Post*, in April 1978, sketched how members of a

House committee were seeking to amend a new federal highway law to aid their districts. James J. Howard (D–N.J.) submitted a $30 million request for a "seagoing jetfoil service to connect his district with New York City." Don H. Clausen (R–Cal.) desired a $50 million road built as "a demonstration to determine how much the road would divert motor vehicle traffic around the Prairie Creek Redwood State Park" in his district. James C. Cleveland (R–N.H.) wanted federal law changed to allow New Hampshire to sell lottery tickets along its interstate highways. Robert C. McEwen (R–N.Y.) asked that the law be changed "to allow placement of a duty-free store on an interstate highway in his district near the Canadian border." These were a few of the election-year requests, prompting a Congressional aide to exclaim, "They're turning this bill into another Christmas tree!" Senator Edmund S. Muskie, Chairman of the Senate Budget Committee, in an emotional address to his colleagues in April 1978, warned that Congress was repeatedly ignoring its own formal spending guidelines. Like the city, it was spending according to perceived political need rather than estimated revenues. "During the debate last year on the energy tax bill," Muskie chided, "we witnessed again this eagerness to sacrifice budget reform in favor of spending proposals when political opportunity becomes more attractive for the moment."

The same melody—*politics*—flows through the short-term decisions that helped bring New York to its knees. There are reasonable explanations for many of these. The word *moral* derives from the word *mores*, which means "customs." During the sixties and early seventies, spending, borrowing and taxing were the accepted custom in New York. There was no organized opposition. "We would always report what the Citizens Budget Commission said in a little sidebar deep inside," recalls former *Times*man Richard Reeves. "We thought the budget tricks were clever." The same point was made by former Budget Director Fred Hayes in an interview with the *Times*: "The newspapers created the impression that we had phony problems and real solutions. Actually, the problems were real but the solutions were phony."

"The presence of so much media skews New York politics," Special Deputy Comptroller Steve Clifford told me just days before leaving his post in late 1977. "Media is all politicians come to care about. If you can get a shot on the six o'clock news, it's more important than changing pension benefits. . . . Politicians see their job as running for office, not providing vision or persuasion. Part of the blame, though, is the public's. We have the most irresponsible electorate anywhere." As Clifford suggests, many of these past decisions were popular, or appeared to be. Rent control was popular, as was free tuition, subsidized rents, school aid, the anti-Arab boycott bill, business taxes, spending now and paying later. "Democracy is a device that insures we shall be governed by no better than we deserve," observed George Bernard Shaw. Citizens complain about garbage collection—but it is, after all, our garbage. Critics complain about television executives who offer braless Charlie's Angels —ignoring the public, which gave the show its number one rating.

When he was about to depart city government after five long years, former Deputy Mayor John Zuccotti told a reporter, "You know, if you ever worry about America becoming socialist, it's an interesting idea. I'll tell you why. You believe in the American dream, private enterprise, etc. You're raised on that. You work hard. You'll get somewhere, etc. That's the whole series. . . . You get in the government five years and you begin to see that people want you to solve all their problems."

Politicians come to judge themselves, and be judged, by whether they deliver the pork; whether they offered grants rather than their own best judgment and wisdom; whether their decision was in the immediate interest of their district or city rather than the long-term interest of the nation. Wisdom and good management are not easily quantified. Hard cash counts. More grants, more programs, more roads, more dams, more malls. John Lindsay baldly justified his seconding speech in behalf of Vice President Spiro Agnew in 1968, saying it guaranteed the city would have a friend in Washington. Abe Beame justified his 1976 support of candidate Jimmy Carter on the same grounds. The unspoken assumption was that from these political acts would flow public monies. That legitimized their decisons.

Obviously, it's not always easy to be a leader. The fundamental tension between a democracy and a republic, between our social and our economic system, is reflected in our politicians. Should they follow what voters want or their own best judgment? Polls or their conscience? Most of us are not immune to this conflict. During the early stages of the Vietnam war, like others of my generation I protested that the war was immoral, no matter what Lyndon Johnson's pocket polls said about "popular" support. Yet in the latter stages of the war, when the polls reversed, we demanded that Nixon terminate this "unpopular war." Many of us are enraged at members of Congress who follow their constituents and vote against federal loans to New York—and at imperious politicians who ignore popular campaign finance reforms. It is in New York's long-term interest to drastically reduce taxes. But how do you tell a worker to sacrifice a raise in order to increase business profits?

The public doesn't help. The word "politician" has come—particularly in the post-Watergate period—to carry more negative freight than it should. We forget that a free society presupposes consent, which in turn presupposes compromise. Abe Lincoln, we forget, was a politician. He made deals, compromised, trimmed his sails, worried about tactics. So do reporters who try to seduce sources through flattery. So do business executives who ingratiate themselves with their bosses; teachers, with their principals; principals, with their superintendents; union leaders, with their members; lawyers, with juries. Americans suffer a double standard. On the one hand we resent politicians for "compromising," and on the other we all compromise. In theory, the only people who don't are dictators.

All of us like to feel morally superior. Unfortunately, New York politicians make it easy. Over the years, most have flunked Publius' test. They failed to distinguish between what was popular and what was in the public interest, between immediate political gratification and the city's long-term interests. Most of us can be selfish, foolish, hypocritical. But we're not paid public money; nor are we granted a public trust. In this sense, politicians should be held to a higher standard. It's not enough for them to explain that everyone was doing it; that it was the times, the pressures, the public thirst. Public officials are elected to lead, as well as follow. "Your representative owes you, not his industry only, but his judgment," Edmund Burke admonished the Electors of Bristol; "and he betrays instead of serving you if he sacrifices it to your opinion." Democracy requires that the electorate exercise self-restraint, the famed Austrian economist and philosopher Joseph Schumpeter wrote in *Capitalism, Socialism and Democracy*; but democracy also requires that when institutional checks fail, the ultimate check be the restraint and good judgment of leaders.

After completing his survey of fifty-one cities, the University of Chicago's Terry Nichols Clark concluded, "The most consistent message of these findings is that local leadership can make a substantial difference. Fiscal strain is greater on local officials with weak tax bases and large numbers of poor residents. But some cities are fiscally healthy (like Pittsburgh, Schenectady and St. Louis) even though they share many socioeconomic problems with Boston and New York."

Mayor Wagner wasn't being a leader when he muddled his way out of crises and commenced deficit financing; neither was John Lindsay when he surrendered huge labor settlements and accelerated local spending while the economy declined; or Abe Beame when he ballooned short-term debt and treated the gathering fiscal storm as if it were a public relations crisis; or Nelson Rockefeller when he crafted "moral obligation" bonds and approved or winked at city budget gimmicks; nor a generation of city and state politicians who spent, borrowed and taxed more than the city could afford.

After a two-year study of the city, the Temporary Commission on City Finances concluded its 17th and "Final Report" with this observation:

Each of the policy areas . . . evidences a common trend, the proclivity of the City to engage in policies and practices that were inconsistent with rather obvious long-term needs. Taxes were raised beyond the point of economic rationality and helped drive out mobile businesses and individuals; debt was issued beyond the capacity of the market to absorb it at competitive rates and ultimately, to absorb it at all; salaries and benefits were negotiated beyond the capacity of the local government to finance the increases except by reducing the work force, cutting essential public services, and worsening the quality of life in New York City. In each instance, it clearly was in the short-run interest of City officials (and City employees and creditors as well) to pursue policies that were destructive to the future. If the fiscal crisis proves anything, it is that short-term and long-term needs are not always consistent.

To excuse these leaders is to accept the assumption that no one is responsible for their acts, that we are all victims. On this point, at least, two opposing devil theories of the fiscal crisis merge. One—advanced by Beame and others—argues that the fiscal crisis proves the city is ungovernable, the victim of social and historical forces beyond its control; the other—advanced by the left—argues that the city is the victim of Washington or the banks. Both implicitly assume there is little New York could do for itself. Both accept what might be called the trapped insect theory—offering moral support to public officials who spend careers avoiding blame.

After spending a tranquil summer in England reading Anthony Trollope, former Deputy Mayor Zuccotti shared a drink with me and reflected on his time in City Hall. Did *politics* explain many of the bad decisions made by New York over the years? He thought a while, looking rested but older than his forty years.

"It's hard to generalize," he said. "I suppose you could say New York tried to do too much, and possibly for the wrong reasons. It's fair to say New York tried to solve its social problems. On the other hand, officials tried to help their own political position. It wasn't all for uplifting moral reasons. They were trying to get votes. . . . There's nothing surprising about it. If you read Trollope, you know it's the oldest game in the world."

Chapter Nine

Liberalism's Vietnam

IF *politics* IS THE MELODY of the fiscal crisis, *liberalism* provides the chorus. New York City is the left's Vietnam. Their traditional weapons—more money, more programs, more taxes, more borrowing—didn't work here; just as more troops, more bombs, more interdiction, more pacification programs didn't work there. And as that miserable war should have instructed military adventurists on the limits of American power, New York's fiscal war, unavoidably, teaches the limits of government intervention.

The domino theory did work in New York. Goaded by liberalism's compassion and ideological commitment to the redistribution of wealth, New York officials helped redistribute much of the tax base and thousands of jobs out of New York.

Yes, the city was, to some extent, the victim of federal policies, of historical and migratory patterns beyond its control, of local and state decisions whose origins were political, not ideological. But many of its wounds were ideologically self-inflicted. New York was not compelled to create a vast municipal hospital or City University system, to continue free tuition, institute open enrollment, ignore budget limitations, impose the steepest taxes in the nation, borrow beyond its means, subsidize middle-income housing, continue rigid rent control, reward municipal workers with lush pension, pay and fringe benefits, graduate kids who couldn't read, pay too much attention to "issues" and too little to management and the delivery of services. These decisions were designed not just to win votes. They sprang as well from a genuine sense of compassion, a desire to help people. That is what the liberal tradition is about.

"New York has been the laboratory for social innovation in this country," observes urban historian Richard Wade, a City University professor. "The welfare state was invented in this state." Led by Governors Al Smith, Franklin Roosevelt, and Herbert Lehman, New York pioneered social legislation to help poor people. Inspired by a New Yorker, FDR, the federal government helped put people back to work and saved the country from the chaos of unfettered capitalism. Liberalism spurred the successful effort to replenish the South's lagging economy, introduced Social Security, outlawed sweatshops and child labor, strengthened antitrust laws, fathered the progressive income tax and social legislation to care for the old, the sick, the infirm, the poor. The Wagner Act, named after New York Senator Robert Wagner, Sr., granted full citizenship to beleaguered labor unions. The left was in the forefront of two of the most important movements of this century: civil rights and the women's movement. States like Texas do indeed enjoy budget surpluses and pro-business climates, but they also ignore their poor and often treat workers as indentured servants.

New York, the Statue of Liberty city, has been home for courageous immigrants fleeing oppression or poverty and seeking freedom and new opportunity. "America"—New York—"was in everybody's mouth," wrote Mary Antin, who immigrated here in 1891. It was, she said, "this magic land." The streets were paved with gold. The dreams and energy of immigrants charged New York's unique sense of compassion, built and infused the world's capital of culture, commerce, ideas. New York's melting pot boasts more Jews than Tel Aviv, more Irish than Dublin, more Italians than Florence. Long before FDR or the New Deal, we learned a different lesson from the one taught by our skeptical, aristocratic Founding Fathers: government could be a friend, an ally, an agent for social reform. We learned to identify with the underdog. As the West incubated an individualistic frontier spirit, New York incubated social idealism.

"I do not exaggerate when I say that New York is unique in the history of human kindness," Mayor Koch eloquently declared in his inaugural address. "New York is not a problem. New York is a stroke of genius. From its earliest days, this city has been a lifeboat for the homeless, a larder for the hungry, a living library for the intellectually starved, a refuge not only for the oppressed but also for the creative. New York is and has been the most open city in the world and that is its greatness and that is why in large part it faces monumental problems today. . . . Without question, this city has made mistakes. But our mistakes have been those of the heart."

Over the last twenty years or so, New York often thought with its heart. Suffused with a commitment to help people, when the federal or state government wouldn't, the city reached to do the job alone. To comfort black and Hispanic immigrants from the South, it offered the most generous welfare benefits in the nation, encouraging more immigration. When private jobs began to disappear, it expanded the public payroll. When labor unions asked for more than the city could afford, they were viewed not as another special interest but as the underdogs of another era. When more revenues were needed to pay for mushrooming costs, the city assumed it was the obligation of the wealthy to pay, and hiked business and personal income taxes. When the budget was unbalanced, we obeyed Mayor Wagner's incredible dictum—"I do not propose to permit our fiscal problems to set the limits of our commitments to meet the essential needs of the people of the city"—and borrowed or tricked the budget. Open enrollment at the City University was instituted to achieve a more egalitarian society, with scant attention paid to cost or academic standards.

Like Prince Prospero, New York leaders often acted as if the city were a nation unto itself, its walls sealed. Until the courts blocked him, Mayor Wagner, with widespread support, ignored the nation's policies and unilaterally tried to raise the city's minimum wage to $1.50 an hour. Wagner wanted to do what he thought was right, sealing his eyes to the many jobs that would shift to other states with no such laws. Just as the Lindsay administration, also with widespread support, didn't believe Wall Street firms would flee to New Jersey when the stock transfer tax was imposed.

Businesses came to be viewed as a source of taxes, not jobs. Liberal politics dominated sound economics. Profits were somehow wicked. Unlike many cities and states, New York discouraged tax and other incentives for private enterprise. We worried about rip-offs, the rich soaking the poor, the inequality of wealth. The sound proposition that the rich should pay more doesn't work unless it's uniform national policy. It wasn't. This is a free country; as local and state taxes climbed, people were free to move—or go out of business.

When businesses moved, many liberals, including Episcopal Bishop Moore, charged they were "immoral." Righteousness infused our politics. When the transit fare was raised in 1975, a City Hall rally attended by a cross-section of political and labor leaders urged citizens to resist. Who would pay the wages of the transit workers? Who would subsidize the deficit-ridden Transit Authority? It didn't matter. Consequences were less important than speaking out, than taking a "moral" position. In their 1977 mayoral campaign, liberal candidates Bella Abzug and Herman Badillo urged a public takeover of Con Edison, the giant utility. In their book *The Abuse of Power*, Jack Newfield and Paul Dubrul summoned the city to sock Con Ed with higher taxes. Ignored in this tumult of liberal and left posturing is a glaring fact: 23 percent of each citizen's Con Ed bill is already earmarked to pay city and state taxes. This is six times greater than Detroit's tax rate, five times Philadelphia's, four times Los Angeles'. If Con Ed were publicly owned, how would the city, which can't tax itself, make up the $470 million in city and state taxes Con Ed says it paid in 1977? If taxes were raised, how would that translate into reduced utility bills for consumers? A compelling argument can be made for public ownership or at least a feasibility study—even after taking into account high taxes and fuel costs (60 percent of a resident's electricity bill), Con Ed's rates exceed those of neighboring utilities. Its management, materials and services, and wage costs exceed, for instance, those of Long Island Lighting Co. or the New Jersey Public Service Electric and Gas. Under public ownership, 4 percent dividends would not be paid. But before the public could own Con Ed, it would have to purchase their reported $10 billion worth of plant and equipment (unless the city were to expropriate this private property, which is illegal). Such action would invite the escape of other businesses—and jobs. To make the public ownership argument, one must be prepared to show that the gains from public ownership will exceed the expenditure or tax loss.

A similar confusion extends to the city's credit crisis. The banks, many liberals charge, are to blame for refusing to lend New York money. The private credit market—composed of thousands of individuals and investment opportunities, of amorphous terms like "investor confidence"—are abstractions. It's assumed that a handful of avaricious individuals conspire to make decisions, and that pure selfishness is to blame when they say no. Banks and investment houses can be faulted for many things—including lying to small investors—but not for acting selfishly. They're in business to make money, not to be social reformers. Because they're amoral about their money, since the spring of 1975 investors have been unwilling to bet on city securities because they fear a city default. Neither David Rockefeller of Chase nor Walter Wriston of Citicorp can change that.

The same confusion surfaces when liberals fault landlords for acting like landlords. When landlords urge legislation to pass on increased fuel costs to tenants, City Council members, galvanized by a bleacherful of critics, blast it as a give-away. Raising rents to cover inflationary costs is also a give-away. Of course, landlords can be predators. But many liberals try to have it both ways: claiming they believe in private enterprise—yet condemning business profits. One might differ with Marxists, but at least they're consistent.

Not only did New York liberalism believe too little in profits, they believed too much in money. "The ultimate problem is money —or rather, the problem of not enough money," intoned John Lindsay's 1969 book *The City*. The "problem" was not defined as a declining economic base, steep taxes, crime, the way services weren't delivered. No, the city could not be held responsible for helping drive people and businesses out. Since the absence of money was defined as the cause, it logically followed that more money would be the cure.

Money was free. New York would get it from a "Marshall Plan for cities," from "reordering national priorities," from a new President, from new spending by Washington. It was assumed that the nation's taxpayers would pay more in taxes but city taxpayers wouldn't. Billions for national welfare reform or health insurance would, somehow, be free.

"I used to say, 'Get it from the Defense Department,' " Jean Larkin, an early foe of the Vietnam war and a supporter of businessman Joel Harnett for mayor, told an audience of the reform-oriented Village Independent Democratic Club (VID) in 1977. "I must confess, I've been wrong. There's no way to restore the city to solvency without encouraging the private sector to create jobs." Ms. Larkin now knew that HEW's budget dwarfed the Defense Department's. She had become a realist.

Bella Abzug had not, as her visit to the VID Club demonstrated. The peeling paint and wall posters of past liberal glories— MCGOVERN FOR PRESIDENT, KRETCHMER FOR MAYOR, ABRAMS FOR ATTORNEY GENERAL—were an appropriate backdrop for

Bella's old-time religion mayoral campaign. She would seek this club's endorsement by spouting the same message she had for years. "The money and the programs are there in Washington," boomed Arnold Weiss, former Chairman of the liberal New Democratic Coalition, introducing Bella. "Why Bella? Because Bella's the one person who can break those doors open. . . . Bella Abzug is what we need."

Enter Bella, sliding a cape from her shoulders, adjusting her hat, letting loose on "the issues"—her issues. All this recent right-wing talk about austerity and fiscal responsibility and management and productivity and what the city must do for itself—*STOP!*

These were not her issues. Although Bella was speaking on Manhattan's West Fourth Street, her mind was in Washington. She lugged a copy of the new city budget—but only to point out those programs she helped navigate through Congress. "Much of what we have to get is from the outside," she declared. ". . . we're gonna have creative managers, we're gonna have manager-managers. But I'm gonna fight for this city. . . . I'm gonna lead a national policy, a national urban coalition."

In a sense, Bella wasn't really running for mayor. Like Lindsay, she was campaigning for something else: a "national urban policy." The unglamorous task of governing more than sixty agencies, policing the expenditure of almost $14 billion, balancing budgets, economic development, fighting for productivity improvements and changes in union work rules . . . boring. What was of interest? More programs, more money, the hidden pot of gold in Washington. When Bella complained about the poor education system, she was not wondering what taxpayers get for the $2,600 the Board of Education spent on each child. Instead, she wondered why we didn't spend more. Spending money was assumed to equal the delivery of service.

Bella's belief was central to the liberal faith. "I think it's fair to say," economist John Kenneth Galbraith told a *New York Times* symposium in July 1975, "that no problem associated with New York City could not be solved by providing more money." He said it was "remarkable" and "outrageous" that "so many people of wealth had left." The "fiscal crisis would be over," declared author Michael Harrington, if Washington passed "three laws"—federalized welfare costs, national health insurance, and the Humphrey-Hawkins full-employment bill. These views were echoed by others on the left, including economists like Robert Lekachman. As General Westmoreland would say, if only we had a few more troops . . .

This preoccupation with money leads, as the social scientists would put it, to a preoccupation with "inputs" rather than "outputs." *Whether* money is spent becomes more important than *how* it is spent. New York State's liberal Medicaid law was "good" because it promised money and "free medicine," though, as some warned, it led to inflated medical costs and outrageous abuses. "To dismiss policemen, firemen, sanitation workers, park employees and teachers is not an alternative when the greatest need of a city is for more police protection, more fire protection, better recreation and competent education," Galbraith exhorted *Times* Op-Ed page readers in 1977. The assumption, commonly shared, was that better services come from more money, not better management; by hiring more cops rather than getting those on the force out from behind their desks or inducing sergeants to sacrifice any of their forty-six vacation and chart days off. Though labor allies say it represents a return to the sweatshop, the Koch administration did say taxpayers could potentially receive 20 million extra hours of service if all city employees worked a forty-hour week, as most other Americans do. Yet most liberals were silent. Fewer layoffs would have been necessary if all workers volunteered to forgo some of their bloated fringe benefits. Yet most liberals were silent.

This concern with "inputs" surfaces throughout recent city history. The liberal impulse argued that it was better to borrow from the capital budget rather than cut expenses. Their passion blinded them to the consequences. In the long run, it cost more. And in the winter of 1978, New York couldn't remove snow from its trench-pocked streets because 40 percent of its equipment had broken down and there was no money for repairs. More federal training funds were good, even though Comptroller Goldin found, in 1978, that thirty days and $10 million after graduation almost one-half of the trainees were unemployed. "Why can't liberals . . . talk about fiscal responsibility and productivity without feeling uncomfortable?" Senator Muskie asked the state Liberal party in a 1975 address. His own answer: "Our emotional stake in government is so much that we regard commonsense criticism almost as a personal attack."

Ed Koch learned this lesson early in his term as mayor. He and Deputy Mayor Herman Badillo had zeroed in on what they called the "poverticians," who siphoned federal poverty funds to build local political machines. "The resistance to change is enormous," the usually ebullient Mayor told me three months into his first term, his vest unbuttoned, his shoulders now slightly stooped. "Everyone protects their own turf. They storm into your office like you're supposed to roll over and play dead." Then Koch recounted the problems he was having with black officials. For years, guilt-ridden liberals exempted their programs from criticism for fear of being called racist. But Koch wasn't a traditional liberal. When he thought Mike Holloman, the black head of the Health and Hospitals Corporation, was incompetent, he was the first prominent white official to say so. With the exception of labor leader Victor Gotbaum, he was almost the only one. "I invited the Council of Elected Black Officeholders to a reception at Gracie Mansion," Koch recounted. "Yet today I was told they had a meeting and none of them liked what I was doing to change the way poverty funds were spent to ensure that the poor received them. Some said they were going to picket the reception. Others said they wouldn't cross a picket line. One official called me up and said, 'What do we do?' I said, 'Easy. I'm canceling the reception.' "

Early in the 1976 Presidential campaign, the late Hubert Horatio Humphrey, the knight-errant of American liberalism, tore into critics of big government while attending a dinner at the Americana: "Ronald Reagan is setting the rules for this campaign. Less is good. Government is too big. . . . Well, I'll tell you, I'm not about to fall for it." Humphrey was getting into the old rhythm, cranking up the old-time religion, whacking the podium first with his right hand, then with his left. "I am not ashamed to tell you I am a New Dealer," he proclaimed. "I want to warn you, my friends, that when people turn their back on our family, your heritage . . . you will lose, and deservedly so. . . . There are some people today who are running against Washington [presumably Jimmy Carter]. They are not positive. . . . The 'less government' theme is just a code word for neglect, a code word for ignoring our cities. . . . Neglect of our cities is a new form of racism."

Wild cheering. Humphrey's enthusiasm was always infectious, but this time he reached his audience because he reminded them of their faith in money and programs; of their faith in compassion, their desire to right wrongs—immediately. Liberalism's appeal has always rested on a big heart. For all his flaws, Humphrey touched a wide range of people because of his obvious humanity and concern. But liberals' very humanity led to an overheated conscience, to demands for instant solutions. After the blackout rioting and looting of 1977, there were loud demands for the federal government to do something. The solution, *Daily News* columnist Pete Hamill briskly declared, was to "Ask Congress for immediate authorization to create 200,000 goods-producing jobs to be located in New York. Not make-work jobs, shoveling sidewalks or cutting grass. The army can do that work. But building factories that employ New Yorkers in the creation of material goods that can be sold to other people. The government can do that in partnership with private enterprise." Just like that—presto!—200,000 jobs. In partnership with private enterprise in the sixties, President Johnson initiated the National Alliance of Businessmen to attract jobs for the hard-core unemployed. In 1968, their first full year, they created but 100,000 jobs in the entire nation. It's not easy to induce profit-making institutions to make socially desirable decisions. Even when government tax or training subsidies are available, white-dominated business is not adept at dealing with the minority-dominated unemployed.

The spreading blight of the South Bronx must be stopped— immediately! Ditto Bushwick. Ditto Bedford-Stuyvesant. Ditto Harlem. Ditto South Jamaica. The answer, declared with absolute certainty, is more jobs, more housing, more government, more money, more inputs. Humility in the pursuit of social justice is no virtue. When confronted with the reality that the people of this country are resistant to new social spending, that President Carter and the Congress will not be forthcoming with the massive funds required—assuming we would know how to spend it if they did— there is a general unwillingness to retreat. To make hard-headed choices about what is do-able as opposed to desirable. So when Jimmy Carter visits the South Bronx and offers a money cure, the city leaps to accept, forgetting that the amount of money Carter offered is inadequate to the task, that there are still viable neighborhoods that could better use limited resources. No, the South Bronx is an outrage! We will not tolerate outrages! While we feel better, neighborhoods like Coney Island or Bushwick slip away.

Such passionate politics leads, inevitably, to a Manichaean view of the world—good guys vs. bad guys, liberals vs. conservatives. To an unusual degree, New York's politics was bursting with a quasi-religious fervor. Rather than questioning which candidate was the most realistic or what policy would work, we often asked who or what was most liberal? Mayor LaGuardia's truism—"There is no Republican or Democratic way to clean streets"—was ignored. Essentially nonideological local questions—how to balance the budget, provide services, retain and attract jobs, educate kids, control crime—were transformed into moral issues. James Schuer's 1969 mayoral candidacy began to unravel when the *Voice*'s Jack Newfield—a valuable muckraker but also a notorious labeler—branded Schuer a "conservative" for raising the "law and order" issue. Yet, that same year, writers Norman Mailer and Jimmy Breslin were treated kindly by the press when they proposed a frivolous but "liberal' idea to make New York City the fifty-first state.

Wagner, Lindsay, Beame and Rockefeller got away with their budget and borrowing tricks partly because they were trying to do the "right thing." Candidates who talked about "the *causes* of crime" were good guys, even if they ignored the *effects* of crime. People who talked about balanced budgets were "fiscal conservatives"; those who spoke of incentives for private enterprise worried lest they be labeled "pro-business"; critics of union contracts were dismissed as "anti-labor"; community groups who organized to save their neighborhoods were disparaged as "bigots."

People who take "moral" positions don't like to make unpleasant choices. During periods of growth and expansion, these choices were easier to avoid. Liberals could both do good and feel good, could keep their moral edge. Liberalism remained strong because citizens, quite accurately, believed they cared. But when public expectations rose and the economy began to decline in the late sixties, that strength of conscience became a vice. The right moral posture became the wrong governmental position. Those who, loosely, subscribed to the liberal label, refused to recognize that there were now limits to what the city could spend, borrow or tax; local limits to providing *more*. The unwillingness to make choices, Senator Moynihan reminds us, was on display when the state offered to assume the city's welfare and higher education costs in the sixties. But, as he says, the city's "powerful political culture" resisted for fear of sacrificing administrative control and free tuition. A decade later, the city clamored for a state takeover of these costs. In the spring of 1978, the city's labor unions demanded raises, though the city faced a huge four-year deficit and was asking Congress for a federal bailout. Labor leaders and the prevailing wisdom in the city held that it would be "an outrage" if raises were not granted. The emphasis was on the "outrage" rather than whether the city could afford it.

The unwillingness to make choices is obviously not peculiar to New York or liberalism. Herbert Allen, president of Allen & Company, one of Wall Street's largest firms, criticizes "politicians"—yet Allen dubbed President Carter's advisers "hopelessly naive" for opposing what he calls "dubious payments" to foreign leaders. Americans want free trade—yet they condemn imports which rob American jobs. We want to attract middle-income people back to our cities—but not to outbid and displace poor people from their old yet restorable homes. We want higher farm subsidies—and cheaper food prices. More government spending—and less inflation. More guns and butter. But, as Peter Jay notes, "So far the only road to paradise lies through the grave."

In New York, the failure to make choices speeded the fiscal crisis. One of the best explanations of *why*, not *how*, the city arrived at its present state is contained in a book that does not mention the fiscal crisis. Nor does it mention Abe Beame, John Lindsay, Robert Wagner or Nelson Rockefeller. Nor such now-familiar terms as investor confidence, bonds, notes, rollovers, deficits or default. In fact, it doesn't even mention the City of New York.

The book, *The Morality of Consent*, is the work of the late Alexander M. Bickel, a Yale University scholar. Bickel wrote of a series of decisions and events in the sixties and early seventies: If the public and the Congress had to be deceived to gain support and "defeat" communism, so be it. When reform legislation crawled too slowly through state legislatures or the Congress, the Supreme Court skipped legal precedents and passed its own laws. To protest the war, it was necessary to deny Defense Secretary McNamara freedom of speech at Harvard. After Karl Armstrong bombed the University of Wisconsin, historian Gabriel Kolko apologized: "To condemn Karl Armstrong," Bickel quotes Kolko, "is to condemn a whole anguished generation. His intentions were more significant than the unanticipated consequences [one dead, four injured] of his actions." If we had to discriminate with racial quotas to end discrimination, conduct illegal wiretaps or invent "the plumbers" in the name of "law and order"—so be it.

Bickel found a common denominator in these decisions: an abuse of either power or "the process," as he called it. "The [social] fabric," he said, "is held together by agreement on means. . . . The derogators of procedure and technicalities, and other anti-institutional forces who rode high, on the bench as well as off, were the armies of conscience and ideology. . . ." The ancient question of means and ends.

What does this have to do with New York? The same common thread stretched through many—not all—of the often well-intentioned decisions which helped hobble the city. It was Nelson Rockefeller's liberal impulse—not to mention megalomania and desire to get reelected—that drove him to devise "moral obligation" bonds in order to build more housing and avoid the danger of voter disapproval. It was the liberal impulse to centralize executive power that prompted the drafters of the 1961 City Charter to remove the comptroller and Board of Estimate as a check on the mayor's power to estimate revenues. It was the liberal impulse to reward labor as a valued friend, to tax and borrow and fraud rather than balance city budgets. No one compelled New York State to spend 60 percent more than the national average for elementary and secondary education; to offer scholarship and tuition assistance that is three times that of the next highest state; to offer the most generous Medicaid program in the U.S.—the state has 8.5 percent of the nation's population yet accounts for 23 percent of all Medicaid spending.

Obviously, these decisions can be attributed to such nonideological truisms as "politics," weak leadership, a docile electorate or human nature. As noted, New York was the victim of forces and decisions beyond its control. But we learn something about what happened to New York when we also view past local decisions as violations of fiscal and legal restraints—of "the process." New York forgot about Adam Smith's "invisible hand" that guides a free market and turned it away from city bonds to more secure investments; forgot that expedient means (excessive borrowing and taxation) would inevitably lead to a bad end (deep debt and loss of jobs); that each city is not an island; that the social contract is violated when leaders lie, be it about budgets or Vietnam body counts.

Another failure was at work in New York—an excessive faith in people. Liberals succumbed to the blissful notion, promulgated more than 100 years ago by Marx and Engels, that the concept of "human nature" was silly. The left believed that institutions, society, capitalism, determined how people would behave. "Does it require deep intuition," they wrote in The Communist Manifesto, "to comprehend that man's ideas, views and conceptions, in one word, man's consciousness, changes with every change in the conditions of his material existence, in his social relations and in his social life?"

To acknowledge a people problem is to acknowledge complexity, the futility of relying on just money for solutions. It's not always society's or the teacher's fault when kids can't read. Contrary to Jesse Jackson's preachments, few criminals are "political prisoners." Jobs would have prevented some but not all of the looting after the 1977 blackout. Brooklyn District Attorney Eugene Gold reported that 48 percent of those arrested were employed; more comprehensive studies suggest 65 to 73 percent were unemployed. Whichever figure you accept, it is true that many of the looters were employed. Put more money into the education system and more than likely it will go to increase teacher pay and benefits, not pupil instruction. There is little class solidarity between workers who sacrifice their union brothers to layoffs while they continue to receive salary increases. Even clichés can be true. Welfare *can* create a cycle of dependency; shorter work weeks and more time off *can* make people lazy. Landlords steal, but so do poor and middle-income people in subsidized housing.

Many are the victims of racism, joblessness, hopelessness—of a capitalist system that often punishes the least efficient, the ugly or the old. But some people, determinists prefer not to concede, are bad people, unreachable. Bushwick's Crazy Homicides, one suspects, would as soon knife you as step on a roach. In just that sense, they are probably little different from the redneck killers of civil rights workers, who killed as a political act. Writer William Bradford Huie once speculated that James Earl Chaney, Michael Schwerner and Andrew Goodman were trying to reason with and appeal to their common humanity when some racist Southerners took them on a back road in 1964 and blew their heads off. The rednecks were as difficult to reach as the Crazy Homicides or the youth gangs of the South Bronx. And yet our schemes to rebuild the South Bronx, for instance, tend to ignore this reality. What if the new South Bronx is torched just like the old?

Most of us are afraid to talk about this problem of an underclass for fear—the most dreaded fear among liberals—of being called "racist." Pat Moynihan, despite his unfortunate reliance on hyperbole, once tried to show how the breakup of black families contributed to crippling black youngsters. He was roundly condemned as a "white racist," among the gentler epithets. Senator Ted Kennedy, exercising considerably more skill, escaped the epithets because he did not appear to be blaming the victim when he told Detroit's NAACP: "Every measure we have tells us that these children are the most likely to be victims of parental abuse, the most likely to be dropouts from their schools, the most likely to be unemployed, the most likely to be on welfare, the most likely to be delinquent, the most likely to be jailed, the most likely to be found in an early grave."

Interestingly, Kennedy placed a large part of the blame for the breakup of black families on the welfare system devised by liberals. "The heart of the problem is a welfare system that too often works against the welfare of those the system is supposed to serve," he said. "There is ample evidence that the welfare system itself, in combination with other factors, has helped to produce the very disease we now seek to cure. . . . we say to this child—wait, there is a way, one way, you can be somebody to someone. We will give you an apartment and furniture to fill it. We will give you a TV set and a telephone. We will give you clothing, and cheap food, and free medical care, and some spending money besides. And in return, you only have to do one thing: just go out and have a baby. And faced with such an offer, it is no surprise that hundreds of thousands have been caught in the trap that our welfare system has become."

Epithets and scapegoating, sadly, also extend to liberals' interpretation of the fiscal crisis. On the first page of their book about New York, Newfield and Dubrul ask, "What is killing New York City?" Their answer: dope, highways, Vietnam, the banks, racism, Defense spending in the Sunbelt, Sirhan Sirhan, national unemployment, recessions, Rockefeller's moral obligation bonds and "a generation of municipal politicians who could not tell the truth." Of these eleven factors, only the last two were self-inflicted. And even these did not represent a failure of ideology or people, since, according to this view. Rockefeller and municipal politicians were just being selfish. The main culprits were Washington and the banks. A similar approach is taken by Richard S. Morris, an otherwise intelligent political activist and consultant to liberal Democrats. The "real villains of the urban crisis," he writes in *Bum Rap on American Cities: The Real Causes of Urban Decay,* are not "liberals" but the robber-baron federal government and greedy bankers. He adds, "Liberals are, indeed, taking a bum rap" because New York's crisis is "not the result of any error in direction or approach." Former Lindsay administration officials blame "the system" or the "ungovernability of cities"—when they're not blaming Washington. Beame, as we've seen, blamed everyone, and therefore no one. The

Marxian analysis—which is closer to the truth in its analysis if not its answer—is presented by Roger E. Alcaly and David Mermelstein in their book *The Fiscal Crisis of American Cities.* "Ultimately," they write, "the origins of the urban fiscal crisis lie in the process of capitalist accumulation, in a system of economic growth dictated by capital's needs to seek ever greater profits." On the other hand, in the Soviet Union, for example, citizens are not permitted to move freely, a natural consequence of a government-dictated economic system.

Rather than accept blame for at least part of what happened to New York, the left too often portrays the city as a victim of a giant right-wing conspiracy. "Our true sin, in the eyes of Philistine skinflints and neo-conservative ideologues," writes Irving Howe, editor of the socialist magazine *Dissent*, "has been the decency—if not sufficient, still impressive—with which New York has treated its poor. . . . The assault on the city is an assault on maintaining, let alone extending, the welfare state. The assault on the welfare state is an assault on the poor, the deprived, the blacks, the Puerto Ricans." No doubt, many conservatives use the New York example as a weapon to bludgeon liberalism—a central thrust of William Simon's book. But the thrust of my argument is practical, not ideological. Not whether New York often tried to do the right thing but whether, alone, it could afford to; whether it worked.

The New York crisis can be seen from many perspectives—from the left, as the result of capitalism's need to search out cheap labor and reduce costs; from the right, as the logical consequence of intrusive government. Both arguments are, simultaneously, true. But the left tends to get so exercised that it overlooks some other truths. Take, for instance, the city's 40 percent subway fare increase in 1975. Many cried, with considerable justice, that this was counterproductive and would lead to the loss of many more riders. That September, the city needed to borrow $906 million to meet its monthly cash needs. Sixty-five percent of this sum was earmarked to repay interest and principal on previous loans, much of which could have been eliminated if previous mayors had not borrowed so promiscuously. Just one-fifth of this September 1975 debt service payment—$120 million—could have spared the 35¢ subway fare.

An ideological view of the fiscal crisis—either from the right, which just blames the left, or from the left, which just blames Washington or capitalism—broadens the risk of bankruptcy. In truth, New York will not be able to dig itself out of its hole without additional federal help, particularly from restructuring its growing debt burden but also in the form of continued federal pressure for local reform. More important is what the city must do for itself. If New York accepted the excuse that it was solely a victim of outside forces, there would be little impetus to alter past habits. Again, as in the South Bronx, the city would fail to confront cold reality or make choices. If it's not New York's fault, how can it be our responsibility? Therefore, if vast new federal assistance is not forthcoming, if federal loans are not renewed indefinitely, if the banks don't open their vaults, if the immutable laws of capitalism don't change—if the city continues to avoid radically restructuring its budget and service delivery system—bankruptcy is almost inevitable. An unelected federal judge will then be empowered to make the budget cuts refused by the city—perhaps choosing to cut social programs for the poor, perhaps deciding that debt obligations to creditors rank ahead of people services.

As long as liberals and many New Yorkers assume that the answer to the $1 billion budget deficit lies in Washington or bank vaults, they shall lack the political will to balance their budget, as other local governments must. They will probably lack the ammunition to sell Washington and the rest of the country the need for further assistance. They will lack the drive, and pressure, to reform the management of the government bureaucracy. They will, like Senator George McGovern, rail against the "undertones of racism" lurking beneath the populist tax revolt, ignoring the public's legitimate anger at government waste.

Ironically, by railing against "racism" and villainous outsiders, those on the left often behave like "conservatives." They come to protect their programs, their traditions, their record. To favor the status quo. To stress the pain and what's already been accomplished, rather than what remains to be done. Some warn that attacks against government are aimed at democracy itself. In his book *The Limits of Legitimacy*, Alan Wolfe, a self-proclaimed Marxist, suggests, "The attack on government activity has become . . . a not particularly well disguised attack on democracy itself." By this logic, the two-thirds of California voters who supported reduced property taxes in 1978 were not just anti-poor but anti-democratic. An act is democratic only if Mr. Wolfe agrees with it. Others warn that change must come gradually and not be disruptive. Echoing Robert McNamara, in late 1977 Mayor Beame declared he saw "light at the end of the tunnel." Governor Carey and the municipal unions stated similar views about "the progress" made. Symbolizing their status quo approach, most of the municipal unions endorsed Beame's reelection bid. "The Mayor is the only candidate able to maintain a relationship with public employees," said Barry Feinstein, head of Teamsters Local 237 and Treasurer of the Municipal Labor Committee. Teachers' union president Albert Shanker also endorsed Beame, declaring he was "best equipped to continue to lead the city out of its fiscal crisis and toward economic and social health." Jack Bigel, perhaps the single most powerful labor official because of his brains, lined up support for his friend Beame, as did John DeLury, chief of the sanitation union. One of the few major union holdouts was Victor Gotbaum—who called Beame "a disaster" but remained neutral.

In May 1976, when then MAC Treasurer Donna Shalala penned an Op-Ed page article for the *Daily News* suggesting the city would have to make further cuts and cease "business as usual" if it were to avoid bankruptcy, Bigel lashed back. "It is a call for confrontation," he wrote on the same page, "confrontation between the city and its employees. But even worse, it is a call for confrontation between the city and all New Yorkers." We must, cautioned the wealthy "conservative" who claims he is a socialist, "thwart the hotheads like Ms. Shalala, and avoid confrontation. . . ." These former allies of the underdog protested not a peep when the city, as required by a union-promoted state seniority law, laid off a disproportionate number of blacks, Hispanics and women. The United Federation of Teachers, in 1977, displayed full-page newspaper ads headlined NEW YORK CITY'S PUBLIC SCHOOLS: THE UNTOLD STORY. Taking negativists to task—"nattering nabobs of negativism"?—the union admonished, "But what the public doesn't see or hear is the enormous *success* [emphasis in original] story of the New York City public schools." It's important to the union that parents not think otherwise. God, what if they demanded a better education for the $2,600 spent annually per pupil? Or fewer teachers' prep periods, sick days, paid sabbaticals? What if citizens, who pay the freight, demanded performance standards for city employees?

Despite the evidence to the contrary, the left continues to treat most labor unions as if they remained the cutting edge of reform, a beleaguered rather than sometimes privileged class. It was easy to attack George Meany's blatherings about communism or the war in Vietnam, but when it comes to many local issues people genuinely committed to reform adopt a conservative pose. When mayoral candidate Bella Abzug strayed and tentatively questioned generous municipal pension benefits, Geoffrey Stokes wrote in the *Village Voice* that she was "union-baiting." Ellen Willis, in *Rolling Stone* magazine, described the municipal unions—who are now the city's primary bankers—as "powerless." Before union leaders consented to withdraw a few of their fringe benefits in 1975, writer Nat Hentoff condemned Shalala and Councilman Robert F. Wagner, Jr., as "anti-labor" for suggesting such blasphemy. The same people who favor strengthened consumer protection and oppose monopolies, blindly support municipal labor monopolies against growing consumer demands to get what they pay for.

All of this has an Alice in Wonderland quality to it. By opposing more local "sacrifices," the chances of bankruptcy grow, as do the odds that the real Huns will step in and demand the wrong kind of cuts or much deeper slashes in worker pay and benefits. If that happens, the nation's foremost liberal city will flash to the rest of the country a message liberals want to avoid: liberalism doesn't work. Some conservative colonialists will be granted license to speak of New York the way they do of "primitive" Africa. The liberal compact would break down as growing numbers of New Yorkers join other Americans in viewing not just liberalism, but government, as the enemy.

This may be the real danger—not that liberalism will be discredited but that government will be. Here, labels do matter. For while the old liberal or left litmus test issues—Vietnam, McCarthyism, domestic spying, unionism, dump LBJ, McGovern vs. Nixon— have receded, what tends to separate those on the left (loosely defined) from those on the right (also loosely defined) is a commitment to use government as an *effective* tool to help people. While many from my post–New Deal generation may reject the liberal label—preferring "progressive"—they would plead guilty to a bias in favor of the less fortunate, an emphasis on what remains to be done, a commitment to seek change; in a word, hope. Obviously, many who are called "conservatives" possess some or all of these qualities. And there are honest differences over the *means* to achieve these ends; people can be "left" on some issues and "right" on others.

But as the child of a working-class home, I know that while liberals may be bleeding hearts, at least they bleed. If you've ever covered or attended a national Republican convention, perhaps you know what I'm trying to say. These are the people who tend to agree with neo-conservative cynics like Irving Kristol, who urges what he calls "benign neglect" for cities: "The cities are bottoming out. Leave them alone and they'll recover." That is the voice of a comfortable man. Similar voices opposed advances in civil rights and women's rights, the antiwar struggle, tax reform, antitrust, consumerism. The status quo. "All great discoveries," C. H. Parkhurst once said, "are made by men whose feelings ran ahead of their thinking."

The challenge to progressives—both nationally and locally—is to think a little more clearly; to learn from, rather than embrace, past mistakes; to make government work. The Depression taught Americans the limitations of unfettered free enterprise and the more important role government could play in solving social problems. The New York crisis teaches the limitations of what government can do.

Perhaps New York's experience will finally rob liberalism of its innocence. As was true for America in Vietnam, in New York liberalism has been identified with the wrong side.

Chapter Ten

1975-78: The More Things Change, the More They Stay the Same

THREE YEARS LATER—after the bouts with bankruptcy, the layoffs, the service cuts, the new bookkeeping systems and the loud threats have been replaced by Big Apple lapel pins and congratulatory speeches—has anything changed?

Not really, laments Edward Costikyan, who was fleetingly a candidate for mayor in 1977. To make the point, he recalls a story his father used to tell about an Armenian sultan with a herd of healthy horses who captured a particularly clever horse thief. Without a moment's pause, the sultan ordered immediate execution.

"No!" cried the thief. "Spare my life and I will teach your horses to fly."

It was an offer the sultan could not refuse, and the thief was granted a year of freedom to perform his miracle.

"But you can't teach horses to fly!" exclaimed a friend.

"Who knows?" responded the thief. "Maybe in a year I'll be dead. Or maybe in a year the Sultan will die. Or maybe in a year the horses will die." He paused, a smile creasing his face. "Or who knows? Maybe the horses really will fly."

Observes Costikyan: "That is what the first three years of the fiscal crisis have been about. New York City has acted as if horses could fly."

In New York's case, the reprieve came from city and employee pension funds and the federal government. New York's ritual execution—bankruptcy—was postponed when the pension funds agreed to risk $3.8 billion of their assets and the Ford administration and Congress narrowly approved a three-year seasonal loan program in late 1975 to provide the city with annual infusions of $2.3 billion in cash it could not raise in the private credit market. The feds, like the sultan, consented to the reprieve after clever people like Governor Carey promised, "We will never need a bailout again, and we won't come back for help; we are going to make it." Three years later, in 1978, New York had not made it and was back before the Congress pleading for an extension of seasonal loans and for new federal loan guarantees. Horses still couldn't fly.

What Has Changed

Much—and little—changed in New York between 1975 and 1978. Political styles changed. In times past, mayoral candidates issued white papers and 14-point platforms, usually crafted by infants fresh from college. Most candidates vied to promise more services, reduce crime, maintain the subway fare, address the "causes" of unemployment, crime and drugs, eliminate business and landlord "ripoffs." The answer to the city's problems, it was commonly assumed, was more money. The critical question was which candidate promised the most new programs, which candidate was most compassionate—who was the most caring liberal, not the most realistic and competent.

All that seemed to change in 1977. Most candidates in that year's mayoral contest acted as if they were aware of the new limits imposed on City Hall. They promised not purification from "the bosses" (as Wagner did in 1961), or Camelot (Lindsay in 1965), or peace and tranquillity (Beame in 1973), but further toil and sacrifice. One candidate, State Senator Roy Goodman, warned that the city's attrition policy was insufficient and that further layoffs would be necessary. Manhattan Borough President Percy Sutton challenged the once-sacrosanct police union and promised 60,000 to 100,000 more auxiliary police volunteers. Builder Richard Ravitch predicted future deficits unless the city cut its budget and slashed its broad range of services. Costikyan vowed to abolish the City University's graduate school. Secretary of State Mario Cuomo promised no-cost labor contracts, with any pay raises funded through increased worker productivity. And the man who ultimately won the contest, Ed Koch, succeeded in part because he was perceived as the most specifically outspoken candidate, lashing out at union as well as business and landlord "ripoffs," seemingly fearless in his condemnation of "poverticians" as well as politicians.

Unlike earlier campaigns, the emphasis was not on "new priorities" for federal dollars. If there was a Maginot Line separating the candidates, it was not between who was the most "liberal" or who made the most promises, but who was primarily responsible—city or federal and bank officials—for the fiscal crisis and its resolution. On one side of the line stood Mayor Beame and former Congresswoman Bella Abzug. The thrust of their argument was that the fiscal crisis was less the fault of past city officials or policies than of federal neglect and avaricious bankers. It followed that those who caused the crisis bore primary responsibility for solving it. Though differing in style and ideology, each ran defensively: Beame was protecting his record as mayor; Bella, her liberal ideology.

Koch, Cuomo, Goodman and several others stood on the opposite side of the line, seeming to agree with the "central conclusion" of the final report of the Temporary Commission on City Finances, issued in June 1977: "The City of New York must be fundamentally reformed before its fiscal problems and the larger economic problems of New York City can be solved: incremental reform of the local government process will not suffice, even in the event that the State of New York and the federal government assume increasing responsibility for functions performed by the City of New York." To drive home its point, Beame's Commission challenged the conventional wisdom which holds that "welfare reform" will untangle the city's budget conundrum. Even if the President and the Congress agreed to assume New York City's $500 million share of welfare costs, they noted, this sum was equal to the then-anticipated 1978 budget gap. Unless the city drastically altered past spending patterns, the additional $500 million would simply be swallowed up by wage increases and new local spending. The new money would not be used—finally—to balance the budget or reduce taxes to help regenerate the local economy. It would be like offering another fix to an addict.

The report was ignored by Beame, but not by many of the other mayoral candidates. For the first time in memory, good politics and good government seemed to be in harmony. None of the contenders would promise to maintain the 50¢ subway fare—not because they didn't want to, but because they didn't know where the money would come from. None promised to slash crime because none of them were sure they could. With the exception of Beame, none promised to hire more police or provide more services. It used to be that citywide candidates trembled at the prospect of being pigeonholed as "pro-business." In 1977, each competed to capture this distinction. Business tax cuts were urged by all the candidates, as were other business incentives. Once, during a September television debate, the nine Democratic and Republican pre-primary candidates were asked which rated a higher priority: cutting taxes or raising wages. Roy Goodman said he would choose to cut taxes. The others emitted indecipherable, noncommittal responses. In previous campaigns, the candidates would have clawed and leaped over each other to promise wage increases.

If the candidates changed, perhaps it was because, in many respects, the public had as well. 1977 was a year when New York voters—like voters across the nation—were registering their distaste for high taxes. They were angry about government spending and waste, about costly municipal labor settlements, about reduced city services. "The tax collector, rather than the employer—at least in New York—is the worker's major adversary. The same tax collector, rather than the worker, is the employer's major adversary." These words emanated not from some Chamber of Commerce spokesman but from Joseph Trerotola, President of New York Teamsters Joint Council 16. During the fiscal crisis, the public suffered reduced services, usually without notable protest. A city that in 1969 hotly debated whether it wanted to become the fifty-first state, quietly surrendered its home rule to the Emergency Financial Control Board. A new consensus was forged: New Yorkers would do what was necessary to restore "investor confidence."

The public chose three candidates—Koch, Cuomo and Goodman—who in prior years might incorrectly have been labeled "conservatives" because of their emphasis on "fiscal responsibility" and "mismanagement." In this campaign, they were perceived as the anti–status quo candidates when they challenged, for example, union "ripoffs," suggesting how much the public's view of who was the enemy had changed. Voters rejected Beame's everything-is-all-right theme and Abzug's line that the federal government offered salvation. They elected Ed Koch not because he was "fresh and everyone else is tired," like John Lindsay in 1965, or because he was against the "bosses," as Bob Wagner was in 1961, or because he was "a mediator," as Abe Beame promised to be in 1973. Koch beat Cuomo and the rest of the field because he came across as the most outspoken, the most specific about how he would do more with less. He convinced people he would represent the public against the special interests. Every time a union leader attacked him, or he harshly called Beame "incompetent," he won points. Koch helped prove that to win a primary or an election it is often better to have the political, business and labor establishment on the other side.

But, as Koch would learn, getting elected is not synonymous with governing. In the first three years of the crisis, two questions—bankruptcy and how to avoid it—dominated City Hall's attention. The people who would help answer those questions were not average voters, or the poor, or blacks, or neighborhood groups. Their influence and power was diminished. Three businessmen were appointed to the Emergency Financial Control Board that would oversee city finances. Labor, too, had its representatives attend Control Board meetings. Yet not one representative of the poor or the city's diverse neighborhoods was represented. Minorities, in particular, lost power. For the first time in twenty-five years, they were not represented on the Board of Estimate. By 1978, blacks, who account for 25 percent of the city's population, held only two of eighteen Congressional seats, three of twenty-five state senate seats, twelve of sixty-five state assembly seats and five of forty-three City Council seats. In place of a far-flung securities market composed of thousands of individuals, a handful of bankers and union leaders decided whether or not to invest in city or MAC securities. A "partnership," as they came to call it, was formed between City Hall, the banks, the municipal unions, the business community, the state and the federal government. All shared a common interest in averting bankruptcy.

Former adversaries—in 1975, the unions blamed the banks and the banks blamed the unions for the fiscal crisis—locked arms. In 1977, Jack Bigel, representing the unions, and Walter Wriston, president of Citicorp, began to meet regularly on an informal basis—leading to the creation of an ongoing committee (called MUFLE) designed to determine areas of mutual interest. To avoid bankruptcy, Mayor Beame, a man fiercely proud of his reputation for fiscal wizardry, silently suffered humiliation and a reduction of his mayoral powers. Governor Carey braved a too-close identification with the city—traditionally unpopular upstate—and risked alienating powerful interest groups while appearing to be the Scrooge-like Chairman of the Control Board. Members of the business and banking community, abandoning the comforts of lecturing politicians, lent their time and financial and managerial expertise to the city. The federal government, stung by the backlash to the callous statements of President Ford and Treasury Secretary Simon in 1975, adopted a more behind-the-scenes role, gently prodding the local partners toward further reforms. And the municipal unions, whose members' wages and fringe benefits form the largest share of the city's budget, made significant sacrifices. For the first time since the Depression, they acceded to 25,000 layoffs. They agreed to defer a pay increase for one year. City workers earning more than $15,000 would defer a full 6 percent raise. To save money, the unions consented to "give back" over $40 million of previously won fringe benefits. At grave risk, employee pension funds also committed to invest $3.8 billion over the three years to keep the city afloat. It became city/union policy to shrink the work force through attrition—a tacit acknowledgment by the unions that there were too many employees.

But the public made the greatest sacrifices. Their taxes went up while their services went down. Free tuition and open enrollment at the City University, library hours, sanitation pickups, city hospitals, day-care centers, the city work force—were cut back or eliminated. The transit fare zoomed 40 percent. According to an analysis for the *City Almanac* by Charles Brecher and Miriam Cukier, between 1975 and 1977 total funding for the Board of Education rose 9 percent while the staff was reduced by 20 percent and pupil enrollment by 6 percent; total refuse collection by the sanitation department dropped 2 percent; police arrests declined by 6 percent; the budget of the Board of Higher Education remained about the same —while the number of college students plunged 24 percent. In his second management report, Koch conceded that streets were dirtier, the city's parks were in a state of "disrepair" and over half the $1.1 billion in back taxes and bills owed the city could be collected but wasn't.

The city government also changed. The growth rate of its budget slowed. The city's bookkeeping system was overhauled. Under a new computerized system—called IFMS, for short—New York will soon enjoy perhaps the most advanced financial management system of any municipality in the world. Gone were the days when a Jim Cavanagh or Abe Beame could project Off-Track Betting revenues on the back of an envelope, as they did in urging the state legislature to create OTB in 1970. Gone too was the myth of "the expert"—that one individual who, alone, knew where funds were buried. Today, there are seven different auditors, including those from the Control Board, MAC, the federal Treasury and the Congress, peering over City Hall's shoulders. The press, more attuned to the nuances of budgets, polices City Hall with greater vigor. "Two major things have changed," observes Sidney Schwartz, Deputy State Comptroller and the Control Board's chief auditor. "One is a change of attitude—I'm referring strictly to fiscal matters. The top management under Zuccotti and Kummerfeld, and now under Koch, realized they had to cut down. They slowed the spending rate. The other thing is, despite all the different numbers, the numbers given out are more reliable."

Even the city's official documents changed. Greater candor was evident, for instance, in the city's May 1977 official prospectus to investors. Mindful of the SEC scathing criticism, New York's problems were not sugar-coated. The prospectus acknowledged that that year's pensions were underfunded by $160 million, warned that "no assurance can be given that the City will realize the projected amount of funds" from the sale of Mitchell-Lama mortgages "in a timely manner," sketched how real-estate taxes were declining, debts rising, and how future city deficits would also grow. Displaying his commitment to the new candor, Mayor Koch announced soon after his election that he would speed the eight remaining years allowed by the state legislature to remove expense items from the capital budget. Koch would complete the task in three. He also would increase appropriations in order to eventually eliminate underfunded pensions.

The city's management also improved. Acceding to the commands of the new City Charter and the Control Board, City Hall installed a management reporting system requiring monthly and annual productivity goals from each city agency. These goals were then monitored by a director of operations, a new office manned by a complement of full-time business executives whose salaries are paid by their companies. Beame had begun to surround himself with a better team of executives. Koch enlarged the pool of talent and began addressing management questions his predecessor chose to ignore. He asked Albany, for instance, to exempt an additional 3,000 city managers from union membership, to reform the civil service laws. He directed his Investigations Department to hire an additional 161 inspectors and search out not just corruption, but sloth and incompetence. In the first four months of the Koch administration, disciplinary actions against nonproductive employees increased—the Human Resources Administration instituted 450 disciplinary actions, the Parks Commissioner reassigned twenty-nine foremen who were not doing their jobs and promoted twenty-nine workers who were.

New York taxes began to inch down. In 1977, Mayor Beame announced the phasing out of the stock transfer tax, a 10 percent reduction in the commercial rent tax, a slight reduction in the real-estate tax. In 1978, Governor Carey proposed and the legislature approved a $750 million reduction in state taxes. New York was struggling to make itself economically more competitive. But this change must be placed in some perspective. The tax bite, conceded Assistant Budget Director John Fava, is deeper in New York City today than it was when the market collapsed in 1975. Responding to pressure from the "conservative" Ford administration, in 1975 the corporate tax rate jumped 50 percent, the financial tax doubled, the retail sales tax was extended to personal and business services, the personal income tax climbed by as much as 25 percent, the real-estate tax soared by $1.40 for each $100 of assessed value. Still, the trend is toward reduced taxes, with the major parties— Democrats, Republicans, Liberals and Conservatives—now vying to convey their greater commitment to tax reduction.

City Hall's attitude toward labor negotiations also seemed to change. "I believe the most dramatic change since I took over City Hall," Koch told me in June 1978, seated in his office between Fiorello LaGuardia's former desk and massive portrait, "is that the municipal labor leaders no longer own the mayor's office. They did." To demonstrate his independence, Koch took the unusual step of releasing a list of sixty-one "give-back" demands he was making of the municipal unions in their 1978 contract negotiations. The new mayor was proclaiming that he, representing the taxpayers in those negotiations, had to win something positive from the negotiations besides the negative of avoiding a strike. Elected with a mandate to shake the cages, Koch applied his favorite expression— "I am outraged"—to actions Beame and others regarded as commonplace. Koch had higher expectations, which filtered through to his commissioners and radiated to the public, accounting for the new mayor's 70 percent approval rating in the fall of 1978. One state auditor recalls a meeting he held with Beame when the latter was comptroller. They met to discuss a state audit which found that Beame's employees were working an abbreviated day. " 'You mean your people put in a full day?' " he recalls Beame asking. "His attitude was, 'Why get excited?' " If anything, Koch got too excited, arousing fears that he was impetuous, unreliable. But that is a fear engendered by all reformers.

What Hasn't Changed

Compared to past practices and rhetoric, much changed in New York during the first three years of the crisis. But given the magnitude of the city's problems, little had changed. "I would say we've only moved the ball from our own seven- or eight-yard line to our own 15 yard line," observed Ray Horton, principal author of the Temporary Commission's reports, in November 1977. In their final report of June 1977, the Commission used the word "decremental" to describe the actions of the Beame administration between 1975 and 1977. Which means going backwards. In the months since, Koch has tried to throw some passes. But the yards are gained slowly. "When I came here," he told me after his first three months in office, "I thought, you know, I would look at something and say, 'This is the reasonable, rational thing to do'—and I'd say, 'It's done.' Oh, no. You have to every day go out there and ask, 'What's happened?' And even then, it's only half done."

A review of the city's finances suggests the snail-like pace of reform. In 1975, the city's three-year fiscal plan predicted that by 1978—excluding the approximately $700 million of expense items sequestered in the capital budget—the city's budget would be honestly balanced and the credit market reopened. By mid-1978, the public credit market was still closed and the city's four-year fiscal plan projected that the budget wouldn't be balanced till 1982. Despite the promises made in 1975, by early 1978 Mayor Koch announced that the city's real deficit—the gap between what it took in and what it spent—would be $1,022 billion in fiscal 1979, and this tidy sum did not include the cost of expiring labor contracts.

The city's future budget projections were still predicated on some big ifs. They cautiously allowed that local revenues would grow slowly. But the city's chief revenue source, the property tax, was expected to decline between 1978 and 1982. And, according to a study by Ray Horton for the Lehrman Institute, "total proceeds from the four other general fund taxes are projected to grow only

22.7 percent" in that period—"a rate that may approximate the rate of inflation but will fall short of the 'natural' rate of expenditure increase by a substantial amount." The budget plan also assumed no further subsidies for the City University, the Health and Hospitals Corporation or the Transit Authority, though in April 1978 the city agreed to increase its transit subsidy by $18 million; and experience suggests the others, particularly the deficit-ridden Hospitals Corporation, will also win increases. The city's budget plan also assumed the continued expansion of federal and state aid, ignoring President Carter's January 1978 budget message with its promise to curb aid, his anti-inflation pledge to slash federal spending; it also ignored the city's dwindling share of the state's population (down from 53 percent in 1950 to 42 percent in 1975) and pledges to cut state taxes; ignored the spreading taxpayer rebellion which threatened Congressional renewal of revenue sharing and helped eliminate countercyclical aid (costing the city $34 million in fiscal 1979), and placed new curbs on the Comprehensive Employment Training Act (CETA).

After the House and Senate passed new federal loan legislation, cracks in the city's four-year plan began to surface. A June 21, 1978, Control Board staff report, which received scant press notice, projected a city budget gap of $928 million in fiscal 1981 and $1,014 billion in fiscal 1982, the year budget balance is supposed to be achieved. In fairness to the city, the staff report did not take into account Koch's projected attrition savings, which would reduce the gap by $272 million in 1981 and $422 million in 1982; nor did it count such unanticipated windfalls as the $24.6 million the city received from Penn Central for back taxes in the fall of 1978. On the other hand, the Control Board report warned that their computations did not take into account the cost of new labor contracts which begin on July 1, 1980, when union leaders say they will seek "substantial raises." (The same 8 percent wage hike won in 1978 would cost about $700 million.) The city's first four-year plan, for instance, made no allowance for continuation of cost-of-living or COLA II payments (now called "bonuses"). The staff report said these, alone, would consume an additional $335 million in 1981 and $310 million in 1982.* By July, officials were beginning to raise the possibility that the city would not achieve a balanced

---

* Nor was provision made, for instance, for the $1.8 billion of property tax claims made against the city which Corporation Counsel Alan Schwartz believes the city could lose in court.

budget by 1982. "Factoring in the full costs of the new contract for city employees and taking into consideration the likelihood of additional costs in the next round of bargaining two years from now," an analysis from Jac Friedgut, vice president of Citibank and one of the active "partners," alerted customers, "true budget balance in fiscal 1982 cannot be considered a foregone conclusion. . . . The city must run very fast to stand still . . . to close what now looks like a rapidly growing budget gap after fiscal 1980." In October 1978, Senator Moynihan—who thanked the President for "saving" the city in August—warned the budget gap was "as bad as it's ever been, and it's gonna get worse."

The gap remained because the city's expenditure patterns did not appreciably change during the fiscal crisis. According to the city's Budget Bureau, between 1975 and 1977 the local budget grew annually by 7.7 percent, compared to a 12 percent average over the previous fifteen years. Thus retrenchment, as defined in New York, meant not cutting but slowing the budget growth rate. Despite an almost 50 percent increase in federal dollars over these years, city spending rose to sponge up the extra funds. Instead of dramatically altering its spending patterns—drastically cutting back the broad range of city services, eliminating whole departments, slashing taxes to make the city more economically competitive—like one of Parkinson's plants, the budget simply sprouted new leaves. By 1978, New York was back before the Congress requesting fresh federal loans it said in 1975 it would never again need. It would not be unreasonable for a member of Congress to wonder how the city could truly balance its budget by 1982 when it had failed to do so, as promised, by 1978.

Were New York a private business, it would be a classic candidate for bankruptcy—with lagging revenues and rising expenditures and debt. As the Municipal Assistance Corporation struggled to provide financing, over the first three years of the fiscal crisis the city's debt grew almost 20 percent—from $12.3 billion in April 1975 to $14.2 billion in April 1978. This sum did not include the $753 million (as of February 28, 1978) that the City Comptroller says was owed for "debt-like commitments to public benefit corporations"; nor did it include the unfunded pension liabilities, pegged at over $8 billion in 1977. Thus the city's true debt was over $23 billion. And, despite the illusion of fiscal progress, despite the dramatic reduction in short-term debt, despite assurances to the Congress and the public that in four years the horses would in fact fly, then MAC board member Richard Ravitch told me private MAC calculations—based on the city's original four-year plan—projected that New York's debt burden could swell to $16.5 billion in fiscal 1983. These calculations were shared with neither the Congress nor the public. Were these calculations true? "It sounds a little high," responded MAC's Executive Director Gene Keilen, "but $16.5 billion is not out of the ball park." Several days later, he phoned to report that new arithmetic, based on fairly optimistic assumptions, showed the total debt could reach $14.4 million by 1990. None of these figures, he cautioned, were fixed, since this was "not a scientific exercise." No one knows what the interest rate will be, what the size of the city's future capital budget will be.

The bad news was kept from the Congress because "the game," in the words of one principal, "was to get the feds in. I think Senator Proxmire was right. The city had the local resources. We didn't need to borrow $4.5 billion of long-term aid, including $2 billion in loan guarantees from the federal government. We don't even know how to spend the $4.5 billion." According to this official, who said he would jeopardize his career by publicly speaking out, Rohatyn and Goldin and Bigel and a few others knew this but chose to mislead the Congress (and the public). Why? Because once the federal government bit the bait and was hooked for a long-term loan guarantee, it wouldn't be able to free itself without taking responsibility for the city's bankruptcy. In three or four years, the city could then go back and ask the feds to take another bite. Then another . . .

The city's annual debt service payments continued to devour an astounding portion of the budget—24¢ of each locally raised dollar in 1978. The $2 billion tab was the same the city paid in 1975, though slightly less than the $2.3 billion paid in 1976. In the long run, admitted Keilen, "total debt service will rise somewhat." MAC had succeeded in stretching out the city's debt repayments, but such stretches also swell the interest charges for future taxpayers. In July 1977, for instance, MAC refinanced $2.5 billion of city and MAC securities held by the banks and city pension funds. MAC Chairman Rohatyn boasted that between 1978 and 1984, the city had reduced its debt service payments by $1.3 billion. What he didn't advertise was that this stretch would burden future taxpayers with an additional $1.7 billion in interest over the longer life of the new bonds. To gain breathing room, the city was doing what it had always done: pay less now, pay more later.

"The cure for New York's fiscal crisis may prove worse than the disease," warned Howard Samuels in 1975. Instead of pushing for lower interest rates or demanding Washington's help to radically restructure and reduce the debt service burden, or, more drastically, seeking relief in the courts, the city and its new fiscal overseers once again made decisions on the basis of short-term rather than long-term consequences. "In retrospect," reflects a city official who has been at the center of the fiscal recovery effort, "bankruptcy would have been the best thing for the city in 1975. You could have refinanced the city's debts rather than refunding more costly MAC bonds. The city could have received relief from costly pension contractual obligations. Bankruptcy would have ended the viselike power of the unions [and the banks]. It might have changed the political make-up of the city."

I have always believed bankruptcy was intolerable. But so is what the city has done. As was true in Vietnam, the city ignored past lessons and was pulled deeper and deeper into debt. By 1978, Rohatyn—ignoring the lessons of the UDC's 1975 collapse—urged the state to place its "moral obligation" behind the city's bonds because they could not be sold without it. When the State Comptroller and Senate Majority Leader Anderson wondered aloud why the state's moral obligation backing was needed if the city's bonds were truly secure, Rohatyn and others double-talked, obfuscating the issue. Simply put: New York bonds were not yet credit-worthy.

By 1977, Mayor Beame—ignoring the fiscal crisis and the city's future deficits—acted as if the war was over. His reelection year budget was stuffed with goodies. Rather than slashing the city's work force by 7,523, as he had promised on January 6, 1977, he announced the hiring of 9,400 additional workers. For the duration of his campaign, Beame stopped the attrition clock from running, temporarily ending the agreed policy of shrinking the work force. Many laid-off workers were given federally funded CETA jobs, with the city paying the difference between their former city pay and the federal CETA ceiling of $10,000. Workers were promised cost-of-living adjustments; taxpayers got longer library hours, more police, the reopening of subway toll booths; the crime-fighting District Attorney offices got a 20 percent budget boost. As Lindsay once shut his eyes to a shrinking tax base, Beame shut his to the city's spreading deficit. "I estimate we came out of the year 1977 with an expenditure base that was $200 to $300 million higher than it had to be," claims former State Budget Director Peter Goldmark.

The city's new fiscal monitors—the state MAC and Control Board and the federal government, which were invited to police and check the excesses of City Hall—often did not blow the whistle. They chose to certify that Beame's last budget was "technically balanced," winking at the city's use of gimmicks which included the ten years the state legislature and the Governor granted the city to remove expenses from the capital budget.* But by that definition, each of the last seventeen city budgets would have been balanced as well. In truth, all the actors now had a stake in demonstrating the city's progress, in justifying their own efforts, in convincing Washington the city deserved more aid. A fraternity was formed—the watchers and the watched were in it together.

"There was a time in 1975 and 1976," recalls a former state official who was then an architect of the rescue efforts, "when all of us were very honest and called a spade a spade. Now we've gone back to buttering the apple even when we know it's rotten."

Seeing the firestorm unleashed by their 1975 opposition to city loans—FORD TO CITY: DROP DEAD, declared the October 30, 1975 front page of the *Daily News*—President Ford and Treasury Secretary Simon in 1976 began extolling "the progress the city was making." Seeing how Ford was trounced in New York in the 1976 election, the Carter administration maneuvered to avoid the appearance of placing unpopular pressure on City Hall. Beame had a political stake in advertising the progress made under his tutelage. Governor Carey, Chairman of the Control Board, had a political stake in freeing himself from unpopular city decisions so he could plan his 1978 reelection campaign. Comptroller Goldin was scheming to run for state comptroller in 1978. Felix Rohatyn had a three-year record to defend, and was eager to return to private life before his financial artifice collapsed. The banks had investments to protect and an interest in keeping the city afloat until the statute of limitations expired on potential noteholder suits in 1982. The unions worried that bankruptcy would not only threaten their pension fund investments but would permit a judge to abrogate all of their contracts, something the state constitution prohibited—except in case of bankruptcy. The *Times* and the *News*, without informing their readers, purchased MAC securities and, more often than not, lauded their local gladiators. The only persistent and informed

* The actual deficit, an independent audit by Peat, Warwick, Mitchell & Co. later found, was $712 million.

opposition to this fraternity of interests came from Wisconsin's Senator Proxmire. By June 1978, he was complaining of an inability to locate people of substance to testify against New York's request for an extension of seasonal loans and for $2 billion of federal loan guarantees.

New York's economic and social indicators did not appreciably change during the first three years of the fiscal crisis, despite Mayor Koch's ludicrous claim that the city was on the brink of a "renaissance." Yes, the local economy showed a gain of 7,000 private jobs from February 1977 to February 1978, the first gain in eight years. But one year does not make a trend. The city's job growth in this year was, we should note, the slowest of any major city in America. And it came in a period when the nation's economy was expanding at a faster rate than projected for the remainder of this decade. And the Bureau of Labor Statistics continued to predict future job losses for New York. *The Economist*, an admired British publication, completed a twenty-two-page survey of the city's economy, optimistically concluding: "New York is not so much declining as changing." The survey was trumpeted by those who affix Big Apple stickers to their lapels. The weakness of this upbeat analysis is that it focused on mid-Manhattan, which is not New York (except to the British chap who wrote the survey). The hotel and restaurant and retail and foreign investment boom in Manhattan is foreign to the other four boroughs, which comprise 80 percent of the city's population and 93 percent of its land mass.

There was little prospect that the conditions which made New York unattractive for many businesses and for people with the means to move—high taxes, high energy and living costs, high crime, reduced services—would suddenly disappear. Though Candidate Koch suggested he would reduce "excessive" city taxes, Mayor Koch's four-year recovery plan called for no such reduction. And, as noted earlier, the tax bite was steeper in 1978 than in 1975. By 1978, the most dangerous people in New York were the same as they were in 1975 and before: those who acted as if they believed the horse thief. Or as Margaret Mead, thinking in a world context, once said, "If we build . . . thinking in too rosy terms, people will become apathetic and not do the things that need to be done. We have to realize that everything we say about the future will influence the future."

It is hard to be sanguine about the city's future when we recall that there were, in the spring of 1978, 25,000 abandoned buildings or lots, each no longer paying property taxes. Another 27,300 buildings, according to Koch's Community Development Budget, would be abandoned by landlords—caught between inflation and impoverished tenants on the one hand and rent control on the other —by June 1979. A total of 71,000 occupied dwelling units would fall into the city's hands by then—four times the number in January 1978—Koch ominously reported later in the year. Thus the City of New York will, conservatively, become the landlord for approximately 500,000 people—a population larger than those of all but twenty-four American cities. Besides not paying taxes, these properties will require City Hall to provide fuel and maintenance. And, as experience dictates, the city will fail to collect rents from many tenants who live in these buildings. Worse: "My biggest worry is, what happens on the first cold day of winter?" says Housing Commissioner Nat Leventhal. Will the city be able to turn on the heat? That this cancer was allowed to fester and multiply can be traced, in part, to the Beame administration, which treated abandoned buildings as it treated budget gaps. They didn't exist. Instead of gearing up to cope with and try to manage these properties, Beame and Deputy Mayor John Zuccotti ignored a confidential April 1977 report from their own Office of Management and Budget. In fact, someone ordered most copies destroyed. It was an election year and abandoned buildings were bad news. Perhaps they would go away.

Another problem that won't go away is the underclass, which few public officials dare talk about. One of the few progressives who has is Senator Edward Kennedy. This problem, he told Detroit's 23rd annual NAACP dinner in May 1978, is "the great unmentioned problem of America today—the growth, rapid and insidious, of a group in our midst, perhaps more dangerous, more bereft of hope, more difficult to confront, than any for which our history has prepared us. It is a group that threatens to become what America has never known—a permanent underclass in our society. . . . They are the other side, the untold side, of our statistics of self-congratulatory progress." Kennedy produced data revealing that more than 50 percent of all New York blacks were born to mothers without husbands (vs. 20 percent in 1956); among Hispanics, almost 50 percent of all children were born out of wedlock (vs. 11 percent in 1956). "But the life of welfare," Kennedy continued, "is not the life of independence and freedom. When Martin Luther King spoke of his achievement, and yours, and we thrilled to his words, he did not say 'Comfort at last' or 'Welfare at last.' He said, 'Free at last.' . . . There is ample evidence that the welfare system itself, in combination with other factors, has helped to produce the very disease we now must seek to cure."

It would be a tough cure to bring off even if we were willing to talk about it. Though New York has reduced welfare rolls and fraud, the number of people on welfare remains staggering. Almost one of every seven city residents—930,000—was on welfare in 1978. Another 500,000 to 1.5 million illegal aliens, most of them desperately poor, were, in effect, declared non-persons—not counted, not taxed, ignored. There are too few job opportunities for these aliens or for the hard-core unemployed and teenagers. And what growth there is in jobs tends to be in the white-collar service sector, which doesn't match a blue-collar population.

The picture was considerably brighter for the banks. The major New York banks emerged in far better shape in 1978 than they were in three years earlier. During this period, they liberated their portfolios of most of their city notes and reduced their investment in city securities, converting the majority to more secure MAC bonds (unlike employee pension funds, which invested three times as much but got stuck with more precarious city paper). The banks had reason to celebrate. *The Wall Street Journal*, in a June 29, 1978, editorial, explained why, despite the city's spreading deficit, the banks agreed in the summer of 1978 to purchase $500 million of MAC bonds to help the city through 1982. "It grows increasingly plausible," the *Journal* said, "that the answer lies in what is known to insiders as the '10–b–5 issue.' That is the section of the securities law that outlaws fraud. The banks underwrote huge volumes of New York City notes just before its fiscal crisis exploded in 1975; their critics have charged that they knew the crisis was mounting and made fraudulent misrepresentations to buyers of the notes. The significance of 1982 is that by then the statute of limitations will have run out. . . . As long as there's a strong public market for MACs, the banks can argue that money losses were relatively small. . . . The [banks'] liability would obviously be far more serious in the event of a city bankruptcy, which could drag down MAC as well. So the bank defendants have an obvious interest in keeping the city afloat until a Friedlander settlement [noteholder suits] or the statute of limitations closes off any more damage suits." Though the *Journal* overstated the case—all current suits will be adjudicated and will not be cut off by a 1982 statute of limitations—it is true that a city bankruptcy would invite a flood of lawsuits.

Senator Proxmire revealed still another reason to celebrate: the assets of the largest city banks jumped by 23.5 percent between September 30, 1975, and September 30, 1977. Yet their holdings of city and MAC securities dropped 3.4 percent. By the spring of 1978, the six major city banks had less than 1 percent of their assets tied up in city paper, compared to a scheduled 38 percent by the city's pension funds. If the banks simply returned to their 1975 level of investment (0.92 percent of assets), Proxmire complained in 1978, "this would net New York City about $2.3 billion in long-term financing over the next four years." "Certainly," Proxmire and Massachusetts Senator Edward Brooke wrote in a joint letter to President Carter on December 23, 1977, "there is no reason to assume that such investments would be more risky than some of these banks' foreign loans, which consume a far larger proportion of assets."

Despite unprecedented "sacrifices," the municipal unions didn't do as badly as their rhetoric suggests. "The unions have been without any increase for almost three years," declared PBA President Sam DeMilla in late 1977. A 1978 advertisement signed by Victor Gotbaum, Executive Director of D.C. 37, wailed: "After three years without raises . . ." Jack Bigel thundered, "We haven't had a wage increase in three years." These views were echoed by and widely believed both by the general public and the press. After all, the Emergency Financial Control Board legislation, passed in September 1975, ordered a three-year "pay freeze."

Or so we were told. Buried in a black, 300-page transition briefing book for Mayor-elect Koch, was a five-page memorandum which suggested there was no "freeze." Since December 1974, the memorandum revealed, city employment had been slashed almost 23 percent—yet city labor costs, which totaled $5.5 billion in 1977, declined by less than 1 percent.

How could it be? There had been 25,000 layoffs, another 36,000 workers had retired or resigned, there was a one-year 6 percent pay deferral, a three-year "pay freeze." If all this were true, it would be as if the city had been on a treadmill for three years—pumping its legs, straining, sweating, yet standing still.

"How could it be that labor costs did not go down?" Edward Costikyan, at that time slated to be first deputy mayor for Koch, asked me in November 1977, revealing the memo. "It can't be!"

exclaimed Deputy City Comptroller Martin Ives when I called. After a day of computations, he called back to say it appeared to be so. Who was lying? In a sense, no one was. When union leaders refer to a "pay raise," they're talking about their pay rate or base salary. Pay rates were frozen. But the take-home pay of workers was not.

Here's why: In the spring of 1974, the unions negotiated new citywide contracts calling for an 8 percent pay rate hike beginning July 1, 1974 (fiscal 1975) and another 6 percent hike for the year beginning July 1, 1975 (fiscal 1976). As an act of statesmanship, union leaders volunteered to defer this 6 percent increase for one year, beginning October 1975. But most workers did not defer the full 6 percent. Those who earned less than $10,000 were allowed to keep 4 percent, thus deferring only 2 percent; those earning between $10,000 and $15,000 got to keep 2 percent; only those workers whose base pay exceeded $15,000 actually deferred the full 6 percent. Since the deferral was for only one year, for two of the first three years of the crisis all workers got to keep their full 6 percent hike; and for that one year, the majority of workers received either 2 or 4 percent increases.

In addition, all city workers received annual cost-of-living bonuses. The first, called COLA I, was a carryover from the 1974 contract and provided annual payments averaging about $400 per employee. The second, called COLA II, was approved by the Control Board in 1976. It allowed further cost-of-living adjustments, provided that these were funded through increased productivity, "other savings" (budget cuts), or "other revenues" (increased state or federal aid). In the first year, 1976–77, COLA II added $199.50 to the paychecks of most city employees. In 1977–78, COLA II added another $672 per worker. To understand what this means, take the case of an accountant whose base salary was $11,550 in the spring of 1975. On July 1, 1975, the accountant was supposed to receive a 6 percent pay raise. Four percent of this raise was deferred for one year. Over the next three years, he or she received the full 6 percent, plus three COLA I payments ($1,200) and two COLA II payments ($872). By June 1978, the same accountant was receiving $13,413—a 14 percent increase from July 1975 to June 1978. Over the same period of time, the cost of living jumped 17.1 percent. Since cost-of-living adjustments were lump sums, the lower the pay of the worker, the greater the percentage jump in pay. According to the Office of Labor Relations, a senior clerk in the middle of the salary scale got a pay raise of 17.4 percent over this period; a higher-paid patrolman 1st grade went up 12.6 percent.

From this, four conclusions can be deduced: (1) there was a "pay freeze" in name only since workers were bringing home more money in 1978 than in 1975; (2) the pattern of previous years—trading reduced public services for increased employee compensation—continued; (3) higher-paid workers did not keep pace with the cost-of-living increases; (4) lower-paid workers about kept pace. When I reported this in my *News* column in December 1977, Victor Gotbaum lashed back, writing in the same paper that it was "absolutely not true" that city "salaries have kept up with the cost-of-living since 1975." Three months later, in a March 16 interview with the respected publication *The Fiscal Observer*, the very same Gotbaum matter-of-factly said, "In real wages over the past five years, lower-economic workers have about broken even."

From the worker's point of view, the scorecard is incomplete. It does not count the 2 to 2.5 percent extra the state legislature now requires each employee to contribute to his or her pension (a worker earning $11,000 pays an additional $300 annually) or the roughly $40 million in fringe benefits City Hall and the unions claim were sacrificed by workers; nor does it compare these raises against increases elsewhere, which have often grown faster; it neglects those low-paid city workers, mostly represented by Gotbaum's union, whose pay is below that of comparable jobs in the private sector and, in some cases, even below the official poverty level. And it does not account for the perceptions of city workers, who blame their low wages for low morale—knowing or feeling they are slipping in the race with inflation.

But the scorecard is also incomplete from the taxpayer's point of view. It does not include other parts of a worker's compensation package: paid overtime, which cost the mayoral agencies $46 million in 1978; night-shift differentials ($45 million); pay increments, which are based on length of service ($30 million); pay differentials, which are based on education degrees ($5.5 million); and pay hikes due to promotions, which have been plentiful with the attrition of 36,000 senior employees. Counting longevity pay, night-shift differentials, uniform allowances, holiday pay and cost-of-living adjustments, the base pay of detectives, for example, jumps by more than $4,000. Yet union leaders exclude these benefits when moaning about their base pay.

"If we count increments and overtime and differentials and promotions, most city employees will have kept ahead of the cost of living over the last three years," the Control Board's Sidney Schwartz told me in December 1977. According to an Economic Development Council study, the 33,000 transit workers—who unlike other workers did not defer any of their pay or benefits—averaged a 16.6 percent hike in their compensation over the three years. According to a 1978 unpublished City Comptroller's study of the W-2 forms of 171,398 city employees on the payroll from January 1975 through December 1977, the average worker's pay jumped 9.8 percent—from $16,600 in 1975 to $18,276 in 1977. But this figure is somewhat understated, as the Comptroller's Office concedes. It does not include the bulk of the workers' COLA I and II payments; or the overtime and other benefits received from January to June 1978.

After a Koch-ordered study, the Budget Bureau certified that labor costs over the three years had indeed dropped by less than 1 percent. But there were complex reasons for this, including increased Social Security, pension, and fringe benefit costs beyond the city's control; the axing of mostly lower-paid workers; and the city's policy of supplementing the pay of many CETA workers. True, actual payroll costs declined by an estimated 9 percent. Yet in a March 1, 1978, response to Senator Proxmire, Koch declared, "Roughly 10 of the 20 percent decrease in the work force was offset by increased payments to city employees approved by the Emergency Financial Control Board." A confidential memorandum, prepared by a Koch ad hoc task force from the Bureau of the Budget, the Office of Labor Relations and Deputy Mayor David Brown's office, startlingly revealed: "Even during one of the most austere periods in the City's history, municipal workers were able to keep relative pace with the general rate of inflation." They found, for instance, that a senior clerk received an *annual* increase of 5.5 percent over the three years. This contrasted with an *average* annual increase of 6.2 percent in the pre-"crisis" period.

New York was thus left with a smaller, better-paid work force. Unlike labor leader Sidney Hillman, who during the Depression urged his brothers and sisters to share equally in the sacrifice, early in the "crisis" municipal labor leaders vetoed proposals to avoid layoffs of some of their members by asking that *all* share in the sacrifice of fringe and other benefits. Because of the state law mandating that layoffs be based strictly on seniority—which, it is worth recalling, no leading union or city official protested—a disproportionate number of blacks, Hispanics, women and young workers suffered. Rather than alienate current members, union leaders also agreed to slash by 10 percent the salaries of those few workers hired after June 1976. In addition, instead of four weeks' paid vacation, these junior workers would receive only three; they would be ineligible for COLA II payments, and would be required to contribute a greater percentage of their salaries toward their pensions.

Seniority provisions affected workers in another way. While 25,000 Indians were getting laid off, their chiefs, who enjoy seniority, became a privileged, untouchable class. Between May 1975 and February 1977, according to a Budget Bureau survey of those laid off, the percentage of city managers actually increased. In that period, employees earning less than $10,000 were reduced by 36.9 percent; those earning between $10,000 and $15,000, by 41 percent; those earning from $15,000 to $20,000 by 4 percent. Yet those earning from $20,000 to $25,000 climbed 8.1 percent; those between $25,000 and $30,000 soared 17.6 percent; and those making more than $30,000 went up 1.4 percent. The staffing of the City of New York now resembles that of the Mexican army.

So managers did not "sacrifice." The pay of city workers was not frozen. And the cost-of-living adjustments were not funded, as claimed by labor leader Barry Feinstein, "by increased worker productivity." Nor was there "no cost to the city," as claimed by Gotbaum, because COLA II payments were funded by "productivity." In what Steve Berger, former Executive Director of the Control Board, called "the first great loophole," in 1976 the Board required that only 50 percent of these cost-of-living adjustments be funded through "increased productivity." Hoisting the white flag, they declared it permissible to fund the remaining 50 percent from budget cuts or increased state or federal aid. Thus New York, in its very own peculiar way, came to define reduced services (attrition) as improved "productivity." And, ignoring a rather sizable budget gap, the city came to earmark any budget cuts or increased state and federal aid to increased worker compensation. Admittedly, it is often difficult to measure productivity, and workers were correct to charge the city and the Control Board with inexcusable delays in making payments to workers who met their productivity goals. But in June 1978 the Koch administration and the Control Board quit trying to define productivity and agreed to surrender the requirement altogether to expedite the remaining $567 COLA II payment that would have been due most workers. They also agreed that future payments would be called "bonuses" and would not require matching "productivity," "other savings" or "other revenues." The real problem with productivity seemed to be political, not definitional.

Labor leaders were not the only ones misleading the public. Governor Carey told the Congress in early 1978 that the city had reduced its work force by 66,000 over the three years. To arrive at this total, he counted 5,000 court workers who had been transferred to Albany's payroll when the state assumed the cost of the courts, a bookkeeping change. City officials certified that the work force was slashed by 61,000, claiming 25,000 layoffs and another 36,000 through attrition. A careful check reveals this total is also false.

"These are 61,000 real bodies," Budget Director James Brigham told me on March 20, 1978. But, he admitted, these numbers were "very rough" since the calculations "were done by hand" and they were "guessing" the exact number laid off vs. attrited.

"Does the 61,000 total include the more than 9,000 laid-off employees Beame rehired?" I asked.

"Yes, it does."

"Does it include the 8,094 laid-off mayoral agency employees rehired on federal CETA lines?"

"It does."

"Are you sure?"

He called back to say these CETA employees were not counted. Nor were the 10,000 rehired Board of Education employees, nor the 19,306 additional CETA employees working for the city as of June 30, 1978. Nor the other city employees supported by federal funds—like those financed by the Law Enforcement Assistance Administration or the Commerce Department—for which Brigham says the city has no numbers. Assuming there are another 1,000 of these, the total number of city workers supported by the federal government in mid-1978 exceeded the 25,000 laid off. Even if Brigham's claim is correct that laid-off workers who have been rehired and other new hires should not be counted, at best the city work force had been reduced by about 25,000, as opposed to the 66,000 or 61,000 proclaimed. This should not suggest there have been no layoffs, no suffering. Many city workers who were rehired went months without a job.

But the city's CETA trick does suggest how little has changed.

Once again, City Hall was making short-term decisions with long-term consequences. Having braved the trauma of laying off 25,000 workers one year, the city turned around and hired an equal number back the next. CETA employees now comprise about 10 percent of the work force. Instead of planning for a long-term scaling down of its service delivery system, City Hall merely found a new device to pay for it. Thus the city set itself another trap. Since the Carter administration has already announced plans to cut back CETA employment, and Congress in October 1978 restricted employment to no more than eighteen months, City Hall and workers will likely be forced to undergo the trauma of layoffs once again. No matter. "My real future worry," Barry Feinstein told me in March 1978, "is that the CETA program will lapse. The city has to make plans to pick up the slack by *expanding* the tax levy budget."

The use of CETA lines helps demonstrate why city labor costs have not gone down, and how the poor once again took it on the chin. Under federal law, these jobs are supposed to be earmarked for the poor. But New York, like other cities, pilfered these funds to rehire laid-off workers. To discourage this, the federal government placed a cap of $10,000 on what it would pay a CETA worker. That didn't stop City Hall. To make up the difference between this $10,000 and a worker's former salary, New York decided to subsidize the difference—$35.5 million worth in fiscal 1978.

Perhaps the real lack of change was in perceptions. The principal actors in the fiscal drama seemed to suffer a collective reality gap. They often spoke the right lines, sometimes risked the boos of an audience, but more often than not they were oblivious to the cold reality of the massive budget deficit. For Abe Beame, it was business-as-usual. He treated his final budget numbers as if they were Vietcong body counts, except that he deflated the totals. Instead of a long night, he proclaimed "light at the end of the tunnel." So he eased up. The mayor who had asked city workers to sacrifice used the occasion of his final days in office to make two commissioner appointments to the seldom-show Board of Water Supply. This is the same board Comptroller Goldin claimed could have been abolished, saving taxpayers $2.6 million. These lifetime posts, requiring attendance at one weekly meeting and offering a chauffeured limousine, secretary and $25,000 salary for the chairman and $20,000 for the two other commissioners, permit full-time outside employment. Beame awarded the chairmanship to his deputy mayor, Stanley Friedman. To deflect anticipated criticism, he gave a commissionership to Simeon Golar, a black former judge. (In mid-1978, spurred by Mayor Koch, the legislature voted to terminate the Board.) Also in his final hours in office, Beame appointed fifteen judges, many being political cronies who failed to win Bar Association approval. When I asked him about these appointments at a Channel 13 lunch one day, Beame reacted as if he didn't understand the question. With doleful eyes he looked at me. Hadn't Lindsay appointed his friends? he asked. Hadn't Wagner? Didn't Carey? Why should he be singled out and picked on?

Nor did the fiscal emergency sink in with others at City Hall. Ignoring the so-called fiscal crisis, top executives of the outgoing Beame administration submitted claims of over $5 million for accumulated overtime, sick days and vacation days not taken. The City Council waited until after the November 1977 elections and then passed legislation raising their part-time salaries from $20,000 to $30,000. After a loud public outcry, the legislation was shelved. No matter. In June 1978, the Council voted themselves an $11,000 increase in each member's expense account. Mayor Koch, who joined the original outcry, approved this later increase, saying in a prepared statement, "I chose not to veto the increase for the Council because I was assured by the Council leadership that the additional funds for the Council members represented vouchered expenses and not 'lulus.' " In truth, the Mayor's support was the price he paid for Council approval of his 1979 budget. Koch also paid a price for the budget approval of the Board of Estimate. The borough presidents of Brooklyn, Queens, the Bronx and Manhattan walked off with $210,000 extra in staff for each of their offices; Staten Island, being smaller, received $190,000. "So the upshot is that everybody got more," observed Senator Proxmire, the Wisconsin Democrat who often seemed to be speaking for city taxpayers, "except, perhaps, the more than seven million private citizens of the City of New York."

New York's economically uncompetitive position didn't sink in with Ray Corbett, President of the state AFL-CIO. In May 1978, he called on the state to unilaterally raise the minimum wage from $2.30 to $3.35 by 1981 (mission accomplished). It didn't seem to sink in with Victor Gotbaum, who, like other principals, looked at a temporary cash "surplus" for fiscal 1978 and declared, "There is no deficit." Gotbaum was trying to win a wage hike for his members, and as long as New York could induce the federal government to help finance a $1 billion deficit over four years, he would worry about next year, next year.

It didn't seem to sink in with Governor Carey. When he was not running for reelection, the Governor was gutsy. But 1978 was an election year. Though he had no legal or legislative authority to do so, nor might he be around by then, Carey coaxed Mayor Koch's support of the controversial Westway project—a $1.1 billion highway and economic development project along the West Side of Manhattan—by pledging to retain the 50¢ subway fare through 1982. Carey, like Governors Rockefeller and Wilson before him, also reduced state taxes in an election year, paying for these, according to Steve Weisman of the *Times*, "by the shuffling of cash between fiscal years, a practice that politicians tend to deplore except when it serves their purposes." The Governor, whose first speech to the legislature in 1975 cautioned that "the days of wine and roses are over," now urged citizens to imbibe some election-year champagne. In addition to a $755 million tax cut and a subsidized transit fare, Carey promised $398 million of new state aid to localities, including more than $200 million to help New York City balance its budget, a $177 million increase in spending for state operations, additional middle-income housing subsidies, elimination of the one-year probation for public employees who break the state law and strike, as well as a cornucopia of other goodies. Each community Carey visited during the campaign seemed to win a government grant. It was like an early Christmas. Buffalo's Sheehan Memorial Emergency Hospital got $22,000 for a burn center; Oswego got $480,000 for its railroad; neighborhood groups, $5 million for preservation work. Intent on proving he was fiscally responsible, Carey's Republican opponent, Perry Duryea, at first called Carey "irresponsible" for pledging to retain the 50¢ city subway fare through 1982. Then, when he was roundly condemned for being "anti-city," Duryea matched Carey's pledge. The state, as it had done in years past, was setting an example for the city, proving that budgets were political documents—not a set of limits imposed by how much revenue you had, but rather by what those in power wished to spend to remain in power.

The state legislature was hardly an inspiration. In addition to expanding their already bloated staffs, the Albany lawmakers ignored the pleas of Koch and others to reform the antiquated civil service system; to exempt an additional 3,000 city executives from union membership, strengthening the mayor's ability to manage the bureaucracy; to reform the "Heart Bill" so that it would not be so easy for workers to win tax-free disability pensions; to slash the patronage-rich city marshals programs; to grant City Hall greater control over appointments to the Board of Education, lessening the influence the United Federation of Teachers (UFT) exercised over appointments made by the borough presidents. Though he pleaded, cajoled and romanced, Koch won none of these reforms from the legislature. It was a defeat, Koch told me. "You can't get anything through the state legislature in an election year that the unions don't want," he groused. "I used to have some feeling of the power of the municipal unions, but I never comprehended the extent of their power. I was told the UFT put a hold on the education bill. I was called yesterday and told by a legislative leader we could get something out of the legislature—we could get two more seats on the Board of Education, four out of nine. 'But what would I have to do?' I asked. You know what I was told? I was told I would have to reappoint the UFT guy, Louie Rivera. I said, 'Screw them. The UFT is not making any appointments.' So we're not getting our legislation through." So we get a picture of the legislature's concept of public service.

The city's basic methods of delivering public services also did not appreciably change. Sure, the most egregiously incompetent commissioners were gone, the Management Advisory Board achieved some of their excellent recommendations, a director of operations was implementing a management plan for each agency. But it remained accepted city policy, as stated in Beame's 1977 Management Plan as well as Koch's 1978 version, that services would continue to decline. The City Council would get their raises. City employees would get their raises. The budget would go up. The banks would secure their investments. Politicians would get reelected. And the public would continue to receive reduced services.

Restrictive union work rules were not amended. The introduction of additional inspector generals checking on sloth was rabidly denounced by labor leaders as "a spy system." The hot breath of competition was not introduced into the city's muscle-bound, monopolistic service delivery system. Sixty-five percent of all American cities with a population of 25,000 or more encourage competition by contracting out for the delivery of sanitation services, according to former Deputy City Administrator E. S. Savas, now a professor of public systems management at Columbia. Oklahoma City, he says, saved $850,000 by contracting out two of its five sanitation districts. Neighboring Newark, New Jersey, recently awarded a bid for one district to the New York Carting Company, · the city's largest private carting service. "The city of Newark was spending $4 million to do the job themselves," said the president of the company, Charles Macaluso. "Our bid guarantees that we'll do the job for half that, or $2 million." Experience in other cities shows contracting out not only saves money—Savas estimates New York's sanitation department could save from $25 to $60 million annually—but also improves the efficiency of the city's effort. Savas' study of the city of Minneapolis disclosed that after the introduction of competition the municipal sanitation agency "achieved a 35% reduction in direct labor hours per household per year, a 37% increase in tons collected per man hour, and a 51% increase in the number of households serviced per shift, while the number of complaints by residents has been declining."

Since the late 1960's, New York officials have prated on about introducing such competition. Savas proposed it then, and was left an orphan when Mayor Lindsay succumbed to the powerful opposition of the sanitation union. Environmental Protection Administrator Jerome Kretchmer, reacting to a Citizens Budget Commission study that claimed the city could save up to $77 million by contracting out sanitation services, proposed an experiment on February 6, 1972. That was the year Lindsay was running for President, and it was never undertaken. Sanitation Commissioner Martin Lang also proposed an experiment in 1975. Three months after offering the job, and under pressure from the sanitation union, Beame abruptly invited Lang to become Parks Commissioner. As a candidate for mayor, Ed Koch pledged to initiate such a program. Yet six months after he became mayor, Carol Bellamy, President of the City Council, chided Koch for appropriating "no funds to the Sanitation Department for such activities." Koch, after he was elected, conferred with sanitation union consultant Jack Bigel about his choice for commissioner. Koch intended to appoint the first choice of his search committee, Nathan Leventhal, an outsider presumably open to experiments. When Bigel huffed, Koch backed off and reappointed Anthony T. Vaccarello, a lovely man but also no boat-rocker. As an added pacifier, Koch anointed Frank Sisto,

President of the Sanitation Officers union, as First Deputy Commissioner.

Koch seemed to be impersonating Beame. Vaccarello and Sisto won the confidence of their men, but in the first six months did little to change the way sanitation services were delivered. (By October 1978, Koch had a new commissioner.) In a June interview, Koch defended the glacial pace of government reforms: "Look, we haven't had a chance to govern. For five and one-half months we've been going from abyss to abyss." Crisis to crisis. Because of this, he said, he had not been able to focus on his director of operations' conclusion that sanitation services could be improved by 10 percent with the introduction of two rather than three men to a truck, a practice followed by most cities. The sanitation union has traditionally opposed this practice, but since it is not prohibited by their contract the city could unilaterally begin such operations in many districts. That it didn't was a management failure. All Koch had to do was give the policy go-ahead for his commissioner to proceed. Koch was offering an excuse, not an explanation—or at least not a very good one. A mayor is supposed to delegate authority and responsibility to his commissioners.

Koch was copping a plea, something Beame did when he ignored the recommendation of the Temporary Commission on City Finances that $100 million could be saved in the Police Department alone through better management; something labor leaders do when they caution that change must come slowly or it will further undermine "worker morale"; something management and labor have both done while ignoring proposals to farm out the delivery of some city services to worker cooperatives, permitting workers and taxpayers to share in the savings. Such cooperatives, which admittedly would alter the concept of public service as a sacrifice of sorts, would work in the following way: Assume it now costs $10 million to provide sanitation services in one district. The city would provide the worker co-op with $8 million to do the job, a $2 million saving for the taxpayers. If the co-op could perform the work for less than $8 million, it would get to keep, say, 50 percent of the difference. The worker thus has an incentive to improve productivity, to work harder, and the taxpayer saves money and receives improved services. As is the case with contracting out to private firms, which could go on simultaneously, competition would have been introduced to a moribund bureaucracy. Yet despite an agreement in 1977 to experiment with worker co-ops in the sanitation department (called gainsharing), by mid-1978 the plan remained on the shelf.*

But neither the city nor its workers has the luxury of time. As the taxpayer revolt of the late seventies demonstrates, government will either reform itself or taxpayers will force it to. With a lagging economy, the best way to ensure future worker raises is to stream-line government management. That is the stated view of Victor Gotbaum, who told his union members in mid-1978, "We can no longer cop a plea and exempt ourselves from the effort to bring about a more productive work force in this city."

There is no substitute for City Hall leadership. And, sadly, the wrong kind of leadership sometimes emanated from Koch's City Hall. "The only 'perk' in my administration," claimed the press release accompanying one of his first executive orders curbing city limousine privileges, "will be the privilege of serving the public." Within days, the public began to pay for that privilege. The mayor who had promised "suffering" and "equal sacrifice," who had op-posed a City Council pay raise because the negative "symbolism" would cost more than the dollars, blithely raised the salaries of more than two dozen City Hall aides by from 20 to 140 percent. They could now afford to take taxis to work. Ronay Menschel, who earned $33,000 as administrative assistant to Congressman Koch, was boosted to a deputy mayor at $57,500. Victor Botnick, a legis-lative assistant to the Congressman at $15,000, became a special assistant to the Mayor at $30,000. Campaign manager John LoCicero, who earned $33,000 as an office manager with a man-ufacturing firm, jumped to $47,000 as a special assistant. Ad-mittedly, the pay of campaign workers is often deflated, making comparisons with former salaries potentially misleading. But most of Koch's City Hall aides came directly from other government or private sector jobs. At a time when the new mayor was threatening no raises for city workers, he was taking good care of his own—ignoring his campaign admonition: "I will insist that my adminis-

---

* Admittedly, the issue of gainsharing is complex. From the taxpayer's point of view, it alters the traditional definitions of public service, institu-tionalizing a kind of gimme-gimme mentality. From the city worker's point of view, it risks rewarding the least efficient agencies. A well-run agency may not be able to grant the same raises because it cannot achieve the same savings.

tration take the attitude that all city workers are 'public servants,' that is, our job is to serve the public, not ourselves."

Asked about these and other raises for Koch insiders, a deputy mayor sighed deeply, confessing that he felt "defensive." "Look," he lamented, "I see people coming into the government who are like looters, all waiting for the first person to go through the broken window. It doesn't matter whether they're reformers or regulars. We've all got lust in our eyes, and it's sickening."

There followed, shortly after, the disclosure that Mayor Koch had raided the staffs of fifteen city agencies to borrow at least ninety-two people to work in City Hall. If these people could be yanked from their agency tasks to work elsewhere, perhaps they hadn't been needed in the first place? Or, if they had been needed at City Hall, perhaps they should have been openly added to the Mayor's budget? Instead, the Mayor's spokesperson defended the subterfuge by telling Don Singleton of the *News*, "We certainly didn't invent the practice." It was traditional.

Koch's bending of the stated job qualifications for the head of the Municipal Broadcasting System was also traditional. Awarding this $40,000-a-year plum to his old friend Mary Perot Nichols, Koch defended the appointment by sermonizing that she would do a "great" job. Which, of course, is not the issue. The appearance of political favoritism during a period of austerity was. So was the question, ignored by the Mayor, whether a city with a cumulative deficit of over $1 billion could afford its own television station and two radio stations. It wasn't as if the city were culturally deprived, enjoying as it does ninety-five radio and thirteen television stations.

By practicing what appeared to be the traditional patronage game, Koch weakened his credibility with city workers on the eve of important contract negotiations. Why should already underpaid secretaries forgo a raise, as the Mayor was then asking them to do, when Koch would not ask his friends to sacrifice? Koch also undermined his credibility by reneging on his campaign opposition to the $1.1 billion Westway project. This highway was, he said then, "an economic and environmental disaster" and "will never be built." He betrayed that public pledge when he joined Governor Carey—who had also called Westway a "disaster" in his 1974 gubernatorial effort—and announced plans in May 1978 to complete the long-delayed project. Politicians, like the rest of us, have the right to change their minds. But citizens also have the right to question Koch's sincerity when he vowed Westway would "never" be built.

Besides, Koch's reversal suggests he had learned precious little from past city mistakes. Once again, the city was leaping to embrace federal funds no matter what the purpose. Once again, city policy would reward a handful of speculators—the construction unions and the "David Rockefellers and a lot of real-estate interests who are going to make a lot of money," Koch warned in the campaign. Once again, the city was pouring limited resources into roads, not mass transportation. And once again, a public figure acted as if a campaign commitment were not a contract with voters. Politicians usually enjoy boasting to each other that their word is their bond; they have fewer compunctions about lying to voters.

Perhaps nothing illustrates how little has changed in New York so much as the 1978 labor negotiations. Because labor costs are the principal component of the city's budget, and because labor contracts impinge on the city's ability to deliver services, a detour is instructive. Witnessing the negotiations, one would think there were no fiscal crisis. Union leaders and others agreed it would be "an outrage" for the city not to grant "substantial" raises, not to keep pace with raises granted elsewhere. To union leaders, the city's ability to pay seemed as much an abstraction as Koch's Westway pledge to voters. The first union to negotiate was the Transport Workers Union, whose contract expired on March 31, 1978. The union commenced the duel by demanding, among other things, a 20 to 25 percent pay hike, two additional paid holidays, free public transportation for the spouses of their 33,000 workers, the elimination of all "beakies" (undercover inspectors), the payment of all unused sick days at retirement, lunch money allowances to be increased from $3 to $5, the three-day death in family allowance increased to five days and extended to cover the death of grandparents.

The Transit Authority countered by calling for contract changes which it said would save $120 million over two years. These included: elimination of paid lunch periods and wash-up and check cashing time, no pay for the first day of sick leave, reduction in vacation allowances, "eight hours work for eight hours pay" (ending swing time, etc.), elimination of premium pay for snow work and two hours' pay on Election Day, limiting pensions to 120 percent of the final year's base pay, and purging the contract of the prohibition against hiring part-timers. Union leader Mathew Guinan thundered, "We're not going to negotiate away things we achieved over the last forty years."

Tradition. As always, the duel was perceived as a contest between labor and management, with the public unrepresented except through its officials, who placed a lid on all public discussion of issues and costs once the negotiations became serious. Samuel Pierce, Jr., chairman of the mediation panel and a law partner of the ubiquitous Theodore Kheel, didn't sound like an impartial referee when he said, "I'm sure both sides realize it's important to keep the fare as low as is humanly possible. But it's a very difficult thing to do because you have 33,000 transit workers who have the problems of inflation thrust upon them and need to meet that problem through increased wages." Pierce seemed to be dismissing the Transit Authority's contention that raises should come out of increased productivity. As always, he implied that maintaining the fare was less important than providing raises. Like almost everyone else, Pierce ignored the study which found that over the three years of the fiscal crisis most transit workers kept pace with inflation.

The negotiations ended on April 1. The union captured a 6 percent pay raise over two years, plus a $250 bonus for each worker, plus a cost-of-living boost, making it a 9 to 10 percent pay hike. Over the two years, the average transit worker was expected to jump from $17,092 to $19,542. In a letter to its members, the union leadership proudly declared, "We gave back absolutely nothing." Also, they wrote, the Control Board would no longer "have any voice in evaluating our productivity." In its place, a friendlier three-member panel would make that determination, with a union leader as one of the members. "Even making allowance for inflation since 1968," the letter intoned, "this new contract—won without a strike—is better than the contract that cost twelve days on the picket line twelve years ago."

The city and the Transit Authority won labor peace without a strike, as was not the case twelve years before. But that's about all they won. Faced with the Hobson's choice of paying more for a contract or a crippling strike, the Carey and Koch administrations decided to sweeten the state's contribution by $80 million and the city's by $18 million. A settlement was reached, but not before the Koch administration backed down on all its demands for "givebacks." The dollar cost was relatively modest. The cost of failing to win modifications in work rules was expensive. How much so can be gauged by recalling that the Authority spent $55 million for overtime in fiscal 1977—more than half the cost of the new settlement. The only "victory" the formerly tough-talking Mayor claimed was that the Authority had won the right to experiment and hire up to 200 part-time change booth collectors. But closer inspection reveals what kind of "victory" this was. "Their sole assignment can only be to open booths not now in service," declares the union letter. "Clearly, this is not a 'give-back,' since any hiring of part-time railroad clerks can only mean an additional cost to the TA. What the TA really fought for was the right to hire part timers as bus operators and in other titles to cut down on overtime. That right they did *NOT* get." The proclaimed give-back was really a "give-in." As ever, the workers got more; the city got peace; and the public got higher costs and no improvement in service.

It was the same with the Patrolmen's Benevolent Association. Negotiating separately from the other municipal unions, the PBA insisted on once again becoming the "number one" paid police force in the nation, issuing a thick powder-blue loose-leaf book containing its demands for $10,000 pay and benefit hikes for each cop. Perhaps no single document speaks more eloquently of the reality gap than this; none better underlines the assumption, shared by other special-interest groups, that the city prints money which, somehow, taxpayers don't have to pay for. The police demands included:

■ "All employees shall be guaranteed a work schedule which provides for no greater than 232 tours (days) and no greater than 1,856 hours per year"—compared to the 2,088 hours worked in 1978.

■ *Christmas bonus:* "An employee shall be entitled to a Christmas bonus of one (1) month's pay payable on or before December 25. For employees who served a portion of the year, each amount shall be pro rated."

■ *Birthday pay:* "For an employee who actually works on a day which is his birthday, his hourly compensation shall include, in addition to his regular day's pay, holiday pay, Saturday pay, Sunday pay, or other entitlements, compensation payable at the rate of his base annual salary divided by the number of days a year the employee is scheduled to work multiplied by eight (8)."

■ *Free college:* "Employees, attending college and promotional courses, shall be compensated for the cost of tuition, fees, books, and supplies necessary for the proper completion of the courses. An employee shall be given paid leave for the purpose of attending college and promotional courses."

■ *Free life insurance:* "The City shall provide a life insurance policy for each active and retired employee and his family in the amount of $100,000, with a double indemnity clause in the event of accidental death to the employee or any member of his family."

■ *Guaranteed employment:* "The City will not lay off for lack of work during the term of the contract. . . ."

■ *Free Parking:* "The City shall provide locations adjacent to, near, or part of police precincts, headquarters and the courts as parking facilities for the personal use of police officers."

■ *Free pensions:* "The City shall absorb the full cost of the pension contributions, and the employees present five (5%) percent contribution shall be eliminated."

■ *New pensions:* "The City shall increase the contribution to the Annuity Fund for each employee [from $1] to Two ($2.00) Dollars per day for each day for which such employees is paid by the City."

■ *Sick days:* "An employee shall be entitled to twenty-six (26) sick days a year, which may be accumulated without limitation. Each employee shall be credited with the full twenty-six (26) days on July 1 of each fiscal year." *Additionally:* "An employee, who is on sick leave . . . may leave his residence or place of confinement at any time, and the City may not check, in person or by other means, on his whereabouts."

■ *Free subways:* "An employee and his family shall be entitled to the free usage of the subways and buses when travelling to and from duty or while otherwise off duty."

■ *Limousine service:* "Foot patrol employees shall not be required to maintain their post and shall be picked up by radio motor patrol car operators when the temperature falls below thirty-two degrees fahrenheit (32° F), the wind chill factor being taken into consideration."

■ *Blood days:* "The present entitlement of blood days for each bleeding [donation] shall be increased [from one] to two (2)."

■ *Vacation days:* "From one (1) to three (3) years of continuous service—thirty (30) working days. In excess of three (3) years of continuous service—forty (40) working days." *Additionally:* "Each employee shall receive 14 paid holidays annually"—an extra three days. *Additionally:* "An employee shall be given five paid leave days if he receives an award for outstanding police service." *Additionally:* "An employee shall be entitled to eight (8) personal leave days for each fiscal year"—an increase of seven days.

■ *Rewards for shooting people:* "An employee shall be granted forty-five (45) days of leave of absence with full pay in the case where he is subjected, in the line or performance of duty, to a traumatic situation which shall include but not be limited to such instances as the fatal shooting of a criminal suspect, etc."

The total cost of these demands, said the city, came to about $750 million extra just for the 18,000 members of the PBA. At the beginning of the negotiations, in March 1978, the Koch administration countered the PBA's demands with its own list of "give-back" demands. At the end of the negotiations, in July, the city once again "gave in." Each cop was offered a two-year 8 percent pay boost, or about $2,400. In addition, each would continue to receive a cost-of-living adjustment of about $1,200 annually. The holiday and night differential pay—which Koch pledged to eliminate—rose to match higher salaries. As was true of previous contracts, the city agreed to pay more for less work. City Hall offered to "give back" six chart days off in exchange for lengthening the average daily tour of duty by twenty minutes. Thus a cop would not work eight hours and thirty-five minutes daily. Koch claimed cops would still be required to work 2,088 hours annually, so this represented no diminution of police service. But as the city learned when Lindsay granted chart days off in return for fifteen minutes of daily "briefing time," these extra minutes cannot match six lost days of work.

"It's a total capitulation," complained one city negotiator. "Deputy Mayor Zuccotti went through a miserable summer but refused to budge and give back any chart days off. His successor, Don Kummerfeld, wouldn't give in. Abe Beame, as miserable as he was, at least held the line, refusing to 'give back' any chart days. The cops pissed on his lawn, and he took it. Now Koch gives in without a fight." True, Koch sought and won some changes—the police gave up their day off for donating blood, and their three annual training days at the Police Academy would be replaced by twenty-four one-hour sessions in the station house. But after PBA delegates twice rejected the pleas of their leaders to support the contract proferred by the city, and after rowdy police demonstrators blocked the delivery of the *Daily News* to protest their sensible editorials, Koch sweetened the pot. He withdrew the city's demand for a curb on sick day abusers and a provision giving precinct commanders authority to schedule more police during high-crime periods. Both of these demands had earlier been accepted by the leadership of the police union.

The negotiations ended the way most previous negotiations had. Deputy Mayor for Labor Relations Basil Paterson, who acted more like a mediator than an advocate throughout, announced, "There are no winners or losers in collective bargaining." Pressed by reporters, Mayor Koch, lacking his usual ebullience, declared, "I do not feel that we have caved in." True, the number of scheduled police hours did not go down. But it was a cave-in because the number of productive police hours did go down. Within days, police officials conceded the pact would result in an average loss of seventy-five cops daily. The important point is that the long-term trend of reduced police coverage continued. To have won a "victory" for the taxpayers, as Koch promised in his campaign, the city would have had to persuade police officers to work more days—not fewer, not even the same number—each year.

The demands made by the Municipal Labor Committee, representing over 200,000 workers whose contracts expired on June 30, 1978, were not as absurd, though Mayor Koch's behavior was. Like John Lindsay, Koch would prove to be an amateur at the bargaining table—leader of The Gang That Couldn't Shoot Straight. The jockeying began during the campaign when Koch declared there was no money for pay raises. "The municipal labor unions will no longer run this city," he announced often. On November 1, 1977, during a mayoral debate sponsored by *The New York Times*, Koch linked the transit and all other labor negotiations, claiming that "whatever is negotiated by the Transit Authority . . . will be the bottom line for all other contracts." In March, the Mayor released a list of sixty-one "give-back" demands and said any pay increase for municipal workers would have to be financed from these because he would "not extend the deficit." The unions parried, demanding a 12 percent pay increase plus new fringe benefits. Koch, sharing Lindsay's penchant for theatrical poses, said their demands were "outrageous." In truth, the unions knew the Mayor was posing; the new mayor did not know he was. In December 1977, a major city labor leader told this reporter, "Don't quote me, but I would be glad to settle for a straight 6 percent." That would have been 6 percent for two years. But Koch's public bluster, like Lindsay's, hardened their demands, bringing greater membership pressure on union leaders to humiliate their City Hall foe.

Which is what they did. In April, thinking the transit settlement too rich to extend to the other city unions, Koch suddenly denied saying what everyone knew he had said. "There is no linkage" between transit and the other contracts, he now professed. Justifiably enraged, D.C. 37's Victor Gotbaum called Koch "a bald-faced liar." "It was," says Alan Viani, one of D.C. 37's negotiators, "like having two kids and saying to one, 'Here's an ice-cream cone,' then turning to the other and saying, 'You can't have one.'" After the Mayor's turnaround, and because many workers felt he made them scapegoats, Viani and his fellow negotiators were put in a box. "I've never seen such disdain for a mayor as I've seen at our delegates' meeting," he said. "It makes it very difficult for us."

And Koch made it difficult for himself. Like Lindsay, he promised to come to the bargaining table prepared. He was not. The public would pay for his education. And that of Deputy Mayor for Finance Philip Toia, who told me in June that the negotiations were "a fascinating experience. I learned to lot." Koch and Toia started by saying there was no money in the fiscal 1979 and 1980 budgets for raises. When the professionals on the union side found temporary cash "surpluses"—additional federal aid and underspending by city agencies, for instance—they began to small blood. "Koch is already at a higher level than he could have been at," claimed one city negotiator in early June. "We could have settled for 6 percent if the city had leveled with us in March. Koch turned to Toia and said, 'Look, I'm the mayor. Tell me what we have to pay for a labor settlement.' Toia said we had nothing. So as time went on and the unions pulled more and more out of Toia, they got tougher."

And the price got higher. By May, the same candidate who denounced Mayor Beame for "pulling a rabbit out of his hat" when Beame discovered $1 billion in 1976 to pay off moratorium noteholders, suddenly fleeced $757 million from the city's budget to pay for a two-year settlement. Under pressure to complete a contract before the start of Senate hearings on the city's loan legislation, a subdued Mayor Koch, on June 5, announced his unconditional surrender. The contract, he said, called for an 8 percent pay rate raise over two years, but because the city postponed the dates these raises would begin, over the two years workers would actually receive 6.7 percent in real money. At the start of their next contract period, however, their pay rate will be up 8 percent. In addition, workers won a continuation of their COLA I payments, being raised to an average of $441 per year (from $395). In place of COLA II, the city agreed to drop the productivity requirement and grant each worker an annual "bonus" of $750—$78 more than they received in fiscal 1978 and $550 more than they received in 1977.

Appearing before Senator Proxmire's Banking Committee on June 6, Koch held aloft a copy of the *Times* front-page story by Jerry Flint. The settlement was, he quoted approvingly, "an enormous achievement"—only 6 percent. (He later amended this to 6.7 percent.) Koch was assuming, as did Flint and others, that since the cost-of-living adjustments were continuations of previously won benefits, they should not be counted as part of the pay hike. Supposedly, they did not represent new money. But they did. The $1,500 in productivity "bonuses" workers would receive over the next two years was $628 more than they received in 1977 and 1978, when they were required to demonstrate productivity improvements.

As is often the case in these matters, it pays to wait until the dust clears and the press's attention shifts elsewhere, then study the contract as viewed by the workers. The city traditionally understates the cost of contracts. D.C. 37's point of view was presented in a circular to their membership—"Terms of the Wage Pact." They claimed the pact called for a 15.84 percent "pay rate" raise. In an accompanying chart, the union explained that they arrived at this total by adding a 4 percent pay raise the first year, 4.34 percent the second, and the annual $750 bonus (7.5%). A worker earning $10,000 in June 1978, they said, would receive an even higher percentage in "actual cash"—an additional $2,525 over the two years. According to Teamsters leader Barry Feinstein, "There is a minimum salary increase of $2,663 in this contract for you." According to *The Chief*, the newspaper that is the bible of civil service workers, "For an employee with three or more years of service the additional cash or so called "grocery money" over the two year period adds up to $3,279.50."

This is only part of the cost. The Koch administration also agreed to abandon all its sixty-one "give-back" demands—including uniform allowances for those who don't wear uniforms, the proposed forty-hour work week, the elimination of excessive sick days, heat days off and restrictive work rules. "The real question is whether in the context of reality . . . could I get, without a strike, the give-backs?" Koch told Proxmire's Committee. What about "give-backs"? "I don't think there is anything else that could be given back," Jack Bigel astonishingly told the Committee. In reality, City Hall did more than "give in" on the "give-backs." Union negotiators actually maneuvered The Gang That Couldn't Shoot Straight to make "give-backs." As a result of the agreement, the city administration consented to "give back":

■ *The productivity requirement on all outstanding 1978 COLA II payments.* For many workers, this came to a bonus of $567, since they had already earned $105. The remaining workers received a full $672 cash bonus. Being "new" money—no longer requiring "productivity" savings and $628 more than they received the two previous years—this sum could be, but was not, counted when City Hall computed the percentage raise.

■ *The productivity requirement and the need for Control Board approval of 1979 and 1980 COLA II payments (now dubbed "bonuses").* "COLA under the new contract no longer is 'if' money," wrote Frank J. Prial II, publisher of *The Chief.* "The $750 a year, effective July 1, is fixed, certain and unrelated to productivity. While this sum is not counted for pension purposes, it will be used to compute overtime, night shift differential pay, and other fringes. In a real sense it is a *new* benefit."

■ *Most of the unions' $24 million 1976 "give-backs."* Meter maids and many other outdoor workers or those in non-air-conditioned offices would again get their shortened summer hours (thirty-hour weeks). New employees would get back one week's vacation, again giving them four weeks a year. New employees would no longer be required to start at a 10 percent lower salary and would now be eligible for cost-of-living adjustments. The reduction by 50 percent in the cost of meals to hospital and other institutional employees would be restored. Workers would again be able to credit vacation and sick leave toward the forty hours per week in excess of which there is premium pay for overtime. The original reason for the give-backs was to ease the city's budget woes. Presumably, the fiscal crisis was now over.

The city also agreed to "give in" and:

■ *Increase holiday and night differential pay, which is tied to base pay.* Detectives, for instance, will receive several hundred dollars more each year—totaling about $1,200 annually.

■ *Agree to binding arbitration over the question whether the city would continue to owe its workers the one-year wage deferrals of 1975*, totaling between $180 and $200 million. (In July 1978, the arbitrators ruled in the workers' favor, declaring the city owed this money to its employees.)

■ *Include COLA I payments in the wage rate in the second year.*

■ *Agree to raise COLA I payments from an average of $395 to $441.* Some employees whose contracts expired at different times, namely, teachers, would receive their $441 in the second year.

■ *Continue to pay increments for teachers, Board of Higher Education professors and uniformed employees.* Most uniformed employees receive increments for just the first three years on the job. After the first year, for instance, cops, firemen and corrections officers receive pay increments of $2,443, in addition to their regular wage hike and cost-of-living adjustments. In year two, they receive $675 more; in year three, an additional $671. Sanitation men get about 10 percent less. Teachers receive about $1,000 annually in pay increments over their first eight years. All increments also become part of the base pay, being counted for future wage hikes, overtime and pensions.

■ *Agree to grant pensions to all part-timers who work for the Board of Education.* These 10,000 paraprofessionals were now to be paid on an annual rather than hourly basis.

■ *Restore the three increments (about $1,650) teachers did not receive in 1977 and 1978 because of the "fiscal crisis."*

■ *Cede to the teachers' union the right to grant larger than 8 percent raises to those with seniority, and smaller raises to junior teachers.* This deed was done when the Koch administration agreed that once they decided how big the pie would be—$757 million of city funds for raises over the two years of the contract—the unions, not the city government, could decide how to slice their share. Faced with an internal union challenge, UFT President Shanker, with the approval of the Board of Education, decided to gift larger slices of the pie to more numerous senior teachers. In fiscal 1979, the increments for seventh-year teachers were increased by $250 (to

$1,250) and eighth-year teachers were given $1,180 extra (a total of $2,180); in fiscal 1980, seventh-year teachers will receive an additional $250 and those in their eighth year an extra $1,250 (or $2,250 in increments). Also, over the two years of the contract, teachers with ten to fifteen years on the job will receive an additional $500 bonus, bringing their longevity pay to $2,000. Those with more than fifteen years' service will receive an extra $1,000 over the two years. Instead of a flat 8 percent raise, Shanker chose to increase increments and longevity pay by an amount greater than 8 percent. However, those teachers with five years or less of service will not share in these raises. Over the two years they will receive their COLA I payments ($777), their cost-of-living bonus ($1,500), their four increments ($2,000) and their three back increments ($1,650). It's not peanuts, but it's less than most teachers will get. "It was a brilliant move by Shanker," observed Michael Rosenbaum, a city negotiator who used to work for D.C. 37. "All of the younger teachers were laid off. Few have been hired. Only about 10 percent of the teachers will not benefit, I would guess." He guessed about right. Shanker's union approved the pact by a vote of 44,858 to 4,485.

Thus, in "grocery money," over the two years of the contract many teachers could receive 40 percent above their base salary. Assuming an $18,000 base salary, watch:

$ 777 = COLA I
             ($336 the first year + $441 the second)
1,500 = bonus
1,650 = three restored increments
1,180 = increment for 7th-year teacher
             (3 mo. into contract)
2,410 = increment for 8th-year teacher
_____
7,517 = additional "grocery money"

Depending on what you count, the two-year pay increase ranged from 6.7 percent to about 40 percent. When you count just "grocery money," the cost of the two-year settlement can be seen as rivaling the 39 percent three-year contract won earlier that year by the coal miners. When you confront city and union officials with these higher percentages, they complain that it's unfair to count as "new money" benefits that have previously been received (as we have seen, this is not what union leaders say to their members). There is merit to this argument, but those who make it usually try to have it both ways. On the one hand, they argue that workers went three years without a raise; on the other, they claim post-1978 raises should not be counted because they are similar to the raises received over the previous three years.

"Measured by the normal standards of labor-management relations," pronounced labor attorney Theodore Kheel, "the settlement is quite reasonable." But these were not "normal" times. Measured against Koch's pledge for "a no-cost labor contract," the settlement was extravagant. Measured against the city's proclaimed four-year budget deficit of over $1 billion, and the knowledge that New York was asking federal taxpayers to take some risk to help finance this deficit through loan-guarantees, the settlement seems less modest. Measured against the management changes the city sought and lost, the contract represented business-as-usual. Once again, the city was deciding to divert whatever cash "surpluses" or budget savings it achieved not to reduce the overall deficit, not to cut taxes to make the city more competitive economically, not to improve services or rebuild crumbling streets and bridges, but to grant wage increases. "We gave them all the money we have, no question about that," Koch softly conceded.

Throughout the negotiations, people asked the wrong question. The question was not whether it is an "outrage" when workers' salaries fall behind rising inflation (it is); nor whether workers had borne a burden throughout the crisis (they had); nor whether their pay was slipping in comparison to the pay of other workers (it was). The right question is: What can New York afford? The settlement widened New York's four-year budget gap, increased the price to be paid two years hence when the contracts expire and union leaders say they will demand "substantial increases," and continued the past pattern of higher costs for reduced services.

After six months in office, things didn't go as Ed Koch had planned. "Mayors of New York have governed by the politics of consensus, making short-sighted, destructive attempts to steer a middle course between strongly differing groups," candidate Koch declared in an August 22, 1977, Op-Ed page article in the *Times*. "If New York City is to survive, it must elect a Mayor who will risk his personal popularity to govern this city along the course of necessity—not convenience. . . . The battle for this city will not be won by steering the middle course that compromises our future. It is by reaching for excellence, not acceptability, that we will survive, and we can prosper." A nice speech. Assuming Koch meant what he said—and I believe he did, and does—the relevant question is: *Why has so little changed?*

The answer is complex, and goes to the heart of many of New York's and the nation's ills. First, with bigness comes a breakdown in responsibility. We see this on the national level, where officials shape one-half-trillion-dollar budgets and quibble over whether the deficit will be $30 or $50 billion. When dealing with one-half-trillion-dollar budgets, $5, $500,000 or even $50,000,000 seems a pittance. With so much money, so many programs, so many constituent groups to be pacified, what's another program? The numbers defy human scale. We're all ants when viewed from 30,000 feet.

Like Ed Koch, Jimmy Carter was an outsider who swept into office promising to be frugal with the public purse. One of his first acts was to boost the salaries of his former campaign aides. James Gammill, who at twenty-two was making $7,500 in the campaign, now earns $45,496 as the White House's personnel director. The President's closest aides, Hamilton Jordan and Jody Powell, saw their campaign salaries more than double to $56,000. Richard G. Hutcheson, who at twenty-four earned less than $10,000 in the campaign, now receives $45,496 as the White House's staff secretary. Midge Costanza, who earned $15,000 as a member of the Rochester City Council, received an almost 400 percent increase to $56,000. Even after she was demoted in 1978, Costanza lost her prestigious office next-door to the President but got to keep her full salary before she ultimately resigned. The taxpayers are abstractions—ants—when viewed from the lofty heights of the powerful.

It's not as if it's your money—or, for that matter, anyone else's. So Mayor Koch conferred huge raises on members of his staff. And so union leaders who struggled to avoid bankruptcy demanded hefty wage and benefit gains. So Assembly Speaker Stanley Steingut, who once slipped on a city sidewalk and broke his toe, insisted, though fully recovered, on suing the city. So former Deputy Mayor John Zuccotti filed a delayed claim for sixty-three days of overtime pay after leaving city government in 1977.

So it was for me. When I resigned as executive director of the city's Off-Track Betting Corporation in 1973—two years before the fiscal storm hit—a check arrived one day in the mail. It was for $5,984. Since I'd taken few vacation days, I assumed it was for back vacation pay. There was nothing to sign, no itemization of what the money was for. Yet here was this big fat check. Terrific.

Or so I thought, until a *Daily News* reporter called in December 1977 to inform me that $2,498 of this sum was for compensatory time (overtime). Ridiculous, said I. Over the years, I'd written several pieces criticizing the practice of paying overtime to city executives.

A call to OTB revealed that the *News* had its facts right. No matter that at the time I didn't know the compensatory time was included. No matter that the money was officially due me, or that I immediately sent a check to reimburse the city for all of the compensatory time (as did Zuccotti, who also claimed he didn't know). The moral of this tale is that I didn't think to ask what the original check was for. It was as if the money rained from heaven. Certainly not from the taxpayers.

To those in or supported by government, taxpayers become abstractions. They were abstractions to the teachers' union and the Board of Education, who in 1975 agreed to shorten the school week so that teachers could retain some of their free preparation periods. They were abstractions to police sergeants, who threatened a strike rather than give up one of their eighteen to twenty-eight extra chart days off; to members of the City Council and Board of Estimate, who voted themselves lavish new staff support; to Abe Beame, who increased city spending to aid his reelection effort; to Hugh Carey, who behaved likewise with state monies in 1978; to Strom Thurmond, who connived federal crop support for his constituents; and to California state officials, who invited Proposition 13 to pass when they allowed a $5 billion state surplus to accumulate while property taxes soared. The prevalent view of government as a communal trough was given voice by a deputy to former city Police Commissioner Michael Codd. Cornering Jay Goldin in early 1978, the aide berated the City Comptroller for blocking Codd's request for a tax-free heart disability pension: "Why did you have to do that to Mike Codd? What do you care? It wasn't your money."

How can people who preach and believe in fiscal restraint, or those who have worked so hard and believe so deeply in saving New York from bankruptcy, behave so greedily? How can someone be a principal actor in the fiscal drama one moment and behave as a detached observer of a newsreel the next? The obvious answer is selfishness. But it's more than that. Government becomes the giant commissary where free lunch is served. To the public, government dispenses protection but also programs, grants and subsidies the way a counterman dispenses mashed potatoes and meat loaf. Soon farmers come to expect their crop support subsidies, tenants their rent subsidies, Lockheed and Chrysler their federal loan guarantees, doctors their huge Medicaid fees and elaborate equipment, cities and counties and states their federal grants. Appetites grow.

To those in government, success is achieved only if the commissary expands fast enough to feed nearly everyone, or at least keep important customers reasonably happy. Politicians know that few care about the chef's wisdom, judgment or diet recommendations. They know that few think about whether there will be enough food to feed many more customers ten years from now, whether there is money to pay next year's bills. They know the press tends to focus on *now*, on politics not government. Liberal democracy has become a service business, and the service that counts is *MORE*. Besides, who'll notice? Government budgets are so big, departments so large, rewards so plentiful, that a sense of personal responsibility breaks down. Everyone's doing it, so how can it be wrong? What's the big deal when the city has a $14 billion budget, 60 commissioners and 300,000-odd employees? The federal government has a $500 billion budget and over 3 million employees. What's a few million?

The future is mortgaged for the present. Ultimately, when the food supply stops growing, there is cannibalization. Liberal democracy, as Peter Jay observed, begins devouring its own tail. Taxpayers lose, but so does the concept of public service. Like us, the people we elect to think about the future and give us their best judgment often fail Publius' test. Public service does not become quite the sacrifice our public officials enjoy proclaiming it to be. Yes, members of the City Council, the state legislature, the Congress, moan about their salaries. But not about the outside income they're allowed—the legal and lecture fees, the investment opportunities. Or about the perks that come with the office—the chauffeured cars, swollen staffs, free phone and mail privileges, fat pensions, future job connections, the honor, like royalty, of being addressed by their title. Yes, they receive public abuse. But most folks don't get their pictures in newspapers, don't enjoy the ego gratification and sense of power we confer on people in public life. This rarefied atmosphere helps desensitize officials, divorcing them from the people they're meant to serve. Public life can be ennobling, but it is rarely humbling.

These universal reasons partially explain why so little changed in New York over the first three years of the fiscal crisis. Still, wasn't

New York a special case? Didn't everyone agree the fiscal crisis was for real? That bankruptcy was an immediate threat? Why weren't local appetites curbed? Why didn't the outside mechanisms imposed to police the city—MAC, the Control Board, the federal Treasury, the outside auditors—function as they were meant to? The answer to this riddle goes back to a commonly shared assumption. All of the actors—City Hall, Albany, Washington, the banks and financial community, the municipal unions, the business community, even the press—agreed: bankruptcy was unthinkable. Start with that common assumption and it follows that each would bend, do what was necessary, to avoid it. Differences revolve around tactics, not strategy. All are scaling the same peak. Since each climber has the power to cut the lifeline, they cling to each other, synchronizing their steps, their every movement. There are no sudden lurches. Alone, the mountain cannot be conquered. A team effort is required, the sharing of each other's days and nights.

Inching up the mountain together, overcoming the same obstacles, surviving one seemingly hopeless crisis after another, the natural tendency is to celebrate the distance covered rather than the distance to go. One's constituency becomes each other. The means becomes the end. Success requires continued team effort. Failure is the plunge into bankruptcy, not the failure to fundamentally reform city practices. That would mean risking a break. Instead of criticizing the banks for their shrinking investment in city securities or the unions for their raises and work rules, the other members of the team praise their cooperation. The pressure is off.

Rather than risk offending New York voters by scolding the city, as the Ford administration did in 1975, since the beginning of 1976 first Ford, then Carter, performed more as cheerleader than cop. With the approval of the teachers' contract in early 1977, Governor Carey started to think of his reelection and began to rein in the Control Board. Hoping to restore investor confidence and seduce additional federal support, MAC Chairman Rohatyn, speaking for the "conservative" local establishment, declared in 1977: "We've cut away all the fat. From now on, we'll only balance the city budget and pay off debts by cutting away New York's muscles, bones and vital organs." Teachers' union president Al Shanker found those words so comforting he reproduced them in paid advertisements in the city's newspapers. Yet, the next year, Mayor Koch announced he planned to cut $993 million of "fat" from the city budget over the next four years. Because he was committed to avoiding bankruptcy and Senator Proxmire demanded a labor settlement before considering loan legislation, Mayor Koch says "we had to" achieve labor peace at almost any price (though the same excuse did not apply to Koch's police settlement, which came after the senate committee had acted). So, too, when the labor settlement was reached, the business/banking establishment, and the editorial pages of the *Times* and *News*, swallowed hard and chimed their support. That was preferable to tarnishing the Big Apple's image in Washington.

Thus there grew, over the first three years of the crisis, the local equivalent of a military/industrial complex—what one might call a public/profit complex. The same absence of opposition, of rigorous checks and balances, which helped cause the fiscal crisis now rendered it nearly impossible to cure. Former adversaries were now on a first-name basis. Labor leader Victor Gotbaum hosted a dinner party at his Brooklyn Heights home for Ellmore C. Patterson, Chairman of the Morgan Guaranty Bank. Felix Rohatyn and Gotbaum celebrated a joint Southampton birthday party in 1978. William Ellinghaus, the vice president of AT&T and former member of MAC and the Control Board, agreed to chair a New School dinner in honor of Gotbaum. Rohatyn and Carey are feted as celebrities at chic watering holes like Elaine's. Gotbaum is featured in Scavullo's latest book. Jack (Bigel) is a friend of Walter's (Wriston). Barry and David and Jack and Felix and Abe and Punch and Mike and Jay and Max and Tex and Victor and Don and John are all friends. Despite the 1975 legislation empowering the Control Board to police and approve all city contracts, Don Kummerfeld, its executive director, sat in on the 1978 labor negotiations, as did Governor Carey. "I don't think it's appropriate for the executive director to be an active participant in labor negotiations when he's supposed to look at the contract," whispered one banker, refusing to be quoted by name. Interestingly, Kummerfeld and Carey's participation evoked not a word of public criticism. In 1978, the legislature extended the Control Board's life but gave the mayor, as well as the governor, a veto over the selection of its executive director.

Nor has there been any public notice of why municipal labor officials seemed to know the budget better than the new Koch administration officials and thus were able to extract money from negotiators who claimed there was none. In March 1978, Jack Bigel's Program Planners, Inc., chief consultant to the Municipal

Labor Committee, reached into the Budget Bureau and hired Allen Brawer, the staff assistant to the director of the Bureau. "They hired a guy right out of our Bureau of the Budget who gave them all of our figures," Ed Koch told me, adding that there was "nothing illegal or immoral about it." Such things are common in Washington, where Defense Department officers regularly join aerospace firms whose contracts they monitored.

But Section 2604 of the City Charter seems to prohibit such switches, proclaiming: "No . . . employee of the city or any city agency, whether paid or unpaid, within a period of three years after termination of his employment, shall appear before any city agency or receive compensation for any services rendered on behalf of any person, firm, corporation or other entity, in relation to any . . . matter with respect to which during his employment he was directly concerned, or in which he personally participated, or which was under his active consideration, or with respect to which knowledge or information was made available to him." The city's Board of Ethics, which rules on this section of the Charter, was never asked by Mr. Brawer, Mr. Bigel or Mr. Koch for a ruling on the propriety of a former city budget official gifting "all of our figures" to another "entity."

Mr. Brawer is not alone. Laura Page, once the Budget Bureau's education budget examiner, now studies—among other duties—the city's budget for the teachers' union. She is joined by Joyce Levinson, once a colleague in the Budget Bureau. The deputy to Al Shanker, head of the teachers' union, is William Scott, former First Deputy City Comptroller. D.C. 37 lured Bernard Rullman from the Comptroller's Office; Arthur Van Houten, once the Executive Director of the New York City Employees Retirement System, is now their pension consultant. Basil Paterson, the city's chief negotiator, used to receive lucrative labor mediation contracts from the same unions he was now negotiating with. In the midst of the 1978 contract bargaining, Anthony Russo, the city Labor Commissioner, told me he received a job offer from one of the unions he was negotiating with.

It gets very cozy.

As former antagonists sit together, they come to understand how "complex" issues are. United as they are by a common foe, bankruptcy, they come to believe that all other issues are "manageable." For good reasons, each party sincerely believed bankruptcy would be ruinous to New York. But, it was often forgotten, avoiding

bankruptcy was not just an act of statesmanship. It was also pure
· self-interest. The unions knew a bankruptcy judge would almost
certainly abrogate their contracts and menace the solvency of their
pension funds. The banks and financial community knew bankruptcy would open the floodgates to note and bondholder suits. No
mayor, governor or President wants to be remembered for, or stuck
with, New York's colossal bankruptcy. Not only would it be bad for
New York, it was bad politics. The case of Assembly Minority
Leader Perry Duryea is instructive. In 1975, Duryea condemned
the city as "profligate," and voted against both the MAC and Control Board legislation which helped the city skirt bankruptcy. In
1978, as the Republican candidate for governor, Duryea suddenly
appeared as a faithful friend to New York, roaming the halls of the
Congress to buttonhole support for city loan legislation, issuing
press releases commending "the progress" the city had made.

The press, too, often abandoned its adversary role. The fiscal
crisis was not just another story. The life and death of a city—our
city—was thought to be at stake. We were now all on the same side.
New York against the reactionaries, the bigots, the Huns out there
who hated us. The issue almost became one of patriotism. Unite to
save New York. If New York was threatened, it followed that businesses here were threatened as well. And the city's three major
newspapers, ninety-five radio stations and thirteen television stations are very much businesses. The publishers of the *Times* and the
News, Punch Sulzberger and Tex James, respectively, had their
papers invest $500,000 and $100,000 in MAC securities, served on
various Big Apple committees, including one urging the construction of Westway, and encouraged editorials supporting their local
gladiators. Why did the *Times* make the investment? According to
their spokesman, Lin Whitehouse, the purchase came "at a time
when the city was trying to corral big companies. It was a show of
good faith."

With the exception of the New York *Post*'s Rupert Murdoch, who
doubles as editor-in-chief, the publishers do not control the news that
appears in their papers. Reporters often wrote stories that displeased
the local team "partners." Still, the pattern of their coverage was
friendly. So friendly that Rohatyn, in a July 12, 1978, Op-Ed page
article in the *Times,* unself-consciously thanked them. Rohatyn
claimed the city's progress was largely "due to the public support we
gained as a result of a supportive press. . . . The press . . . once it
understood what we were trying to do and why, treated us with fair-

ness, supported us and created the climate in which political leaders could do difficult and painful things." Clearly, a "supportive press" was not infused with the same zeal to puncture untruths or wrong-doing as they were, say, in the case of Vietnam, CIA spying, Watergate or Bert Lance. Implicitly, the press took the city's side. During Senate Banking Committee hearings on the city's loan legislation in June 1978, I asked a *Post* reporter why the critics of the legislation—Senators John Tower, Richard Luger, Jake Garn—were not attending. "It's just as well the critics are not attending," he said. "They'd hurt *our* case." Former Treasury Secretary William Simon describes being confronted in 1975 by one of New York's better reporters, WNEW-TV's Gabe Pressman: "On camera, he lunged at me with the question 'Do you mean to say you're going to let millions of innocent people go down the drain?' "

The daily press also operated with a handicap not of its own making. Journalists are trained to search out at least two sides of an issue. But what happens when both sides are really one? When Felix agrees with Jack? Or Jack agrees with Walter? Abe with Barry? And because the story is so complex, the numbers so confusing, journalists are compelled to keep going back to the same handful of "experts" for information. Dependency, trust, friendships, develop. Felix Rohatyn and Victor Gotbaum, for instance, are not only very smart men, they are also very charming, open, helpful to reporters. It was not hard for those covering the story to grow too close to the people involved; to assume they were all trying to save New York, forgetting they were also desperately trying to save their own ass.

What happened to City Comptroller Goldin is pregnant with meaning both about the role of the press and about the workings of the local version of the military/industrial complex. In the summer of 1977, an agreement was reached between MAC, the city, the unions and the banks to trade in their shorter-term securities for longer-term MAC bonds. This stretch eased the city's immediate debt service payments, but it also ballooned the city's long-term costs because a higher rate of interest over a longer period of time was called for. At first, the only major public official to protest was Goldin. "Our major complaint," said one of his principal aides, "was the outrageous interest rate. The banks were making $150 million on the deal. That's a lot of money. So Goldin publicly protested. We couldn't interest the press in writing about it. I got a call from one newspaper reporter who said, 'I lost a lot of respect for you for opposing the stretch.' I blew up. That night, someone from MAC called to say, "We have the *Times* and the *News* editorially supporting the stretch tomorrow.' The next day Goldin got quiet. He was worried." The stretch passed without opposition. Felix had, cleverly, made sure to first brief his friends on the *Times*, the *News* and the *Post*.

Assessing the first three years of the partnership before the state assembly's Committee on Banks, Ellmore C. Patterson of Morgan Guaranty proudly exclaimed, "It is pride which I am happy to share with many others, not only in the financial community but also in the labor unions, the Municipal Assistance Corporation, and the State and Federal governments." Patterson had reason to be proud. The partnership had, together, kept the city from plunging into bankruptcy.

But they had not fundamentally altered the city's government. They had not balanced the city's budget or returned the city to the private credit market. They had not ended the city's reliance on federal credit or reduced the city's debt; had not imposed a "wage freeze"; had not reversed the trend of rising budgets and reduced services; had not drastically overhauled the city's management. New York could not have avoided bankruptcy without them, yet it couldn't change ingrained habits with them. A veto power was conferred on each partner. City Hall entered the fiscal crisis as the victim of too many special interests and emerged as the victim of too few.

The banks and the municipal unions and the other partners have a hammerlock on City Hall. The city asks the banks to purchase city securities, and the banks successfully demand that the city grant unprecedented powers to nonelected business auditors. Committed to shaking up the government, Mayor Koch in January asked the state legislature to approve a bill to remove 3,000 city managers and supervisors from union membership. By May, he could not persuade a single Democratic member of the Assembly to sponsor his bill. He asked the City Council to pass legislation declaring that the city's ability to pay be the paramount consideration in any labor arbitrator's ruling. Yet he couldn't muster the votes to get the bill out of committee. "I called in the City Council's committee," recalls Koch, a note of disbelief in his voice. "Miriam Friedlander said to me, 'That's anti-labor.' I said, 'Miriam, don't you understand, you're part of management.' I was later told that of the nine committee members, seven were against me and two were noncommittal." Normally, the only difference between the Council and a rubber stamp, Councilman Henry Stern once observed, "is that at least a rubber stamp leaves an impression."

In 1975, the employee pension funds agreed to purchase $683 million worth of city securities in the spring of 1978. The unions, led by the wily Jack Bigel, made sure the purchase date coincided with the date of the expiration of their contracts. During the 1978 labor negotiations, the unions balked, refusing to make the purchase. Mayor Koch cried that the city was being "held hostage." No matter. When the contract was settled, Bigel announced, "Everything will now be considered." The pension funds then purchased the securities. Why are the unions so powerful, particularly within legislative bodies? Seated in a soft leather chair, his long legs crossed over the plush red carpet of his City Hall office, Ed Koch answered, "One, they give to candidates, either by way of groups or to individuals, the funds to run a statewide campaign. Lots of candidates, and certainly a statewide party, cannot run without them. Secondly, the unions threaten to support their opponents or to run someone against them."

There is also the matter of ideology. Labor has traditionally been perceived as the good guy, the underdog. Habits of thought change no less slowly than habits of governance.

No contract, no loan, said the unions. No Control Board, no agreement on future loans, said the banks. No labor contract or agreement with the banks, no loan legislation, said the federal government. No city agreements, no extension of the Control Board and MAC's borrowing authority, said the state. "The system will never respond," says the Control Board's chief auditor, Deputy State Comptroller Sidney Schwartz. "It's inherent in the system. You have a kind of democratic environment which provides certain protections for established groups, such as labor. It's almost impossible to make sudden changes. Under dictators it's easy—'Off with your head!' "

Labor is not the only culprit. The banks and the investment community and a host of lesser special interests are carrying out, as they should in a democracy, the task of advancing their interests. The problem is that public officials, who are supposed to represent the broader public interest and check the power of special interests, find it difficult to do so. Democratic government cannot function without the consent of powerful groups; it must persuade, not command. And yet, when it succeeds, it does so slowly and at great cost. Confronted with the fiscal crisis, New York could make only incremental reforms. "I really do believe in the system," Koch's thirty-year-old press secretary, Maureen Connelly, says. "But after six months I've decided it can't be done. I mean, little things can be done." Shell-shocked from being bombarded by interest groups and buffeted from crisis to crisis, she added, "There is a Murphy's law corollary: A crisis will emerge to fill the vacuum created as another crisis subsides. You don't have time in government to look ahead. You're always putting out fires."

New York's woes are not uncommon. Detroit and Rutgers University, like New York, chose layoffs of a few of their workers or teachers rather than cuts in benefits for all. Detroit and other cities chose to use federal CETA funds to rehire laid-off city workers rather than give jobs to the poor. President Carter announces a voluntary effort to curb inflation, but business refuses to curb prices, labor to scale down wage demands. By mid-1978, Washington lobbyists had gutted or blocked tax reform, labor law reform, a Consumer Protection Agency and hospital cost containment legislation. Despite proclamations that the energy crisis was America's most pressing problem, almost two years later President Carter still couldn't navigate legislation past powerful interest groups in the Congress. The oil companies demand higher profits. Consumer groups demand lower prices. Sometimes the enemy, as Pogo said, is us. Twenty years ago, scientists predicted the energy shortage. That didn't deter Americans from purchasing electric hair driers, toothbrushes and can openers. If New York now suffers from too few special interests, the country suffers from too many. In all cases, they are too powerful. In a large, diverse nation, interests inevitably collide. Oil-producing states have different interests from nonproducers. The Sunbelt doesn't want to take fewer federal dollars so that the Snowbelt can take more. The rich and the poor don't share the same interest in tax reform. Cities vie with counties and suburbs and rural areas for a bigger piece of the federal pie. It usually takes a startling event or crisis—a hot or cold war, Sputnik, Barry Goldwater's smashing electoral defeat, the civil rights revolution, Watergate—to get the system to respond.

Democracy becomes a kind of Tolstoyan drama in which interests and events and institutions, not individuals, often hold sway. Ed Koch came to City Hall determined to shake up the system. He captured a public mandate to do so. He had the opportunity created by the fiscal crisis. The sign on his City Hall desk, the same desk that Fiorello LaGuardia once used, reads:

> If You Say 'It' Can't Be Done
> You're Right—
> *You* Can't Do It.

"I have persevered," Koch told me in March 1978. "I never give up. Don't tell me it can't be done. That's the sign I have on my desk. . . . The bastards are not going to beat me down. They'll have to carry me out of here." So every morning New York's ebullient Mayor rises, anxious to get to City Hall, to unleash a new reform proposal, to condemn some ancient wrong as "an outrage." Like most people in government, Ed Koch is an optimist by choice as well as by chemistry. It would be difficult to get out of bed in the morning and face the day's problems if he were as cynical as most journalists. Koch honestly believes he can make a difference.

But, imperceptibly, a change comes over most officeholders. It's not just the crush of responsibility that accompanies public office, a greater appreciation of complexity. It's also something basic, like ego. After a while, you come to label defeats as victories, not because you're a liar but because you can't tell the difference between the two. You also come to believe your own press releases. Knowing that you're judged not always by what you do but by what you appear to do, a good press becomes all-important. Soon you're spending part of each day laboring over your image. Success comes not from resolving problems but from skirting or appearing to solve them. From holding press conferences, giving speeches, issuing press releases, creating photo opportunities. The daily press's preoccupation with a steady diet of news feeds the politicians' preoccupation with making news.

Soon much of what you do becomes gloss. New York City's economy looks better to Mayor Koch since *he* assumed office. Why? Because "I feel it," Koch says. Like his partners, Koch claimed the labor settlement was an "extraordinary achievement," as was "the progress" made by the city generally. To claim otherwise is to disparage your own work; all the backbreaking hours of toil and sweat. Besides, your staff and the local military/industrial complex agree. Together, you're making progress.

Soon you lower your sights. You aim not for the moon but for the top of the trees. "The chains of habit," Samuel Johnson once said, "are too weak to be felt until they are too strong to be broken." For the first three years of its fiscal crisis, New York could not break with past habits. In his first ten months in office, Mayor Koch could not break the chain, either. He achieved a labor contract, won the continued investment of the banks and pension funds, helped persuade the Congress to pass new loan legislation. He survived some difficult crises. He got by the year.

But as long as the city's debt and budget grow faster than its revenue base, bankruptcy lurks just over the horizon. As long as no dramatic moves are made to make the city economically more competitive or to improve services, it is unlikely New York will maintain a tax base to support its budget. As long as the city spends more money than it collects, investors will be wary of making loans. As long as the rhetoric of the fiscal crisis is not matched by the actions, the Sturm und Drang of the fiscal crisis will become a permanent fixture, like the Brooklyn Bridge. Someday, the public will no longer believe the rhetoric.

Yet an almost eerie sense of optimism prevails among the partners. "We avoided bankruptcy," Jack Bigel almost cheerfully told me in September 1977. "No one knew how we were going to refinance $8 billion in 1975. That we did. No one knew how we could come up with $983 million to pay moratorium noteholders in 1976. Yet we did. Ibsen can write and bring a play to a close in three acts. For us, it's just another four weary years of continuing the formula we started in 1975. Call it a loose coalition, a process of exchange among partners. If you ask me how, I don't know. I have to fall back on history." The partners were, again, emboldened when the Congress passed additional loan legislation in the summer of 1978. Each congratulated the other for the truly brilliant lobbying effort. One of the few sour notes was sounded by *The Wall Street Journal*, which over the three years had earned the right to say I-told-you-so. "The doctors are concocting a patent cure for anemia, but the patient has a severed artery," they editorialized. The city's budget, they reminded readers, still wasn't balanced. Nor was it soon likely to be. In 1978, as in 1975, the city was granted loans for essentially political, not economic reasons. In both years, the big change was that the loans came not from the public credit market but from the federal government, the pension funds and a handful of banks.

Over the first three years of the fiscal crisis New York's witch doctors were often asking the wrong question—how do we avoid bankruptcy? The questions they should have constantly asked were: How do we make New York whole? Restore its economy? Improve its services? Truly balance its budget?

ONE PART OF ME is beginning to believe that perhaps bankruptcy is the answer. Since 1975, I have accepted the prevailing wisdom that bankruptcy would be a calamity for New York—an official declaration of death, an admission that democratic government had failed. I recoil at the thought of a nonelected judge ordering around elected officials. And at the ugly prospect of a fractious struggle among the city's creditors—welfare recipients, bondholders, city workers, printers, landlords, bus drivers—for their slice of the city's tangible assets. I worry about the psychological impact of bankruptcy: businesses or middle-income people who feel they have a bright future will not long remain in a city that has declared it may not have any future at all. I worry that Felix Rohatyn is right when he warns that the bankruptcy of America's premier city could further undermine the dollar and convulse the international economy.

Yet, increasingly, I wonder whether to save New York we don't have to destroy the stranglehold of our very own local military/ industrial complex. Maybe New York's system of consent can't work and only a judicial command will compel solutions. Maybe bankruptcy is inevitable and by postponing it through witchcraft New York is simply digging itself deeper into debt. If forced to choose between immediate or inevitable bankruptcy, I would choose the former because it is cheaper. Maybe the Wizard of Oz had a point when he told Dorothy, "I'm really a very good man, but I'm a very bad wizard." Maybe horses can't fly.

That's the pessimist in me talking. Another part of me truly believes that New York is governable—that people, not just events, shape history, and that courageous and skillful leaders can make a difference. New York can capture additional federal aid without becoming a permanent ward of the federal government; need not remain a hostage of powerful special interests. The city can cut its budget, make its economy and business climate more competitive; reform its management and civil service system; inspire citizen volunteers, neighborhood improvement efforts, hope. "I have always held," wrote Albert Camus after long and dangerous service as a member of the French Resistance, "that if he who bases his hopes on human nature is a fool, he who gives up in the face of circumstances is a coward."

I am haunted by Prince Prospero. The Prince was a fool because he insisted on gaiety in the face of death, insisted on walling himself and his minions off from the truth, thinking they had "saved" themselves. While they partied and dreamed of a renaissance, the plague spread. The Prince wasn't murdered. He committed suicide.

Index

About the Author

KEN AULETTA was brought up in Coney Island, attended New York City public schools and the State University of New York at Oswego, and received an M.A. from the Maxwell School of Citizenship and Public Affairs at Syracuse University. He worked for the federal and city governments and participated in national and state political campaigns. A former contributing editor of *New York* magazine and writer for the *Village Voice*, he is now a writer for *The New Yorker*, a columnist for the *New York Daily News* and a regular commentator and host on New York public television. He is also a contributing editor of *Esquire* magazine, and his work has appeared in the *New York Review of Books* and the *New York Times*.